# Airman's Guide

# Airman's Guide

## 8th Edition

MSgt. Boone Nicolls
USAF (Ret.)

STACKPOLE
BOOKS

Published by
STACKPOLE BOOKS
5067 Ritter Road
Mechanicsburg, PA 17055
*www.stackpolebooks.com*

*Cartoons by Jake Schuffert*
*Cover design by Tessa J. Sweigert*

Printed in the United States of America

10  9  8  7  6  5  4  3  2  1

This book is not an official publication of the Department of Defense or Department of the Air Force, nor does its publication in any way imply its endorsement by those agencies.

ISBN 978-0-8117-0794-7

**Library of Congress Cataloging-in-Publication Data**

Nicolls, Boone.
  Airman's guide / Boone Nicolls. — 8th ed.
      p. cm.
  Includes bibliographical references and index.
  1. United States. Air Force—Handbooks, manuals, etc. I. Title.
  UG632.43.N53 2011
  358.400973—dc23
                                    2011032786

# Contents

# Preface

This eighth edition of *Airman's Guide* includes a wide range of information about current policies and procedures that relate to pursuing a successful career in the U.S. Air Force. It has been prepared for new airmen, airmen-to-be, career airmen, and family members—all of whom will find it a convenient way to stay abreast of formal policy changes and other matters.

*Airman's Guide* was written with two primary purposes in mind: to serve as a convenient personal reference, since most airmen don't have access to a "five-foot shelf" of all the pertinent directives and information that directly affect their careers and their families; and to present in one volume some of the most important Air Force programs and to discuss them in everyday terms. The guide also includes sources of further information.

*Airman's Guide* could not have been written without the strong support and input of many interested people, including noncommissioned and commissioned officers (both active-duty and retired), spouses and family members, civil service personnel, public affairs representatives, employees of Air Force-related private associations, and many others. All of them have given generously of their time and their thoughts to help ensure that the book is timely and that it represents current policies and guidance.

Stackpole Books has published *The Airman's Guide* through fourteen editions from 1949 through 1968. Publication resumed in a newly numbered series in 1988 as *Airman's Guide*, 1st Edition, in response to the continuing need for a first class reference work for the modern airman. The author and the publisher take pride in presenting this thoroughly updated eighth edition of the new series, to serve those who serve. We invite your continuing comments for future editions.

# Acknowledgments

There has been a wide range of transitions since the release of the last edition of the *Airman's Guide*. Some have been evolutionary changes in internal Air Force programs and policies. Others have been much more far reaching, such as the advances in aerospace, communications, and information technology and the commitment of the U.S. Armed Forces to new engagements around the globe.

The United States Air Force continues to evolve and adapt, much like this eighth edition of the *Airman's Guide*, to meet the needs of the Nation we serve. Many thanks go to those who have made this work possible. I remain grateful to the countless professionals who have been everyday heroes in action by living out the Air Force's core values of integrity first, service before self, and excellence in all they do.

My wife Pam and children Christopher, Sarah, Catherine, Joshua, Elizabeth, Titus, and Levi have been a continual inspiration. They have endured many separations and hardships through the years. The Lord has been very kind to me in both my natural and Air Force families. I am truly grateful.

I must also acknowledge the work of Capt. Wayne A. Valey, USAF Ret., who authored the first through fifth editions of the new series of this book during the years 1988 to 2001. His understanding of the professional needs of airmen was unexcelled, and this edition contains much of the structure and content that he produced. Last, but certainly not least, I want to thank Kathryn Fulton from Stackpole Books for her counsel and guidance in producing this updated and expanded eighth edition.

# Introduction

Serving in the U.S. Air Force is like embarking on a journey. It's a brand-new experience, full of opportunity—an opportunity to serve one's country; an opportunity to participate in a team effort with people from all walks of American life; and, in the process, an opportunity to achieve personal goals and fulfillment.

Whether you're a young airman who just recently entered the USAF, a career-minded noncommissioned officer, or a family member, this book is for you. It talks about life on and off duty. It provides information about Air Force policies, programs, and opportunities. It includes examples that illustrate programs. And it answers commonly asked questions. Each chapter also includes references so that you can follow up if more information is required.

The term *airman* is used throughout the book, sometimes in a dual context. It specifically refers to enlisted personnel in grades airman basic through senior airman. It's also used in a universal sense to denote any military member in the USAF. Similarly, *Airman's Guide* has been written primarily for those presently serving in the grades of airman basic (pay grade E-1) through technical sergeant (pay grade E-6), and also for those who are looking toward the future in the broader context by pursuing a USAF career in positions that require further increases in grade and responsibility.

Air Force members' understanding of their role, and the part they assume within the organization, increases the longer they are in the service. We can see this evolution in personal growth and commitment by comparing new trainees with those who have progressed in their careers. Initially, trainees have very little understanding of how the USAF as a whole functions. As they progress through training, they are exposed to wider ranges of information. They also learn teamwork and gain experience by performing tasks and communicating with others. By the time they graduate, they have a much fuller understanding of the USAF and the role they are expected to assume.

As airmen progress in their careers, they assume supervisory responsibilities and positions of leadership. They need to be technically competent within their career field and familiar with other aspects, such as security and facility management. They establish contact with their counterparts at other bases to get crossfeed and ideas.

Senior personnel have much broader responsibilities. They are ultimately responsible for ensuring that operational requirements are met, as well as maintenance requirements; support requirements ranging from medical to chaplain, finance, personnel, civil engineers, transportation, the base exchange and commissary, community relations, and protocol functions; and a variety of other activities. At headquarters levels, they oversee programs at many bases, ranging from personnel issues to deployment of weapons systems.

In the U.S. Air Force there are two commonly used terms—*the big picture* and *the bottom line.* Being able to see the big picture means understanding how individual actions and programs work, how they affect each other, and what they mean collectively. A summary of the big picture, usually in a sentence or two, is the bottom line. Bottom Line Up Front (BLUF) is a term often used as a high-impact summary to announce purpose or results first, then include background or discussion as warranted.

The USAF distributes a large amount of information to keep its personnel informed about the big picture. Much of this information was reviewed during the process of writing this book; for obvious space reasons, however, topics that relate more directly to general career issues, rather than to specific career fields, are discussed. Changes in Air Force policy do occur occasionally and may, in time, modify some of the policies outlined here. When pursuing an action or interest, it's always best to review the current directive. The same applies for career field descriptions and designations, which can be affected by shifts in technology or in force structure.

In several instances, the words of airmen—noncommissioned officers and officers, young and old, past and present—have been used to clarify concepts and programs. These comments help provide insight to the topics discussed.

The following pages should help you look into the big picture as you embark on a career in the Air Force. As a bottom line, consider the information here as a starting point toward, and a reference for, gaining more knowledge and preparing to meet tomorrow's challenges and opportunities, and remember this adage: "Every exit is an entry somewhere else." At the very least, you will want to consult other experienced Air Force members and referral services, to keep informed through internal information programs and professional readings, and to increase your knowledge through professional military education (PME) courses.

# PART I

# The Air Force

# 1

# A Professional Approach

*The Air Force is not a social actions agency. The Air Force exists to
fight and win wars. That's our core expertise; it is what allows us to
be called professionals. We are entrusted with the security of our
Nation. The tools of our trade are lethal, and we engage in operations that involve much national treasure and risk to human life.
Because of what we do, our standards must be higher than those of
society at large. The American public expects it of us and properly
so. In the end, we earn the respect and trust of the American people
because of the professionalism and integrity we demonstrate.*

—Gen. R. R. Fogelman,
former Chief of Staff, USAF

Professionalism is a broad topic that doesn't come with a simple formula. There is,
however, common agreement about the importance of certain core values and their
role in an institutional framework. Gaining a basic understanding of these values
today is an important first step toward meeting the challenges of tomorrow.

## COMMITMENT: A TWO-WAY STREET
The first step in a professional approach is understanding and accepting responsibility for commitment. In general, commitment is an act of pledging, entrusting, or
putting something to a purpose. In the U.S. Air Force, a commitment considers the
interrelationship of the individual, relationships with others, the mission of the Air
Force, and the needs of the nation.

Everyone's Air Force career begins with an oath of enlistment, involving
pledges and solemn promises: "I do solemnly swear . . . support and defend the
Constitution of the United States . . . bear true faith and allegiance . . . so help me
God." In making that oath we undertake a series of commitments. The Air Force
itself also undertakes commitments: to provide for the needs, aspirations, and welfare of its members and the security of the nation.

## LEADERSHIP AND "FOLLOWERSHIP"

As you pursue your career and assume positions of increased rank and responsibility, your individual commitment will require deeper levels of involvement. As part of the leadership of the Air Force, you will become more entrusted to help assure that members' needs and mission requirements are met.

Leadership is a well-recognized ingredient for success in any organization, but "followership" is equally important. Robert D. Gaylor, a former chief master sergeant of the Air Force, described some of the responsibilities of followership.

> Aristotle, that famous Greek Chief Master Sergeant, once remarked, "One who has not learned to follow can never lead." It might very well be the smartest thing the great philosopher ever said. . . .
>
> Everyone in the Air Force works for someone so we all qualify as followers. Let's ask ourselves the question, "What do I want from my boss?" I can't answer for you, but I can answer for myself. See how many of my points you agree with:
>
> - I want to be treated with respect and human concern. Since those are two-way streets, I have to be respectful to my boss.
> - I don't want preferential treatment, but I expect fair and just play. I have to be fair and honest with my boss to earn equality in return.
> - I want work that is meaningful and challenging. I've got to show my boss that I possess the skill and training necessary to do my assigned job.
> - I want enough authority to make decisions and become involved in planning and organizing my work. It's important that I don't abuse and misuse the authority I'm given.
> - I want my boss to communicate, listen, and keep me informed. My responsibility is to keep my boss advised of problems and solutions that I might be aware of and to promote open lines of communication.
> - I want a boss who inspires me—one who can bring out the best in me. I have to display self-discipline and motivation so my boss will know I'm receptive to instructions and capable of innovation.
> - I want a boss who is not impulsive—one who does not act in haste. I have got to show that I can obey rules and standards so I don't place the boss in a compromising position.

One point becomes crystal clear: The relationship between a leader and a follower is a two-way street—a give and take. You cannot be an effective leader or follower unless you do what you can to promote that kind of an agreement.

## RESPONSIBILITY AND AUTHORITY

Responsibility and authority increase with grade and experience. Whereas younger airmen go through trainee and worker phases, noncommissioned officers evolve through worker, technician, and supervisor phases. Senior noncommissioned officers, in turn, dedicate less time to technical duties and more to broader leadership and management issues.

Responsibility and authority go hand in hand. Being responsible means accepting and executing duties and instructions in a timely manner with a minimum of supervision. It begins when you point the finger at yourself and not at someone else. Authority is the right to act and command. There are two kinds of authority: legal and earned. Legal authority is provided for in the Uniform Code of Military Justice (UCMJ) as a means of enforcing standards and obedience. Earned authority is the best kind; it's derived from respect, which inspires cooperation.

## INITIATIVE AND INVOLVEMENT

Initiative is recognizing and doing what needs to be done before being asked to do it. This positive character quality is recognized and respected by everyone who has ever had to supervise people. Those that demonstrate this particular quality often distinguish themselves by their work ethic and duty performance. Being involved in the success of both the mission and the people you work with will bring great rewards when done with right motives. Gen. Wilbur Creech, former commander of Tactical Air Command, encapsulated the quality of initiative with his motto, "make it happen, make it better."

## A POSITIVE ATTITUDE

A positive attitude is a major plus in any walk of life. It's also a primary factor in achieving a professional reputation. People with positive attitudes are usually realistic, optimistic, helpful, and confident without being overbearing. They chalk up a lot of accomplishments and, in general, have a positive effect on the people around them.

In an article titled "Positive Attitudes," MSgt. Julian R. Lucero discussed several observations that he had made as a first sergeant in the USAF. He noted three specific ways personnel of all grades can use a positive outlook to enhance productivity and motivation within a work center.

1. Set the example. Be on time, look sharp, and have a positive attitude. It's very common for people to reflect the tones, feelings, and stresses of their supervisors and contemporaries.
2. Be competent. When people see your ideas and results being recognized, others will begin to follow the example. Everyone likes to be part of a winning team.
3. Develop and use "personal power." It's just as important as positional power. Think of the best supervisor you ever worked for and about his

or her leadership style—or better yet, his or her attitude. Was it proud, positive, and professional? What was it that really made you want to respond with a total effort? Have you adopted part of that style to enhance motivation and productivity in your work environment?

## STANDARDS

The Air Force emphasizes high standards of performance, conduct, discipline, and appearance (outlined in part II). These are important because they affect the overall image and efficiency of the Air Force. Accepting these standards is a direct reflection of personal pride and commitment.

## PROBLEM SOLVING

As airmen are promoted to noncommissioned officers and positions of increased responsibility, they become, by definition, part of management and should be oriented more toward problem solving than problem finding. Identifying potential problems is a valuable service, of course, but it is also important to help identify options for resolving them.

You can contribute to problem solving in three ways:
1. Make recommendations for each problem you've found.
2. Think of all the possible impacts your proposals might have. For example, introducing new procedures for the rapid repair of jet engines could reduce processing times, but it might also result in safety hazards and reduced engine reliability.
3. Help and follow through on any subsequent actions that may be necessary.

## CONSTRUCTIVE CRITICISM

Criticism is usually the result of frustration with another's performance or opinion. It happens from time to time in all walks of life; not everything goes perfectly 100 percent of the time. At the same time, it's important to remember that comments should be offered in a positive and constructive way. Putting yourself in your supervisor's shoes may help you understand the reasons behind an action or decision. Remember that those in key positions are considering many factors; they're looking at the mission from a big-picture perspective.

Should a situation arise where you disagree with a decision, first discuss it with someone above your pay grade and try to minimize the impact of your disagreement on those you supervise. Point out potential problems and recommend alternative courses of action. Keep the emphasis on *what* is right rather than *who* is right. Once a final decision has been made, support it and press on to other matters of importance.

## UNDERSTANDING THE DIRECTIVES

Air Force directives contain a wide range of guidance and information. They provide sound foundations on which to base decisions. When using them, remember to go with the spirit and intent of the directive. Requirements that are critical and must be followed to the letter usually are prefaced by *must* or *will.* They normally address subjects where specific procedures must be followed because of operational necessity, safety considerations, or the control of funds and resources. Passages that begin with *should* or *may* usually imply the best course of action but allow for interpretation and flexibility at local command levels. Always check that directives are current. Policies and procedures are updated regularly, and passages used one year cannot automatically be assumed to be in effect the following year.

## SELF-IMPROVEMENT

Self-improvement opportunities, including both Professional Military Education (PME) and off-duty education programs, yield benefits for you and for the Air Force. PME provides valuable experiences for gaining insight into Air Force–related disciplines through formal instruction and interaction with contemporaries. Off-duty education programs provide information in a specialized field of your choice. Active participation in such programs is frequently viewed as an indicator of your commitment to excellence and your potential for future success.

## AIR FORCE CORE VALUES

All of the above military professionalism traditions have been summarized in the Air Force's core values. The three words that epitomize the core values of the military profession are integrity, service, and excellence. The foundation is integrity, fortified by a commitment to the service of our country and fueled by a drive in excellence in all that we do. These are the core values every member of the Air Force must believe in and, more importantly, must live by.

### Integrity

Integrity is the essential element and foundation on which other values are built. Integrity is being honest with others, as well as with yourself, and doing what's right at all times. Integrity is the very bedrock of the military profession. Service members possessing integrity will always do what's right, regardless of the circumstances, even when no one is looking. They will make no compromise in being honest in small things, as well as in great ones.

### Service Before Self

The next is military service—an uncommon profession—that calls for people with an enduring commitment and dedication to the mission. It requires us to have a sense of duty and an understanding that our personal needs are secondary to the needs of our great country. Military service is a twenty-four-hour-a-day commitment that requires many personal sacrifices. Personal goals are important and often coincide with Air Force goals. However, there is no room for personal agendas that interfere with the needs of the Air Force or the interests of our government.

## Excellence in All We Do

This brings us to excellence, our third core value. Military members have been entrusted by all Americans with our nation's security. This encompasses many things, among which is the care of the resources of our nation, the most treasured of which are the lives of those who serve. This makes competence or excellence in all things we do paramount. Doing the very best you can is not just a professional obligation but a moral one as well.

Integrity first, service before self, and excellence in all we do. These core values serve as our road map and set the standard for our behavior. They serve to remind us of the importance of the profession we have chosen, the oath we have taken, and the demands that have been placed upon us as members of the profession at arms.

## THE AIRMAN'S CREED

In 2007 Air Force Chief of Staff Gen. T. Michael Moseley and Chief Master Sergeant of the Air Force Rodney McKinley introduced The Airman's Creed to encourage the often felt but previously unspoken "warrior ethos" in airmen. The creed guides the hearts and minds of all Air Force warriors:

I am an American Airman.
I am a Warrior.
I have answered my nation's call.

I am an American Airman.
My mission is to fly, fight, and win.
I am faithful to a proud heritage,
a tradition of honor,
and a legacy of valor.

I am an American Airman,
Guardian of freedom and justice,
My nation's sword and shield,
Its sentry and avenger.
I defend my country with my life.

I am an American Airman:
Wingman, Leader, Warrior.
I will never leave an Airman behind.
I will never falter,
And I will not fail.

# 2

# Customs and Courtesies

Customs and courtesies are important aspects of military life. They reinforce and reward common goals, unity, and teamwork. Some have their roots in tradition; others create an environment that fosters mutual respect and commitment to duty. Where customs and courtesies are noted, they are extended to members of other U.S. Armed Forces (Army, Navy, Marines, and Coast Guard) and armed forces of friendly nations.

## DUTY, HONOR, COUNTRY

The concept of duty, honor, and country is a recognized code for military professionals in all branches of the U.S. Armed Forces. It places a twenty-four-hour-a-day responsibility on each member for a commitment, undertaken with honor, to put the needs of the country and the mission first, without regard to personal wants and preferences. Acceptance of this responsibility contributes to the continued success of each branch of service and is also critical in maintaining the trust and confidence of the American people.

## THE AMERICAN FLAG AND THE NATIONAL ANTHEM

The American flag and the national anthem symbolize the democratic principles of our country. To members of the armed forces, they further symbolize the commitment to uphold those principles and the sacrifices made by their fellow men and women in uniform during America's history. Respect to the flag is shown most frequently during reveille and retreat ceremonies. During the raising and lowering of the flag, those in formation are called to attention and render salutes from the first note of the national anthem or "To the Colors" to the last note of music. Those not in formation should face the flag, or the sound of the music if the flag is not visible, and salute. All motor vehicles should stop at the first note of the music, and those inside should sit at attention until the music stops. Personnel indoors are not required to stand or salute during reveille or retreat, or usually when the national anthem is played on the radio, on television, or in movies. It is, however, a commonly expected form of respect to stand at attention when the national anthem is played in the base movie theater.

## THE SALUTE

The salute is deeply rooted in military custom and tradition. It binds military members together, regardless of rank, through a greeting based on mutual respect. Salutes are rendered to the American flag, to the President of the United States, to all commissioned and warrant officers of the U.S. Armed Forces, to officers of other friendly foreign nations, and to other officials and dignitaries when deemed appropriate.

Salutes are rendered first by the person junior in grade and are held until returned. Turn your head toward the person being saluted, and raise your right hand smartly until the tip of the forefinger touches either the lower part of your headgear (except for flight caps) or your forehead above and slightly to the right of the right eye. The thumb and fingers are extended and joined, palm to the left, upper arm horizontal, forearm inclined at a forty-five-degree angle, with the hand and wrist straight. To complete the salute, drop the arm to its normal position by the side in one motion, at the same time turning your head and eyes to the front.

While the salute itself is a standard procedure, the circumstances under which it is rendered can vary. General guidelines include the following:

- *Outdoors:* Salutes are exchanged between individual members upon recognition and also rendered to senior personnel in properly marked staff cars and government vehicles. For formations and work details, the person in charge renders the salute. For informal groups not in formation, the first person to see the officer should call the group to attention, and all members of the group should face the officer and salute.
- *Indoors:* Salutes are required for formal reporting situations, such as reporting to a commander. Otherwise, they are not normally required.
- *Other situations:* Salutes are not required when a person is encumbered (arms full) or when approaching an officer from the rear. In these cases an exchange of a verbal greeting is appropriate. In some public situations, salutes may be inappropriate or impractical, for example, at religious gatherings or sporting events. In uncertain situations, the best rule of thumb is, when in doubt, salute.

## MILITARY TITLES

Standard titles are used in addressing and introducing all Air Force members. The following accepted forms of rank/grade designation can be used on their own or in conjunction with the person's last name:

| | |
|---|---|
| Generals of all grades | **"General"** |
| Colonels and lieutenant colonels | **"Colonel"** |
| Majors | **"Major"** |

| | |
|---|---|
| Captains | **"Captain"** |
| First and second lieutenants | **"Lieutenant"** |
| Doctors and dentists | **By grade or "Doctor"** |
| Chaplains | **"Chaplain" or by grade** |
| Chief master sergeants | **By full title or "Chief"** |
| Senior master sergeants | **By full title or "Sergeant"** |
| Master sergeants | **"                          "** |
| Technical sergeants | **"                          "** |
| Staff sergeants | **"                          "** |
| Sergeants | **"                          "** |
| Senior airmen | **By full title or "Airman"** |
| Airmen first class | **"                          "** |
| Airmen | **"                          "** |
| Airmen basic | **"                          "** |
| Cadets of the Air Force Academy | **"Mister" or "Miss"** |

**Rank, Recognition, and Respect.** Formal procedures for recognition and respect are established to facilitate the conduct of military affairs and aid in maintaining standards of discipline. Most are based on grade and tradition. They include five general practices:

1. Airmen and noncommissioned officers are addressed by their grade. During informal work situations within a duty section, personnel of the same grade sometimes refer to each other by first name, but only by mutual consent.
2. Officers are addressed by their grade or "sir" or "ma'am."
3. When speaking to an officer, you should always rise and remain standing, unless directed otherwise.
4. When a senior officer enters the rooms, the first person who sees the officer should call the group to attention, and all should rise and stand at attention. The exception to this procedure occurs when an officer who is equal to or senior to the one entering the room is already in the room—for example, when a colonel enters a room where another colonel or a general officer is present.
5. Senior members, whether officer or enlisted, are always given the position of honor, which is on the right side. This applies to walking, sitting, or riding in a vehicle. The senior officer enters a vehicle or aircraft last and exits first.

Other forms of mutual respect, based on commonly accepted acts of courtesy and good human relations, are also expected by members of all grades.

**Retirees of the Armed Forces.** A fall 1995 article in *The Inspector General Brief* titled "Earning the Title for Life," written by former Chief of Staff Gen. Ronald Fogelman, outlined the contributions put forth by Air Force retirees and the special reasons why they should, as a courtesy and a sign of respect and dignity, be addressed by their rank. General Fogelman noted the following:

> The retired officers and noncommissioned officers of all services earned their rank through hard work and determination. They endured hardships, made sacrifices, and often risked their lives in serving our country. Our Air Force retirees laid the foundation for the world's premier air and space force. We owe these dedicated professionals, who have given so much to our nation, the courtesy of using the rank they earned. So it is appropriate to use rank when addressing a retired officer or noncommissioned officer who introduces himself or herself by rank when coming into the clinic for medical care or calling the Military Personnel Flight for assistance. As a source of habit, I encourage it because it accurately reflects the esteem with which we hold our retirees.
>
> While some may consider this a small thing, it is an important concern for retired Air Force members and it is important to me. Our retirees believe they earned their rank for life and should be addressed accordingly—and I agree with them. So, I urge all Air Force people to realize that military retirees from every service deserve to be called by their military rank. It is rightfully theirs because they earned it—for life.

## CEREMONIES

Ceremonies formally recognize and reward excellence, pay respect, and stimulate teamwork, morale, and esprit de corps. Some familiar ceremonies are described here.

Two *flag ceremonies,* reveille and retreat, are conducted at most installations. Reveille (pronounced "rev-uh-lee") signifies the start of the official duty day and is associated with a ceremony for raising the flag. Retreat signifies the end of the official duty day and is a ceremony for formally paying respect to the flag. Times and sizes of troop formations are specified by the base or installation commander.

*Drill ceremonies* teach the value of teamwork. Although ceremonial in nature, they enhance individual performance on the job and in group situations. Because they promote understanding the need for authority, discipline, and following orders promptly and precisely, these ceremonies help develop personal confidence, military bearing, and assertiveness.

*Recognition ceremonies* honor individual achievements and important events that happen during a member's career. They can take place in either formal environments (staff meetings, commander's calls, parades, or special social functions, such as awards banquets) or informal environments (such as in a work center or a supervisor's office). Examples are awards, decorations, reenlistment, promotion, and retirement.

Military social functions include formal gatherings, such as awards banquets, special-occasion functions (such as the anniversary of the Air Force, Christmas, and so forth), dining-ins, dining-outs, and the Order of the Sword. The dining-in is a formal dinner for members of a military organization or unit. Ceremony, tradition, and good fellowship abound. Guest speakers are frequently invited, awards may be presented, new and departing personnel may be recognized. Those attending wear the formal Air Force mess dress uniform or the semiformal uniform. The dining-out follows the same basic format except that spouses, friends, and civilians may also attend. The Order of the Sword is a special program where noncommissioned officers of a command recognize individuals they hold in high esteem and wish to honor. Those selected for induction are usually honored during a formal ceremony at a dining-in.

## THE USAF THUNDERBIRDS

The USAF Thunderbirds serve as a source of personal pride and symbolism and inspire esprit de corps, teamwork, self-discipline, and the pursuit of excellence. The U.S. Air Force's official aerial demonstration team, the Thunderbirds, gave their first performance in 1953. Since then the Thunderbirds have traveled throughout the United States and to sixty countries around the world. Frequently referred to as America's "Ambassadors in Blue," they have logged over four thousand performances before more than 325 million people, including members of the USAF, prime ministers, presidents, foreign dignitaries, celebrities, and countless fans.

The most visible part of the Thunderbird team is its aircraft, the General Dynamics F-16 Fighting Falcon, a multirole combat fighter. During a typical performance, the red, white, and blue aircraft perform a variety of graceful, intricate maneuvers, sometimes in formations where their wing tips are separated laterally by only three to five feet.

The Thunderbird team is composed of more than 130 personnel. Each member is a volunteer, hand selected from the stacks of special-duty applications. They are chosen because of an ability to perform their jobs to the squadron's exacting standards.

Approximately 120 highly skilled enlisted men and women support the operation in over thirty different career fields. United States Air Force Maj. Nicole

Malachowski became the first woman pilot selected to fly as part of the USAF Thunderbirds. Her first public performance was in March 2006 and she spent the 2006 and 2007 air show seasons flying the Number 3 (right wing) aircraft in the diamond formation.

If you are interested in information about applying for a special-duty assignment with the USAF Thunderbirds, see chapter 19, "How to Get the 'Right' Assignments."

## SOURCES OF ADDITIONAL INFORMATION

Air Force Pamphlet 36-2241, Volume 1, *Professional Development Guide.* See chapter 8, "Military Customs, Courtesies, and Protocol for Special Events."

Consult your supervisor or your unit's first sergeant.

# 3

# Who's Who: Grades, Roles, and Responsibilities

As of October 2010, there were more than 329,000 individuals on active duty, and more than 138,000 civilian employees. The Air National Guard and Air Force Reserve add approximately 177,000 more to these numbers. Their roles and responsibilities are based on their grade and status and on the traditions and standards established and subscribed to by the Air Force community.

## THE ENLISTED FORCE STRUCTURE

The enlisted force structure has three tiers, each with specific grades that correspond to levels of training, technical competence, and leadership and management responsibilities.

As members of the profession of arms, all enlisted members are sworn to support and defend the Constitution of the United States and to obey the orders of the officers appointed over them. As enlistees progress from airman basic to senior airman, they acquire the necessary discipline and professional military education and may be appointed candidates for noncommissioned officer (NCO) status by their commanders. Attaining NCO status is a special point in an airman's career. It is recognition that he or she is capable of assuming positions of increased grade, assuming responsibilities for providing leadership through example, and upholding Air Force policies, traditions, and standards.

Within the enlisted ranks, NCOs take precedence over all airmen and other NCOs according to grade and within grade. Within each grade, leadership responsibility rests on the individual who is senior in rank. The specific responsibilities within each tier are described below.

**The Airman Tier.** The airman tier, also referred to as the entry tier, is the first tier of the enlisted force structure. It consists of the grades airman basic (AB), airman (Amn), airman first class (A1C), and senior airman (SrA). When they enter the USAF, these airmen pursue training programs and develop skills in their specialties.

## The Enlisted Force Structure

| | | | | |
|---|---|---|---|---|
| **SENIOR NONCOMMISSIONED OFFICER TIER** | Chief Master Sergeant | Superintendent | | Manager |
| | Senior Master Sergeant | Superintendent | | Manager |
| | Master Sergeant | Craftsman | Supervisor | Manager |
| **NONCOMMISSIONED OFFICER TIER** | Technical Sergeant | Craftsman | | Supervisor |
| | Staff Sergeant | Craftsman | | Supervisor |
| **AIRMAN TIER** | Senior Airman | Journeyman | | Supervisor |
| | Airman First Class | Apprentice | | Worker |
| | Airman | Apprentice | | Worker |
| **ENTRY** | Airman Basic | Apprentice | | |

As airmen progress in grade, they are assigned more responsibilities in their specialties and, at the senior airman level, enter a transition phase to prepare for the second tier and the role of noncommissioned officer. All airmen in the first tier are expected to understand and conform to Air Force standards. As they increase in grade, they develop supervisory and leadership skills and become role models for other airmen.

**The Noncommissioned Officer Tier.** The NCO tier includes the grades of staff sergeant (SSgt) and technical sergeant (TSgt). The technical and supervisory roles of NCOs increase in scope consistent with their grade and responsibilities. NCOs are responsible for the development of all enlisted personnel under their supervision and must continually strive to ensure that assigned tasks are effectively and efficiently accomplished to meet the needs of the Air Force mission. They have further responsibility for self-development within their specialties through professional military education and off-duty education programs. They establish rapport and maintain open communication with their subordinates, contemporaries, and superiors. They also ensure fair and equitable treatment of personnel and ensure that Air Force standards are met.

**The Senior Noncommissioned Officer Tier.** The senior noncommissioned officer tier includes the grades of master sergeant (MSgt), senior master sergeant (SMSgt), and chief master sergeant (CMSgt). Senior NCOs are thoroughly trained in their specialties, and they are also used as leaders and managers with supervisory responsibilities. They are assigned duties commensurate with their skill level and status, for example, as chief of a section or branch, superintendent of a division or unit, or in special circumstances, detachment chief or commandant. They are responsible for developing personnel under their supervision into a cohesive team capable of meeting challenges and effectively accomplishing mission requirements. They provide counsel and guidance to subordinates and provide feedback to commanders and others in their chain of command. They also take the lead in assuring fair and equitable treatment and in achieving, maintaining, and enforcing Air Force standards.

**The Life Cycle of Education, Training, and Grade (Rank).** The Air Force training review of 1992 created more rigorous training standards for the future and standardized training concepts and procedures. It also aligned skill level advancement with professional military education (PME) and established career phase points. Along with the changes in the new training program came newly defined terms for the skill levels awarded to enlisted personnel:

- The 3 skill level is referred to as the *apprentice* level. It is awarded to formal technical training school graduates.
- The 5 skill level is referred to as the *journeyman* level. It is awarded when commanders ensure that trainees are at least senior airmen, have been in upgrade training at least twelve months, have completed the required career development course (CDC) for their Air Force specialties, and have completed all of the training requirements listed in their career field education and training plans (CFETP).
- The 7 skill level is referred to as the *craftsman* level. It is restricted to staff sergeants and above. To be awarded, the airman must be entered into upgrade training and complete eighteen months of on-the-job training, the required 7-level CDC, and all training requirements listed in the CFETP. Trainees are awarded the 7 skill level when they graduate from the craftsman technical training course.
- The 9 skill level is referred to as the *superintendent* level. The new policy restricts the 9 skill level award to senior master sergeants upon graduation from the senior noncommissioned officer academy (SNCOA) for active-duty personnel or completion of the SNCOA correspondence course for AFR and ANG personnel.

The accompanying illustration shows enlisted education and training paths that coincide with the grades and ranks of USAF enlisted personnel.

**Special NCO Positions.** The *first sergeant* plays a vital role in every unit. He or she is a senior noncommissioned officer in the grade of master sergeant, senior master sergeant, or chief master sergeant. First sergeants ensure that assigned personnel are aware of and understand their commanders' policies, and they also represent the interests of enlisted personnel to their commanders. They are actively involved in morale, welfare, and career issues that affect members on and off duty. Personnel in these positions frequently interact with other key personnel and agencies on base. As such, they are good points of contact for information, guidance, and assistance.

## ENLISTED INSIGNIA OF GRADE

| AIR FORCE | ARMY | MARINES | NAVY |
|---|---|---|---|
| Chief Master Sergeant of the Air Force (CMSAF) | Sergeant Major of the Army (SMA) | Sergeant Major of the Marine Corps (SgtMajMC) | Master Chief Petty Officer of the Navy (MCPON) |
| Chief Master Sergeant (CMSgt) / Command Chief Master Sergeant | Command Sergeant Major (CSM) / Sergeant Major (SGM) | Sergeant Major (SgtMaj) / Master Gunnery Sergeant (MGySgt) | Fleet/Command Master Chief Petty Officer / Master Chief Petty Officer (MCPO) |
| Senior Master Sergeant (SMSgt) / First Sergeant (E-8) | First Sergeant (1SG) / Master Sergeant (MSG) | First Sergeant (1stSgt) / Master Sergeant (MSgt) | Senior Chief Petty Officer (SCPO) |
| Master Sergeant (MSgt) / First Sergeant (E-7) | Platoon Sergeant (PSG) or Sergeant First Class (SFC) | Gunnery Sergeant (GySgt) | Chief Petty Officer (CPO) |
| Technical Sergeant (TSgt) | Staff Sergeant (SSG) | Staff Sergeant (SSgt) | Petty Officer First Class (PO1) |
| Staff Sergeant (SSgt) | Sergeant (SGT) | Sergeant (Sgt) | Petty Officer Second Class (PO2) |
| Senior Airman (SrA) | Corporal (CPL) / Specialist (SPC) | Corporal (Cpl) | Petty Officer Third Class (PO3) |
| Airman First Class (A1C) | Private First Class (PFC) | Lance Corporal (LCpl) | Seaman (Seaman) |
| Airman (Amn) | Private E-2 (PV2) | Private First Class (PFC) | Seaman Apprentice (SA) |
| Airman Basic (AB) (no insignia) | Private E-1 (PV1) (no insignia) | Private (Pvt) (no insignia) | Seaman Recruit (SR) |

# OFFICER INSIGNIA OF GRADE

| AIR FORCE | ARMY | MARINES | NAVY |
|---|---|---|---|
| General of the Air Force | General of the Army | (None) | Fleet Admiral |
| General | General | General | Admiral |
| Lieutenant General | Lieutenant General | Lieutenant General | Vice Admiral |
| Major General | Major General | Major General | Rear Admiral (Upper Half) |
| Brigadier General | Brigadier General | Brigadier General | Rear Admiral (Lower Half) |
| Colonel | Colonel | Colonel | Captain |
| Lieutenant Colonel | Lieutenant Colonel | Lieutenant Colonel | Commander |
| Major | Major | Major | Lieutenant Commander |

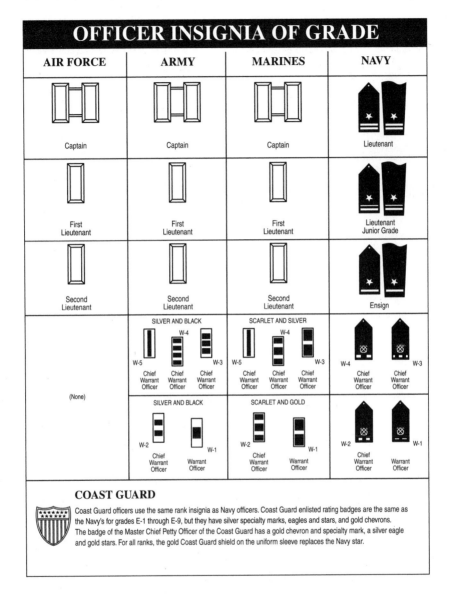

## OFFICER INSIGNIA OF GRADE

| AIR FORCE | ARMY | MARINES | NAVY |
|---|---|---|---|
| Captain | Captain | Captain | Lieutenant |
| First Lieutenant | First Lieutenant | First Lieutenant | Lieutenant Junior Grade |
| Second Lieutenant | Second Lieutenant | Second Lieutenant | Ensign |

**COAST GUARD**

Coast Guard officers use the same rank insignia as Navy officers. Coast Guard enlisted rating badges are the same as the Navy's for grades E-1 through E-9, but they have silver specialty marks, eagles and stars, and gold chevrons. The badge of the Master Chief Petty Officer of the Coast Guard has a gold chevron and specialty mark, a silver eagle and gold stars. For all ranks, the gold Coast Guard shield on the uniform sleeve replaces the Navy star.

The *command chief master sergeant (CCMS)* occupies a position at most major installations and at the major commands, numbered air forces, air divisions, direct reporting units, and separate operating agencies. The incumbent is a chief master sergeant who has the responsibility of maintaining liaison between the commander and the enlisted force. He or she works closely with other key personnel and staff agencies to ensure that the commander's policies are known and understood, and advises the commander on issues of concern for the enlisted force.

CCMSs also monitor compliance with Air Force standards, serve on advisory councils, maintain liaison with officials and programs in the local community, and perform other duties related to their positions based on local command needs. The command chief master sergeant role went into effect on November 1, 1999, and it offers a new insignia. The title and star let everyone know who the top NCO in their organization is.

The *Chief Master Sergeant of the Air Force (CMSAF)* is the senior enlisted member of the U.S. Air Force and takes precedence over all enlisted members while serving in the position. The incumbent acts as the personal advisor to the Air Force Chief of Staff and the Secretary of the Air Force on matters concerning the morale, welfare, effective use, and progress of the enlisted force.

## CADETS
Cadets of the U.S. Air Force Academy are presidential appointees and are officers in the constitutional sense. They do not have a military rank and neither outrank nor are outranked by enlisted personnel. Cadets are not on active duty, are not saluted by enlisted personnel, and are not placed in supervisory positions over enlisted personnel. However, since they are officers in a constitutional sense, they hold a position below commissioned officers for protocol purposes.

## COMMISSIONED OFFICERS
Commissioned officers perform in leadership and management roles and also in specialized and technical fields. For certain USAF positions, a commission is a prerequisite (for example, exercising command authority or other authority as required by law and other statutory provisions, such as the Uniform Code of Military Justice, appropriations acts, and so forth). Officers' responsibilities increase with grade and are based on a three-tier formation: (1) company-grade officers include second lieutenants, first lieutenants, and captains; (2) field-grade officers include majors, lieutenant colonels, and colonels; (3) general officers include brigadier generals, major generals, lieutenant generals, and generals.

## CIVILIAN PERSONNEL
Civilian employees constitute approximately one-third of the U.S. Air Force's workforce and perform in a wide range of capacities. Civilian positions are subject to either the General Schedule (GS) or the Federal Wage System (FWS). At base level, the focal point for questions about the civilian work force is the Civilian Personnel Office.

**FOREIGN NATIONAL EMPLOYEES**
As of October 2010, the U.S. Air Force employed about 13,000 foreign nationals
on overseas installations and bases. Foreign nationals are normally used in support
roles, as stipulated in Status of Forces Agreements and local laws. At base level,
questions regarding their policies or use should be referred through USAF supervisory channels or the host nation's civilian personnel office.

**SOURCES OF ADDITIONAL INFORMATION**
> Air Force Instruction 36-2618, *The Enlisted Force Structure.*
> Air Force Pamphlet 36-2241, *Professional Development Guide.*

# 4

# Mission and Organization

The U.S. Air Force, like the other U.S. Armed Forces, is organized and operated in the interest of national defense. The basic institutional framework for the armed forces is derived from the Constitution, which places the military under civilian control—under the President, who occupies the position of Commander in Chief.

The President delegates authority to the Office of the Secretary of Defense, the Department of Defense, the Office of the Joint Chiefs of Staff, unified and specified commands, and the military departments: the Air Force, the Army, and the Navy (including the Marine Corps, and in times of war, the Coast Guard). In turn, each military department develops and trains its forces to perform the primary functions that support national objectives and policies, and the efforts of the other services.

## THE AIR FORCE MISSION
The mission of the United States Air Force is to fly, fight, and win—in air, space, and cyberspace. Teamed with the Army, Navy, and Marine Corps, the Air Force is prepared to fight and win any war if deterrence fails. To achieve that mission, the Air Force has a vision of *Global Vigilance, Reach and Power*. That vision orbits around three core competencies: Developing Airmen, Technology-to-Warfighting, and Integrating Operations. These core competencies make six distinctive capabilities possible:
- **Air and Space Superiority**: With it, joint forces can dominate enemy operations in all dimensions—land, sea, air, and space.
- **Global Attack**: Because of technological advances, the Air Force can attack anywhere, anytime—and do so quickly and with greater precision than ever before.
- **Rapid Global Mobility**: Being able to respond quickly and decisively anywhere we're needed is key to maintaining rapid global mobility.

- **Precision Engagement**: The essence lies in the ability to apply selective force against specific targets because the nature and variety of future contingencies demand both precise and reliable use of military power with minimal risk and collateral damage.
- **Information Superiority**: The ability of joint force commanders to keep pace with information and incorporate it into a campaign plan is crucial.
- **Agile Combat Support**: Deployment and sustainment are keys to successful operations and cannot be separated. Agile combat support applies to all forces, from those permanently based to contingency buildups to expeditionary forces.

The Air Force bases these core competencies and distinctive capabilities on a shared commitment to three core values—integrity first, service before self, and excellence in all we do.

## AIR FORCE ORGANIZATION

The Air Force mission is planned and carried out at different organizational levels. Airmen are assigned at every level throughout the Air Force.

At the top level, the Department of the Air Force is administered by a civilian secretary and is supervised by a military Chief of Staff, an Air Force four-star general. Both of these officials are appointed by the President, with the consent of the Senate. The *Secretary of the Air Force* exercises authority through civilian assistants and the Chief of Staff but retains immediate supervision of activities that involve vital relationships with Congress, the Secretary of Defense, other governmental officials, and the public.

The *Chief of Staff of the Air Force (CSAF)* serves as a member of the Joint Chiefs of Staff and the Armed Forces Policy Council. He also presides over the *Air Staff*, transmits Air Staff plans and recommendations to the Secretary of the Air Force, and acts as the Secretary's agent in carrying them out. To assist the Secretary and the Chief of Staff, the Secretariat and the Air Staff (also referred to as HQ USAF) establish programs and policies to implement objectives. These, in turn, become mission requirements. The Air Staff operates out of the Pentagon in Washington, D.C., and several other locations.

Below the HQ USAF level, there are nine major commands (MAJCOMs), twenty-eight field operating agencies (FOAs), and five direct reporting units (DRUs) that, along with their subordinate elements, constitute the field organization that carries out the Air Force mission.

## MAJOR COMMANDS (MAJCOMS)

The major commands group similar functions together and provide an intermediate level of command between base-level operations and Headquarters USAF. They are organized by function in the United States and by geographical location in overseas areas. Their missions are either operational or support. Operational

# Department of the Air Force

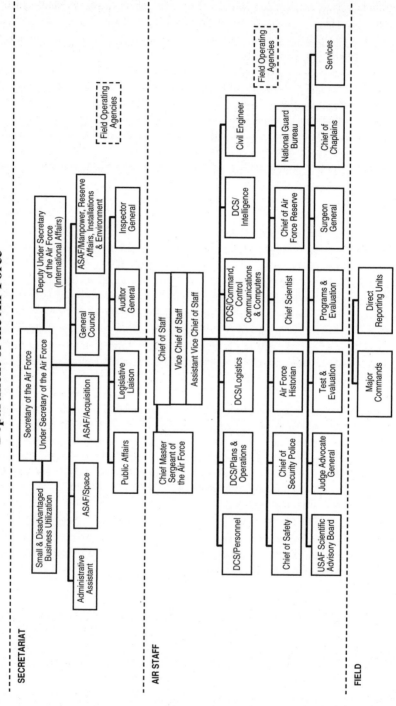

**SECRETARIAT**

Secretary of the Air Force
Under Secretary of the Air Force
Deputy Under Secretary of the Air Force (International Affairs)

- Administrative Assistant
- Small & Disadvantaged Business Utilization
- ASAF/Space
- ASAF/Acquisition
- Public Affairs
- Legislative Liaison
- General Council
- Auditor General
- ASAF/Manpower, Reserve Affairs, Installations & Environment
- Inspector General

Field Operating Agencies

**AIR STAFF**

Chief of Staff
Vice Chief of Staff
Assistant Vice Chief of Staff

Chief Master Sergeant of the Air Force

- DCS/Personnel
- DCS/Plans & Operations
- DCS/Logistics
- DCS/Command, Control Communications & Computers
- DCS/Intelligence
- Civil Engineer
- USAF Scientific Advisory Board
- Chief of Security Police
- Air Force Historian
- Chief Scientist
- Chief of Air Force Reserve
- National Guard Bureau
- Chief of Safety
- Judge Advocate General
- Test & Evaluation
- Programs & Evaluation
- Surgeon General
- Chief of Chaplains
- Services

Field Operating Agencies

**FIELD**

- Direct Reporting Units
- Major Commands

commands are composed, in whole or in part, of strategic, tactical, space, or defense forces; or of flying forces that directly support such forces. Support commands may provide supplies, weapons systems, support systems, operational support equipment, combat material, maintenance, surface transportation, education and training, or special services to the Air Force and other supported organizations.

The Air Force has undergone significant organizational and mission changes to reflect changes in the world situation. Many familiar Air Force organizations and missions have been realigned. Some of the major changes include:

- Military Airlift Command (MAC), Strategic Air Command (SAC), and Tactical Air Command (TAC) were inactivated, and two new commands, Air Combat Command (ACC) and Air Mobility Command (AMC), were activated. These commands were organized with the realization that airplanes have both tactical and strategic capability and should not be constrained by artificial distinctions. Lessons learned during Desert Storm clearly demonstrated that the line between tactical and strategic airpower had become blurred. During this armed conflict, fighter and attack-designated aircraft that belonged to TAC and bombers that belonged to SAC were employed together against tactical and strategic targets.
- Air Force Systems Command (AFSC) and Air Force Logistics Command (AFLC) merged to become the Air Force Materiel Command (AFMC). This move was, in part, an outcome of the Air Force's commitment to streamline its headquarters organizations. AFMC is now a single organization responsible for fielding and maintaining quality weapons systems. As such, it gives the operational commands a single point of contact for research, development, acquisition, modification, maintenance, and long-term weapons systems support.
- Air Force Communications Command (AFCC) was reclassified from a major command (MAJCOM) to a field operating agency (FOA). As a part of the restructuring effort, the size of AFCC dropped dramatically due to the transfer of field operational communications and computer responsibilities to the new MAJCOMs and agencies they supported.
- Air Education and Training Command (AETC) was formed in July 1993 to combine the missions of the Air Training Command (ATC) and Air University (AU).

As a result of the restructuring initiative, the USAF now has ten MAJCOMs. Their names, roles, and missions are as follows.

### Air Combat Command (ACC)

The ACC integrates capabilities across air, space, and cyberspace to deliver precise, coercive effects in defense of our nation and its global interests. ACC is the lead command for the combat Air Force. The command organizes, trains, equips, and deploys combat-ready forces to support combatant commanders around the globe. Additionally, ACC provides the air component headquarters to U.S. Northern, Southern, and Central commands and supports the in-place air components of U.S. European and Pacific commands. ACC also provides air defense forces to North American Aerospace Defense Command. To accomplish the objectives of the National Defense Strategy, the command operates fighter, attack, bomber, intelligence, surveillance and reconnaissance, combat search and rescue, battle-management, electronic combat, and unmanned aircraft system platforms. In addition, ACC conducts information operations and provides command, control, communications, and intelligence systems to theater commanders and combat forces. Headquarters: Langley AFB, Virginia.

### Air Mobility Command (AMC)
AMC provides global air mobility—the right effects, in the right place, at the right time. AMC Airmen—active duty, Air National Guard, Air Force Reserve, and civilians—provide airlift and aerial refueling for all of America's armed forces. They also provide aeromedical evacuation and Global Reach laydown. The command has many special-duty and operational support aircraft and plays a crucial role in providing humanitarian support at home and around the world. Headquarters: Scott AFB, Illinois.

### Air Force Space Command (AFSPC)
Air Force Space Command is responsible for organizing, training, and equipping mission-ready space and cyberspace forces and capabilities for North American Aerospace Defense Command, U.S. Strategic Command, and other combatant commands worldwide. AFSPC oversees Air Force network operations to provide capabilities in, through, and from cyberspace; manages a global network of satellites; and is responsible for space system development and acquisition. It executes spacelift to launch satellites with a variety of expendable launch systems and operates them to provide space capabilities in support of combatant commanders around the clock. It provides positioning, navigation, timing, communications, missile warning, weather, and intelligence warfighting support. AFSPC personnel operate sensors that provide direct attack warning and assessment to U.S. Strategic Command and North American Aerospace Defense Command. The command develops, acquires, fields, operates, and sustains space systems and fields and sustains cyber systems. Headquarters: Peterson AFB, Colorado.

### Pacific Air Forces (PACAF)
Pacific Air Forces provide Pacific Command integrated expeditionary Air Force capabilities to defend the homeland, promote stability, dissuade/deter aggression, and swiftly defeat enemies. PACAF organizes, trains, equips, and maintains resources prepared to conduct a broad spectrum of air operations—from humanitarian relief to decisive combat employment—in the Department of Defense's largest area of responsibility. PACAF conducts multinational exercises and hosts international exchange events to foster partnerships for regional security and stability in an area covering thirteen time zones and one hundred million square miles, with 60

# EMBLEMS OF MAJOR AIR COMMANDS

**Air Combat Command**

**Air Mobility Command**

**Air Force Space Command**

**Pacific Air Forces**

**U.S. Air Forces in Europe**

**Air Education and Training Command**

**Air Force Materiel Command**

**Air Force Special Operations Command**

**Air Force Reserve Command**

**Air Force Global Strike Command**

percent of the world's population, one-third of the world's economic activity, and five of the six largest armed forces. Headquarters: Hickam AFB, Hawaii.

### U.S. Air Forces Europe (USAFE)
U.S. Air Forces in Europe executes the U.S. European Command mission with forward-based air power to provide forces for global operations, ensure strategic access, assure allies, deter aggression, and build and maintain partnerships. USAFE promotes regional stability, supports combatant command missions, develops and cares for Airmen and their families, and sustains forward-based infrastructure. USAFE consists of 2 numbered Air Forces, 7 main operating bases and 114 geographically separated units. Headquarters: Ramstein Air Base, Germany.

### Air Education and Training Command (AETC)
AETC develops America's airmen today, for tomorrow. It is responsible for recruiting, accessing, commissioning, and training USAF enlisted and officer personnel. This includes basic military training, initial and advanced technical training for enlisted and commissioned personnel, and flying training. AETC also conducts and manages the Air Force Recruiting and the Air Force Reserve Officer Training Corps (ROTC) programs and administers the Community College of the Air Force (CCAF) program. With the integration of Air University (AU) programs into this new MAJCOM, AETC is also responsible for conducting Professional Military Education (PME), graduate education, and professional continuing education programs for commissioned officers and noncommissioned officers. Headquarters: Randolph AFB, Texas.

### Air Force Materiel Command (AFMC)
AFMC researches, develops, tests, acquires, delivers, and logistically supports every Air Force weapons system. It works closely with its customers (the operational commands) to ensure that each has the most capable aircraft, missiles, and support equipment possible. AFMC's involvement is ongoing, from the initial inception of a weapons system on the drawing board to support through its operational life and its final disposition and retirement from use. It operates major product centers, logistics centers, test centers, and laboratories. The command was created in July 1992 from the integration of the Air Force Logistics Command and the Air Force Systems Command. This integration was driven by budget reductions, streamlining of the Air Force, and defense management reforms. The new command emphasizes continuous process improvement and strong partnership with the operational commands and industry. Headquarters: Wright-Patterson AFB, Ohio.

### Air Force Special Operations Command (AFSOC)
AFSOC organizes, trains, and equips Air Force Special Operations forces for worldwide deployment and assignment to regional unified commands for conducting unconventional warfare, direct action, special reconnaissance, counterterrorism, foreign internal defense, humanitarian assistance, psychological operations,

personnel recovery, and counternarcotics. It is responsible to U.S. Special Operations Command for the readiness of Air Force special operations forces to conduct the war on terrorism and to disrupt, defeat, and destroy terrorist networks that threaten the United States, its citizens, and its interests worldwide. The command's mission areas include shaping and stability operations; battlefield air operations; information operations; intelligence, surveillance and reconnaissance; specialized air and space mobility; precision engagement; and agile combat support. Headquarters: Hurlburt Field, Florida.

### Air Force Reserve Command (AFRC)

AFRC became a MAJCOM with the enactment of the 1997 Defense Authorization Act. The Chief of the Air Force Reserve serves as the Commander of the AFRC. Located at Robins AFB, Georgia, HQ AFRC carries out the Chief of Staff's responsibility for command of Air Force Reserve (AFR) forces. It provides about 20 percent of the Air Force's capability with only about 4 percent of the total Air Force budget, while spanning a wide variety of missions. It's the only Department of Defense unit that conducts fixed-wing aerial spray missions. It also flies hurricane hunter missions for the National Weather Service and is administratively responsible for the Air Force's individual mobilization augmentee program.

### Air Force Global Strike Command (AFGSC)

AFGSC became a MAJCOM in 2009 and contributes to the Air Force strategy of providing nuclear deterrence and global strike forces for combatant commanders, allies, and joint forces. The AFGSC's mission is to develop and provide combat-ready forces for nuclear deterrence and global strike operations to support to President of the United States and combatant commanders. The B-52 Stratofortress and B-2 Spirit are two airframes that became part of the AFGSC's forces in 2010. The command has three bomb wings and three missile wings, and is headquartered at Barksdale AFB, Louisiana, with approximately 900 people at the headquarters and more than 20,000 across the six wings at five installations.

### Air National Guard (ANG)

The Air National Guard is administered by the National Guard Bureau, a joint bureau of the departments of the Army and Air Force, located in the Pentagon, Washington, D.C. It is one of the Reserve components of the United States armed forces that augment the active components. Although the ANG is not a MAJCOM, it plays a vital role in the Total Force with both federal and state missions. The dual mission, a provision of the U. S. Constitution, results in each guardsman holding membership in the National Guard of his or her state and in the National Guard of the United States.

### SUBCOMMANDS AND LOWER LEVELS OF COMMAND

Below the major command level, intermediate levels of command and organization are established to meet mission requirements. They include numbered air forces, wings, groups, squadrons, and flights. Air divisions (ADs), which were intermediate levels of command between the numbered air forces and wings, were eliminated during 1993 with the restructuring initiative and the decision to delegate more power and authority down to the wing level. This action shortened operational command lines and reduced overhead staff functions.

Numbered Air Forces (NAFs) were also restructured during 1993 to a strictly operational and warfighting role. With the elimination of support functions, staffing has been reduced by approximately 50 percent. Usually commanded by a two- or three-star general, the remaining NAF staff is dedicated to operational planning and employment of forces for several wings.

Wings are the basic Air Force units for generating and employing combat capability. They may have an operational mission (such as air combat, airlift, or flying training) or a specialized mission (such as an intelligence wing). They may also have the responsibility for providing support to a MAJCOM headquarters or geographically separated units. Each wing has a commander who is responsible and accountable for that wing's mission results. A new wing structure, referred to as the objective wing, was designed and implemented to streamline and consolidate responsibilities and move toward clear lines of command. In the majority of cases, the objective wing organization will only have operations, logistics, support, and medical groups assigned. Additional groups, such as security police, civil engineering, and communications, may be added to larger wings. Each of these groups has a commander who is responsible and accountable to the wing commander for mission accomplishment. The Air Force has composite wings that operate more than one kind of aircraft and wings that continue to operate a single type of aircraft. Both may be configured as self-contained units designated for quick air intervention anywhere in the world.

Groups are flexible units composed of two or more squadrons that may have identical, similar, or different missions. Their role may be operational, supporting, or administrative. Groups have numerical designations and usually take the number of the wing to which they are assigned. For example, the groups assigned to the 123 Wing would be designated the 123 Operations Group, the 123 Logistics Group, the 123 Support Group, and so forth.

Squadrons are the basic unit of the Air Force. Each squadron formation is based on either operational commands or the functional grouping of specific tasks and responsibilities (for example, aircrew or missile operations, security police, civil engineering, aircraft maintenance, or transportation).

Detachments are elements of a large unit (squadron, group, or wing) that are geographically separated from the parent unit.

Flights are the lowest unit level in the Air Force. Numerically designated flights exist for small mission elements that need to be incorporated into an organized unit. Alphabetically designated flights are used to group similar functions within a unit. For example, A, B, C, and D flights could be used to designate certain personnel within a Security Police squadron. In turn, those designations could

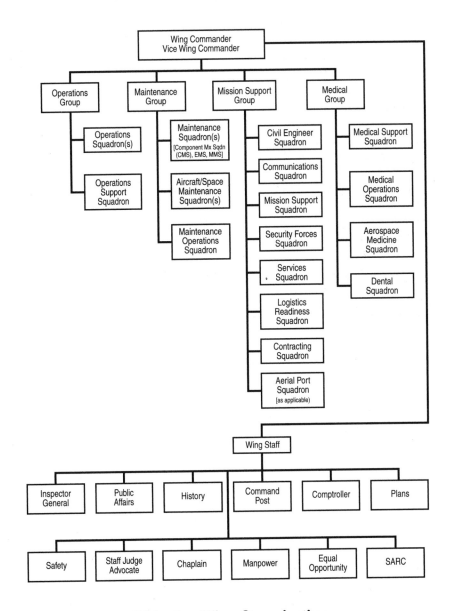

**Objective Wing Organization**

## Example of a Composite Wing

| CAPABILITY | | AIRCRAFT |
|---|---|---|
| MULTI-ROLE | 24 | F-16C |
| NIGHT/UNDER WEATHER ATTACK | 12 | F-16C (LANTIRN) |
| LONG RANGE/PRECISION GUIDED MUNITIONS | 12 | F-15E |
| AIR SUPERIORITY | 24 | F-15C |
| AIR REFUELING | 6 | KC-135R |
| SURVEILLANCE/CONTROL | 3 | E-3A |

NOTE 1.   The mission of a wing, such as the one shown above, would be air intervention.

NOTE 2.   A composite wing tasked for ground support could also include a mix of A-10s, F-16s, and AC-130 gunships.

NOTE 3.   A composite wing tasked for special operations could also include a mix of MH-53J pave low and MH-60G pave hawk helicopters, MC-130 combat talons, and AC-130 gunships.

NOTE 4.   Bombers and electronic support aircraft, such as the EF-111 Raven, could also be included in composite wings whose missions require the support of such aircraft.

be used to schedule training requirements and periods of duty (day shift, swing shift, mid-shift, and breaks). The term *flight* can also be used to denote a parade formation of two or more squads.

## FIELD OPERATING AGENCIES (FOAS)

A field operating agency (FOA) is a subdivision of the Air Force that carries out field activities under the operational control of a USAF functional manager and beyond the scope of the MAJCOMS. The USAF has many FOAs, whose missions complement, but remain separate from, those of the major commands.

**Air Force Agency for Modeling and Simulation, Orlando, Florida.** AFAMS supports development and use of the joint synthetic battlespace for training, analysis, acquisition, test and evaluation, experimentation and operations. It manages, coordinates, and integrates Air Force and joint modeling and simulation programs and initiatives; manages the Air Force modeling and simulation resource repository; and staffs the Air Force modeling and simulation help desk. (http://www.afams.af.mil)

**Air Force Audit Agency, Washington, D.C.** AFAA provides all levels of Air Force management with independent audit services. It also produces audit products that evaluate the efficiency, effectiveness, and economy of Air Force programs and activities. (https://www.afaa.af.mil)

**Air Force Center for Engineering and the Environment, San Antonio, Texas.** AFCEE manages Air Force military construction, military housing, and environmental restoration programs. It also oversees military family housing privatization by maintaining an extensive housing portfolio and training base asset managers. The center employs more than 500 civilians and 48 military professionals, who specialize in archeology, architecture, chemistry, engineering, geology, planning, and toxicology. Three regional environmental offices serve as advocates for the Air Force. Two overseas branches are located at Ramstein Air Base, Germany, and Joint Base Pearl Harbor-Hickam, Hawaii. Contractor partners augment the center's in-house staff. Many of these contractors are the nation's most respected private firms. The center's multi-billion dollar contracting capacity covers the entire range of environmental and construction management services that take place worldwide. (www.afcee.af.mil)

**Air Force Civil Engineer Support Agency, Tyndall AFB, Florida.** AFCESA maximizes base civil engineers' capabilities in base and contingency operations. It provides professional engineering support; training; vehicles and equipment; utility rate intervention and negotiation; airfield pavement evaluations; depot-level repair support of power generation, electrical distribution, and aircraft arresting systems; as well as technical support for heating, ventilating, and air conditioning systems. (http://www.afcesa.af.mil)

**Air Force Cost Analysis Agency, Arlington, Virginia.** AFCAA performs independent component cost analyses in support of major Air Force programs. It is responsible for Air Force cost estimating and analysis, develops cost models and databases, and maintains a cost library and the Air Force total ownership cost database. (http://www.saffm.hq.af.mil)

**Air Force Flight Standards Agency, Oklahoma City, Oklahoma.** AFFSA consistently increases the effectiveness and combat capability of Air Force global air operations by ensuring access to worldwide airspace in all weather conditions. The agency provides accurate, relevant, and timely flight information and support services to DOD, national, and coalition aviators. AFFSA establishes U.S. Air Force flight rules, standards, and policy, and ensures congruity with DOD, joint, Federal Aviation Administration, NATO, and ICAO standards. It develops, revises, coordinates, and ensures joint interoperability of global Air Force visual/instrument flight procedures. AFFSA acts as lead command for the creation and application of criteria, procedures, and precision equipment for worldwide instrument flight operations, air traffic control, airfield management, and landing systems for the Air Force.

**Air Force Historical Research Agency, Maxwell AFB, Alabama.** AFHRA archives historical documents, responds to inquiries for historical data, approves unit heraldry and emblems, records official aerial victory credits, tracks organizational lineages, and provides research facilities for military scholars and the public. (http://www.afhra.af.mil)

**Air Force Inspection Agency, Kirtland AFB, New Mexico.** AFIA provides Air Force leaders with independent assessments to improve Air Force operations and support. It is the single comprehensive inspection agency of Air Force medical organizations. It conducts nuclear surety inspection oversight, nuclear inspection training and certification, health services, and radioactive material inspections. AFIA performs by-law compliance inspections of Air Force-level field operating agencies and direct reporting units. It publishes the Air Force's oldest magazine, "TIG Brief." The agency has the capability to provide independent assessments of acquisitions, operations, logistics, and support for the Secretary of the Air Force, Air Force Chief of Staff, Secretary of the Air Force inspector general, and major command commanders. (http://afia.af.mil)

**Air Force Intelligence, Surveillance and Reconnaissance Agency, San Antonio, Texas.** The agency organizes, trains, equips, and presents assigned forces and capabilities to conduct intelligence, surveillance, and reconnaissance for combatant commanders. It implements and oversees execution of policy and guidance to expand Air Force ISR capabilities to meet current and future challenges. More than 17,000 active duty Airmen, reservists, and Guardsmen as well as AF civilians are stationed worldwide to support the agency's global mission. The 480th ISR Wing, Langley AFB, Virginia, operates and maintains the AF Distributed Common Ground System, conducting imagery, cryptologic, and measurement and signatures intelligence activities. The 70th ISR Wing, Fort George G. Meade, Maryland, integrates Air Force capabilities into global cryptologic operations, directly supporting national-level decision makers, combatant commanders, and tactical warfighters. The Air Force Technical Applications Center, Patrick AFB, Florida, operates and monitors a variety of air, ground, space, and seaborne sensor platforms to ensure compliance with several nuclear treaties. The National Air and Space Intelligence Center, Wright-Patterson AFB, Ohio, is the Air Force's single intelligence analysis center and the primary DOD producer of foreign air and space intelligence. The Air Force Cryptologic Office in Fort Meade, Maryland, serves as the HQ Air Force ISR Agency's primary cryptologic intelligence staff in the National Capitol Region, and represents and coordinates all cryptologic matters for the Air Force within the National Security Agency. The Air Force Geospatial Intelligence Office is the HQ Air Force ISR Agency's principal geospatial intelligence element and serves as the Air Force's primary liaison to the National Security Agency on geospatial matters. The 361st ISR Group, Hurlburt Field, Florida, organizes, trains, equips, and presents ISR to Special Operations, providing direct threat warning and enhanced situational awareness to AFSOC aircrews. (www.afisr.af.mil)

**Air Force Legal Operations Agency, Joint Base Anacostia-Bolling, Washington, D.C.** The agency includes all senior defense counsel, senior trial counsel, and appellate defense and government counsel in the Air Force, as well as all Air Force civil litigators defending the Air Force against civil lawsuits claiming damages and seeking other remedies in contracts, environmental, labor, and tort litigation. The agency includes numerous field support centers to include Tort Claim, Environmental Law, Labor Law, Commercial Litigation, Contract Law, Medical Law, and Accident Investigation Board. It also includes the utility litigation team, the Medical Cost Reimbursement program, and the Air Force Claims Service Center. The agency also includes the Judge Advocate General's school and the Information Systems Directorate. The latter provides IT services to Air Force legal offices worldwide and, as the DOD Executive Agent for Federal Legal Information

Through Electronics, to legal offices throughout the DOD. AFLOA has offices worldwide at more than 76 locations and consists of 571 military and civilian attorneys and 387 military and civilian paralegals and support personnel.

**Air Force Logistics Management Agency, Maxwell AFB-Gunter Annex, Alabama.** AFLMA is the logistics problem-solving organization that conducts a wide variety of studies to produce solutions that improve combat logistics operations. It evaluates, recommends, and tests new or improved concepts, methods, systems, or procedures. (http://www.aflma.hq.af.mil)

**Air Force Manpower Agency, Randolph AFB, Texas.** AFMA determines peacetime and wartime resource requirements through objective and innovative manpower studies to improve mission performance, effectiveness, and resource efficiency. (http://www.afma.af.mil)

**Air Force Medical Operations Agency, Port San Antonio, Texas.** The agency oversees execution of Air Force Surgeon General policies supporting Air Force expeditionary capabilities, health care operations, and national security strategy. The agency provides expert consultative leadership support to seventy-five military treatment facilities and eleven major commands/direct reporting units to ensure a cost-effective, modern, and prevention-based health care continuum for 2.1 million beneficiaries worldwide. AFMOA directs and supports the clinical currency of 43,131 health care professionals providing 6.6 million visits and 133,500 bed days. The agency provides clinical and population health data and analysis to AF/SG and MAJCOM surgeons. Partners with the Assistant Secretary of Defense (Health Affairs) Secretary of the Air Force, Chief of Staff of the Air Force, and Department of Veterans Affairs.

**Air Force Medical Support Agency, Arlington, Virginia.** AFMSA is the surgeon general's primary focal point for policy development, strategies, plans, consultant services and requirements dealing with facilities, supplies, equipment, acquisition, information systems and resources. (https://www.afms.mil/sg/afmsa)

**Air Force Office of Special Investigations, Joint Base Andrews, Maryland.** AFOSI has been the Air Force's principal investigative service since 1948. It reports to the Office of the Inspector General of the Air Force. It provides investigative services to all Air Force activities. Its primary responsibilities are criminal investigation and counterintelligence services. (http://www.osi.andrews.af.mil)

**Air Force Personnel Center, Randolph AFB, Texas.** AFPC manages personnel programs and policies and ensures the right numbers of troops in the right grades and skills are available to perform Air Force missions worldwide. (http://www.afpc.randolph.af.mil)

**Air Force Personnel Operations Agency, San Antonio, Texas.** This agency provides analysis of personnel policies and programs as well as providing automated information system support for the Deputy Chief of Staff for Personnel and local users of the Personnel Data System.

**Air Force Petroleum Agency, Fort Belvoir, Virginia.** The agency is the Air Force service control point for all Defense Logistics Agency fuel-related support issues. The organization provides a full range of technical and professional services related to fuels, propellants, chemicals, lubricants, gases, and cryogenics for all aerospace vehicles, systems, and equipment. It is composed of three directorates, Operations Support, Business Support, and Product Support, and six area aerospace laboratories with worldwide presence. AFPA also develops quality assurance specifications and agreements to ensure interoperability with commercial, interservice, and international partners for sustainment of Air Force, joint, and combined force actions. (www.afpa.af.mil)

**Air Force Public Affairs Agency, Lackland AFB, Texas.** This agency provides an agile and responsive public affairs capability to the Air Force through three combat camera squadrons—1st CTCS, Charleston AFB, South Carolina; 2nd CTCS, Hill AFB, Utah; and 3rd CTCS, Lackland AFB, Texas—and seven operating locations. It provides an archiving and distribution capability for all PA products, manages licensing and branding of the Air Force trademark, and deploys crisis response teams for Air Force PA support to contingencies. It also enhances the future capabilities of the entire Public Affairs career field by conducting research and establishing guidance on emerging technologies for future PA operations. The agency also provides graphics support to all PA offices; manages career field force development through training, career tracking, and assignments; conducts force management and deployment management for the PA community; provides standards and evaluations guidance for PA activities; and procures and field-tests future equipment systems for the PA career field.

**Air Force Real Property Agency, Lackland AFB, Texas.** This is a field-operating agency within the office of the Assistant Secretary of the Air Force for Installations, Environment and Logistics. It acquires, disposes, and manages all Air Force-controlled real property worldwide. (http://www.safie.hq.af.mil)

**Air Force Review Boards Agency, Joint Base Andrews, Maryland.** This agency provides the management of various military and civilian appeals boards for the Secretary of the Air Force. These include the Personnel Council's five component boards, the Board for Correction of Military Records, and the Civilian Appellate Review Office.

**Air Force Safety Center, Kirtland AFB, New Mexico.** AFSC develops, implements, executes, and evaluates Air Force aviation, ground, weapons, systems, space mishap prevention, and nuclear surety programs to preserve combat readiness. It oversees mishap investigations, evaluates corrective actions, and ensures implementation of safety programs. (http://www.afsc.af.mil)

**Air Force Security Forces Center, Lackland AFB, Texas.** AFSFC develops force protection policies by planning and programming resources in support of nuclear, non-nuclear and weapon system security, physical and information security, base defense, combat arms, law enforcement, combating terrorism, resources protection, corrections, and the DOD military working dog program.

**Air Force Services Agency, San Antonio, Texas.** AFSA supports commanders by implementing and sustaining service policies, procedures, and quality-of-life programs that enhance combat readiness. Programs include community support and business activities, human resource activities, a contracting and purchasing agency, data systems network, and worldwide financial and banking systems. (http://www.afsv.af.mil)

**Air Force Weather Agency, Offutt AFB, Nebraska.** AFWA provides weather support worldwide to Air Force, Army, and joint warfighters; unified commands; national programs; and the national command authority. (http://afweather.afwa.af.mil)

## DIRECT REPORTING UNITS (DRUS)

A direct reporting unit (DRU) is a subdivision of the Air Force. These units are directly subordinate to HQ USAF, but they are not under the operational control of an HQ USAF functional manager because of their unique mission, legal requirements, or other factors. The USAF has three DRUs: the Air Force Operational Test and Evaluation Center, the U.S. Air Force Academy, and the Air Force District of Washington.

**Air Force Operational Test and Evaluation Center, Kirtland AFB, New Mexico.** AFOTEC is the USAF's independent test agency responsible for operational testing of new or modified weapons systems and components (for example, aircraft, missiles, munitions, space systems, and so forth) that are being developed for Air Force and multiservice use.

**United States Air Force Academy, Colorado.** USAFA is located near Colorado Springs, Colorado, and provides instruction and experience to all cadets, so that they graduate with the knowledge and character essential to leadership and the motivation to become career officers in the Air Force. The cadets receive a broad military education as a foundation for developing leadership and professional officer qualities. This includes the theory and practice of warfare, with particular emphasis on the application and contribution of airpower. The USAFA provides a four-year academic curriculum leading to a bachelor of science degree. Approximately 50 percent of cadets complete majors in the areas of science and engineering, and 40 percent in the social sciences and humanities. In addition to the academic program, USAFA cadets participate in rigorous physical education and military training.

**Air Force District of Washington.** The Air Force District of Washington is the single voice for planning and implementing Air Force and joint solutions within the National Capital Region. It accomplishes this by providing superior service always, defense support to civil authorities when asked, and effective contingency response when needed. AFDW organizes, trains, equips, and provides forces for air and space expeditionary force deployment, homeland defense operations in support of civilian authorities, and ceremonial support within the National Capital Region and worldwide. AFDW executes specified Air Force responsibilities for administration and support of Air Force headquarters and assigned units, as well as for more than forty thousand Airmen worldwide. AFDW organizations include the 11th Wing, the 79th Medical Wing, the 320th Air Expeditionary Wing, and the 844th Communications Group at Joint Base Andrews, Maryland. Its specialized units include the U.S. Air Force Band and the U.S. Air Force Honor Guard, located on Joint Base Anacostia-Bolling, Washington, D.C. AFDW is also home to the largest helicopter squadron in the Air Force, the 1st Helicopter Squadron, at Joint Base Andrews.

## TOTAL FORCE COMPOSITION
The total force composition is based on military and civilian personnel in the regular Air Force and those in Air Reserve forces. Air Reserve forces include Air Reserve units and the Air National Guard. As of October 2010 the Air Force's strength was 329,638 active-duty personnel, 138,801 civilian personnel, and 177,230 trained reserve forces.

## EXPEDITIONARY AEROSPACE FORCES
In addition to fulfilling traditional organizational missions, roles, and functions, the Air Force has evolved into an expeditionary aerospace force (EAF). An EAF is a force that is:
- Tailored to mission success with the right combination of capabilities and people to match the challenge.
- Rapidly deployable to any part of the world.
- Light and lean with the smallest possible footprint forward.
- Globally connected to reach back for worldwide information and support.
- Able to command and control the assigned forces in near real time.
- Led by a scheduled and seasoned air commander who can decisively apply the gamut of air and space capabilities across the spectrum of crisis.

Since the end of the Cold War, personnel cuts have forced every branch of the U.S. armed services to reexamine their roles as part of the national security puzzle. The Air Force looked closely and saw that it needed to prepare for the changing face of world dynamics. After reducing the size of its force and scaling back its presence overseas, it became clear that the Air Force would need to become more expeditionary (deployable) to meet future global challenges. By definition, expeditionary means "sent on military service abroad." Being expeditionary means that the Air Force will conduct global aerospace operations with forces based primarily in the United States that will deploy rapidly to begin operations as soon as they arrive at a forward operating location. This includes deployment to and operations from austere locales without a robust support infrastructure for an unknown duration in support of joint military operations.

**Operational Concept.** America's Air Force is now organized differently than in the past. Ten deployable AEFs have been constituted. They deploy to steady-state, rotational operations or remain on-call at home stations. The ten AEFs are composed of geographically separated active-duty, Air National Guard, and Air Force Reserve units from across the Air Force. Every wing in the Air Force has personnel aligned under one or more AEFs. There is no one location or base for an AEF.

Each AEF contains sets of USAF forces (aircraft, equipment, and personnel) from which tailored force packages deploy to support the warfighting commanders.

Each AEF has a cross-section of Air Force weapons systems, 150 to 175 combat-capable aircraft, and 10,000 to 15,000 airmen. The AEF also consists of expeditionary combat support (ECS) capabilities, such as security forces, communications, civil engineering, medical teams, fire fighters, transportation, and maintenance. Although some airlift and refueling resources are aligned to the AEFs, most of the global mobility resources (e.g., strategic airlift and aerial refueling that make expeditionary operations possible) are managed by Air Mobility Command (AMC) and the Joint Chiefs of Staff (JCS) airlift priority system.

**Role of Airmen in the AEF.** Approximately 65 percent of Air Force personnel serve in deployable positions. Depending on an airman's AFSC and duty location, the EAF can have a variety of effects. It is designed to bring more stability and predictability in deployment schedules.

### SOURCES OF ADDITIONAL INFORMATION
Air Force Instruction 38-101, *Air Force Organization.*
Air Force Pamphlet 36-2241, *Professional Development Guide.*

# 5

# Looking Back:
# The Importance of
# USAF History

*When I want to understand what is happening today or try to
decide what will happen tomorrow, I look back.*
— Oliver Wendell Holmes, Jr.

History is the continuing story of life and generations—of families, of affiliated groups, and of nations. Since the beginning of recorded history, the armed forces have played a strong role in society. The U.S. Armed Forces represent our country's heritage more than those of most other countries because of their ability to be in harmony with the fundamentals and values of the culture that they have served. For over two hundred years, the members of our armed forces have worked together, overcoming obstacles and adversity to achieve their objectives. They have done so in the pursuit of institutional values—in a spirit of cooperation, discipline, loyalty, and selflessness. At an individual level, members have sensed that they were part of something bigger than themselves, something that was tied irrevocably to the destiny of their society. They recognized that they were part of a special team whose continuing role was to "support and defend the Constitution of the United States of America" and to help safeguard and ensure the security of the nation and the free world.

As members of the U.S. Air Force, our understanding of past events that are related to the military and our country can be extremely valuable. Past events can serve as sources of pride; they can also help us to project visions for the future. By analyzing possibilities and choices that once existed, we can determine patterns, analyze trends, and draw conclusions about present-day situations and the consequences of the choices available.

The following pages provide insight into the value of history, information about the goals and mechanics of the Air Force History Program, and agencies that you may visit or contact for further information.

## THE AIR FORCE HISTORY PROGRAM

A sense of history has been a quality of most great men and women, and nowhere has this sense of history been more prevalent than in outstanding military leaders. The value of the Air Force History Program has been clearly stated and strongly supported by each Chief of Staff of the U.S. Air Force.

Many Air Force personnel use history in performing their daily duties. They use it to gather facts for speeches, briefings, background information, and studies, and to obtain facts to justify individual and unit awards. In a dramatic litigation case, the use of Air Force histories resulted in a $50 million savings to the Air Force. While these are all valid applications of history, some even more important uses are frequently overlooked.

1. History serves as a cultural tradition—a shared body of ideas, values, experiences, and common bonds that unite diverse groups.
2. History serves as memory and as a source of personal identity. It keeps alive the experiences, deeds, and ideas of people of the past. By allowing us to view people from the past as heroes and role models, history connects past and future and can help develop character.
3. History promotes a sense of collective immortality. By rooting human beings on a continuum of the human experience, history provides each man and woman with a sense of immortality.
4. An understanding of history can also broaden an individual's outlook and understanding and serve as a means of learning from the collective experience of others. As such, it can provide an added dimension for decision-making processes.

By reading the history of their organizations or similar organizations (in formats such as general Air Force histories, command histories, Inspector General reports, and special subject studies), leaders can broaden their outlook and develop a basis for action. Although this will not always provide direct answers to specific questions, it will provide a wider frame of reference that can be used as a sound basis for formulating answers.

**History and Its Relationship to Air Force Doctrine.** Air Force doctrine is noted in Air Force Manual 1-1, *Basic Aerospace Doctrine of the United States Air Force.* The content outlines the body of enduring principles, the general truths and accepted assumptions that provide guidance and a sense of direction for the most effective way to develop, deploy, and employ airpower.

The fundamental assumptions that constitute doctrine are based to a large degree on historical experience. Experience makes doctrine practical rather than merely theoretical. Without an awareness of what airpower has done (and has not done), Air Force members would have to derive doctrine solely from hypotheses about the capabilities of air forces. By recording and trying to understand Air Force history, we are in a better position to evaluate and to analyze objectively what airpower has done; we can gain a better understanding of what really happened and why. By drawing on lessons learned and changes that have occurred, we can enter into the future with a heightened awareness of the best courses of action.

**The History Program at the Unit Level—and Your Role in It.** Each organizational level—from shop to branch, squadron, group, wing, numbered air force, major command, direct reporting unit, and separate operating agency—contributes written materials to the Air Force Historical Program. Subjects will cover a unit's broad scope of experience during a specified period of time (e.g., three months, six months, or one year). They usually include, but are not limited to, information about weapons systems performance, inspections, achievements and innovative procedures, problems and the actions undertaken to solve them, significant events, such as exercises and deployments, financial data, personnel, and morale and welfare issues.

At the working level (shop or branch), supervisors are asked to provide data about their operations to a unit (usually squadron) historian. He or she, in turn, forwards it to the base-level historian, who usually works for the wing commander. The base-level historian reviews all of the information and decides what is appropriate for inclusion in the printed history.

97 AMW Historian MSgt. Rich Guinan, USAF (Ret.), describes the wing historian as a fellow warrior whose duty it is to constantly capture the experiences within the wing—good and bad—and record them for future leaders. It is through the historian that the American people learn of how their sons and daughters preserved their nation's freedom. Following the commander's review and approval, the unit submits its final product through channels to HQ USAF. In this way the USAF develops the overall history of the USAF. Air Force history is made available to decision makers, researchers, and members of the USAF.

## AVENUES TO USAF HISTORY

There are numerous facilities and programs that you can visit or contact to review displays and exhibits of USAF heritage and historical records. Many exist at base level. Some of the more extensive ones are described here.

**The USAF Enlisted Heritage Hall.** Established at Gunter AFB, Alabama, in 1984, the Enlisted Heritage Hall has nearly one hundred exhibits, including pictures, replicas, and static displays that provide insight into the development of airpower, trace the USAF's lineage from the U.S. Army to the present, and provide insight into the roles and achievements of enlisted personnel. For additional information, contact the Enlisted Heritage Hall Director, 550 McDonald St., Maxwell AFB-Gunter Annex, AL 36114-3107, DSN 446-1110, or call commercial (205) 279-1110.

**The National Museum of the United States Air Force.** The official United States Air Force Museum is charged with depicting the history and traditions of the USAF. Located at Wright-Patterson Air Force Base near Dayton, Ohio, it attracts over one million visitors each year and is internationally recognized as the oldest and largest military aviation museum in the world.

Approximately two thousand of the museum's fourteen thousand-plus holdings are currently on display. When viewed collectively, they are a dynamic tribute to the ingenuity, technology, and boldness of spirit that lifted men and women to the skies and then into space. The exhibits provide considerable insight into aviation history. The range extends from historic da Vinci designs of helicopters, balloons, and gliders to personal effects of legendary aviators. There are exhibits of props, jets, and space-age vehicles. Aircraft and missiles from eras of World War I, World War II, Korea, and Vietnam are on display, as are experimental and prototype aircraft that were never placed into active service. Tours can be self-guided or by group. The museum also has a good-sized restaurant and a well-stocked shopping center with aviation-related books, souvenirs, and memorabilia.

Behind the scenes, the museum maintains extensive archives for use in maintaining historical data in support of the museum's acquisition, restoration, public-information programs, and exhibits. Included are thousands of books, periodicals, technical manuals, drawings, photographs, test reports, and other aviation-related materials. The holdings are available for reference to qualified researchers, such as historians, authors, engineers, model builders, patent attorneys, and artists. For more information about museum programs, contact your base's Public Affairs office or write to USAF Museum, Wright-Patterson AFB, OH 45433, or call commercial (937) 255-3286.

**U.S. Air Force Historical Research Agency.** The USAF Historical Research Agency (USAFHRA) is the repository for all Air Force historical documents. A direct reporting unit assigned to the Chief of Staff, U.S. Air Force, it is located with the Air University Library in building 1405 at Maxwell AFB in Alabama. The center's collection consists of more than 60 million pages of material relating to the history of the service. It represents the largest and most valuable organized collection of documents on U.S. military aviation anywhere in the world.

The agency provides research and reference services for PME students and faculty and visiting researchers. More than 85 percent of the pre-1955 holdings are declassified, and the majority of documents are recorded on 16mm microfilm. Holdings consist largely of unit histories prepared by the major commands, wings, and other subordinate organizations.

Special collections, some dating back to the early 1900s, complement the unit histories. Among them are monographs, end-of-tour reports, joint and combined command documents, aircraft record cards, and materials from the U.S. Army, the British Air Ministry, and the German Air Force. The agency also houses personal papers of key retired Air Force leaders and a substantial collection of oral history interviews. About six thousand documents and collections are added to the archives annually.

**The Air University Library.** The Air University Library (AUL) is the largest library in the Department of Defense and the largest federal library outside Washington, D.C. Located at Maxwell AFB, Alabama, in building 1405, and named Fairchild Library in honor of Air University's first commander, Gen. Muir S. Fairchild, its mission is to provide professionally directed academic and research library and information services to the Air University and the Air Force.

The Muir S. Fairchild Research Information Center, founded in 1946, is the premier library in the Department of Defense (DoD). It houses well-balanced collections especially strong in the fields of warfighting, aeronautics, Air Force and DOD operations, military sciences, international relations, education, leadership, and management. The library holds more than 2.6 million items: 530,000 military documents; over 429,000 monographs and bound periodical volumes; 615,000 maps and charts; 150,000 current regulations/manuals; and over 909,000 microforms. (*http://www.au.af.mil/au/aul/commun.htm*)

**The USAF Academy Academic Library.** The USAF Academy Academic Library, also referred to as the Cadet Library, has holdings that include over 480,000 books, some 244,000 government documents, and 744,000 microfiche and hard copies of report literature. For additional information, write to the United States Air Force Academy Academic Library, USAFA, CO 80840.

All of these Air Force history centers of information have websites. See chapter 12.

## SOURCES OF ADDITIONAL INFORMATION

Air Force Manual 1-1, *Basic Aerospace Doctrine of the United States Air Force.*

Air Force Pamphlet 36-2241, *Professional Development Guide.* See the chapter on USAF history for a chronology of the major events, ideas, and people that have shaped the course of Air Force history and traditions.

For general information about your present unit's history or Air Force history, contact your unit's historian or public affairs representative. Your base library or overseas Stars and Stripes bookstores can also be good starting points.

# 6

# Looking Forward:
# The Air Force of the Future

Many opportunities and challenges face the Air Force in the twenty-first century. Some challenges are of a near-term nature, and others are focused on the long term. This chapter outlines some of the special reviews that have been conducted by the Air Force to help it meet its future national and international missions, including recognition of the important role airmen will play in future initiatives. Also discussed are other initiatives that are being pursued by the senior leadership to enhance the quality of life for those who serve.

## THE IMMEDIATE FUTURE

For the next ten to fifteen years, the U.S. Air Force will continue to have to deal with the stresses and disorders of the world as it continues the transition from the Cold War era. Defense intelligence analysts predict that no power, circumstance, or condition is likely to emerge in the short term that will be capable of overcoming post-Cold War stresses and creating a more stable global environment.

Within this environment, the "Big C" issues will continue to dominate America's political and military attention. These are (1) counterdrug operations, (2) counterintelligence against the growing variety of potentially hostile forces, (3) activities to counter proliferation of weapons of mass destruction, and (4) counterterrorism operations, especially against threats directed against the United States and its citizens, businesses, and military forces at home and abroad.

Globalization is the principal force driving the "Big C" issues. On the one hand, globalization means the increasing flow of ideas, money, people, information, and technology. It is generally a positive force that will help most in the world to advance economically and democratically. The Internet and the explosion of information available at the click of a mouse has added to and accelerated the drive toward globalization.

On the other hand, the explosion of information has exacerbated local and regional tensions. It has increased the prospects and capabilities for conflict and will be used by those who would harm America. The transfer of information on weapons production technology allows smaller states and groups to gain access to the destructive capabilities of chemical, biological, and nuclear weapons.

What follows is a brief listing of troubled countries and regions where U.S. Air Force personnel are or may have to operate. Improvised Explosive Devices (IEDs) continue to harass both civilians and military, especially in Iraq. Shoulder-fired, infrared-seeking surface-to-air missiles (SA-18, Stinger, SA-7b, etc.) also continue to threaten aircraft during takeoff or final approach when the heat signature of engines is highest, airspeed lowest, and maneuverability most critical. Threats to an airbase itself run the gamut from suicide bombers in trucks to weapons delivered by short or intermediate range ballistic missiles (SRBM/IRBM).

Some of the more specific threat areas include:

**International Terrorism.** The probability of another terrorist attack against U.S. interests, either here or abroad, perhaps with a weapon designed to cause mass casualties, is considered likely.

**The Middle East.** A worsening of conditions in the Middle East has led to expansion of Israeli-Palestinian violence. A continued commitment of the U.S. Air Force to the region combined with regional perception of the United States as Israel's primary military and political supporter greatly increases the likelihood of violence directed at American assets.

**Southwest Asia.** The drawdown of U.S. forces in Iraq and continuing operations in Afghanistan will continue to require significant levels of U.S. forces inside the countries with supporting Air Force lines of communication through bases in the Persian Gulf. U.S. operations in Afghanistan face a similar situation of internal instability requiring a U.S. force presence in these Central Command areas of operations.

**India and Pakistan.** These countries share a very tense border. Each maintains large ground forces in close proximity to that border, and there have been several clashes in recent decades. Both countries have tested nuclear weapons and have the aircraft, SRBMs, and IRBMs to deliver them. The potential for a mistake or miscalculation by either side remains relatively high.

**Africa.** Continuing developments in Libya have created an international concern for the protection of the civilian population. NATO, the United States, and others are looking for ways to help stabilize the political, economic, and government challenges that face this country looking for greater freedom and prosperity.

**Russia.** In the last few years there have been intensifying disagreements with Russia over U.S. actions in Afghanistan and Iraq and U.S. plans to implement ballistic missile defense systems. During its Soviet period, Russia was a major exporter of weapons and weapons technology including shoulder-fired infrared-seeking missiles. While conducting operations against the Taliban in Afghanistan, the U.S. Air Force has made use of air bases in former Soviet republics along Russia's southern tier, countries with large Muslim populations.

**Korea.** North Korea has demonstrated the ability to produce delivery systems in the form of SRBMs and IRBMs. It is believed to have the technological means to produce and test nuclear weapons, which if developed, would place U.S. air-bases in the region under potential threat. A breakdown in the growing rapprochement between North and South Korea would mean a return to high tensions between the two countries. On the other hand, America must also prepare for a move toward reunification of the two countries. This, too, will have security implications as U.S. national interests in the region are great. There is a redeployment of U.S. forces in South Korea, which is designed to reduce tensions without reducing our presence or support in the region.

**China.** There remains a potential for conflict between China and Taiwan as Beijing increases its pressure on Taiwan for reunification. One example of this pressure is China's tests of SRBMs in Taiwan's waters, which coincided with Taiwan's internal debate on declaring independence. China, also a producer of shoulder-fired infrared-seeking missiles, continues to gain influence in Central America through its strong presence in Panama.

**The Balkans.** There is always a possibility of more conflict in the Balkans as the various nationalities continue their demands for increased autonomy or territory at the expense of their neighbors. The commitment of American forces to peacekeeping operations there is likely to continue for the foreseeable future.

In addition to the issues that continue to dominate America's political and military attention, the humanitarian assistance to other nations in times of crisis and natural disasters provides the U.S. government the opportunity to show compassion in action. Although these efforts stretch the vital resources of our nation and military, they have been a hallmark of our democratic republic and an example to the world.

## THE LONGER TERM FUTURE: AIR FORCE 2025

Air University at Maxwell Air Force Base, Alabama, undertook a major study to look thirty years into the future to identify concepts, capabilities, and technologies the United States will require to remain the dominant air and space force in the first quarter of the twenty-first century. The study is called *Air Force 2025* or *2025* for short. It offers a rich glimpse into the future and suggests some clear imperatives, as well as the important risks and opportunities that the Air Force might face in the new century.

The 2025 study team had access to and input from some of the best brains in the country in and out of government. The team used advanced analytical techniques to identify:

- What the world of 2025 could look like vis-à-vis the United States.
- The top ten of forty technology systems currently being evaluated by the Air Force that will have the most merit and be the best investments for assuring the security of the United States in the context of Air Force roles and missions, regardless of which world we face between now and the year 2025.
- The six technologies that will afford the greatest leverage in the next century.

- The five primary trends that will define the Air Force, its weapon systems, and personnel practices between now and then.

## Plausible Future Worlds And Challenges

The 2025 team used the alternate futures technique to describe various plausible future worlds, each separate and distinct, and each offering different security and planning challenges. The six possible future worlds that could exist in 2025 are:

- One where America's military power is constrained by other world players with other forms of power.
- A future where world power is dominated by multinational corporate giants.
- A third, scary future in which information and biogenetic technology is dispersed, giving individuals and small groups untold power to influence world events.
- A fourth potential world, where the United States loses its status as a superpower to an Asian colossus.
- A confused world marked by fundamental changes in the social structure, environment, and the international security system, making it difficult for the United States to determine how best to exert its power and influence.
- A final world, where a major conflict shapes events in 2025.

## Concepts with the Most Merit

Using the six alternate futures as a backdrop, the 2025 study then identified the most significant separate systems capabilities and emerging advanced technologies that had the most relevance for the Air Force mission. These were deemed to be the "best investments" to ensure continued United States air and space dominance in the future.

The resulting top ten systems are:
- Global Information Management System
- Sanctuary Base
- Global Surveillance, Reconnaissance, and Targeting System
- Global Area Strike System
- Uninhabited Combat Air Vehicle
- Space High Energy Laser
- Solar High Energy Laser
- Reconnaissance Unmanned Air Vehicle
- Attack Microbots
- Piloted Single Stage Space Plane

The six highest-leverage advanced technologies of greatest use to the Air Force that emerged from the study are:
- Data fusion
- Power systems
- Micromechanical devices

- Advanced materials
- High-energy propellants
- High-performance computing

The 2025 study also identified five primary trends that will be fundamental for U.S. air power dominance and that will characterize Air Force activity over the twenty-five-year period. These are:

- Humans will move from being more in the cockpit to being more in the loop.
- The medium for Air Force operations will move from air and space toward space and air.
- Development responsibilities for critical technologies and capabilities will move from government toward industry.
- Strategic influence will increasingly be exerted by information more than bombs.
- Military education will move from being rigid to responsive.

The study concluded that preparing now for the military challenges of the twenty-first century is central to our national security. The keys to preserving the military security of the United States are the integration of information technologies with air and space capabilities and the connectivity for distributed, demand-driven systems. Having these capabilities produces what the 2025 team called "the vigilant edge." Investments in technologies that enhance vigilance, decision-making capabilities, and communication architectures will help ensure a future full-service Air Force capable of providing a true "vigilant edge" for America of 2025.

## THE ROLE OF AIRMEN IN FUTURE INITIATIVES

Achieving *Air Force 2025* will require contributions from all airmen. This will involve developing aerospace officer and NCO leaders who can take command of flying forces, unmanned assets, space assets, and information assets and integrate the enormous amount of battlespace information these systems create.

Former Chief Master Sergeant of the Air Force (CMSAF) Eric Benken said the service's single, most important resource for carrying out the Air Force mission—to fight and win America's wars—is its people. The continued strength of the Air Force will depend on the ability to recruit, train, and retain quality people and ultimately to provide a reasonable quality of life for our members and their families as they serve the nation.

### Cyberspace Command

Emerging challenges have created new opportunites to exploit and execute new technology to best serve our nation. One example of creative and flexible foresight by our senior Air Force leaders is the establishing of a command for directing the service's numerous activities in cyberspace, a move intended to combat the ever-growing Internet prowess of terrorist groups. "These future technologies all share a common backbone: they assume that we have Cyberspace dominance, making

Cyberspace a center of gravity to protect and exploit," former Secretary Michael Wynne said. "This is why Air Force Chief of Staff General [T. Michael] Moseley and I are standing up a Cyberspace Command, devoted to exploiting this domain."

## AIR FORCE SYMBOL

The U.S. Air Force symbol was developed and released in January 2000 on a trial basis. It has since been accepted, approved, and integrated into the Air Force culture. The new symbol's elements attempt to capture, in part, Air Force heritage and the service's aspirations for the future. The Air Force symbol has two main parts.

**Air Force Symbol**

In the upper half, the stylized wings represent the stripes of the Air Force's strength—the enlisted men and women of the force.

In the lower half are a sphere, a star, and three diamonds. The sphere within the star represents the globe. It signifies our obligation to secure our nation's freedom with global vigilance, reach, and power. The globe represents our challenge to provide decisive aerospace power worldwide. The star's five points represent the components of our force and family—our active duty, civilians, guard, reserve, and retirees.

The two elements come together to form one symbol that presents two powerful images—at once it is an eagle, the emblem of our nation, and a medal, representing valor in service to our nation.

# PART II

# Service
# in the Air Force

# 7

# Standards of Conduct

The Air Force's core values discussed in chapter 1, when explored in detail, set the standard of professional military conduct. Those values—integrity, service before self, and excellence in all we do—are the benchmark standards for the whole Air Force.

The Air Force exists to fight and win wars—that's its core expertise. Because of what members of the armed forces do, their standards must be higher than those of society at large.

Members of the U.S. Air Force are guided by a wide range of standards of conduct. Some of these standards are explicitly stated and have been prescribed through law and directives. Others have evolved over a period of time and have been passed down through tradition. As a member of the Air Force, you should practice the highest standards of behavior, obedience, and loyalty.

## PROFESSIONAL STANDARDS

Department of Defense and Air Force regulations provide guidance to Air Force personnel on standards of conduct. They also provide a number of useful definitions of ethical conduct.

- **Ethics** are standards by which one measures what is right and what is wrong.
- **Honesty** means being respectfully truthful, straightforward, and candid.
- **Integrity** means having the guts to do what's right at all times and avoiding doing what is wrong.
- **Loyalty** means standing by and keeping faithful to your family, your unit, and your fellow airmen. It means being faithful and committed to the right cause.
- **Accountability** means accepting responsibility for your actions and decisions and the resulting consequences.
- **Fairness** means performing your official duties with open-mindedness and impartiality and treating all personnel in an equal and unbiased manner.

- **Caring** means courtesy, kindness, and understanding. It is essential to maintaining good relationships with others.
- **Respect** means treating others with dignity and consideration, even when you disagree with them.
- **Promise keeping** means keeping the commitments you have made to your family, friends, colleagues, superiors, and subordinates. It also means paying your debts.
- **Responsible citizenship** means doing your civic duty, even in simple matters, such as voting, obeying traffic laws, and avoiding littering.
- **Pursuit of excellence** means striving for the best possible outcomes in all that you do and not being satisfied with performing in a substandard or ambivalent manner.

## THE CODE OF CONDUCT FOR MILITARY OPERATIONS

As a member of the U.S. Armed Forces, it is your duty to oppose all enemies of the United States whether in combat or as a prisoner of war (POW). The Code of Conduct was drawn up in 1955 after the Korean War and amended in 1988 to make its language gender neutral. The code provides a clear statement of commonly understood commitments to how servicemembers meet their obligations to their country, service, unit, and fellow Americans.

### Servicemember Responsibilities Under the Code

The code applies to all members of the U.S. Armed Forces. It has six articles that are based on time-honored concepts and traditions that date back to the days of the American Revolution.

**Article I.** I am an American, fighting in the forces which guard my country and our way of life. I am prepared to give my life in their defense.

**Article II.** I will never surrender of my own free will. If in command, I will never surrender the members of my command while they have the means to resist.

**Article III.** If I am captured, I will continue to resist by all means available. I will make every effort to escape and aid others to escape. I will accept neither parole nor special favors from the enemy.

**Article IV.** If I become a prisoner of war, I will keep faith with my fellow prisoners. I will give no information or take part in any action which might be harmful to my comrades. If I am senior, I will take command. If not, I will obey the lawful orders of those appointed over me and will back them up in every way.

**Article V.** When questioned, should I become a prisoner of war, I am required to give name, rank, service number, and date of birth. I will evade answering further questions to the utmost of my ability. I will make no oral or written statements disloyal to my country and its allies or harmful to their cause.

**Article VI.** I will never forget that I am an American, fighting for freedom, responsible for my actions, and dedicated to the principles which made my country free. I will trust in my God and in the United States of America.

## Government Responsibilities Under the Code

The U.S. government also has responsibilities under the code. The Nation promises:
- To keep faith with you and stand by you as you fight in its defense;
- To care for your family and dependents; and
- To use every practical means to contact, support, and gain release for you and all other prisoners of war.

## STANDARDS OF PERSONAL CONDUCT

Every large organization has codes of behavior. Some codes are written, and some are not. Most deal with personal relationships and with relationships of the individual to the organization. Personal relationships affect morale and discipline. We have all seen or heard stories about favoritism: "teachers' pets," people who "take care of their friends," and so forth. You may have also seen or heard about people who abuse their position and act in their own selfish interests. We tend to be suspicious of the decisions and motives of people who engage in favoritism or misuse their position. Imagine how you would feel if your assignment to combat was based on the personal likes and dislikes or financial interests of your superiors. Avoiding favoritism and misuse of authority are two good reasons to maintain all duty relationships on a professional basis.

### Professional and Unprofessional Relationships

Professional relationships describe personal interactions that add to morale, discipline, and respect for authority. Open communication about careers, duties, performance, and the mission is always encouraged. Participation in unit, base, or civic activities normally contributes to esprit de corps and has a positive effect on others.

Unprofessional relationships describe personal interaction that results in the appearance of favoritism, misuse of position or authority, or the abandonment of organizational goals for personal interests. Relationships of this type have a negative effect and, when they begin to break down or destroy morale, discipline, or respect for authority, they become a matter of official Air Force interest.

AFI 36-2909, *Professional and Unprofessional Relationships,* establishes command, supervisory, and personal responsibilities for maintaining professional relationships. It applies to all active-duty, reserve, and Air National Guard members. It provides insight into how professional relationships contribute to the effective operation of the Air Force and discusses how military missions require absolute confidence in command and how relationships have to be consistent with Air Force core values.

Certain kinds of personal relationships can present high risks by having the potential to negatively affect morale, discipline, respect for authority and/or unit cohesion. Examples include, but are not limited to:

- Relationships between subordinates, supervisors, government contractor personnel, and commanders within an organization that become too personal.
- Dating and close friendships when they adversely affect mission accomplishment, even when members are not in same unit or chain of command.
- Sharing living accommodations, vacations, transportation, and off-duty interests on a frequent or recurring basis that are or are perceived to be unprofessional. Two of the key indicators in determining whether or not the relationship is professional are (1) the frequency of the activity and/or (2) the absence of official purpose.
- Relationships formed during or at recruiting, training, schools, and Professional Military Education (PME) are now bound by special rules, which are discussed below.

## CONDUCT OF PERSONNEL IN CERTAIN ASSIGNMENTS

### Recruiting and Training Assignments

Air Force officers, noncommissioned officers, and other enlisted ranks will in the course of their military service be involved in recruiting efforts, basic military training, initial technical training, and a variety of PME schools. The recruiting experience is a critical step in the development of Air Force members since it establishes expectations and begins the initial process whereby Air Force core values are formed. Drill sergeants, instructors, and staff members at Air Force schools exercise considerable influence and authority over trainees and students who have limited experience with Air Force standards, and there is a recurring risk that those standards could be compromised. As such, recruiters and instructors are not permitted to engage in any of the following activities with a recruit or student:

- Date or carry on a social relationship.
- Seek or engage in sexual activity with, make sexual advances to, or accept sexual overtures from.
- Use grade, position, threats, pressures, or promises to gain any personal benefit.
- Gamble with, lend money to, borrow money from, or become indebted to each other.
- Use personal resources to provide lodging, transportation, or other benefit.
- Solicit donations other than for Air Force–approved campaigns.

These restrictions also apply to immediate family members of the recruit, trainee, or student.

**Treatment, Care, and Counseling Settings**

Persons receiving medical, psychological, pastoral, legal, or other professional care or counseling may be vulnerable to the provider of these services. Personnel who are providing treatment, care, and counseling will not use their position to gain any personal benefit from the recipient. They are also prohibited from engaging in any of the above activities with the patient or immediate family members of persons receiving services.

Commanders of reserve component organizations should tailor the application and enforcement of the above rules to address unique situations that arise from part-time military service. When on active duty, reserve component personnel follow the rules of conduct as stated.

## FRATERNIZATION

Fraternization is a personal relationship between a commissioned officer and an enlisted member that violates the customary bounds of acceptable behavior in the Air Force. It can prejudice good order and discipline, discredit the armed services, or operate to the personal disgrace or dishonor of the officer involved. The custom against fraternization extends to all officer/enlisted relationships. Under current policy, commissioned officers are prohibited from engaging in the following activities with enlisted members.

- Gambling.
- Lending money to, borrowing money from, or becoming indebted to enlisted members.
- Engaging in sexual relations or dating.
- Sharing living accommodations except when military operations require it.
- Engaging on a personal basis in business enterprises with or soliciting or making solicited sales to, except for one-time sale of a house, car, piece of furniture, or similar transaction.

Because officers serve in the higher levels of leadership and exercise considerable authority over those members junior to them, it is recognized that the potential harm from their unprofessional conduct can have a significant negative impact on morale, discipline, and respect for authority. For this reason, officers are forbidden from entering into certain relationships. It is also for this reason that airmen should not seek to enter into relationships of this nature with commissioned officers.

When considering responses to cases involving dating or sexual relationships, it is the impact or foreseeable consequences of conduct, not the characterization of the conduct, that determines the seriousness of the action to be taken. Present policy specifies that unprofessional relationships should not be excused simply because the parties marry or one of the parties leaves the service. Officer/enlisted marriages do exist, but they are rare. They are not always the result of fraternization. However, when fraternization occurs, current Air Force policy states that a subsequent marriage does not preclude appropriate command action. Members from the officer and enlisted ranks who do marry are expected to respect all customs and courtesies when on duty, in uniform in public, or at official social functions.

## CONFLICTS OF INTEREST

A servicemember's private business or professional interests should not conflict with the public interest of the United States and the activities that are related to his or her Air Force duties. This also applies to the private interests of his or her spouse, minor children, and any other members of the household. In general, you are not permitted to use your Air Force position on or off of duty as a means to:

- Persuade any person or group to provide a financial benefit to you or others.
- Engage in any commercial solicitation or sale to any military personnel or civilian subordinates that are junior to you in rank or grade. There is an exception to the above general rule. The one-time sale of personal property, such as a vehicle or a private dwelling/house, to a person who is junior in rank is permitted.

Unprofessional conduct can also have serious and punitive legal repercussions for airmen, just as they do to public officeholders or corporate leaders, and airmen are cautioned to be alert for any attempts to involve them in such conduct as the following.

**Bribery and Graft.** Air Force members can be subject to criminal penalties if they solicit, accept, or agree to accept anything of value in return for performing (or refraining from performing) an official act.

**Gratuities.** Except as provided for in Air Force and DOD directives, you and your immediate family may not solicit or accept any gift, gratuity, favor, entertainment, loan, or any other thing of monetary value, either directly or indirectly, from any person, business activity, and/or public or private organization, in the performance of your official duties.

**Gifts from Foreign Governments.** Air Force Instruction 51-901, *Gifts from Foreign Governments,* requires all Air Force military and civilian personnel and their dependents to report all gifts from foreign governments that exceed a U.S. retail value of $305. Gifts and gift reports are due to the Air Force Personnel Center, Special Trophies and Awards Section, Promotions, Evaluations, and Recognition Division within sixty days of receiving the gift. This requirement also includes gifts that recipients desire to retain for official use or display. Failure to report gifts in excess of $305 can result in a penalty in any amount, not to exceed the retail value of the gift plus $5,000.

**Misuse of Government Facilities, Property, and Manpower.** Air Force members may not directly or indirectly use or allow the use of government property of any kind, including property leased to the government, for other than officially approved activities. This includes equipment, supplies, or other property that is under your control.

**Misuse of Civilian and Military Titles in Connection with Commercial Enterprises.** All civilian employees and military personnel on active duty are prohibited from using their civilian or military titles or positions in connection with any commercial enterprise. They are also prohibited from endorsing any commercial products.

**Gambling, Betting, and Lotteries.** Servicemembers may not participate in any gambling activity, including conducting a lottery or pool, conducting a game for money or prizes, or selling or purchasing a "numbers" slip or ticket, while on government-owned or government-leased property or while on duty for the government. These restrictions do not apply to Air Force recreational activities specifically authorized by instructions, such as bingo in base clubs.

## FINANCIAL RESPONSIBILITY

Air Force members are expected to satisfy their financial obligations in a proper and timely manner. Nothing will make your first sergeant or unit commander more upset than having to repeatedly counsel you on your financial obligations. This has become a serious problem, especially for junior airmen who are incurring debt far greater than their salaries can support. Administrative or disciplinary action may be taken against Air Force members in cases of continued financial irresponsibility.

AFI 36-2906, *Personal Financial Responsibility,* places responsibility on commanders and the Family Support Center for providing counseling on financial matters. The Personal Financial Management Program (PFMP) offers information, education, and personal financial counseling to help individuals and family members maintain financial stability and set financial goals. Subjects such as checkbook maintenance, budgeting, buying with credit, and local fraudulent business practices are common examples of topics covered. For additional information concerning these offerings, contact your first sergeant or your base PFMP manager.

Another popular easy-to-read source for financial planning geared to servicemembers is the *Armed Forces Guide to Personal Financial Planning*, 6th Edition (Stackpole Books, 2007).

## DEALING WITH UNPROFESSIONAL CONDUCT

In instances where unprofessional relationships have been confirmed, unit commanders and NCO leaders will take appropriate action. Administrative actions that can be considered include counseling, reprimand, unfavorable information file (UIF), removal from position, reassignment, demotion, delay of or removal from a promotion list, adverse or referral comments in performance report, and/or separation. More serious cases may warrant nonjudicial punishment or trial by court-martial.

In some cases, you may be ordered to cease the unprofessional relationship. The violation of such an order would be subject to the UCMJ and would be the basis for punishment of the offending party. Instances of actual favoritism, partiality, or misuse of a position may also constitute violations of the UCMJ or the *Joint Ethics Regulation.*

## SOURCES OF ADDITIONAL INFORMATION

*The Code of Conduct*

DOD Regulation 5500.7-R, *Joint Ethics Regulation.*

Air Force Instruction 31-213, *Armed Forces Disciplinary Control Boards and Off-Installation Liaison and Operations.*

Air Force Instruction 35-101, *Public Affairs Policies and Procedures.*

Air Force Instruction 51-901, *Gifts from Foreign Governments.*

Air Force Instruction 51-902, *Political Activities by Members of the U.S. Air Force,* and AFI 51-903, *Dissident and Protest Activities.*

Air Force Instruction 36-2906, *Personal Financial Responsibility.*

Air Force Instruction 36-2909, *Professional and Unprofessional Relationships.*

# 8

# Rights, Benefits, and Restrictions

Being a servicemember in the U.S. Armed Forces calls for a great deal of personal responsibility, sacrifice, and commitment. Servicemembers are also citizens. While in service, they retain nearly all of their rights as citizens. Moreover, when on active duty, they receive other rights, protections, privileges, and benefits that civilians do not have. Many of these rights, protections, privileges, and benefits are considered compensation for the dangerous and difficult duty of protecting the nation.

The Air Force is also part of the U.S. government. Air Force duty involves command and leadership direction over vast quantities of people, money, facilities, and equipment. Much of its work is of a classified and restricted nature. Because of this, there are restrictions that officers and NCOs must enforce and that airmen of all ranks must obey. Most of the restrictions contained in this chapter are common sense, and as you read them, you will understand why they are needed.

## RIGHTS OF AIRMEN

There are a number of rights that are extended to servicemembers while they are fulfilling their obligations to military service. It is important to understand that a right is a benefit established for military people by federal law. If a benefit is not established by law (for example, if it is only offered through a departmental policy), it is a privilege and can be subject to administrative change or withdrawal, without recourse.

A citizen who has taken the oath of office becomes entitled at once to certain rights of military service, such as the right to wear a uniform. Other rights accrue only by completing specified requirements, such as the right to retire after completing a stipulated period of service.

## The Right to Wear the Uniform

Members of the military service have the right to wear the uniform of their service. Members of the reserve components on inactive status, retired personnel, and former members of the service who have been honorably separated have the right to wear the uniform only at stipulated times or circumstances, and unless these conditions are met, the right is denied.

## The Right to Draw Pay and Allowances

Pay scales for grade and length of service are established by law. The rights as to pay and allowances may be suspended, in part, by action of a court-martial or forfeited, in part, by absence without leave.

## The Right to Receive Medical Attention

Members of the armed services and, with restrictions, their families are entitled to receive medical and dental treatment of their wounds, injuries, or disease. Servicemembers cannot function at peak performance if they are not fit and in good health. Individuals who are distracted by sickness or health problems of family members are also incapable of full concentration on their military duties. Consequently, the Air Force provides medical and dental care, in varying degrees, to airmen and their families. Many consider medical and dental care as primary benefits of service in the Air Force. Medical and dental care for servicemembers is free of charge. See chapter 24.

## The Right to Individual Protection Under the Uniform Code of Military Justice (UCMJ)

All members of the military service are under the jurisdiction established by the articles of the Uniform Code of Military Justice. In part, it specifies that:
- Servicemembers may not be compelled to incriminate themselves before a military court.
- No person shall be tried a second time for the same offense without his consent.
- Cruel and unusual punishments of every kind are prohibited.
- Although the punishment for a crime or offense is left to the discretion of the court, it shall not exceed such limits as the President may prescribe.

## Rights Under the Servicemembers' Civil Relief Act of 2003

A new law replacing the Soldiers' and Sailors' Civil Relief Act of 1940 was signed by President Bush on December 19, 2003. The new law, called the Servicemembers' Civil Relief Act (SCRA), clarifies, updates, and strengthens the previous Soldiers' & Sailors' Civil Relief Act of 1940 by providing servicemembers greater protection for their personal financial and legal obligations.

Among the significant changes is an automatic 90-day stay of civil proceedings upon request of the servicemember. This applies to both judicial and administrative hearings. Previously, stays were discretionary with the courts. Other significant changes include a six percent limitation on interest rates for pre-service debts and expanded protection against eviction from your dwelling. Under the old act, servicemembers and their families who entered into a dwelling lease for $1,200 or less could not be evicted without a court order. This amount is increased to $2,400, to which is added an annual inflation adjustment. The new act also gives the servicemember who has received PCS orders, or who is being deployed for 90 days or more, the right to terminate a housing lease with thirty days' written notice. New also are provisions for the protection of motor-vehicle leases. Any active-duty servicemember who has received PCS orders outside the continental United States, or who is being deployed for 180 days or more, may terminate a motor-vehicle lease without early termination charges. There are many protections under the law that benefit servicemembers. Your unit judge advocate or installation legal assistance officer can provide further information.

### The Right to Seek Redress of Wrong
Each of the armed services provides a procedure by which all members may seek redress of wrong when they feel they have been wronged by a superior. In most instances, these issues are submitted to, and responded to, by a commander in the complainant's chain of command. They can also be submitted through inspector general channels.

### The Right to Profit from Inventions
Air Force members have the same rights as other citizens to profit from their ideas and creations as long as the invention was not created in the line of duty. In the latter case, the Air Force often awards prizes or incentive awards for in-the-line-of-duty inventions, especially those that save money. There is no right, however, to awards.

### The Right to Request Correction of Military Records
Military records serve as the basis for recording the fact, nature or character, and duration of military service. For any individual military record that contains an error, means have been made available for the affected servicemember to petition for correction.

### The Right to Vote
Air Force personnel are encouraged to exercise their right to vote in federal, state, and local elections. To encourage and assist eligible servicemembers to vote, the Department of Defense maintains liaison with the various state election authorities to obtain current voting information, which, through Air Force channels, is

promptly disseminated to all. Voting officers are available to answer pertinent questions concerning forthcoming elections in the servicemember's state of domicile and to provide printed postcard applications for absentee ballots, which are transmitted postage free to the appropriate state. Although the Air Force provides information and assistance concerning elections and voting procedures, the actual decision to vote rests with the individual airman. No airman will be required or ordered to participate in political elections. The determination of eligibility and the specification of requirements for voting are completely governed by the appropriate state. To vote, all servicemembers must meet such requirements and must be declared eligible to vote by the state in which they desire to exercise their voting privilege.

## The Right to Retire
After satisfying specific requirements of honorable service for a specified period of time (usually twenty or more years) or, under some conditions, having endured a physical disability, members of the armed forces have a right to retire.

## The Right to Access Department of Veterans Affairs (VA) Programs
Former members of the armed forces and retired personnel may be eligible for a range of VA benefits for themselves, their spouses, and their beneficiaries. Examples of VA benefits include:
- Servicemembers' group life insurance.
- Educational aid.
- Guarantees of loans for the purchase or construction of homes, farms, or business property.
- Readjustment allowances for veterans who are unemployed.
- Disability compensation.
- Vocational rehabilitation.
- Physical examinations, hospital care, and outpatient medical and dental treatment.
- Domiciliary care and guardianship service.
- Pensions.
- Death benefits to survivors.

## Military Funeral and Burial Rights
Federal law requires the Department of Defense to provide, upon request, military funeral honors to each eligible retiree or veteran. The law directs DOD, at the minimum, to provide the ceremonial flag folding, the flag presentation to the next of kin, and the playing of Taps. At least two uniformed military personnel, in addition to a bugler, if available, shall perform the ceremony. The next of kin or appropriate individual must request the funeral honors; they are not provided automatically. DOD requires that funeral directors, rather than the next of kin, contact the military

to coordinate funeral ceremonies and burial. The web site is www.militaryfuneral honors.osd.mil.

## RIGHTS WITH LIMITATIONS

### Writing for Publication
Active-duty personnel are permitted to write for publication as long as the message is not prejudicial to military discipline and as long as the content does not include classified military information. Authors are required to obtain clearances on proposed public speeches and publications related to military issues from the public affairs office. Air Force members, however, may not write for unofficial publications during duty hours. These may not be produced using government or nonappropriated fund property or supplies. In cases where a publication contains language that is punishable by the UCMJ or other federal laws, the person(s) that are involved in its printing, publication, or distribution may be subject to prosecution or other disciplinary action.

### Religious Accommodation
The Air Force recognizes the importance of worship and spiritual health. Accommodating religious practice is an established American military tradition. Chaplains from many denominations are available in the Air Force. When accommodation is not possible—or when the belief jeopardizes military readiness, unit cohesion, standards, or discipline—the individual must conform to military requirements or face disciplinary or administrative action.

Religious apparel that is a part of the religious faith practiced by a servicemember may be worn if it is not visible and if it does not interfere with the proper wear of the uniform. Any visible religious item must be authorized individually.

### Political Activities
AFI 51-902, *Political Activities by Members of the U.S. Air Force,* and AFI 51-903, *Dissident and Protest Activities,* provide policy and guidance about participation in political activities. In general, airmen have the same rights and responsibilities as other American citizens. They have the right, with some limitations, to:
- Vote in all national, state, and local elections. This right is unlimited as noted above.
- Voice their opinions on political matters. In exercising this right, care must be exercised so that personal opinions are not directly, or by implication, represented as those of the U.S. Air Force.
- Make personal monetary contributions to legal political parties.
- Stand for election to public office. In some instances, members of the active-duty Air Force may become candidates for election to public office. If elected, they must not act in their official capacity as the holders of the

office or perform any of the duties during military duty hours. Because this particular privilege has been questioned several times in recent years, servicemembers who are considering becoming candidates for office should consult the base legal office prior to becoming actively involved.

- Engage in fund-raising activities. In exercising this right, servicemembers may not solicit or otherwise engage in fund-raising activities in federal offices or facilities, including military reservations, for a partisan political cause or candidate. They are also prohibited from making campaign contributions to a partisan political candidate or to another member of the armed forces or an officer or employee of the federal government for promoting a political objective or cause.
- Participate in political groups and events or rallies as a spectator when not in uniform. There are restrictions on participating in partisan political management, campaigns, or conventions; making speeches; being listed as a sponsor; providing transportation to polling centers; conducting public opinion polls; and/or attending as an official representative of the armed forces.
- Serve as an election official if such service is not as a representative of a partisan political party, does not interfere with military duties, and is performed while out of uniform. Performing as an election official also requires the prior approval of the servicemember's major command commander or equivalent authority (this authority may be delegated, but not below the level of the installation commander).
- Participate in political speech. Servicemembers are permitted to sign petitions as long as they do so in their capacity as private citizens and not as a representative of the armed forces. They can write letters to the editor, display bumper stickers on their private motor vehicles, and wear campaign buttons on their civilian clothing.

Some political activities are not permitted. Servicemembers may not:

- Allow, or cause to be published, partisan political articles signed or authorized by the member for soliciting votes for or against a partisan political party or candidate.
- Speak before a partisan political gathering of any kind for promoting a partisan political party or candidate.
- Participate in any radio, television, or other program or group discussion as an advocate of a partisan political party or candidate.
- March or ride in a partisan political parade.
- Use contemptuous words against the officeholders, described in Title 10, *United States Code,* Section 888.
- Display a large political sign, banner, or poster on the top or side of your private vehicle.

## PRIVILEGES

Privileges, as compared to rights, are enjoyed subject to certain criteria being met. When the criteria is not met, the privilege is withdrawn.

### Rank Has Its Privileges

This, in concept, is very similar to the respect that, in the civilian community, is expected to be customarily extended to dignitaries, seniors, or elders. More information on Air Force customs and courtesies is in chapter 2.

### Leave

Military personnel are entitled to accumulate leave and apply for permission to take it when their duty schedules permit. If they are absent without permission, they may be subject to disciplinary action. Since there are conditions attached to leave usage, it is considered a privilege instead of a right.

### Base Exchange and Commissary Privileges

These are extended to active-duty personnel, military retirees, and their dependents upon presentation of an official identification card. The privileges may be revoked if they are abused, for example, if purchases are made for personnel who are not granted the privilege of using these facilities.

### Membership in Air Force Clubs

Air Force members have the privilege of joining Air Force clubs (e.g., airmen's clubs and NCO clubs) based on their rank. They must follow the rules of the clubs regarding payment of dues and bills, dress codes, behavior, and so forth. If they do not, this privilege may be curtailed or withdrawn.

### Outside Employment

Off-duty jobs are permitted when the prior approval of the servicemember's supervisor and commander is obtained. However, servicemembers must not engage in outside employment or other activity, with or without compensation, that interferes or is not compatible with the performance of their duties. Airmen are also required to avoid outside employment that may reasonably be expected to bring discredit to the United States, the Department of Defense, or the Air Force.

## RESTRICTIONS

Just as airmen have rights, privileges, and benefits, they also face a number of restrictions, most of which have been instituted to ensure the dignity of the individual, the morale and integrity of the service, and good order and discipline in the unit.

### Unlawful Discrimination

Commanders and supervisors—all airmen—must work together to ensure that unlawful discrimination based on race, color, national origin, religion, or sex does not occur in the Air Force. Unlawful discrimination degrades human beings, negatively affects the mission, and violates Air Force policy. It often results in lack of team cohesiveness, poor morale, reprisal, breakdown in communications, and withdrawal due to fear of being discriminated against.

Any activity that attempts to deprive individuals of their civil rights is incompatible with military service and will be dealt with accordingly.

## Sexual Harassment

Sexual harassment is a form of discrimination that involves unwelcome sexual advances, requests for sexual favors, and other verbal or physical conduct of a sexual nature when (1) submission to such conduct is made either explicitly or implicitly a term or condition of a person's job, pay, or career; and (2) such conduct has the purpose or effect of unreasonably interfering with an individual's work performance or creates an intimidating, hostile, or offensive working environment.

Any person in a supervisory or command position who uses or condones any form of sexual behavior to control, influence, or affect the career, pay, or job of a military member or civilian employee is engaging in sexual harassment. Similarly, any airman or civilian employee who makes deliberate or unwelcome verbal comments, gestures, or physical contact of a sexual nature in the workplace is also engaging in sexual harassment. The Air Force position is clear—unlawful discrimination and sexual harassment in today's Air Force is prohibited and will not be tolerated.

## Homosexual Conduct

The legal status of homosexuals and homosexual behavior in the armed forces has been guided by policy that was instituted during the Clinton presidency. Under the Obama presidency, the policy has been repealed to allow homosexuals to serve openly. Homosexuality is no longer a disqualifying factor for entering military service and servicemembers are no longer subject to administrative separation on the basis of "lawful" gay, lesbian, or bisexual conduct. Sexual *mis*conduct, *regardless of sexual orientation,* that violates a Service standard, rule, regulation, policy or law, will still be considered grounds for administrative or legal action, to include possible discharge.

Servicemembers occupy a unique position in society and represent the military establishment. This special status brings with it a *responsibility* to uphold and maintain the dignity and high standards of the military services at all times and in all places. Violations of standards of conduct pertinent to professional relationships and public displays of affection may be punished as violations of lawful regulations or orders, or derelictions of duty, as the case may be, under the UCMJ. Servicemembers may be involuntarily separated prior to the expiration of their term of service for various reasons established by law and military regulations, *to include* violations of standards of conduct.

## Participation in Certain Groups

Active participation in publicly demonstrating, rallying, fund-raising, recruiting and training, and organizing and leading the following types of activities is incompatible with military service and therefore prohibited:

1. Organizations that support supremacist causes or attempt to create illegal discrimination based on race, creed, color, sex, religion, or national origin.
2. Organizations that advocate the use of force or violence or otherwise engage in efforts to deprive individuals of their civil rights.

## Searches and Seizures

Servicemembers are subject to searches and seizures when legally authorized. These are usually authorized by installation commanders after they have consulted with the staff judge advocate and determined that they have probable cause to conduct a search. Searches are the examination of an individual, property, or premises with the purpose of finding criminal evidence, such as illegal drugs, contraband, or stolen property. Seizures are the meaningful interference with property and/or evidence that is an individual's possession and is reasonably believed to be associated with a crime.

## Illegal Drug Use

Air Force members are prohibited from using illegal drugs. The urinalysis program is used to detect and deter drug use. Positive urinalysis tests can be the basis for administrative and Uniform Code of Military Justice (UCMJ) action.

## Off-Limits Areas

AFI 31-213, *Armed Forces Disciplinary Control Boards and Off-Installation Liaison and Operations,* allows commanders to place certain areas or establishments off limits to military personnel. This means you may not go there or participate in activities being carried on there. Establishments and areas can be placed off-limits if their activities include counseling servicemembers to refuse to perform their duties, to desert, or to involve themselves in acts that could result in significant adverse effects on health, welfare, or morale of military members.

## Smoking

DOD and Air Force policy is to promote a healthy work environment and healthy servicemembers. Programs have been initiated to help smokers quit, and restrictions have been imposed to limit smoking in official duty environments.

## Classified Information

Military information or equipment to which access is restricted is classified as confidential, secret, or top secret. The unauthorized use or release of classified material or information is a serious offense that is subject to imprisonment and fine.

Egregious violations of classified information restrictions could even be subject to laws dealing with espionage.

## Public Statements

AFI 35-101, *Public Affairs Policies and Procedures,* provides policy for making public statements on official Air Force matters. It stipulates that commanders (or their authorized public affairs representatives) are the appropriate approval authorities for public statements. The goal of this practice is to reduce the risk of the release of statements that do not reflect Air Force policy or that, if taken out of context, could be misleading to the public. Personnel who make releases should make certain that the information is accurate, prompt, and factual. It should be presented simply, honestly, and professionally. Comments should be confined to their particular area of expertise. Hypothetical and speculative comments should be avoided.

## Political Dissent

The basic mission of the Air Force is to safeguard the security of the United States. In striving toward this goal, there's a need to balance the servicemember's right of expression, consistent with good order, discipline, and national security. Most issues can be resolved based on the particular facts of a situation and according to the various constitutional, statutory, and regulatory provisions and the UCMJ. More complex cases may require advisement by command officials and the staff judge advocate offices. Examples of activity that can be characterized as political dissent include the following.

*Possessing or Distributing Printed Materials.* Written or printed materials related to political dissent activities may not be distributed on an Air Force installation if the installation commander or authorized designee determines that they are a clear danger to the loyalty, discipline, or morale of members of the armed forces or if they interfere with accomplishment of the military mission. If so, these materials may be impounded and then returned to the owners when they leave the installation. These materials may be kept if they have been determined to be evidence of a crime.

*Demonstrations and Similar Activities.* There are three major prohibitions related to demonstrations and similar activities.

1. Air Force members are prohibited from participating in demonstrations when they are on duty, in a foreign country, in uniform, when their activities constitute a breach of law and order, or when violence is likely to result.
2. Demonstrations or other activities near an Air Force installation that could result in interfering with or preventing the orderly accomplishment of a mission of the installation or that could present a clear danger to loyalty, discipline, or morale of the armed forces are prohibited.

3. It is a crime for any person to enter a military installation for any purpose prohibited by law or lawful regulation or for any person to enter or reenter an installation after having been barred by order of the installation commander.

## Personal Restrictions

Restrictions have been imposed on some outside activities, including the following, which are specifically prohibited:

- Acting as a consultant for a private enterprise.
- Providing assistance to persons preparing for civil service examinations.
- Soliciting contributions for gifts for those in a superior official position.
- Accepting gifts from subordinates, except for nominal ceremonial items.
- Personal use of franked envelopes and Air Force letterhead stationery.

## SOURCES OF ADDITIONAL INFORMATION

Department of Defense 5500.7-R, *Joint Ethics Regulation,* provides guidance to Air Force personnel on standards of conduct that relate to possible conflicts between private interests and official duties.

Air Force Instruction 31-213, *Armed Forces Disciplinary Control Boards and Off-Installation Liaison and Operations.*

Air Force Instruction 35-101, *Public Affairs Policies and Procedures,* provides policy for making public statements on official Air Force matters.

Air Force Instruction 51-901, *Gifts from Foreign Governments.*

Air Force Instruction 51-902, *Political Activities by Members of the U.S. Air Force,* and AFI 51-903, *Dissident and Protest Activities.*

Air Force Instruction 36-2906, *Personal Financial Responsibility.*

Air Force Instruction 36-2909, *Professional and Unprofessional Relationships.*

# 9

# Your Uniform and Standards of Appearance

## AIR FORCE UNIFORMS

Air Force Instruction 36-2903, *Dress and Personal Appearance of Air Force Personnel,* contains a description of each item of the military uniform and the way it should be worn. The Air Force Uniform Board, in conjunction with personnel experts, monitors uniform design with periodic reviews. Changes are implemented when required to meet the needs of the entire force or those of specific career fields. Special consideration is given to ensure that uniforms present a neat, dignified appearance that is plain, not too ornate, and distinctively Air Force. Other important factors include functional use, military image, cleanliness, and safety.

The type of uniforms that may be worn is often determined by the nature of duties performed or by a specific occasion.

1. Service dress, dress, battle dress, and standardized functional uniforms for men and women include service dress uniforms, long- and short-sleeved blue shirts, long- and short-sleeved blue blouses, men's blue service trousers, women's blue service skirts and slacks, maternity service uniforms, fatigue uniforms, maternity fatigue uniforms, camouflage fatigue uniforms, white food-service uniforms, and white hospital-service uniforms.

2. Pullover sweaters and outer garments include blue pullover sweaters, lightweight blue jackets, all-weather coats, raincoats, overcoats, and headgear.

3. Organizational clothing and equipment items are issued to meet unique work requirements. Functional clothing items, designed for specific duties, include parkas, protective footwear, coveralls, and specialized flight clothing. Distinctive uniforms and items are issued for members of certain organizations while they are performing distinctive duties; for example, USAF honor guard uniforms, USAF band uniforms, and security police uniforms.

4. Dress uniforms for men and women include black mess dress uniforms, blue mess dress uniforms, black formal dress uniforms, blue formal dress uniforms, semiformal dress uniforms, and black, white, or blue ceremonial dress uniforms.

## Men's Service Dress Uniform (Enlisted)

*Notes:*

1. Place highly polished U.S. insignia halfway up the seam, resting on but not over it. Bottom of insignia is horizontal with the ground.

2. Aeronautical badges are mandatory. Others are optional. Center aeronautical and occupational badge $1/2$ inch above the top row of ribbons. Center additional badge $1/2$ inch above first one. Wear highly polished badges only.

3. Center ribbons resting on but not over edge of welt pocket. Wear three or four in a row. Wear all.

4. Center duty badge $1^1/2$ inches below top of welt pocket and centered, and/or on right side centered between arm seam and lapel, $1/2$ inch below name tag. *EXCEPTION:* Missile and missile maintenance badges are worn $1^1/2$ inches below top of welt pocket and centered. Wear highly polished badges only.

5. Center new 4-inch sleeve chevron halfway between shoulder seam and elbow bent at 90-degree angle.

6. The metallic name tag must be worn on the wearer's right side of the service dress jacket with the bottom of the name tag level with the bottom of the ribbons. It should be centered between the sleeve seam and the lapel. If a duty badge is worn on the wearer's right side of the service dress jacket, men will center the badge $1/2$ inch below the new name tag.

[Notes apply also to the men's semiformal dress uniform.]

## Women's Service Dress Uniform (Enlisted)

*Notes:*

1. Place highly polished U.S. insignia halfway up the seam, resting on but not over it. Bottom of insignia is horizontal with the ground.
2. Aeronautical badges are mandatory. Others are optional. Center aeronautical and occupational badge $1/2$ inch above the top row of ribbons. Center additional badge $1/2$ inch above first one. Wear highly polished badges only.
3. Center ribbons resting on but not over edge of welt pocket. Wear three or four in a row. Wear all.
4. Center duty badge $1^1/2$ inches below top of welt pocket and centered, and/or on right side centered $1/2$ inch above the name tag. *EXCEPTION:* Missile and missile maintenance badges may be worn $1^1/2$ inches below top of welt pocket and centered. Wear highly polished badges only.
5. Center new $3^1/2$- or 4-inch sleeve chevron halfway between shoulder seam and elbow bent at 90-degree angle.
6. The metallic name tag must be worn on the wearer's right side of the service dress jacket with the bottom of the name tag level with the bottom of the ribbons. It should be centered between the sleeve seam and the lapel. If a duty badge is worn on the wearer's right side of the service dress jacket, women will center the badge $1/2$ inch above the new name tag.

[Notes apply also to the women's semiformal dress uniform.]

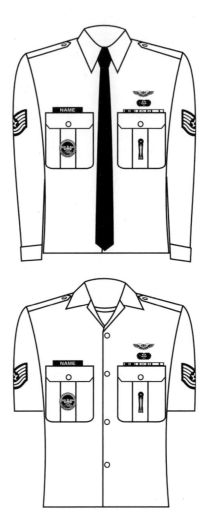

## Men's Long-Sleeved and Short-Sleeved Shirt

*Notes:*

1. Aeronautical and chaplain badges are mandatory. Others are optional. Center aeronautical and occupational badge $1/2$ inch above ribbons or pocket if not wearing ribbons. Center additional badge $1/2$ inch above the first one. Wear satin finish or highly polished badges.
2. Center ribbons resting on but not over edge of pocket between the left and right edges. Wear all.
3. Center duty badge on lower portion of left pocket between left and right edges and bottom of flap and pocket, and/or on right pocket between left and right edges and bottom of flap and pocket. *EXCEPTION:* Missile and missile maintenance badges are worn on left pocket.
4. (Optional) Center tie tack or tie clasp (Air Force coat of arms, grade insignia, or wing and star) between bottom edge of knot and bottom tip of tie.
5. Center name tag on but not over edge of pocket.
6. Officers place shoulder mark insignia as close as possible to shoulder seam. Airmen center 3-inch or $3^1/2$-inch sleeve chevron halfway between shoulder seam and elbow bent at 90-degree angle on the long-sleeved shirt, or halfway between shoulder seam and bottom edge of sleeve on the short-sleeved shirt.

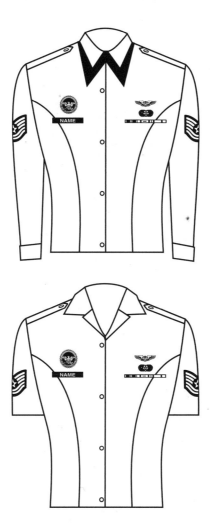

## Women's Long-Sleeved and Short-Sleeved Blouse

*Notes:*

1. Aeronautical and chaplain badges are mandatory. Others are optional. Center aeronautical and occupational badge $1/2$ inch above the ribbons. When not wearing ribbons, center badge parallel to the name tag. Center additional badge $1/2$ inch above first one. Wear satin finish or highly polished badges.

2. Center ribbons on left side parallel with ground. Align bottom of the ribbons with the bottom of the name tag. Wear all.

3. (Mandatory for major generals and below.) Pointed Collar: Center name tag on right side, even with to $1 1/2$ inches higher or lower than the first exposed button. Rounded Collar: Center name tag on right side $1 1/2$ to $2 1/2$ inches below bottom of the tab, parallel with ground.

4. Center duty badge $1/2$ inch above name tag. Wear satin finish or highly polished badges. Airmen: Center 3- or $3 1/2$-inch sleeve chevron halfway between shoulder seam and elbow when bent at 90-degree angle on the long-sleeved shirt, and halfway between shoulder seam and bottom edge of sleeve on the short-sleeved shirt.

### Men's and Women's Battle Dress Uniform

*Notes:*

1. Aeronautical and chaplain badges are mandatory. Others are optional. Center subdued embroidered badge (aeronautical, occupational) $1/2$ inch above U.S. AIR FORCE tape. Center additional badge $1/2$ inch above the first badge. A third badge may be worn on lower portion of left pocket between left and right edges and bottom of flap and bottom of pocket. NOTE: Missile and missile maintenance badges are worn in this location.

2. Center U.S. AIR FORCE tape immediately above left breast pocket. Center name tape immediately above right breast pocket. Cut off or fold tapes to match pocket width. Maternity: Place in same relative position.

3. (Commanders' discretion) Center subdued emblems on lower portion of pocket between left and right edges and bottom of flap and pocket. Center emblem over right pocket $1/2$ inch above name tape. When wearing a badge on an emblem-designated area, do not wear the emblem. Maternity: Place in same relative position. *NOTE:* Personnel attached to Army units may wear associate unit patch only while attached to unit.

4. Airmen: Center 3-, $3^1/2$-, or 4-inch (women) or 4-inch (men) sleeve chevron halfway between shoulder seam and elbow when bent at 90-degree angle. Wear the new style rank insignia.

5. NAME/USAF tapes are mandatory. Do not wear the Aircrew Style Name Patch.

## Airman Battle Uniform

*Notes:*

The Airman Battle Uniform (ABU) is the new battledress uniform for the United States Air Force. It is currently in the beginning stages of being phased into service and will replace the Battle Dress Uniform (BDU) by Fiscal Year 2011. The ABU will be "wash and wear," meaning the only care needed will be to wash and dry it. The ABU will replace the familiar camouflage-pattern BDU.

## Men's Mess Dress Uniform

*Notes:*
1. Aeronautical and chaplain badges are mandatory. Others are optional. Center aeronautical and occupational badge $1/2$ inch above top row of medals or when not authorized medals, midway between shoulder and top button. Wear either highly polished or satin finish badges, cuff links, or studs. Wear cuff links and studs as a set. Do not mix highly polished or satin finish.
2. (Mandatory) Center miniature medals between lapel and arm seam and midway between top shoulder seam and top button of jacket.
3. (Optional) Center duty badge $1/2$ inch below bottom row of medals or comparable position when no medals are authorized, and/or on top right side in same relative position as those badges worn on left.
4. (Mandatory) Airmen: Center 4-inch sleeve chevron (either aluminum color on blue background or new style rank insignia) halfway between shoulder seam and elbow bent at 90-degree angle.

## Women's Mess Dress Uniform

*Notes:*

1 and 2.    Aeronautical and chaplain badges are mandatory. Others are optional. Center aeronautical and occupational badge $^1/_2$ inch above top row of medals or when not authorized medals, midway between shoulder and top button. Wear second badge above first badge when authorized. Wear satin finish or highly polished badges. Do not mix highly polished or satin finish.

3. Center miniature medals between lapel and arm seam and midway between top of shoulder seam and top button of jacket. Airmen: Center 3-, $3^1/_2$-, or 4-inch sleeve chevron (either aluminum color on blue background or new style rank insignia) halfway between shoulder seam and elbow bent at 90-degree angle.

4. Center duty badge on top right side in same relative position as those badges worn on left.

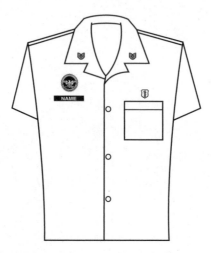

**Hospital White Uniform**

*Notes:*
1. Center name tag on the right side of the shirt with bottom edge parallel to the top of the left breast pocket or on the same relative position if no pocket.
2. Wear metal rank insignia 1 inch up from collar bottom.
3. (Optional) Center metal certification badge or cloth certification patch $^1/_2$ inch above name tag.
4. Aeronautical badges are mandatory, others are optional. Center the metal Air Force occupational badge $^1/_2$ inch above the left breast pocket or same relative position if no pocket.
5. (Commanders' discretion) Center metal or cloth MAJCOM or subordinate unit emblem $^1/_2$ inch above name tag.

**Men's and Women's Pullover Sweater**

*Note:*
1. Officers and senior NCOs wear shoulder mark grade insignia. All other enlisted members wear metal collar insignia centered horizontally on the epaulet with bottom of insignia placed 1 inch from shoulder seam.
2. The metallic name tag will be worn on all pullover sweaters on the wearer's right side with the bottom of the name tag level centered between the middle of the sleeve seam and the seam of the neckline.

## PT Uniform

*Notes:*

The Air Force designed a PT uniform that became mandatory for wear in October 2006. The uniform consists of shorts, T-shirt, jacket, and pants. The shorts are AF blue with silver reflective stripes on the leg, a key pocket attached to the inner liner, and an ID pocket on the outside of the lower right leg. The pants are blue with silver piping and reflective stripes. The T-shirt is a moisture-wicking fabric with reflective Air Force logos on the upper left portion of the chest and across the back. The jacket is blue with silver reflective piping and a reflective chevron on the back.

## ACQUISITION OF AIR FORCE UNIFORMS

Air Force uniforms and articles that are mandatory for wear are issued to all Air Force members when they enter the service. After that, replacement and optional items are purchased by individual members at Army and Air Force Exchange Service (AAFES) outlets and at Military Clothing Sales Stores (MCSSs). Functional and distinctive clothing equipment items, when authorized for wear as outlined in Table of Allowances (TA) 016, are issued through supply channels.

## WEAR OF THE AIR FORCE UNIFORM

The Air Force uniform is worn with pride, and each member is responsible for presenting a neat and clean military image. Items other than those provided for in AFI 36-2903 are not to be worn. Uniforms may be worn to off-base establishments for short trips. This policy, however, may be subject to local conditions, such as in overseas areas where host nation sensitivities may be affected. In some cases, civilian clothing allowances may be authorized.

## WEAR OF AWARDS AND DECORATIONS

Air Force members may wear medals and ribbons for awards and decorations they have received. When worn, they are arranged in order of precedence. The medal or ribbon with the highest precedence is worn nearest the lapel on the top row. Medals are primarily displayed on dress uniforms. Ribbons are displayed on the service dress uniform and on long- and short-sleeved blue shirts and blouses. They are not worn on outer garments, such as raincoats, topcoats, overcoats, sweaters, or lightweight blue jackets.

## WEAR OF INSIGNIA, BADGES, AND DEVICES

Grade insignia is worn by all Air Force members except those in Basic Military Training School or Officer Training School and agents of the Office of Special Investigations (OSI), unless otherwise directed. There are four types, designed for various uniforms: metal collar insignia, subdued cloth insignia, blue and silver cloth insignia, and formal dress insignia with silver-colored chevrons embroidered on a blue background.

**Lapel Insignia.** Lapel insignia identify the wearer as a member of the U.S. Air Force. Following the Air Force chief of staff's vision of "lasting heritage—limitless horizons," the Air Force Uniform Board made minor changes to the enlisted uniform. These changes include returning to the U.S. insignia with circle for the service dress uniform and the deletion of the optional shoulder board rank for the blue uniform, making the sleeve chevrons mandatory. Officers continue to wear the lapel insignia "U.S." without the circle around the device.

**Name Tags.** The standard Air Force name tag is laminated ultramarine blue plastic, $3^3/_{16}$ inches long and $5/_8$ inch wide. Names (last names only) are engraved in block style in white letters usually $1/_4$ inch in size. Letters may be smaller if necessary to accommodate longer names.

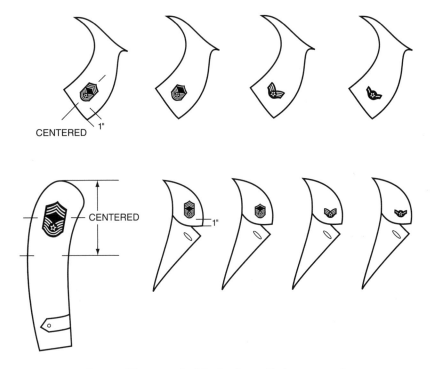

## Proper Placement of Insignia on Outergarments

*Notes:*

1. Full-Length Outergarments and Lightweight Blue Jacket. Enlisted personnel wear 3-, 3½- or 4-inch (women) and 4-inch (men) sleeve chevron on sleeves or metal rank insignia on collar. Wear metal rank insignia centered 1 inch up from bottom collar and parallel to outer edge. Wear the new style rank insignia. *NOTE:* Sleeve chevrons are not worn on the raincoat so as not to compromise its watertight integrity.
2. Pullover Sweater. Officers and senior NCOs wear shoulder mark rank insignia. All other enlisted members wear metal rank insignia. Center horizontally on the epaulet with bottom of insignia 1 inch from shoulder seam. Wear the new style rank insignia.

The new metallic name tag must be worn on the wearer's right side of the pullover sweater and the service dress jacket, with the bottom of the name tag level with the bottom of the ribbons on the latter. It should be centered between the sleeve scam and the lapel.

**Badges.** The Air Force has forty-five badges that may be worn on the service dress, service, and fatigue uniforms. Air Force members are highly encouraged to wear their current occupational badge. Aeronautical and chaplain badges are mandatory; others are optional. The badges fall into three categories:

- Aeronautical badges (9)
- Occupational badges (27)
- Duty badges (10)

**Women's Lightweight
Blue Jacket**

**Men's Lightweight
Blue Jacket**

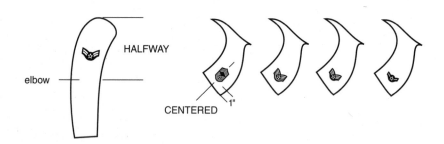

### Men's Lightweight Blue Jackets

*Notes:*
1. Enlisted personnel wear standard 4-inch chevrons on sleeves or metal collar insignia.
2. Officers wear regular metal grade insignia on epaulets.


### Women's Lightweight Blue Jackets

*Notes:*
1. Enlisted personnel wear standard 3- or 4-inch chevrons on sleeves or metal collar insignia.
2. Officers wear miniature metal grade insignia on epaulets.

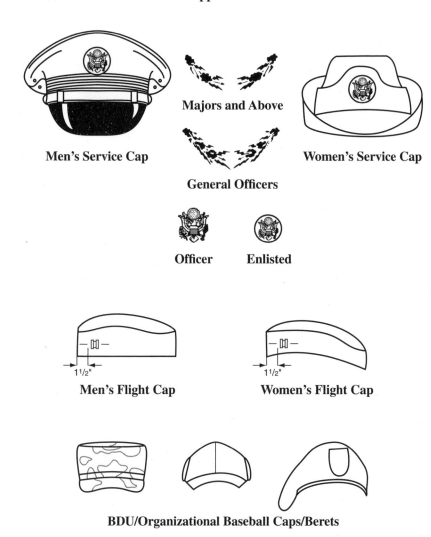

**Men's Service Cap**

**Majors and Above**

**General Officers**

**Women's Service Cap**

**Officer** **Enlisted**

**Men's Flight Cap** **Women's Flight Cap**

**BDU/Organizational Baseball Caps/Berets**

## Men's and Women's Headgear

*Notes:*
1. Officers only wear regular size metal grade insignia.
2. Wear the regular size cloth or subdued metal grade insignia on the camouflage pattern BDU cap. MAJCOM commanders may authorize wear of the bright nonsubdued grade insignia by officers on BDU caps while in garrison. *NOTE:* Chaplains may wear chaplains' insignia centered $^1/_2$ inch above visor of BDU cap.
3. Grade will be centered vertically and horizontally.
4. Officers wear service cap insignia without circle on service cap; enlisted wear service cap insignia with circle.

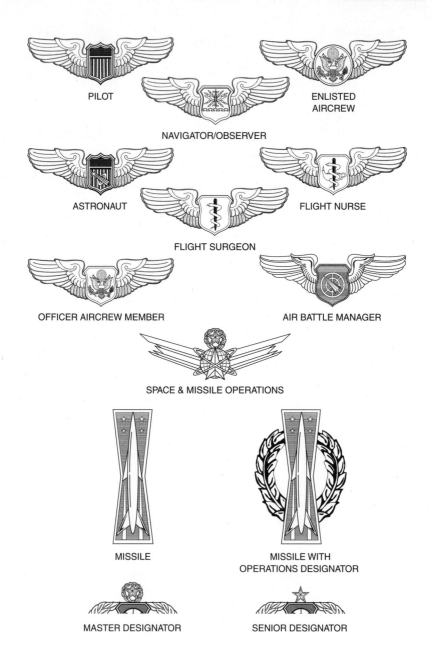

PILOT

NAVIGATOR/OBSERVER

ENLISTED
AIRCREW

ASTRONAUT

FLIGHT SURGEON

FLIGHT NURSE

OFFICER AIRCREW MEMBER

AIR BATTLE MANAGER

SPACE & MISSILE OPERATIONS

MISSILE

MISSILE WITH
OPERATIONS DESIGNATOR

MASTER DESIGNATOR

SENIOR DESIGNATOR

**Aeronautical Badges**

ACQUISITION & FINANCIAL
MANAGEMENT

AIR TRAFFIC CONTROL

BAND

CHAPLAIN SERVICE
SUPPORT

CIVIL ENGINEER
READINESS

CIVIL ENGINEER

COMMAND & CONTROL

COMMUNICATIONS &
INFORMATION

EXPLOSIVE ORDNANCE
DISPOSAL

FORCE PROTECTION

FORCE SUPPORT

HISTORIAN

INFORMATION
MANAGEMENT

INTELLIGENCE

JUDGE ADVOCATE

LOGISTICS

MAINTENANCE

MANPOWER & PERSONNEL

METEOROLOGIST

**Occupational Badges**

OPERATIONS SUPPORT

PARACHUTIST

PARALEGAL

PUBLIC AFFAIRS

SERVICES

SPACE/MISSILE

SUPPLY/FUELS

TRANSPORTATION

WEAPONS DIRECTOR

BIOMEDICAL SCIENCE
CORPS

DENTAL CORPS

ENLISTED MEDICAL

MEDICAL CORPS

MEDICAL SERVICE
CORPS

NURSE CORPS

BUDDHIST

CHRISTIAN

JEWISH

MUSLIM

**Occupational Badges (continued)**

**Presidential Service Badge**

**Vice-Presidential Service Badge**

**Office of the Secretary of Defense Badge**

**Joint Chiefs of Staff Badge**

**Headquarters Air Force Badge**

**Commander's Badge**

**Permanent Professor USAF Academy Badge**

**Duty Badges**

**Recruiting Service**

**AETC Instructor
Insignia**

**Security Police
Badge**

**Fire Protection
Badge**

**Duty Badges (continued)**

The badges are shown on the preceeding pages. Their placement on the various Air Force uniforms is described in the notes on uniforms. Note that the introduction of the metal name tag for the service dress uniform has affected the placement of the duty badges, and that the placement differs for men and women.

The commander's badge has been designed and authorized for officers in the grade of major through colonel who are or have been commanders of a squadron, group, or wing. It features the Hap Arnold star and wings encircled by a wreath.

On 28 September 2005, the Chief of Staff of the Air Force approved the design and development of the Headquarters Air Force Badge. The badge provides a distinct identification of military staff members assigned and, after assignment, indicates that the service member has satisfactorily served on the Headquarters Air Force Staff or Secretary of the Air Force Staff within the National Capital Region. The symbolism incorporated in the Great Seal of the Department of the Air Force on the badge is as follows:

- The predominant colors, ultramarine blue and gold, are the colors of the Air Force through transition from the Air Corps.
- The crest includes the American bald eagle, which is the symbol of the United States and air striking power.
- The shield, divided with the nebula line formation, representing clouds, is charged with the heraldic thunderbolt. The thunderbolt portrays striking power through the medium of air.

A new space badge was introduced in 2004. The new combined Space and Missile Operations Badge replaced the Missile Badge for operators and is no longer limited to pure space and missile operators/maintainers, but is also awarded to 61XX, 62XX, and 63XX (officer) AFSCs who have performed space/ICBM acquisition duties, even if they were non-operational in nature.

## RESTRICTIONS ON WEAR OF THE UNIFORM AND INSIGNIA

Air Force members may not wear the uniform, or any part, in situations that are counter to the interests of the United States or the U.S. Air Force, including the following:

1. A meeting of, or sponsored by, an organization, association, movement, or group that the Attorney General of the United States has named as totalitarian, fascist, communist, or subversive; that advocates acts of force or violence to deny others their rights under the Constitution; or that seeks to change the U.S. government by unconstitutional means.
2. Activities such as public speeches, interviews, picket lines, marches, rallies, or any public demonstration not approved by the Air Force. To do so could imply the Air Force's sanction of the cause for which the demonstration or activity is conducted.
3. When furthering private employment or commercial interests, if official sponsorship might be inferred.
4. When engaged in off-duty civilian employment.
5. When doing so would discredit the armed forces.
6. Any public meeting, demonstration, march, rally, or interview if the purpose may be to advocate, express, or approve opposition to the U.S. Armed Forces.

Air Force members are also prohibited from wearing combinations of uniforms not prescribed in AFI 36-2903 and from wearing or mixing distinctive uniform items (grade insignia, cap devices, badges, insignia, and so forth) with civilian clothing.

Personnel outside of the military are also affected. Any person within the jurisdiction of the United States who, without authority, wears a uniform or distinctive part of a uniform of the armed forces in an attempt to pose as a military member is subject to penalties as outlined in Title 18 U.S.C. 702.

## RECENT CHANGES IN UNIFORMS

The recent Air Force Uniform Board has brought about many changes. One shift will be the return of heritage to the enlisted corps reflected by chevrons on the sleeves and circles around the U.S. insignia. The circle around the U.S. insignia on the service coat was eliminated in 1991, but it is back again. Senior NCOs will no longer be allowed to wear shoulder boards, except on the optional wool sweater. Desert combat uniforms are now only authorized on civilian flights to and from the area of responsibility. Air Force personnel are not authorized to wear desert boots with the battle dress uniform. New guidance about the wear of flight clothing also is incorporated in the latest changes. The new Airman Battle Uniform (ABU) is a new "wash and wear" fabric with lots of new pockets. Air Force deputy chief of staff of personnel Brig. Gen. Robert R. Allardice calls the new ABU "the uniform of the future." The new uniform design is a pixilated tiger stripe with four soft earth tones consisting of tan, grey, green, and blue. The ABU has a permanent crease and is made with a 50-50 nylon-cotton blend, permanent-press fabric that eliminates the need for winter- and summer-weight uniforms.

For additional information about the recent decisions made on the Uniform Board's recommendations, log onto the news site on Air Force Link at *www.af.mil*, or visit your military personnel flight or commander's support staff.

## PERSONAL GROOMING

Standards of appearance include four elements: neatness, cleanliness, safety, and military image. Military image is subjective, not always easy to outline in definitive terms, but it is a major consideration because it instills public confidence in the military. This is why standards were established for the most common appearance issues. These standards specify military members' responsibility for maintaining an "acceptable military image" and their right, within limits, to express individuality through their appearance.

**General Requirements.** Uniforms should be kept in a good state of repair. Shoes should be shined and in a good state of repair. Ribbons should be clean and should be replaced when they become frayed, worn, or faded. All buttons should be buttoned and pocket contents should be concealed from view, except for pens and pencils in the compartment of the left pocket on the fatigue uniform. Visible ornaments may not be worn, except for watches, rings (a maximum of three), and a wrist bracelet less than 1 inch wide if it is neat, conservative, and does not pose a safety hazard. Conservative sunglasses and photosensitive eyeglasses may be worn.

Hair must be clean, well groomed, and neat. If dyed, it must look natural. It must not contain excessive amounts of grooming aids, be worn in an extreme or fad style, or violate safety requirements. The hair must not touch the eyebrows when groomed or protrude below the front band of properly worn headgear (except for women's berets or flight caps). Wigs and hairpieces must conform to the same standards required for natural hair, be of good quality, and fit properly. They must not be worn in aircraft, on the flightline, or during in-flight operations. Hair nets must be worn if required for safety. They must be cotton or synthetic, a conservative solid color similar to the individual's hair color, and strong enough to support and control hair. They must contain no metal fasteners.

**Standards for Men.** Hairstyles must be tapered on both sides and at the back, both with and without headgear, no more than $1/4$ inch thick at the termination point. A block cut is permitted as long as a tapered appearance is kept. Hair may not touch the ears. Only closely cut or shaved hair on the back of the neck may touch the collar. Overall, the hair must not exceed $1^1/4$ inches in bulk, regardless of length. It must not have any visible foreign items attached to it. Beards must not be worn except for health reasons when authorized by a commander on the advice of a medical officer. Mustaches may be worn but must not extend downward beyond the lipline of the upper lip or sideways beyond a vertical line drawn upward from the corner of the mouth. These restrictions do not apply to personnel with a shaving waiver. Sideburns, when worn, must be neatly trimmed and tapered in the same manner as the haircut. They must be straight and of an even width (not flared) and end in a clean-shaven horizontal line, not below the lowest part of the exterior ear opening. These restrictions do not apply to personnel with a shaving waiver.

**Standards for Women.** Hairstyles must present a professional appearance. Plain and conservative pins, combs, and barrettes similar to the individual's hair color may be worn to keep the hair in place. The hair must not be longer than the bottom edge of the shirt collar at the back of the neck, exceed 3 inches in bulk, or prevent proper wear of headgear. Cosmetics may be worn as long as they are conservative and in good taste. Nail polish may be worn when it is uniform, conservative in color, and in good taste. It must not, however, contain any ornamentation.

## Air Force Policy on Body Art

Air Force Instruction 36-2903, *Dress and Personal Appearance of Air Force Personnel,* establishes guidelines on tattoos, branding, and body piercing. It specifies that:

- Tattoos and brands should not be excessive. Those that contain inflammatory, obscene, racist, sexist, or similar content are strictly prohibited. Examples of those that could be considered excessive would include images or brands that cover more than one-fourth (25 percent) of an exposed body limb or are visible above the collarbone in an open-collar uniform.

- Men, on base, in or out of uniform, on or off duty, cannot wear earrings or any other visible body piercing.
- Women may, on duty, on base, in uniform, wear a single, small, spherical, matching earring in each earlobe. When on duty, on or off base, in civilian clothes, they may wear a single, small, spherical, matching earring in each earlobe. When off duty, on base, in civilian clothes, they may wear earrings that are conservative and kept within sensible limits. No other body piercing should be visible.

Commanders, first sergeants, supervisors, and airmen now have clear guidance on what is acceptable body art. They have the latitude to look at the size and extent of the tattoo and determine what is acceptable. Air Force doctors also support the new policy. They note that, in terms of tattooing, piercing, and scarification (cutting into the skin with a sharp instrument), there is the potential for serious medical complications, including blood-borne infections such as HIV and hepatitis B and C, as well as staph and strep infections. Secondary infections might also occur during healing processes. There is, moreover, some question regarding whether any resulting infection or injury falls within the line of duty, that is, whether the Air Force will pay for such treatment. Decisions on this are made on a case-by-case basis.

## AIR FORCE FITNESS PROGRAM

The Air Force is concerned about the weight and fitness of its members for two primary reasons: First, the American public and its elected representatives form opinions about the Air Force based on the appearance of its members. If military personnel look out of shape, perception of the service's effectiveness will not be good. Second, obesity can pose dangerous health risks—heart problems, strokes, and diabetes—that are detrimental to the individual Air Force member and to his or her physical ability to perform military tasks during both peacetime and war.

Recent changes to the USAF Fitness program have brought new vigor to the previous fitness and weight management programs. The emphasis is on health, fitness, and readiness through physical training, personal involvement, and adoption of a warrior culture.

Air Force Instruction 36-2905, dated 1 July 2010, states that it is every airman's responsibility to maintain the Air Force Fitness Standards 365 days a year. Being physically fit allows you to properly support the Air Force mission.

The goal of the Fitness Program (FP) is to motivate all members to participate in a year-round physical conditioning program that emphasizes total fitness, to include proper aerobic conditioning, strength/flexibility training, and healthy eating. Health benefits from an active lifestyle will increase productivity, optimize health, and decrease absenteeism while maintaining a higher level of readiness.

Commanders and supervisors must incorporate fitness into Air Force culture, establishing an environment for members to maintain physical fitness and health to meet expeditionary mission requirements. The Fitness Assessment (FA) provides commanders with a tool to assist in the determination of the overall fitness of their military personnel. Commander-driven physical fitness training is the backbone of the AF physical fitness program and an integral part of mission requirements. The program promotes aerobic and muscular fitness, flexibility, and optimal body composition of each member in the unit.

Scoring tables for men and women by age are shown in appendix D.

## SOURCES OF ADDITIONAL INFORMATION

Air Force Instruction 36-2903, *Dress and Personal Appearance of Air Force Personnel.*

Air Force Instruction 36-2923, *Aeronautical, Duty, and Occupational Badges.*

Air Force Instruction 36-2905, *Fitness Program.*

Consult your supervisor or your unit's first sergeant.

# 10

# Awards, Decorations, and Recognition Programs

*Let him who has won the palm bear it.*

—Latin proverb

Awards and decorations programs were developed to recognize and reward individuals and organizations for outstanding performance. The commonly accepted term *recognition programs* is sometimes used to refer to programs that technically are awards programs. Both have a similar goal: to provide sincere and timely recognition, which fosters morale, incentive, and esprit de corps. They also have a positive influence on career decisions and retention. In the Air Force, as in the civilian community, a large element of job satisfaction and the desire to reenlist or stay with the company comes with the acknowledgment of a job well done. When people feel their efforts are not fully appreciated, they may consider leaving to seek fulfillment in another role.

## DECORATIONS PROGRAMS
A decoration is a formal recognition of personal excellence, such as acts of exceptional bravery, outstanding achievement, or meritorious service. Award of a decoration requires an individual nomination and subsequent approval by designated levels of authority within the Department of Defense or the Department of the Air Force. The types of decorations and their eligibility criteria are listed in Air Force Instruction 36-2803, *The Air Force Awards and Decorations Program.*

**U.S. Military Decorations.** U.S. military decorations include the Medal of Honor (MH), the Air Force Cross (AFC), the Defense Distinguished Service Medal (DDSM), the Distinguished Service Medal (DSM), the Silver Star (SS), the Defense Superior Service Medal (DSSM), the Legion of Merit (LM), the Distinguished Flying Cross (DFC), the Airman's Medal (AmnM), the Bronze Star Medal (BSM), the Purple Heart (PH), the Defense Meritorious Service Medal (DMSM), the Meritorious Service Medal (MSM), the Air Medal (AM), the Aerial Achievement Medal (AAM), the Joint Service Commendation Medal (JSCM), the Air Force Commendation Medal (AFCM), the Joint Service Achievement Medal

# ORDER OF PRECEDENCE
## Awards and Decorations

| | | | | |
|---|---|---|---|---|
| Medal of Honor | Air Force Cross | Defense Distinguished Service Medal | Distinguished Service Medal | Silver Star |
| Defense Superior Service Medal | Legion of Merit | Distinguished Flying Cross | Airman's Medal | Bronze Star |
| Purple Heart | Defense Meritorious Service Medal | Meritorious Service Medal | Air Medal | Aerial Achievement Medal |
| Joint Service Commendation Medal | Air Force Commendation Medal | Joint Service Achievement Medal | Air Force Achievement Medal | Air Force Combat Action Medal |
| Presidential Unit Citation | Joint Meritorious Unit Award | Gallant Unit Citation (GUC) | Meritorious Unit Award | Air Force Outstanding Unit Award |
| Air Force Organizational Excellence Award | Prisoner of War Medal | Combat Readiness Medal | Air Force Good Conduct Medal | Good Conduct Medal |
| Air Reserve Forces Meritorious Service Medal | Outstanding Airman of the Year Ribbon | Air Force Recognition Ribbon | American Defense Service Medal | American Campaign Medal |
| Asiatic-Pacific Campaign Medal | Euro-African Middle Eastern Campaign | World War II Victory Medal | Army of Occupation Medal | Medal for Humane Action |
| National Defense Service Medal | Korean Service Medal | Antarctica Service Medal | Armed Forces Expeditionary Medal | Vietnam Service Medal |
| Southwest Asia Service Medal | Kosovo Campaign Medal | Afghanistan Campaign Medal | Iraq Campaign Medal | Global War on Terrorism Expeditionary Medal (GWOT-E) |
| Global War on Terrorism Service Medal (GWOT-S) | Korean Defense Service Medal (KDSM) | Armed Forces Service Medal | Humanitarian Service Medal | Military Outstanding Volunteer Service Medal |
| Air and Space Campaign Medal | Air Force Overseas Ribbon Short | Air Force Overseas Ribbon Long | Air Force Expeditionary Service Ribbon (AFESR) | Air Force Longevity Service Award |
| Air Force Basic Military Training Instructor Ribbon | Air Force Recruiter Ribbon | Armed Forces Reserve Medal | USAF NCO PME Graduate Ribbon | USAF Basic Military Training Honor Graduate Ribbon |
| Small Arms Expert Marksmanship Ribbon | Air Force Training Ribbon | Philippine Defense Ribbon | Philippine Liberation Ribbon | Philippine Independence Ribbon |
| Philippine Presidential Unit Citation | Republic of Korea Presidential Unit Citation | RVN Gallantry Cross With Palm | United Nations Service Medal | United Nations Medal |
| NATO Meritorious Service Medal | NATO Medal for Yugoslavia | NATO Medal for Kosovo | Article 5 NATO Medal (EAGLE ASSIST) | Article 5 NATO Medal (ACTIVE ENDEAVOUR) |
| Non-Article 5 NATO Medal (Balkan Opns) | Non-Article 5 NATO Medal (ISAF) | Republic of Vietnam Campaign Medal | Kuwait Liberation Medal (Kingdom of Saudi Arabia) | Kuwait Liberation Medal (Government of Kuwait) |
| Republic of Korea Korean War Service Medal | | | | |

(JSAM), the Air Force Achievement Medal (AFAM), and the Air Force Combat Action Medal (AFCAM). The most frequently awarded are the following:

1. The *Meritorious Service Medal (MSM)* is awarded for outstanding non-combat meritorious achievement or service to the United States. It has distinction above and beyond the Air Force Commendation Medal. Nominations are prepared on one side of a sheet of bond paper, typewritten and single-spaced. Emphasis is placed on awarding this decoration to outstanding field-grade officers and senior noncommissioned officers. Under enlisted promotion score systems, each MSM is valued at five points.

2. The *Air Force Commendation Medal (AFCM)* is awarded for outstanding achievement or meritorious service rendered specifically on behalf of the Air Force, acts of courage, and sustained meritorious performance. Awards are restricted to achievements and services that are clearly outstanding and unmistakably exceptional when compared with similar achievements and accomplishments of personnel of like rank and responsibilities. Nominations may be prepared on Air Force Form 642, "AF Achievement Medal and AF Commendation Medal Justification." This form allows room for seven primary job accomplishments and five other accomplishments (special projects, additional duties, and so on). Each entry allows for one concise and factual sentence. Emphasis is placed on awarding this decoration to outstanding company-grade officers and airmen whose achievements and service meet the prescribed standards. Under enlisted promotion score systems, each AFCM is valued at three points.

3. The *Air Force Achievement Medal (AFAM)* is awarded for outstanding achievement and meritorious service rendered specifically on behalf of the Air Force and for acts of courage that do not meet the requirements for award of the Air Force Commendation Medal. In instances where many people are affiliated with an exceptionally successful program, project, or mission, the AFAM is awarded to those few whose contributions clearly stand out from the others and who have contributed most to the success of the program. Emphasis is placed on awarding this decoration to outstanding junior officers and airmen whose achievements and service meet the prescribed standards. Under enlisted promotion score systems, each AFAM is valued at one point.

These nominations originate with a member's supervisor and are forwarded for review and approval through command channels. All decorations can be awarded to an individual more than once. Usually, they are obtained in sequence as an airman increases in grade and positions of responsibility (the AFAM first, the AFCM second, and the MSM third).

There are three keys to obtaining these decorations: outstanding performance, a well-written nomination that is specific and factual, and the support of the nominee's supervisor and commander. This third point can't be overemphasized. I remember a young senior airman (E-4) who was disappointed because an Air

| ☐ AIR FORCE ACHIEVEMENT MEDAL  ☐ AIR FORCE COMMENDATION MEDAL | | DATE |
|---|---|---|
| **JUSTIFICATION** | | 1 Jul 11 |

| 1. NAME (Last, First, MI) | | 2. GRADE | 3. SSN |
|---|---|---|---|
| DOE, JOHN R. | | SSgt | 000-00-0000 |

**4. DUTY TITLES(S) AND INCLUSIVE PERIOD**

NCOIC, Awards and Decorations  (Use multiple titles if held during period of recommendation)

**5. JUSTIFICATION** (Use a short "Bullet" statement for each accomplishment. Minimize description - emphasize results. Use only as many bullets as required. Additional space below the dotted lines may be used for Air Force Commendation Medal Justification only.)

**a. PRIMARY JOB ACCOMPLISHMENTS:**

(1) Designed a new system that has raised average on-time percentage rates from less than 30% to over 95%.

(2) Reduced the average number of recommendations for decorations returned for administrative correction from 18 to less than 3 per month.

(3) Not only met but ensured all suspenses for AFI 36-2805, *Special Trophies and Awards* nominees were sent to higher headquarters before the required suspenses.

(4) Initiated a new system that ensures all approved decorations are updated in a manner that totally prevents the need for supplementary consideration for promotion under WAPS.

(5)

(6)
(7)
FOR ALL RECOMMENDING OFFICIALS:  Please note the justifying statements are short, concise, and factual statements that are devoid of "flowery" phrases and "Atta-Boys."  There are five items under "Primary Job Accomplishments" available for justification of the new Air Force Achievement Medal (AFAM) and seven for the Air Force Commendation Medal (AFCM).  Under "Other Accomplishments" there are three items available for the AFAM and five for the AFCM.

**b. OTHER ACCOMPLISHMENTS:** (Special projects, additional duties, etc.)

(1)

(2)

(3)

(4)

(5)

| 6. NAME, GRADE AND TITLE OF INITIATOR | 7. SIGNATURE |
|---|---|
| JOSEPHINE D. SMITH, CMSgt, USAF  NCOIC, Military Personnel Flight | *Josephine D. Smith* |

AF FORM 642  MAR 85  PREVIOUS EDITION WILL BE USED.

**AFAM and AFCM Justification (AF Form 642)**

Force Commendation Medal nomination was not favorably considered. The supervisor felt that an Air Force Achievement Medal was more appropriate and could be approved, but the sergeant said, "If I can't get the Commendation Medal, I don't want any." On the next promotion cycle, he missed staff sergeant (E-5) by less than one point. Had he been awarded the Achievement Medal, he would have been promoted.

One of the newest medals, the Air Force Combat Action Medal (AFCAM), can be awarded to airmen actively involved in combat operations, on the ground and in the air, for actions from September 11, 2001, to a date yet to be determined. The AFCAM is the highest-level Air Force individual award to not earn points under the Weighted Airmen Promotion System

**U.S. Nonmilitary Decorations.** U.S. nonmilitary decorations are awarded by the President, the Department of Defense, and the Department of the Air Force. Military personnel are eligible to receive the National Security Medal, for distinguished achievement or outstanding contribution on or after July 26, 1947, in the field of intelligence relating to the national security and the Presidential Medal of Freedom, for an exceptionally meritorious contribution to the national security interests of the United States, world peace, or cultural or other significant public or private endeavors.

## AWARDS PROGRAMS

Awards are formal recognition given to a specific group or persons. They fall into several major categories.

**Service Awards.** U.S. service awards recognize active military service personnel or reserve members who have faithfully and honorably served their country during periods of war or national emergency or in specific military operations. Common examples are the National Defense Service Medal, the Vietnam Service Medal, the Armed Forces Expeditionary Medal (for operations such as Beirut, Grenada, and Libya), the Southwest Asia Service Medal, and the Kosovo Campaign Medal.

The Southwest Asia Service Medal has been authorized to those servicemembers who served in the Persian Gulf area in operations Desert Shield and Desert Storm from August 2, 1990, to November 30, 1995. The Kosovo Campaign Medal was approved on May 8, 2000, for those who served in that operation as of March 24, 1999.

In March 2003, President Bush issued an executive order establishing two new U.S. service awards for actions in the global war on terrorism: the Global War on Terrorism Expeditionary Medal (GWOT-E) and the Global War on Terrorism Service Medal. The Global War on Terrorism Expeditionary Medal will be awarded to servicemembers who served in military expeditions to combat terrorism on or after September 11, 2001. Warriors who participated in operations in Iraq, Afghanistan, and the Philippines are examples of servicemembers who will receive the award. The Global War on Terrorism Service Medal will be awarded to

# DECORATIONS, AWARDS, AND SERVICE MEDALS

## USAF AND DEPARTMENT OF DEFENSE
## MILITARY DECORATIONS

**Medal of Honor
(Air Force)**

**Air Force Cross**

**Defense
Distinguished Service
Medal**

**Distinguished Service
Medal
(Air Force)**

**Silver Star**

**Defense Superior Service
Medal**

**Legion of Merit**

**Distinguished Flying Cross**

**Airman's Medal**

**Bronze Star Medal**

**Purple Heart**

**Defense Meritorious Service Medal**

**Meritorious Service Medal**

**Air Medal**

**Aerial Achievement Medal**

**Joint Service Commendation Medal**

**Air Force
Commendation
Medal**

**Joint Service
Achievement
Medal**

**Air Force
Achievement
Medal**

## USAF AND DEPARTMENT OF DEFENSE UNIT AWARDS

**Presidential
Unit Citation
(Air Force)**

**Joint Meritorious
Unit Award**

**Air Force
Gallant Unit Award**

**Air Force
Meritorious Unit
Award**

**AF Outstanding
Unit Award**

**AF Organizational
Excellence Award**

# MILITARY SERVICE AWARDS

**Combat Action Medal
(Air Force)**

**Prisoner of War
Medal**

**Combat Readiness
Medal**

**Good Conduct Medal
(Air Force)**

**Air Reserve Forces
Meritorious Service
Medal**

**National
Defense Service
Medal**

**Antarctica Service
Medal**

**Armed Forces
Expeditionary
Medal**

**Vietnam Service
Medal**

**Outstanding Airman of the Year Ribbon**

**Air Force Recognition Ribbon**

**Air Force Overseas Ribbon (short tour)**

**Air Force Overseas Ribbon (long tour)**

**Air Force Expeditionary Service Ribbon**

**Air Force Longevity Service Award Ribbon**

**USAF Basic Military Training Instructor Ribbon**

**Air Force Recruiter Ribbon**

**NCO Professional Military Education Graduate Ribbon**

**USAF Basic Military Training Honor Graduate Ribbon**

**Small Arms Expert Marksmanship Ribbon**

**Air Force Training Ribbon**

**Southwest Asia Service Medal**

**Kosovo Campaign Medal**

**Afghanistan Campaign Medal**

**Iraq Campaign Medal**

**Global War on Terrorism Expeditionary Medal**

**Global War on Terrorism Service Medal**

**Korean Defense Service Medal**

**Armed Forces Service Medal**

**Humanitarian Service Medal**

**Military Outstanding Volunteer Service Medal**

**Air and Space Campaign Medal**

**Armed Forces Reserve Medal**

# NON-U.S. SERVICE MEDALS

**United Nations Medal**

**NATO Medal**

**Multinational Force and Observers Medal**

**Republic of Vietnam Campaign Medal**

**Kuwait Liberation Medal (Kingdom of Saudi Arabia)**

**Kuwait Liberation Medal (Government of Kuwait)**

servicemembers who served in military operations to combat terrorism on or after September 11, 2001. The new awards do not take the place of the Armed Forces Expeditionary Medal, established December 4, 1961, or the Armed Forces Service Medal, established January 11, 1996.

In April 2002, the Secretary of the Air Force authorized a new Air Force service award called the Air and Space Campaign Medal for qualifying service after March 24, 2002. The medal is awarded to members of the U.S. Air Force who participate in or directly support a significant U.S. military operation designated so by the Chief of Staff. The medal is awarded only to personnel who provide direct support of combat operations from outside a geographic area determined by the JCS. The Air Force Chief of Staff will designate the military operations that qualify for award of the medal.

In October 2003, the Secretary of the Air Force approved yet another service award called the Air Force Expeditionary Service Ribbon to recognize airmen who supported an air expeditionary force deployment. The ribbon will be awarded to any Air Force member of any component who completed a contingency deployment after October 1, 1999, that lasted for forty-five consecutive days or ninety nonconsecutive days. There is no time limit for completing the nonconsecutive days.

In February 2004, the Department of Defense announced the creation of the Korean Defense Service Medal for servicemembers who are serving or have served in the Republic of Korea during the period July 28, 1954, to a future date to be determined by the Secretary of Defense. To be eligible, servicemembers have to have served thirty consecutive or sixty nonconsecutive days or meet one of several other service criteria.

The Afghanistan Campaign Medal (AFGM) and the Iraq Campaign Medal (ICM) were approved by the President per Public Law 108-234, 28 May 2004, and Executive Order 13363, 29 November 2004.

The AFGM is to recognize service members who serve or have served in the country of Afghanistan in direct support of Operation ENDURING FREEDOM (OEF). The area of eligibility (AOE) encompasses all land area of the country of Afghanistan and all air spaces above the land. The period of eligibility is on or after 24 October 2001 to a date to be determined (DTBD) by the Secretary of Defense or the cessation of OEF. The AFGM shall be positioned below the Kosovo Campaign Medal and above the Iraq Campaign Medal.

The Iraq Campaign Medal (ICM) area of eligibility encompasses all land area of the country of Iraq, the contiguous water area out to twelve nautical miles, and all air spaces above the land area of Iraq and above the contiguous water area out to twelve nautical miles. The ICM period of eligibility is on or after 19 March 2003 to a future date to be determined by the Secretary of Defense or the cessation of OIF. Only one award of this medal may be authorized for any individual. Service Stars are not authorized at this time. The ICM shall be positioned below the Afghanistan Campaign Medal (AFGM) and above the GWOT-E.

Non-U.S. service awards that have been accorded presidential acceptance and are authorized for wear by eligible personnel include the United Nations Service Medal (UNSM) and the United Nations Medal (UNM), the two NATO medals the Republic of Vietnam Campaign Medal, and the two Kuwait Liberation Medals (KLM). Of the latter, the first KLM has been awarded by the Kingdom of Saudi Arabia for direct participation in Operation Desert Storm between January 17, 1991, and February 28, 1991. The second KLM has been awarded by the Government of Kuwait for service between August 2, 1990, and August 31, 1993.

**Unit Awards.** Unit awards are presented to U.S. military units that distinguish themselves during peacetime or in action against hostile forces or armed enemies of the United States.

1. The *Presidential Unit Citation (PUC)* is awarded for extraordinary heroism in action against an armed enemy on or after December 7, 1947.
2. The *Joint Meritorious Unit Award (JMUA)* is awarded in the name of the Secretary of Defense to Joint Activities of the Department of Defense for meritorious achievement or service, superior to that normally expected, during combat with an armed enemy of the United States, during a declared national emergency, or under extraordinary circumstances that involved the national interest.
3. The *Air Force Gallant, Meritorious,* and *Outstanding Unit Awards* are awarded for exceptionally meritorious service or exceptionally outstanding achievement that clearly sets a unit above and apart from similar units. It is primarily awarded to wing-level units and below.
4. The *Air Force Organizational Excellence Award (AFOEA)* is similar to the AFOUA but is awarded to higher-level unnumbered organizations, such as major command headquarters, separate operating agencies, and direct reporting units.

The acceptance of foreign service awards is no longer authorized (U.S. service awards are not tendered to foreign military personnel); however, awards that were previously authorized and accepted may be worn.

Army and Navy unit decorations are similar to those for the Air Force. Members of cited Air Force units and other persons who, while Army and Navy members, received unit decorations that they are entitled to wear permanently may wear the appropriate award devices on the Air Force uniform.

**Achievement Awards.** Achievement awards recognize specific types of achievements made while serving on active duty in the Air Force or as a member of the Air Force Reserve. To be eligible, an individual must meet the criteria for each award, and service for the entire period of the award must be honorable. Air Force achievement awards include the following:

Prisoner of War Medal
Combat Readiness Medal
Good Conduct Medal
Air Reserve Forces Meritorious Service Medal

Outstanding Airman of the Year Ribbon
Air Force Recognition Ribbon
Air Force Overseas Service Ribbon
Air Force Longevity Service Award
USAF Basic Military Training Instructor Ribbon
Air Force Recruiter Ribbon
Armed Forces Reserve Medal
NCO Professional Military Education Graduate Ribbon
USAF Basic Military Training Honor Graduate Ribbon
Small Arms Expert Marksmanship Ribbon
Air Force Training Ribbon

**Foreign Decorations.** Congressional authority was given to U.S. Armed Forces personnel to accept and wear decorations proffered by friendly foreign governments and international organizations for military service performed during specific operations during specific time periods, which are outlined in AFI 36-2803. Foreign decorations authorized to date in order of precedence are:

United Nations Medal
NATO Medal
Republic of Vietnam Campaign Medal
Kuwait Liberation Medal (Kingdom of Saudi Arabia)
Kuwait Liberation Medal (Government of Kuwait)

**Special Trophies and Awards.** The Air Force, as well as some private organizations, has established programs that recognize individual contributions and achievements based on grade and level of responsibility. They also recognize units of comparable status (wing, base, squadron) and achievements in established programs (for example, safety, personnel, supply, and fuels).

Nominations are made primarily by a written narrative that notes significant achievements during the period of the award. At the Air Force level, one individual or unit is selected for the top award. However, the nominating process provides recognition for many deserving people along the way.

One example of how a program works is the annual Air Force Outstanding Information Management Awards Program. Over a dozen awards are established. One category is for junior enlisted personnel assigned to the base Information Management Division. This means that there's an opportunity for more than one hundred people to be selected as the "best junior enlisted information manager on base," and that a dozen of them will be selected by their major command (Air Combat Command, Air Mobility Command, and so on) as the "best junior enlisted information manager in the command." Command winners are then forwarded to the HQ USAF level, where a "best junior enlisted information manager in the USAF" is selected. Those selected have significant comments for their next performance reports. In most cases, they also receive presentations, such as letters of appreciation, certificates, or plaques.

These programs are supported very strongly by supervisors and commanders at all levels, and publicity about them is circulated periodically.

Air Force Instruction 36-2805, *Special Trophies and Awards,* describes the special trophies and awards programs sponsored by the USAF and by private organizations that seek Air Force participation. This directive notes the criteria, policies, and procedures for applying for the following special trophies and awards programs that are monitored by the Air Force Personnel Center:

Non-Commissioned Officers Association (NCOA) Vanguard Award
Team of the Year Award
USAF First Sergeant of the Year Award
12 Outstanding Airmen of the Year Award
Theodore Von Karman Air Force Association (AFA) Award
David C. Schilling Award (AFA)
Gill Robb Wilson Award (AFA)
Hoyt S. Vandenberg Award (AFA)
Citation of Honor (AFA)
Joan Orr Air Force Spouse of the Year Award
Verne Orr Award
Lance P. Sijan USAF Leadership Award
Government Employees Insurance Company Military Service Awards (3)
Ten Outstanding Young Americans Award (U.S. Jaycees)
Wright Brothers Memorial Trophy (National Aeronautic Association [NAA])
Norman P. Hays Institute of Navigation (ION) Award
Thomas L. Thurlow Award (ION)
P. V. H. Weems Award (ION)
Superior Achievement Award (ION)
Early Achievement Award (ION)
Katharine Wright Memorial Award (NAA)
Air Force Sergeants Association (AFSA) Pitsenbarger Award

The directive also provides extensive lists for two other categories of awards and trophies:

1. A list of special functional area trophies and awards set up by other Air Force directives (for example, Information Management Awards, Maintenance Awards, and Security Police Awards). The names and numbers of these directives, as well as the name of the monitoring activity, are listed for additional information.
2. A list of special trophies and awards set up by Air Force and private organizations that are not governed by a specific Air Force directive, including lists of agencies to which nominations should be sent.

**Unit Level Awards and Recognition Program.** Air Force Instruction 36-2805, *Special Trophies and Awards,* also provides commanders with the authority to establish recognition programs and awards for personnel in their organizations. The programs available depend on the mission of the unit and the creativity of assigned personnel. They include commonly accepted day-to-day initiatives and local competitions based on grade and categories.

*Day-to-Day Initiatives.* Day-to-day initiatives from Air Force supervisors can include personal messages, oral or handwritten, that tell an individual or group that a job was done well, or formal letters or certificates of commendation giving credit to an individual or a group for a specific accomplishment.

Another way to give public recognition is to submit ideas for articles and photographs about the achievement to the editor of the base newspaper. The focal point for the base newspaper is the Public Affairs Office; staff there are accustomed to providing guidance for newsworthy ideas.

*Special Recognition Programs.* Special recognition programs are developed locally in three primary categories:

1. Grade: such as the airman, noncommissioned officer, or senior noncommissioned officer of the month, quarter, and year.
2. Career area: such as crew chief of the month, maintenance person of the month, personnel specialist of the quarter.
3. In support of a special program: such as the Air Force Suggestion Program or the Foreign Object Damage (FOD) program.

The intervals at which each program is offered usually depend on the number of personnel assigned. A maintenance squadron with more than three hundred airmen would probably initiate an airman of the month program; a maintenance squadron with only fourteen senior noncommissioned officers would probably initiate a senior noncommissioned officer of the quarter or year program.

*Methods of Selection.* Methods of selection vary from unit to unit, depending on the nature of the award. Written nominations are required at some locations; most units convene local selection boards. In general, boards are less time-consuming and a better forum for considering a variety of factors. Under this system, each nominee personally appears before a board of five or six noncommissioned officers and a chairperson, usually a senior noncommissioned officer or a commissioned officer. The board usually convenes in a squadron conference room. Nominees are scheduled at fifteen- or twenty-minute intervals.

When nominees report in, their appearance, military bearing, and communications skills are noted. They are asked about subjects such as current events, Air Force mission and organization, Air Force policies and programs, leadership and management, self-improvement efforts, and community involvement. After each one leaves, members of the board assign scores based on the nominee's presentation and responses. (The chairperson usually votes only in case of a tie.) The board recommends the nominee with the highest score to the commander, who notifies the individual of his or her selection. Those selected receive a letter of notification and congratulations. Tangible awards are certificates or plaques, three-day passes, and in some cases special activities (such as incentive rides in high-performance aircraft). These awards are frequently noted in performance reports and can have a favorable influence on promotion and job placement decisions.

Sometimes the thought of meeting a selection board can be a bit nerve-racking, but it is a fair process that gives everyone an equal chance to compete. It helps to steer clear of written nominations, because polished writing styles often result in the selection of deserving but lesser qualified nominees. Meeting a board can also be a very special experience. It gives you an opportunity to interact with senior personnel and to learn more about the Air Force and about yourself. Also, nomination itself can be a source of personal satisfaction. As one airman put it, "I don't really care if I win or not. I'm just glad that my supervisor thought enough of my performance to recommend me for the competition."

***Other Forms of Recognition.*** Other forms of recognition include special service identification badges (such as the Presidential Service Badge, the Vice Presidential Service Badge, the Office of the Secretary of Defense Identification Badge, and the Joint Chiefs of Staff Identification Badge), lapel buttons, and special devices such as ribbon bars, clasps, arrowheads, stars, and clusters.

## SOURCES OF ADDITIONAL INFORMATION

Air Force Instruction 36-2903, *Dress and Personal Appearance of Air Force Personnel,* concerning the display and wear of ribbons, medals, badges, and devices on the Air Force uniform.

Air Force Instruction 36-2805, *Special Trophies and Awards.*

Air Force Instruction 36-2803, *The Air Force Awards and Decorations Program.*

See chapter 9, "Your Uniform and Standards of Appearance," for wear of awards and decorations.

At the unit level, the best points of contact are your supervisor, the unit awards and decorations monitor, and your first sergeant.

At the base level, contact the customer service section of the military personnel flight.

The web site www.afpc.af.mil has information regarding Air Force recognition programs awards, decorations, and special trophies.

# 11

# The Communication Process

*I know you think you understand what you thought I said, but*
*I'm not so sure you understood what I really meant.*

—Anonymous

Almost everybody can identify with the message in the opening quote. At one time or another, we've all experienced the frustration of being misunderstood. Sometimes it happens more frequently in the USAF because the nature of business is unique. There's a different sense of urgency—it's airpower and defense, it's technology and tradition. It's also a system where we must be fairly specific, because we can't afford to be misunderstood if we are to successfully meet the needs of the USAF mission. On a personal level, your ability to effectively communicate with other people in the USAF will be a key factor in achieving the goals you've set for yourself.

## LISTENING

Of all the communication processes, listening is probably the most important, yet it usually gets the least emphasis. Stop for a moment and think about some of the conversations you've had recently. Did the other people fully understand what you were trying to say? Did you fully understand what they were trying to say? Instead of tuning in to their message, were you really thinking of what you were going to say next?

In the USAF you'll be exposed to a wide range of forums that will require you to listen to others and to draw conclusions from the information provided—from large-scale briefings to small shop meetings—and also to formal and informal discussions with personnel of all ranks. Your ability to develop your listening skills, especially in positions of increased responsibility, will have an effect on almost every other aspect of your career.

Here are some general guidelines to becoming a better listener:
- Define the type of listening that's required. Ask yourself, "Why am I listening?" If it's a formal briefing that conveys information or requires you to make a decision afterward, your attention must be much more focused than in a casual conversation.

- If possible, try to become familiar with the subject matter beforehand.
- Tune in. Give your undivided attention. Try to eliminate as many distractions as possible—put away newspapers and books, turn off the radio, refrain from taking telephone calls, and so forth.
- Don't be afraid to say, "I don't understand." If the message is unclear, ask questions or ask the other person to rephrase the statement.
- When speaking or asking for information, use everyday language. Don't try to make a simple concept seem deep, mystical, and complex.
- Don't overcommunicate. Sometimes it's possible to say too much. When that happens, your main points will be smothered in all the extra words. As a result, you'll confuse your listener and probably lose him or her.
- Separate fact from fiction. Rumors grow by leaps and bounds as they travel through the grapevine. The best rule of thumb: "If in doubt, check it out."
- Take notes if necessary, especially to record specific times, dates, and places. Key words and phrases are sufficient.

## SPEAKING

Your effectiveness and self-confidence as a speaker usually improve over time as you become more familiar with the subject matter and your listeners.

**Using the Telephone.** The telephone is the primary means that USAF servicemembers use to communicate with other Air Force and DOD staff agencies. In many ways, using it is quite easy—a matter of common sense, courtesy, and organization. However, you should be familiar with several unique aspects of the DOD telecommunications system.

Your starting point for obtaining general USAF telecommunications information is the installation telephone directory. Each base publishes one. Revisions are made annually or as required when major changes occur. Most directories list each on-base agency by title, functional address symbol, and telephone number. Some directories note each agency's building numbers. Other items frequently included are general user information, emergency numbers, quick reference lists for agencies that are frequently contacted, maps for the installation, and DSN numbers.

Each primary Air Force base also has telephone switchboard operators who have been trained to respond to inquiries with courtesy, accuracy, and speed. They provide directory assistance, call routing service, and support for geographically separated units (such as off-base sites) that are assigned to the base on which the operators work.

When using the telephone in your duty station, you should keep two primary thoughts in mind:

1. The USAF telephone lines are for official government business; lengthy matters of a personal nature should not be discussed.
2. The telephone lines are not secure for discussing classified information. Military telecommunications facilities and networks, including both owned

and leased telephone circuits, are subject to various types of monitoring (wiretapping, electronic eavesdropping, and so forth) by other nations' armed forces and security agencies. Such agencies do this routinely to collect information with potential intelligence value. Since this can pose serious problems for preserving the national security of the United States, our own forces implement security programs to monitor and safeguard the use of our communications systems. These safeguards include the use of technological innovations. For example, in cases where there is a requirement to discuss classified material over the telephone, special instruments equipped with approved encryption devises (frequently referred to as Automatic Secure Voice Communications [AUTOSEVOCOM] instruments) must be used.

Another safeguard is an ongoing communications security (COMSEC) education program that provides all personnel with information on the proper ways to use unprotected telecommunications. This program continually reemphasizes the prohibition of intentional, willful discussion of classified information over unsecured telecommunications equipment. It also advises personnel of the ways that classified or sensitive intelligence information may be accidentally compromised (for example, during idle gossip or in cases where individuals may be unaware of the sensitivity of the information being discussed) in areas such as operations, plans, programs, strengths, weaknesses, numbers, equipment, deployment, capabilities, and intentions. This second point is very important. In the hands of well-trained analysts, virtually any information can be of intelligence value in and of itself or when pieced together with other collected information.

It's also important to learn any local or government security procedures, such as the Air Force Form 440, *Bomb Threat Aid*. These forms facilitate recording threats called in on government phone lines.

### Some General Tips for Using the Phone.
1. Answer promptly and speak clearly and slowly.
2. Always identify yourself when answering. The common practice for answering the telephone is to first state your duty section and then your rank and name; for example, "Base Operations, Airman Smith speaking." When calling someone else, you would usually provide the same information but in reverse order; for example, "This is Airman Smith from Base Operations."
3. If you are unsure of who is calling, tactfully request the caller's identity.
4. If the call is for someone who is not available, offer to take a message. Offer your own assistance, too. A lot of incoming calls are for general nonsensitive information that you may be able to provide.
5. Take time to organize your thoughts before you place a call. If necessary, jot down a few key points or notes on the items you need to cover.

6. Time is valuable, so conversations should be as brief and concise as possible. If you plan a lengthy discussion, ask whether the person you called has time to talk.
7. If a commitment is made over the phone to pursue a further course of action, make a brief handwritten memo for the record.

```
MEMORANDUM
    OF CALL                          Previous editions usable
TO:
     LT.  SUGGS

[X] YOU WERE CALLED BY—     [ ] YOU WERE VISITED BY—
   SERGEANT  PEGGY  SENKO
OF (Organization)
   THE  PUBLIC  AFFAIRS  OFFICE

[X] PLEASE PHONE ▶      [ ] FTS        [ ] AUTOVON
          432 - 5678

[ ] WILL CALL AGAIN          [ ] IS WAITING TO SEE YOU
[ ] RETURNED YOUR CALL       [X] WISHES AN APPOINTMENT
MESSAGE

   WANTS  TO  DO  AN
   ARTICLE  ON  YOUR
   AWARD  FOR  THE  BASE
   NEWSPAPER. " PLEASE
   CALL  TODAY. "
RECEIVED BY                 |DATE      |TIME
     SGT  COBOS             |18 APR    |0900
63-110   NSN 7540-00-634-4018   STANDARD FORM 63 (Rev. 8-81)
   ☆U.S.GPO:1986-0-491-247/20046   Prescribed by GSA
                                 FPMR (41 CFR) 101—11.6
```

**Standard Form 63, Memorandum of Call**

*Commercial Toll Call Procedures.* Official long-distance calls are placed or received through the base operator. They should be made only when time does not permit the use of any other means of communications (official mail or message traffic).

To make outgoing long-distance calls, you must first obtain authorization from your unit's Telephone Control Officer (TCO). You will need to tell the TCO whom you are calling, the number, and the reason for the call. The TCO will record the information on an Air Force Form 1072, "Authorized Long-Distance Toll Calls" (also referred to as a telephone control log), and will provide you with a government billing number to give the operator.

The same procedure applies to incoming collect calls. Since such calls require expenditures of appropriated funds, they must be approved in advance by the unit TCO. These calls must come in through the base switchboard operator so they can be properly recorded and billed.

*The Defense Switched Network (DSN).* When Air Force personnel need to call long-distance from base to base, they don't call on commercial phone lines; they call DSN. DSN is the principal long-haul, voice communications network within the Defense Communications System. Through a system of government-owned and leased automatic-switching facilities, DSN provides direct-dialing service worldwide to handle unclassified telecommunications traffic for mission-essential functions, such as command and control, operations, intelligence, logistics, and administration. A high-tech digital system, DSN can handle computer, video, and voice communication.

The telephone codes for the DSN system consist of seven-digit numbers. Most base telephone directories include a list of those that are most frequently called. The first three numbers identify the base or organization; the last four numbers identify the extension for a specific agency (e.g., the personnel office or the security police). For example, the DSN number for the U.S. Air Force Academy switchboard operation is 259-3111. 259 is the DSN prefix that identifies the base; 3111 is the extension that connects you with the operator.

The DSN system has an automatic preemption capability for high-precedence calls. This means your call can be cut off if another user has a higher priority call to make. The precedence system is based on four levels of urgency.

1. ROUTINE precedence is reserved for all official communications. This category does not have a preemption capability.
2. PRIORITY precedence is reserved for calls that require prompt completion for national defense and security, for the successful conduct of war, or to safeguard life or property. Normally, PRIORITY will be the highest precedence that may be assigned to administrative matters when speed of handling is of paramount importance. This category can preempt ROUTINE precedence calls.
3. IMMEDIATE precedence is reserved for vital communications that have an immediate operational effect on tactical operations, directly concern safety or rescue operations, or affect the intelligence-community operational role. This category can preempt PRIORITY and ROUTINE precedence calls.
4. FLASH precedence is reserved for telephone calls pertaining to command and control of military forces essential to defense and retaliation, critical intelligence essential to national survival, conduct of diplomatic negotiations critical to the arresting or limiting of hostilities, dissemination of critical civil-alert information essential to national survival, continuity of federal government functions, fulfillment of critical U.S. internal security functions essential to national survival, and catastrophic events of national

or international significance. This category can preempt IMMEDIATE, PRIORITY, or ROUTINE precedence calls.

FLASH precedence calls in progress may be preempted by the application of the FLASH OVERRIDE capability. This special capability is available only to the President of the United States; the Secretary of Defense; the Joint Chiefs of Staff; the commanders of unified and specified commands when declaring either Defense Condition One (DEFCON ONE) or Defense Emergency; and the Commander in Chief, North American Aerospace Defense Command (CINCNORAD) when declaring either DEFCON ONE or Air Defense Emergency.

Sometimes the use of telephones is restricted. MINIMIZE is one such program. It is a condition imposed by commanders to control and reduce electrical communications, both message and telephone traffic, during exercises or periods of emergency. MINIMIZE may be imposed Department of Defense-wide, Air Force-wide, command-wide, or for given countries, states, or areas as conditions warrant. MINIMIZE may be imposed on DSN, telephone, data, or teletype systems. One or all systems or services may be minimized as required, by the imposing authority.

**The Phonetic Alphabet.** In the English alphabet a lot of letters sound similar (B, C, D, E, G, P, T, V, Z). The phonetic alphabet was designed to avoid confusion. With it, you can pronounce isolated letters and spell out words that can be difficult to understand, especially over the telephone and on aircraft radio transmissions.

| | | | | | |
|---|---|---|---|---|---|
| A | = | Alpha | N | = | November |
| B | = | Bravo | O | = | Oscar |
| C | = | Charlie | P | = | Papa |
| D | = | Delta | Q | = | Quebec |
| E | = | Echo | R | = | Romeo |
| F | = | Foxtrot | S | = | Sierra |
| G | = | Golf | T | = | Tango |
| H | = | Hotel | U | = | Uniform |
| I | = | India | V | = | Victor |
| J | = | Juliet | W | = | Whiskey |
| K | = | Kilo | X | = | X-ray |
| L | = | Lima | Y | = | Yankee |
| M | = | Mike | Z | = | Zulu |

Imagine a telephone call between two bases.

"The runway at Robins Air Force Base will close at 2100 hours today."

"Was that Robins Air Force Base or Dobbins Air Force Base?"

Both bases did actually exist, so the confusion could have been real. To clarify, the caller uses the phonetic alphabet: "Robins Air Force Base. R as in Romeo." If he had meant Dobbins, he would have said, "Dobbins Air Force Base. D as in Delta."

**Military Times and Dates.** In the Air Force, as in the other military services, time of day is referred to on a twenty-four-hour basis. This helps reduce the confusion that can arise under the A.M./P.M. system, where two hours in each day have the same numerical designation. Here are the official military times and their A.M./P.M. equivalents:

| | | | | | | |
|---|---|---|---|---|---|---|
| 0030 | = | 12:30 | A.M. | 1230 | = | 12:30 P.M. |
| 0100 | = | 1:00 | A.M. | 1300 | = | 1:00 P.M. |
| 0130 | = | 1:30 | A.M. | 1330 | = | 1:30 P.M. |
| 0200 | = | 2:00 | A.M. | 1400 | = | 2:00 P.M. |
| 0230 | = | 2:30 | A.M. | 1430 | = | 2:30 P.M. |
| 0300 | = | 3:00 | A.M. | 1500 | = | 3:00 P.M. |
| 0330 | = | 3:30 | A.M. | 1530 | = | 3:30 P.M. |
| 0400 | = | 4:00 | A.M. | 1600 | = | 4:00 P.M. |
| 0430 | = | 4:30 | A.M. | 1630 | = | 4:30 P.M. |
| 0500 | = | 5:00 | A.M. | 1700 | = | 5:00 P.M. |
| 0530 | = | 5:30 | A.M. | 1730 | = | 5:30 P.M. |
| 0600 | = | 6:00 | A.M. | 1800 | = | 6:00 P.M. |
| 0630 | = | 6:30 | A.M. | 1830 | = | 6:30 P.M. |
| 0700 | = | 7:00 | A.M. | 1900 | = | 7:00 P.M. |
| 0730 | = | 7:30 | A.M. | 1930 | = | 7:30 P.M. |
| 0800 | = | 8:00 | A.M. | 2000 | = | 8:00 P.M. |
| 0830 | = | 8:30 | A.M. | 2030 | = | 8:30 P.M. |
| 0900 | = | 9:00 | A.M. | 2100 | = | 9:00 P.M. |
| 0930 | = | 9:30 | A.M. | 2130 | = | 9:30 P.M. |
| 1000 | = | 10:00 | A.M. | 2200 | = | 10:00 P.M. |
| 1030 | = | 10:30 | A.M. | 2230 | = | 10:30 P.M. |
| 1100 | = | 11:00 | A.M. | 2300 | = | 11:00 P.M. |
| 1130 | = | 11:30 | A.M. | 2330 | = | 11:30 P.M. |
| 1200 | = | noon | | 2400 | = | midnight |

As you can see, military times have four digits; the first two show the hour and the last two show minutes after the hour. For example, 1417 would be 2:17 P.M., 2347 would be 11:47 P.M., and 0007 would be seven minutes after midnight.

Once you're accustomed to it, the military time system becomes very easy to use. And it can be critically important. Imagine you're a pilot running low on fuel.

Another pilot is going to meet you at twelve, "up in the air," for in-flight refueling. What happens if he's thinking midnight and you're waiting at noon?

The use of calendar dates is much simpler. The format is day, month, and year: 25 December 1987. Sometimes this is abbreviated to the first three letters of the month, all capitalized, and the last two digits of the year: 25 DEC 87.

**Military Briefings.** Briefings are conducted to provide information to decision makers at all levels. They can range from informal discussions with your contemporaries in your immediate duty section to formal presentations for senior managers in conference rooms. If you are asked to provide a briefing, your supervisor will usually give you some basic guidance. Then it's a matter of defining the following five aspects:

1. *Format:* Ask if it will be informal or formal. Analyze your audience, the occasion, and the location. Ask if you will be able to read notes or if you will be required to use special visual aids, such as flip charts, powerpoint slides, 35mm slides, or other computerized systems.

2. *Content:* Determine how much information is required to explain the subject. Some audiences may not need as many details as others. In Air Force jargon, a "wall-to-wall" briefing is fully comprehensive, and that's OK. But a "horizon-to-horizon" briefing is too long and too much in depth; it usually puts people to sleep.

3. *Time:* Ask how much time you have for your presentation. It will often be governed by the audience and the location.

4. *Questions:* Anticipate what questions might be asked, and have answers ready. If you don't know, don't guess. It's always better to say, "I don't know the answer to that question, but I'll find out and get back to you."

5. *Practice:* Give your briefing a dry run beforehand. Solicit feedback from your supervisor and your peers. Revise any parts that could be more clearly stated. By doing this, you'll feel much more comfortable when you're presenting the final briefing.

**"Words for the Wise."** In addition to the English language, over the years the U.S. Air Force has developed a vocabulary of its own. It consists of terms for official programs, often abbreviated, and a wide variety of unofficial jargon, phrases, and sayings that are commonly understood by all members.

*Acronyms.* Terms for programs are often abbreviated and spoken as acronyms. In day-to-day life in the USAF, you may hear something like this: "You'll have to go TDY tomorrow on short notice. I'm short of people because Jones is going PCS, Smith is on OJT, and Doe is AWOL." TDY is short for temporary duty, PCS for permanent change of station, OJT for on-the-job training, and AWOL for absent without leave.

When these terms are used in written correspondence, they are usually spelled out in full the first time, followed by the abbreviation in parentheses; after that, the capitalized abbreviation is used alone. When they are used in conversation, a full description is not always given because they are commonly accepted terms. If you're in doubt about a meaning, it's always best to ask until you learn the language.

Some of the most frequently used acronyms include the following:

| | |
|---|---|
| **AAFES** | Army and Air Force Exchange Service |
| **AD** | active duty |
| **ADC** | Area Defense Counsel; Air Defense Command |
| **ADSC** | Active Duty Service Commitment |
| **AEF** | air and space expeditionary force; American Expeditionary Force (World War I) |
| **AFAS** | Air Force Aid Society |
| **AFPC** | Air Force Personnel Center |
| **AFR** | Air Force Reserve |
| **AFROTC** | Air Force Reserve Officer Training Corps |
| **AFS** | Air Force specialty |
| **AFSC** | Air Force specialty code |
| **AFTR** | Air Force Training Ribbon |
| **ALS** | airman leadership school |
| **AWOL** | absent without official leave |
| **BAH** | basic allowance for housing |
| **BAS** | basic allowance for subsistence |
| **BDU** | battle dress uniform |
| **BMT** | basic military training |
| **BOP** | base of preference |
| **CAA** | career assistance advisor |
| **CCAF** | Community College of the Air Force |
| **CDC** | career development course |
| **CI** | compliance inspection |
| **CLEP** | College-Level Examination Program |
| **COLA** | cost-of-living adjustment |
| **CONUS** | continental United States |
| **DFAS** | Defense Finance and Accounting Service |
| **DIEMS** | date initially entered military service |
| **DOD** | Department of Defense |
| **DOR** | date of rank |
| **DOS** | date of separation |
| **EPR** | enlisted performance report |
| **FAP** | Family Advocacy Program |
| **FPCON** | force protection condition |
| **FSA** | family separation allowance |
| **LES** | leave and earnings statement |
| **MFR** | memorandum for record |
| **MilPDS** | Military Personnel Data System |

| | |
|---|---|
| **MKTS** | military knowledge and testing |
| **MPS** | military personnel section |
| **MSO** | military service obligation |
| **MTF** | military treatment facility; medical treatment facility |
| **NCO** | noncommissioned officer |
| **OJT** | on-the-job training |
| **ORI** | operational readiness inspection |
| **OTS** | Officer Training School |
| **PCM** | primary care manager |
| **PCS** | permanent change of station |
| **PFE** | promotion fitness examination |
| **PME** | professional military education |
| **RNLTD** | report not later than date |
| **ROTC** | Reserve Officer Training Corps |
| **SBP** | survivor benefit plan |
| **SGLI** | servicemembers group life insurance |
| **SKT** | specialty knowledge test |
| **SNCO** | senior noncommissioned officer |
| **TA** | tuition assistance |
| **TAFMS** | total active federal military service |
| **TDY** | temporary duty |
| **TEMSD** | Total Enlisted Military Service Date |
| **TIG** | time in grade |
| **TIS** | time in service |
| **TMO** | traffic or transportation management office |
| **TO** | technical order |
| **TOS** | time on station |
| **TSP** | Thrift Savings Plan |
| **USAF** | United States Air Force |
| **USAFA** | United States Air Force Academy |
| **USAFR** | U.S. Air Force Reserves |
| **UTM** | unit training manager |
| **VA** | Veterans Affairs |
| **WAPS** | Weighted Airman Promotion System |

For a more extensive list of Air Force acronyms, see appendix E.

**Some Common Phrases.** The other category of unofficial jargon—phrases and sayings that have common understanding—is much more extensive. Most of them have been around for quite a while and their origins are not always known. They're usually used with a touch of humor and often to communicate a moral or emphasize a point.

*Above my pay grade:* Up the chain of command, usually in the context of decision making. The captain said, "The decision was made above my pay grade."

*Action officer:* A servicemember who has the primary responsibility for a particular job or project. Does not have to be a commissioned officer. "Sergeant Wilson was the action officer for the foreign object damage program."

*Additional duty:* A job or responsibility given to an Air Force member in addition to his or her primary job; for example, budget/resource monitor, supply/equipment custodian, security manager, safety monitor, or advisory council member.

*Aircraft identification codes:* Different types of aircraft are distinguished and referred to through the use of alphabetical prefixes. For example, B stands for bomber (B-1, B-2, B-52); C stands for cargo (C-5, C-130, C-141, C-17); F stands for fighter (F-4, F-15, F-16); and T stands for trainer (T-38, T-43). In some cases, two letters are used to further distinguish the role of an aircraft. For example, the R in SR-71 and TR-1 stands for reconnaissance, and S and T stand for strategic and tactical, respectively.

*Appropriated funds:* The funds that Congress authorizes and sets aside for Department of Defense expenses.

*Barracks lawyer:* Often used in reference to someone who provides opinions and advice that he is not fully qualified to give. In the majority of cases, he communicates inaccurate information. The first sergeant said, "You were driving a car under the influence of alcohol. I want you to get advice from the base legal office. This is a serious matter; don't seek advice from a barracks lawyer."

*Below-the-zone material:* Someone whose performance has been outstanding and is worthy of rapid promotion before his or her contemporaries.

*Big picture:* How individual actions and programs work, how they affect each other, and what they mean collectively. The young airman said, "Chief Master Sergeant Smith has good judgment and a lot of experience. He really understands the big picture."

*Bite the bullet:* Similar in meaning to "grin and bear it." Often used when telling someone to take responsibility for an action, even if it's unfavorable or controversial.

*Bottom line:* A summary of a complex situation, usually in a sentence or two. It can be a statement of fact or a recommendation on how to proceed.

*Brass:* A high-ranking commissioned officer. The sergeant said, "The brass will be visiting our duty section this afternoon."

*Brown shoe:* Used in reference to military members who have been in the service for many years or to those who take a very firm position on the way standards will be met and duties will be carried out.

*Busted:* To be reduced in rank as a result of nonjudicial punishment (an Article 15) or a court-martial. Airman First Class Doe was busted to airman because he went absent without leave.

*By the book:* To do an action as outlined in official guidance, such as an Air Force Instruction. The sergeant said, "We'll do it by the book."

*Check-six:* Term usually used by fighter pilots to mean "check your tail" or "look in back of you." To other personnel, it means make sure all your facts are correct.

*Chief:* Short title for chief master sergeant, an E-9, the highest enlisted grade.

*CINC:* Abbreviation for commander in chief; pronounced as "sink." Refers to the President of the United States. Prior to the year 2002, the title was also used for commanders of major joint, combined, and theater commands.

*Classified:* Material that has a security classification of confidential, secret, or top secret. The sergeant said, "We can't discuss this information here; it's classified."

*Colonel:* There's always questions about why members of the armed forces pronounce this rank as "ker-nel," instead of the way it looks, "col-on-el." The word colonel derives from the same Italian word that gives us the word for "column." A colonel was the commander of a column of soldiers. Around four hundred years ago, the English followed the Spanish practice and spelled the word "coronel," and they pronounced it the way it looks. After a period of time, the English made the decision to change the spelling of coronel to colonel so that it would more properly reflect the word's Italian origin.

*Comm squadron:* Commonly accepted term to denote a communications squadron, the unit on base that is responsible for all communications, including telephone, message centers, radar, and air traffic control.

*Delta Sierra:* Derived from the phonetic alphabet. Means a bad action or deep trouble.

*Dependent:* By federal law, military dependents are defined as spouses, unmarried children under twenty-one years of age, and children of any age unable to support themselves because of physical or mental handicaps. In some cases, the definition extends to parents dependent on military members for their support, to stepchildren, to adopted children, and so forth. Such status entitles them to be eligible for military benefits, including medical care, commissary privileges, and access to many facilities. Although it is a commonly used term, it is sometimes upsetting to some who are categorized as such.

*Distance yourself:* Usually means to separate yourself from an unfavorable action or person. The first sergeant said, "Distance yourself from Airman Jones. He's being discharged for using drugs."

*Down the tubes:* To fail an inspection and get less than a satisfactory rating. "Sergeant Jones's shop went down the tubes; they got an unsatisfactory rating on the inspection."

*Drawdown:* General term used when discussing the reduction of armed forces units or personnel.

*Dream sheet:* An Air Force form used by all airmen to list the assignments (bases and geographical locations) they would like to be selected for.

*Driver/Jock:* Slang for pilot. "Captain DeMars is an F-16 driver" or "Captain Berres is an F-22 jock."

*Electric jet:* Slang for the F-16 tactical fighter jet, referred to as such because of its sophisticated avionics (aviation electronics) systems.

*Envelope:* Term used by aviators when discussing the testing of new aircraft for determining maximum performance. Pilots talk about "pushing the envelope." They're talking about a two-dimensional concept; the bottom is zero altitude (the ground), the top is maximum altitude, the left is zero speed, and the right is maximum speed. In most cases, pilots try to push the upper right-hand corner of the envelope (altitude and speed). According to the *Collected Journals* of Adm. Rick Hunter, "What everybody tries not to dwell on is that that's where the postage gets canceled, too."

*Esprit de corps:* Pronounced "espree de core." A spirit of devotion and enthusiasm among members of a group for one another, their group, and its purposes.

*Face time:* When an Air Force member tries to make personal contact with a supervisor or commander to become recognized for outstanding performance. Many people believe that in building a professional reputation, this recognition is just as important as doing an outstanding job. It helps supervisors link a success (what) with a face (who was personally responsible for the success).

*Fall on your sword:* Originates from Roman generals who performed badly on the battlefield and threw themselves on their own swords. In modern times, it is identified with servicemembers who, to their own detriment, insist on carrying on with an inappropriate action. The commander said, "I don't think that's the best option; carry on if you like, but don't fall on your sword."

*Fast burner:* Similar to *below-the-zone material.* People who are well respected, highly capable, and successful. As a result, they are usually selected for rapid promotion and positions of increased responsibility.

*First shirt or First skirt:* Slang for first sergeant (male or female).

*Fiscal year:* A twelve-month period for which an organization plans to use its funds. For federal agencies, the fiscal year starts on October 1st and ends on September 30th.

*FOD:* Acronym for foreign object damage. Used primarily by aircraft maintenance personnel and aircrews, this term refers to items (buttons, hats, loose tools, and so on) that can damage jet engines and other moving parts.

*Full bird:* Slang for a colonel, an O-6. Rank insignia: eagles.

*Gig-line:* When a shirt or blouse is worn tucked into trousers with a front fly opening, the bottom front edge of the shirt, the outside edge of the belt buckle (when required), and the edge of the fly will align. This alignment is called a *gig-line.* The gig-line is to be straight and neat. The sergeant said, "Your uniform looks a bit sloppy; straighten your gig-line!"

*GI party:* A mandatory formation to clean up a duty section or a dormitory. It usually involves three or more people and is scheduled by a supervisor, the first sergeant, or the commander.

*Gofer:* Sounds like "gopher." Used to note someone who perpetually runs errands or coordinates matters—one who will "gofer this, gofer that."

*Gung-ho:* This term has two meanings. It can be used to denote a person who is unswervingly dedicated and loyal or someone who is foolishly enthusiastic.

*Hit the ground running:* Refers to talented individuals who are immediately productive; used with respect. The supervisor said, "I'm really pleased with Sergeant Smith's performance. She hit the ground running as soon as she signed in for duty."

*Homesteading:* When a servicemember tries to stay at one duty location for an extended period of time.

*Hot:* Very important. The commander said, "This is a hot project; everything else can wait."

*Integrity:* An important part of building a professional reputation. In the USAF, it denotes a servicemember's strong commitment to honest and sincere support of the mission and all personnel: superiors, peers, and subordinates.

*Last four:* Last four numbers of your Social Security number. Ensures accurate identification of military members. Most frequently used in the personnel office and the hospital/dental facilities.

*Lifer:* Primarily used by first-term airmen during the 1960s and early 1970s, before the elimination of the draft and the introduction of the all-volunteer force. It described career airmen who reenlisted after their initial four-year term. A long term of service was perceived as a lifetime commitment; therefore, someone who made that commitment was referred to as a lifer.

*Line number:* A number given to those who have been selected for promotion. It determines the date a promotion will be effective; the lowest numbers are promoted first.

*Long-winded:* Someone who speaks at length; tediously long.

*Loop (in or out of):* To be aware of. "Sergeant Smith was in the loop concerning aircraft takeoff times during the alert."

*Loyalty:* Faithfulness to those ideals and people that a servicemember is under obligation to defend, support, or be true to. In the USAF, it usually refers to commitment to the mission or to personnel in the chain of command (such as your supervisor or your commander). Not to be confused with blind obedience. The concept of loyalty recognizes that all personnel have a responsibility to respectfully point out errors in judgment or potential problems that may be detrimental to the mission.

*Mess hall:* The dining facility for enlisted personnel; also referred to as the chow hall.

*Mid-shift:* Short for midnight shift. The third shift of a normal day, usually from 2330 to 0730.

*Military brat:* Son or daughter of a military member (although not necessarily a "brat").

*Motor pool:* The office on base that controls and services all the installation's vehicles (cars, trucks, vans, and buses). Sometimes it supplies drivers; sometimes vehicles can be checked out and driven by other personnel who possess a government vehicle driver's license. Sergeant Skopp said, "Call the motor pool for a truck so we can move this mobility equipment."

*Mustang:* Slang term for a commissioned officer who has had prior enlisted service.

*Nonappropriated funds:* Funds generated by Department of Defense military and civilian personnel and their dependents and used to augment funds appropriated by Congress to provide a comprehensive, morale-building welfare, religious, educational, and recreational program, designed to improve the well-being of military and civilian personnel and their dependents.

*OPR:* Acronym for Office of Primary Responsibility. "Security Police is the OPR for issuing identification cards."

*Ops Tempo/Optempo:* Shortened for operations tempo. Term frequently used in the 1990s to note the high pace of global operational tasking with very strained and limited resources (e.g., funding, personnel, and equipment). Since 1986, deployment requirements have increased by more than 400 percent. Missions range from enforcing the no-fly zone over Iraq to peacekeeping and humanitarian operations around the world. An increase in the number of deployments causes unanticipated, long-term burdens on units, equipment, and families.

*Press on:* To continue with a job or program. The commander, proud of the squadron's progress in the aircraft maintenance program, said, "You're doing your job well. Press on."

*Protocol dictates:* Actions accepted as proper and correct in official dealings, such as ceremonies and courtesies. The first sergeant said, "Protocol dictates that the guest of honor will have the seat at the head of the table."

*Punching out:* To eject from an aircraft during flight.

*Rainbow:* Term used to describe new airmen at basic training who are still wearing multicolored civilian clothing instead of the green fatigue uniform.

*RHIP:* Acronym for rank has its privileges.

*Short:* Used to describe the amount of time before a servicemember departs for another unit on a permanent change of station. Airman Jones said, "I'm leaving for my next base in three days. I'm short."

*Sierra Hotel:* Derived from phonetic alphabet. Used primarily by aircrew members to describe an exceptionally good or commendable action.

*Suspense:* A deadline/date for completing an official action.

*Swing shift:* The second work shift of a normal duty day, usually from 1530 to 2330.

*System:* As in "the system." Used in relation to specific programs, such as the promotion system, the assignment system, and so forth. Sometimes used as an overgeneralization during periods of frustration. The sergeant said, "I got passed over for promotion for the ninth time. It's the system, you know. It just isn't fair."

*Ticket:* Slang for a performance report. "Did your supervisor write your ticket yet?"

*Top three:* The top three enlisted ranks or grades in the USAF: master sergeant, senior master sergeant, and chief master sergeant (E-7, E-8, and E-9 respectively).

*TWX:* Sounds like "Twix." Short term for a message transmitted like a telegraph message. Transit time depends on the priority assigned. Some can be transmitted and received within minutes. The majority are processed as routine and usually received within twenty-four hours.

*War stories:* Recollections of past events during a person's military career. Most have a humorous twist or convey a moral relevant to a current situation. You can tell that one is coming when someone says, "I remember when . . . "

*Wiring diagram:* An organizational chart showing clear vertical and horizontal lines of authority. Often used to show who reports to whom, by function or by person (as in a chain of command chart).

*Zulu Time:* Greenwich Mean Time, the standard of time used throughout the world. Used by USAF members when they are in different time zones to assure that there are no misunderstandings as to which time is being referenced. Zulu is the phonetic alphabet designation for Z. When Zulu is referred to orally, the whole word is used. For example, if someone in Washington, D.C., was planning a mission with a USAF base in England, he or she might say, "The President's aircraft will arrive at 1800 Zulu." In written communications, Zulu time is designated with a Z attached to the end, as in 1800Z.

## WRITING

> *Want to see a general cry? Stop by when I'm reading some of your writing.*
>
> —A major general introducing the Executive Writing Course

Over the past decade, the USAF has put increasing emphasis on the quality of written communications, for two reasons: Clear and concise information is needed to ensure that mission requirements are understood and met; it also saves time, money, and materials.

Written communications are presented in a wide range of standardized formats, prescribed by intended purpose. Here are some of the most frequently used formats.

- The formal letter (the most common) is usually prepared on official Air Force letterhead. It's used to convey policy, guidance, or information.
- A memorandum for record (also referred to as a memo for record) is prepared to document an action, sequence of events, or reasons why a certain decision was made. It is then filed for later reference.

- A staff summary sheet is prepared on AF Form 1768 or in an Electronic Staff Summary Sheet (ESSS). It provides senior personnel with a summary of key issues for projects, including potential problems, and offers recommendations on an appropriate course of action. Background information is usually included or attached.
- Messages are the Air Force's equivalent of a telegraph. They're typed on a DD Form 173 and then sent through the Defense Message System to other Air Force bases or to Department of Defense activities.
- Directives, such as instructions, supplements, and operating instructions, provide guidance and policy to Air Force units.
- Performance reports and recommendations for awards and decorations are written on special forms. The way they're written (content, directness, and grammar) can often have a direct effect on a servicemember's career.

Air Force correspondence is expected to be as follows:

1. Factual and accurate, focused directly on an issue (what is right, not who is right).
2. Concise, direct, and grammatically correct. Lots of adjectives and fifty-cent words are discouraged.
3. Timely. A matter that is important should be acted on as soon as possible.

Writing well comes with experience and practice. Start by becoming familiar with the different formats available. Decide on your purpose and choose the appropriate format. Organize an outline that is clear and logical. Support your main points with all the relevant facts. Once you've completed your first draft, take a critical look at it and rewrite where necessary. Ask for feedback from your peers and your supervisor. Make adjustments. Have it typed, proofread it, and have typographical errors corrected. Before you send it out, make sure it has been properly coordinated through your chain of command. This is especially true where the policy expressed is new or introduces any dramatic changes.

## SOURCES OF INFORMATION

There are two ways to learn what's happening throughout the Air Force community: official channels and unofficial channels.

**Official Channels.** Information distributed through official channels originates in different forms at different levels of command. For example, at your base and unit level you will receive information through your chain of command and through personal and group contacts, such as meetings and commander's calls. Other official channels are locally produced printed media, such as policy and information letters, base newspapers, and daily or weekly information bulletins.

Each base also has a Publications Library (also referred to as a Master Reference Library), usually maintained by the Base Information Management Division. This is where copies of directives that may not be available in your immediate duty section are kept. Air Force directives, however, are now all on electronic media.

## STAFF SUMMARY SHEET

| | TO | ACTION | SIGNATURE ( *Surname* ), GRADE AND DATE | | TO | ACTION | SIGNATURE ( *Surname* ), GRADE AND DATE |
|---|---|---|---|---|---|---|---|
| 1 | DOEA | Coord | | 6 | | | *Sign your surname, rank or grade, and date on the bottom line if you* |
| 2 | DOE | Coord | | 7 | | | *are the addressee; sign on the top line if you aren't the addressee.* |
| 3 | DO | Sign | | 8 | | | *If more than 10 coordinators, use another form and fill in all info* |
| 4 | | | | 9 | | | *through Subject line.* |
| 5 | | | | 10 | | | |

| SURNAME OF ACTION OFFICER AND GRADE | SYMBOL | PHONE | TYPIST'S INITIALS | SUSPENSE DATE |
|---|---|---|---|---|
| Harris, CMSgt | OMP | 652-4075 | clp | 14 Jun 11 |

| SUBJECT | DATE |
|---|---|
| Preparation of the Staff Summary Sheet (SSS) | 2 Jun 11 |

SUMMARY

1. The SSS introduces, summarizes, coordinates, or obtains approval or signature on a staff package. It should be a concise (preferably 1 page) summary of the package. It states the purpose, pertinent background information, rationale, and discussion necessary to justify the action desired.

2. The SSS is attached to the front of the correspondence package. If an additional page is necessary, prepare it on plain bond paper. Use the same margins you see here. Summarize complicated or lengthy correspondence or documents attached, or any tabs that are not self-explanatory. If they're self-explanatory, say so. Attach a copy (or extract of appropriate portion) of any document you reference.

3. List attachments to the SSS as tabs. List the document for action as Tab 1. List incoming memo, directive, or other paper—if any—that prompted you to prepare the SSS as Tab 2. (If you have more than one document for action, list and tab them with as many numbers as you need and then list the material you're responding to as the next number: Tabs 1, 2, and 3 for signature, Tab 4 incoming document.) List supplemental documents as additional tabs, followed by the record or coordination copy, and information copies. If nonconcurrence is involved, list it and the letter of rebuttal as the last tab.

4. VIEWS OF OTHERS. Explain concerns of others external to the staff (i.e., OSD, Army, Navy, State, etc.). For example: "OSD may disapprove of this approach."

5. OPTIONS. If there are significant alternative solutions, explain the options. For example: "Buying off-the-shelf hardware will reduce costs 25%, but will meet only 80% of our requirements."

6. RECOMMENDATION. Use this caption when the SSS is routed for action. State the recommendation, including action necessary to implement it, in such a way that the official need only sign an attachment, or coordinate, approve, or disapprove the recommended action. Do not recommend alternatives or use this caption when the SSS is being submitted for information only.

*George Kailiwai*

GEORGE KAILIWAI III, Lt Col, USAF
Commander, AFOMS

2 Tabs
1. Proposed Memo
2. HQ AETC/CC Memo, 1 Jun 99 w/Atch

**AF FORM 1768, SEP 84 *(EF-V4)***      *(FORM FLO2)*           PREVIOUS EDITION WILL BE USED.

Above the base and unit level, the USAF sends out a variety of information to keep everyone up-to-date on current developments that affect the overall mission and the quality-of-life programs. Audiovisual Services produces films on special subjects, such as safety and disaster preparedness, and others on a recurring basis, such as the *Air Force Now* monthly series, which covers current events and programs. Air Force Recurring Periodicals (AFRPs) are also printed and distributed to inform personnel about new policies and ongoing programs. Here are some examples:

AFRP 90-1, *The Inspector General (TIG) Brief*
AFRP 35-1, *Airman* magazine
AFRP 36-1, *Afterburner* (USAF News for Retired Personnel)
AFRP 35-3, *Air Force Policy Letter Digest*

**Obtaining Air Force Publications and Forms.** As of October 1, 1999, all eighty-eight of the Air Force's publishing distribution offices (PDOs) were closed. The PDO was the central warehouse on most bases where customers could retrieve or order forms, publications, technical orders, joint service publications, and more.

In its place is a new electronic system, which is an online ordering system run by an Air Force Publications Distribution Center. For stateside bases, that center will be in Baltimore; overseas, Pacific Air Forces and U.S. Air Forces in Europe will select locations for centers in their respective regions.

People who occasionally use certain forms or publications can still obtain them from their local area network or from the Air Force's web page at http://www.e-publishing.af.mil. These forms can be printed on office printers and/or duplicated on copier machines.

**Unofficial Channels.** Unofficial channels of information are provided by private associations that deal in matters of interest to the armed forces. Many of their contributors are former service personnel. To receive their information, you can either join the organization for an annual fee or look for copies in the base library. Included here are some of the primary organizations that will keep you aware of the major issues affecting the USAF.

1. The *Air Force Association* (AFA) is a professional society committed to peace and freedom through adequate aerospace power. It represents all elements of the Air Force family: military and civilian, officer and enlisted, active and reserve, cadet and veteran, dependent and retiree, civil service and aerospace worker. The AFA publishes *Air Force Magazine* each month. Articles cover a wide range of topics, from historical discussions of airpower to personnel issues and special annual reviews of the military capabilities of U.S. and Russian air forces. A variety of other services and programs are also provided. For additional information, contact the Air Force Association, 1501 Lee Highway, Arlington, VA 22209-1198.

2. The *Air Force Times* is printed each week in a newspaper format. It's a very good source of current information about the Air Force in general and policy changes that affect members and their families. Of special note are the printed lists of those promoted to grades E-5 (staff sergeant) and above and the lists of personnel being reassigned from one base to another. For additional information, contact the *Air Force Times,* Springfield, VA 22159-0250.

3. The *Air Force Sergeants Association* (AFSA) provides a wide range of information and services for its members (noncommissioned officers, grades E-4 through E-9, active duty, retired, or reserve). Of special note is its commitment to represent members' interests to elected government representatives and to spread the word about new programs and changes in benefits. Most bases have a local chapter organized and operated by those in the surrounding area (active duty, retired, and reserve). For additional information, contact Air Force Sergeants Association, Box 31050, Washington, DC 20031.

4. *Aviation Week and Space Technology* is a periodical covering technical developments in the aviation industry and their applications to the military establishment. Often referred to as *"Aviation Leak"* by the intelligence community, it provides insight into current research and development projects—sometimes more insight than military planners and strategists would like. For additional information, contact *Aviation Week and Space Technology,* P.O. Box 1505, Neptune, NJ 07754-1505.

## USE OF COMPUTER SYSTEMS

The USAF has significantly increased the number of personal computer systems for the purpose of communicating and conducting official Air Force business. Routine applications (such as word processing, graphics, and spreadsheets) are commonly used in every major office, and there are specialized programs for operations such as finance, personnel, supply, and aircraft maintenance.

The extent of computer training that is provided depends on the complexity of the applications identified for use and the program or programs they support. Some staff are provided with formal technical training, whereas others are provided with orientations at their base of assignment. For additional information refer to chapter 12.

## SOURCES OF ADDITIONAL INFORMATION

Air Force Handbook 33-337, *The Tongue and Quill*, is one of the best references available for Air Force personnel. The content is easy to follow and is balanced with illustrations and practical advice. It can be found electronically at *http://www.e-publishing.af.mil.*

Air Force Manual 37-126, *Preparing Official Communications.*

Air Force Pamphlet 36-2241, *Professional Development Guide,* chapter 14, "Communicating in Today's Air Force." This publication is used for those studying for promotion. The content is brief but provides valuable information about the importance of effectively communicating in the USAF.

Consult your base library for Air Force recurring periodicals and USAF-oriented magazines, newspapers, and books.

# 12

# Air Force
# Computer Systems
# and Information Technology

The Air Force has entered the information superhighway in a big way with thousands of sites currently online and more being published every day. Computer literacy is increasingly important for airmen and NCOs because it enables them to receive and transmit text and supporting communications across vast electronic networks. No longer do you have to thumb through old copies of the *Air Force Times* or look for paper copies of directives to find information that is important to your career. Now, you can pass along or retrieve almost all of the information you need online, through the web via a modem and personal computer. It is also important to understand that computer systems are not always a secure means of transmitting official information, so it's necessary to be aware of and use the safeguarding procedures that have been prescribed.

Air Force members use personal computer systems for three primary reasons:
1. To use electronic mail (e-mail) to communicate and exchange messages.
2. To use computer software in the performance of their duties.
3. To access and use information that is available through the World Wide Web.

## ELECTRONIC MAIL (E-MAIL)
E-mail is the electronic transmission of messages and documents across one or more networks, computer to computer. It is generally a stand-alone system or a separate module within a software package that uses any one or more of the following to transmit data: local area networks (LANs), wide area networks (WANs), telephone connections, and/or the Internet. E-mail messages are normally sent over

unsecured telephone lines, so you must be aware of the limitations and associated risks that these systems present during the conduct of normal operations within the Air Force. You must also understand that your use of e-mail gives your implied consent to monitoring, regardless of the purpose for which you're using it (this includes incidental and personal uses, whether they are authorized or unauthorized).

Air Force Instruction 33-119, *Electronic Mail (E-Mail) Management and Use,* consolidates in a single reference source many information management, security, and communications policies. It also provides e-mail users many tips to facilitate, optimize, and safeguard information that is processed through this medium. It specifies that:

- E-mail is to be used for official purposes that further the Air Force mission.
- E-mail communications should be respectful and professional.
- E-mail generated through USAF systems is to be used for official and authorized purposes only. You should not share use of your individual mailboxes or passwords or reveal office account passwords to anyone outside of your office or organization.
- Some e-mail messages may be federal records and must be managed in accordance with Air Force Manual (AFMAN) 37-139, *Records Disposition Schedule,* and/or AFMAN 37-123, *Management of Records.*
- E-mail users consent to the monitoring of their messages—whether they are official or personal.

## Personal Use of E-Mail

Personal use of the Air Force e-mail system is permitted under the following conditions:

- A supervisor authorizes it.
- It does not interfere with performance of official duties.
- Use is of reasonable duration and frequency.
- Use serves a legitimate Air Force interest, such as notifying family of travel changes while on temporary duty (TDY), communications from place of duty required during duty hours, or morale purposes if stationed away from home for an extended period.
- The message does not reflect badly on the Air Force, such as uses involving pornography, chain letters, advertising, soliciting, or selling.
- Use does not overburden the communication system and does not create significant additional costs to the Air Force.

## Protocols for Using E-Mail

Air Force members may use e-mail to transmit both formal and informal correspondence. Individually, they bear the sole responsibility for the material that they access and send. As with other forms of communication, there are guidelines and rules that you must follow.

## Official E-Mail

Official e-mail originates from an organization's mailbox (office account) and is transmitted to another organization's mailbox. In some instances, the release of certain e-mail must be authorized by a designated releasing official within your chain of command. When this is necessary, you should prepare the correspondence for release; send it to the appropriate staff members for coordination; and then forward it to the release authority electronically or in hard copy. The release authority can, in turn, send the electronic correspondence via e-mail or return the hard copy to the action officer for release.

E-mail systems may be used to transmit official taskings. When doing so, the senders are responsible for making sure that taskings are received by the intended receiver(s). Some e-mail systems have features that allow users to request acknowledgments or receipts.

You must not enter or transmit classified information via e-mail systems unless you transmit it over an approved secure network from a secure workstation to a secure workstation. You may transmit unclassified information; however, do not transmit information that requires special handling (e.g., Privacy Act, for official use only, exclusive for, personal for, limited distribution, and so forth) on e-mail systems that are not certified for that purpose. For information affected by the Privacy Act, refer to AFI 33-332, *Air Force Privacy Act Program.*

## THE INTERNET AND THE INTRANET

The Internet is the worldwide free enterprise of computers that links distant information sites together. The Air Force goal is to use the Internet to provide Air Force members with access to the maximum amount of information—at acceptable risk and security levels—in order for them to meet mission requirements and conduct official Air Force business.

The Department of Defense originally developed the Internet as a means of transmitting research data. It has only been in the last ten years that the military has started to make use of the "net" to communicate routine electronic mail, as well as to post great quantities of current information. The Internet is, for the most part, open for public use. It is frequently referred to as the *World Wide Web* and is often shortened to www or "the web."

Intranets are different from the Internet. Intranets are proprietary internal versions of the Internet within a large organization. They generally limit the users that can access the information. This greatly enhances document access and information flow between workers.

## Air Force Internet Use

The Internet offers many opportunities to expand the amount of information available to the Air Force. AFI 33-129, *Transmission of Information Via the Internet,* spells out the legal and illegal use of federal and Air Force telephones, facsimile machines, electronic mail, and the Internet.

Airmen and civilian employees are authorized to use the Internet and browse the web to further professional and military knowledge. While there are clear benefits to accessing information from these systems, there are also hazards. As such, users must understand and meet the following conditions, which are largely the same as those for the use of e-mail.

- Access is restricted to authorized personnel only.
- Use does not interfere with the performance of official duties.
- Use is of reasonable duration and frequency.
- Use serves a legitimate Air Force or public interest, such as research, enhancement of professional skills, and TDY support.
- There is no significant additional cost, overburdening of the system, or violation of federal, state, or local laws.
- The material does not reflect badly on the Air Force.
- It is not used for personal financial gain.
- It may not be used for transmitting or receiving offensive material, such as hate literature, sexually harassing materials, or pornography.

Similar to the use of the telephone, brief personal communications are authorized as long as the above criteria are met. Individual commanders or supervisors can provide more detailed guidance.

## PROTECTING AIR FORCE INTERNET SYSTEMS

### Viruses
To protect against downloading viruses from the Internet and introducing potential risk to Air Force networks, users should check all files downloaded off the Internet for viruses. This applies to sound files, video files, and files attached to e-mail messages. If possible, files should first be downloaded to a floppy disk and checked for viruses before placing them on the computer's hard drive. Additionally, users should obtain certification and approval for any software loaded on an Air Force automated information system. The use of shareware, freeware, and public-domain software without testing violates Air Force Internet policy and AFI 33-114, *Software Management,* and can put Air Force networks at risk.

### Information Vulnerability and Operations Security (OPSEC)
The World Wide Web has had a profound effect on how we find and distribute information. It is both an asset and a liability to the Air Force. It serves as an asset by providing us online access to a vast library of information, and it connects users to a valuable tool for research, learning, and the exchange of information. It can also be a liability because it offers opportunities for data mining and other techniques that result in the aggregation of information. This increases the potential for the inadvertent disclosure of sensitive or critical information.

It is Air Force policy to provide the public and Congress maximum information about Air Force operations and activities. At the same time, OPSEC concerns must be considered when decisions are made about which types of Air Force information to post (or not post) on the public access web. Information must be protected through risk assessment and risk management. Everyone must take an active role in their processes of reviewing and releasing information. For additional information, consult AFI 33-129, *Transmission of Information via the Internet,* for more detailed guidance and policy related to public web site procedures.

## USING THE WORLD WIDE WEB

Recent DOD policy encourages use of the World Wide Web, since it is a powerful communications tool. At the same time, the policy calls for tighter security controls and a stronger focus on matching web sites to the organization's mission.

The new web policy clarifies and extends the rules for posting information on public DOD web sites. In the past, restrictions on web publication applied to information that was either classified, sensitive in nature, or not cleared for public release. The new policy broadens these restrictions to include information of questionable public value that creates a potential security risk if made easily available to a worldwide audience. Just like attempted break-ins at home call for special security, increased threats to mission-critical information and information networks warrant a defensive posture that improves information protection throughout both the Air Force and the DOD.

## ON-LINE INFORMATION ABOUT THE AIR FORCE

### Air Force Link: The Official Air Force Web Site

The Air Force's official web site is Air Force Link. People visit the site each week to read news, download photographs, hear Air Force Radio news, and access speeches and other publications. The site can be found on the Internet by pointing your browser to http://www.af.mil. After you log in, you will be able to go into the following primary links:
- Home
- News
- TV
- Social Media
- Photos
- Art
- Information
- Public Web Sites

### Air Force-Related Sites

*Air Force Association (AFA).* AFA is a private nonprofit organization. Its web site provides links to *Air Force Magazine* and other AFA publications. Its web site address is *www.afa.org.*

*Air Force Sergeants Association (AFSA).* AFSA is a federally chartered nonprofit organization that represents the professional and personal interests of more than 150,000 active-duty and retired enlisted members of the U.S. Air Force, Air National Guard, and Air Force Reserve. Its web site address is *www.afsahq.org.*

**The Air Force Times.** The *Air Force Times* is a very popular weekly newspaper for airmen of all ranks. Its web site address is *www.airforcetimes.com.*

**The Department of Veterans Affairs.** When you plan to leave the service, this is one of the key sites you will want to study. Its web site address is *www.va.gov.*

**The Federal Web Locator.** Federal Web Locator is a one-stop shopping point for federal government information on the World Wide Web. It lists all offices of the legislative, judicial, and executive branches. It also lists a large range of other federal agencies, boards, committees, and commissions. Its web site address is *www.infoctr.edu.fwl.*

*Military City.* Military City is a network of sites operated by the Army Times Publishing Company. It offers a wide range of information about the military community for servicemembers in the Army, Navy, Marine Corps, and Air Force and their families. It contains news and special reports, military pay guides, installation guides, military links, vacation tips, benefits, message boards, and information about weapons and warfare. Its web site address is *www.militarycity.com.*

*Red Cross.* This is always a useful site to keep in your favorites. Its web site address is *www.redcross.org.*

*TRICARE.* This is the military medical system. Its web site address is *www.tricare.osd.mil.*

*United Service Organization (USO).* The USO has been assisting servicemembers since World War I. It continues to do so today. Its web site address is *www.uso.org.*

## SOURCES OF ADDITIONAL INFORMATION

Air Force Instruction 33-119, *Electronic Mail (E-Mail) Management and Use.*
Air Force Instruction 33-129, *Transmission of Information via the Internet.*

# 13

# The Inspector General and the Inspection System

Two little letters—IG—solicit undivided attention from almost every Air Force member, from young airmen to seasoned noncommissioned officers to four-star generals.

IG stands for Inspector General and is commonly used to refer to those responsible for implementing the USAF complaints program and inspection system. Their purpose and role are frequently misunderstood, but with some insight into their reason for being and the ways they accomplish their mission, a deeper appreciation for the work they do may be gained.

## INSPECTOR GENERAL COMPLAINTS PROGRAM

"At the end of every complaint is a person who needs help."

—Lt. Col. James Berres,
325th FW Inspector General

The Air Force IG Complaints Program was established to address the concerns of Air Force active duty, reserve, and Guard members, civilian employees, family members, and retirees, as well as the interests of the Air Force. The first responsibility of the IG is to operate a credible complaints program that investigates personal complaints; Fraud, Waste, and Abuse (FWA) allegations; congressional inquiries; and issues involving the Air Force mission.

Personal complaints and FWA disclosures to the IG help commanders correct problems that affect the productivity, mission accomplishment, and morale of assigned personnel, which are areas of high concern to Air Force leaders at all levels.

Full-time installation IGs were established to remove any perceived conflict of interest, lack of independence, or apprehension by Air Force personnel. The installation IG reports directly to the installation commander. The IG is the "eyes, ears, and conscience" of the commander. He or she keeps the commander informed of potential areas of concern as reflected by trends and acts as the fact-finder and honest broker in the resolution of complaints. A good IG will maintain objectivity while protecting both the best interest of the Air Force *and* of the individual.

More information on how to file a complaint, complaints not appropriate for the IG system, and complainants' rights and responsibilities can be found in AFPAM 36-2241V1, *PFE Study Guide*, or at your local IG office.

## USAF INSPECTION SYSTEM

Historically, the IGs have been viewed as the guys in the black hats. They went out and found problems. An inspectee was either right (in compliance with the regulation) or wrong (not in compliance)—there wasn't very much middle ground. Careers could be seriously affected by the stroke of a pen. Even today war stories circulate about the general who removed people from his staff and wanted them "off base by sundown" (meaning permanent reassignment) because of comments made by a visiting IG team.

Today's inspection system was designed to give the Secretary of the Air Force, the Chief of Staff USAF, and MAJCOM, separate operating agency (SOA), and NAF commanders feedback and information on the state of USAF readiness and on the efficiency and effectiveness of units, functions, programs, and guidance. The system uses a two-pronged approach: first, to find problems and help fix them; and second, to stimulate and reward excellence. Policies, procedures, and responsibilities are set by the Inspector General at HQ USAF and those in similar positions appointed by MAJCOMs, SOAs, and NAFs who conduct inspections of subordinate units.

### Types of Inspections

Types of inspections and reviews vary, based on the nature of each command's requirements. Some of the most common are the following.

*Operational Readiness Inspection (ORI).* The most direct measure of a unit's warfighting readiness is through an ORI. All units with a wartime mission are evaluated on their ability to conduct combat operations in wartime. These evaluations assess how well a unit can prepare, deploy, and employ forces, as well as survive and operate in a combat environment.

*Nuclear Surety Inspection (NSI).* NSIs assess compliance with procedures for the handling and employment of nuclear weapons. Because of the critical nature of nuclear weapons programs, these inspections can pose the most difficult tests for the activity inspected. Unsatisfactory performance in any nuclear surety area may result in an overall unsatisfactory unit rating, regardless of the ratings earned in other areas.

*Health Service Inspection (HSI).* HSAs are designed to evaluate medical readiness and management of the health-care system. The focus is on performance

**"A bunch of guys from the IG team dropped by to see you, but I told them to come back tomorrow because you were napping."**

and HSIs compliance and is designed to provide a broad look at medical treatment facility operation.

*Management Review.* Management reviews are not inspections; they are reviews that are conducted to provide senior leadership with information concerning topics with Air Force-wide significance. There are two categories of review: functional, such as contingency contracting, aircraft engine oil analysis, USAF regional nuclear weapons maintenance, and unfavorable information files (UIFs); and acquisition, such as aircraft battle damage repair, realignment of space launch operations from Air Force Materiel Command to Air Force Space Command, and initial operational test and evaluation. Ratings are not given for these reviews. Recommended solutions may be included in written reports; however, the program or process owner is responsible for developing the method that will best correct problems that are identified.

*Compliance Inspection (CI).* CIs focus primarily on those actions required by law, executive orders, DOD directives, and safety guidelines that, if not complied with, could result in significant legal liabilities, penalties, or significant mission impact. The Air Force specifies a number of CIs that must be reviewed. MAJCOM commanders may identify other CIs that should be assessed at the units under their control. Following the review of a compliance inspection item (CII), ratings (such as in compliance/not in compliance, satisfactory/unsatisfactory, pass/fail, and so forth) are used. The following is a brief list of some of the CIIs that are presently monitored Air Force-wide.

- Environmental
- Intelligence oversight
- Contracting
- Leave Management
- Transition assistance programs
- Command, control, communications, and computers
- Voting Assistance Program
- Sexual harassment education and prevention
- Safety
- Fitness Program

***Special Interest Items (SIIs).*** The SII process provides a system to focus management attention, gather data, and/or assess the status of specific programs and conditions in the field. It may also be used to determine the degree of compliance with directives, policies, and procedures; gather information on known or suspected problems; identify specific deficiencies; or to confirm that a problem has been resolved. The use of the SII process is also a source of feedback to command officials that has proved to be of value in facilitating decision-making and policy adjustments. There are two types of SIIs:

- A long-term SII is used when an issue is pervasive and is of major importance Air Force-wide or when assessing compliance in a specific area of concern. The time period for a long-term SII is normally six months to a year.
- A short-term SII includes subject areas within a limited scope or issues that are analyzed from data based on past inspections or from the results of a one-time survey. The time period for a short-term SII is less than six months.

When inspections are conducted, observations and findings must be based on facts that can be validated for accuracy. These facts are usually documented in a formal written report that outlines the finding, the impact, the cause, and a recommendation. The effectiveness and efficiency of a program are then measured, using a rating system.

## HOW TO SURVIVE AN INSPECTOR GENERAL TEAM VISIT

Now that you understand the purpose of Inspector General teams, here are some things to think about.

**Be Ready at All Times.** The best way to prepare is to be ready at all times. Ratings usually have a direct relationship to a unit's daily effort. Outstanding operations are built over a period of time, not two weeks before the inspection.

**Be on the Same Wavelength as Your Supervisor and Commander.** Develop a full understanding of your current programs and responsibilities and their importance to your unit's mission.

**Actively Seek Out New Ideas to Improve Your Operations.** Think about more efficient ways of doing things. Streamline procedures to enhance mission responsiveness or customer service. Take advantage of new technology. Look for actions that are cost-effective without loss of quality. Remember that you get a satisfactory rating by meeting mission requirements. Excellent or outstanding ratings are earned by going above and beyond the requirements. Submit innovative ideas as a "Best Practice" so others can employ your great idea to improve their mission success too.

**Use a Self-Inspection System to Check Yourself and Be Honest.** Carefully review your checklists if you've marked everything "yes, yes, yes, OK, OK, OK." This will indicate one of three things: your program is indeed outstanding; your checklists are out of date; or someone is "pencil-whipping" the answers. If you fall into category 2 or 3, you should back up and regroup. Remember, the inspectors have experience in your career field; they won't be easily misled. When they do find adverse trends, they usually look harder and deeper. They will find problems where they exist. If you find problems that are beyond your ability to fix, talk to your supervisor or your commander. They won't be able to help if they aren't advised. If you are not in compliance, fix it. Have a plan to correct deficiencies and an expected completion date. As long as your deficient area is identified and you are working towards compliance, you can justify not being in compliance, as you are working towards compliance.

**Read the Results of Other Units' Inspections.** Your supervisor should be able to get copies. These reports can tell you what the inspector looks at closely and what things denote an outstanding or excellent unit. Read the Best Practice submissions from others who have found smarter, better, faster ways of accomplishing their mission or program. You can also learn from the mistakes and poor ratings from other units. Don't let their lessons learned go to waste!

Get crossfeed information from supervisors in your chain of command, from your counterparts at other units (especially if they've been inspected recently), and from higher headquarters personnel who conduct staff assistance visits. Also check the IG web site.

**Think Beyond Your Specialty.** This is especially true for special-interest items and facility appearance. The way your shop looks is a reflection of the pride you take in your overall operation. There's an old IG saying: "I never saw a good unit that looked bad. I've seen a lot of bad units that looked good, but I never saw a good unit that looked bad."

**During the Inspection.** During the inspection itself, there are some things you should do and some things you definitely should not do.

*Dos*

1. Do be positive and professional. It makes the inspector's job easier, and it demonstrates your knowledge and control of your area. At the same time, it's important to relax and be yourself. Everyone has a slightly different approach or style.
2. Do be open and honest. It shows you have nothing to hide and establishes your credibility.
3. Do ask questions to get feedback. Make sure that you fully understand the observations and recommendations of the inspection team.
4. Do expose working-level personnel. They're tomorrow's supervisors and leaders. Let them talk to the inspectors and explain what they do. This demonstrates your trust in them and helps build their confidence for the future.
5. Do update your supervisors at the end of each duty day. They may be able to shed more light on items that, on the surface, appear to be problems. You can pass this information on to the inspectors and eliminate some items that might otherwise wind up in the printed report.

*Don'ts*

1. Don't resent the inspectors' visit. Their sole reason for visiting your unit is to enhance the efficiency and effectiveness of the U.S. Air Force.
2. Don't try to use delaying tactics (war stories, excessive coffee breaks, scheduling conflicting appointments, "mislaying" important documents, and so forth). Inspectors are well aware of all the time-wasting tricks. They also have to analyze a lot of information in a very short time. If they see that you are trying to mislead them, they may think you have something to hide, and they'll usually look at your programs a lot closer to find out why.
3. Don't argue, philosophize, or rationalize. It's all right to disagree, but explain why—and be diplomatic. It's important to keep the focus on *what* is right, rather than *who* is right.

## SOURCES OF ADDITIONAL INFORMATION

Air Force Recurring Periodical 90-1, *The Inspector General (TIG) Brief.*
Air Force Policy Directive 90-2, *Inspector General—The Inspection System.*
Air Force Instruction 90-201, *Inspector General Activities—The Inspection System.*
Air Force Instruction 90-301, *Inspector General Complaints Resolution*

# PART III

# Getting Ahead

# 14

# Careers and Goals

*However long you live, and whatever you accomplish, you will find that the time you spent in the [military service] was the most profitably spent portion of your life.*

—Gen. Robert E. Lee, 1863

The people who join the U.S. Air Force come from all parts of the country and all walks of life. They join for a variety of reasons, and they pursue their careers, brief or long, with different goals in mind. This chapter will help you put your finger on some of your own needs and goals. It will also help you develop a plan, a road map, for achieving those goals by the most direct route.

## WHO JOINS THE AIR FORCE AND WHY

Each man and woman who joins the USAF is unique. On the surface they seem very different. Their actions, feelings, and values have been affected by their backgrounds and by the people they've met throughout their individual lives. So why have they decided to join the Air Force? To some it's a job, providing the security and income they need to be self-reliant and independent. Others join because it's a well-respected family tradition. To many, it's a way to gain valuable education and training benefits. It's also a way of life—the desire to serve one's country, the camaraderie, the feeling of belonging, the excitement, the travel, the love of aircraft. Sometimes it's the intangible feeling of achievement, success, and self-satisfaction. Overall, the USAF does offer a system where common goals and individual roles are well defined; that kind of stability and order is an important consideration for many people.

Everyone who joins the Air Force—regardless of background, rank, or reason for joining—meets certain standards. Almost all those in the enlisted force are high school graduates (over 99 percent during the past two fiscal years); some have university degrees. For commissioned officers, a college degree is mandatory. These achievements are indicators of future success; they show that a person has persistence, the ability to stay with a program and succeed. In addition, each candidate must meet a range of preset standards before being accepted. After meeting basic educational requirements, prospective airmen undergo a very selective screening process: They take aptitude tests and physical examinations, and they must meet the requirements of a background investigation. They are also put through a screening process in basic military training school or officer training programs to ensure that they have "the right stuff." Failing to meet the criteria at any step along the way can shorten their career.

## WHAT IS SUCCESS?

According to the dictionary, success is the achievement of something desired, planned, or attempted. But success means different things to different people. Your personal feeling of success will depend on the values and needs that have meaning for you. Here are some examples:

- Job satisfaction: a sense of belonging, challenge, achievement, recognition, and progression.
- Status: an enhanced self-image, position, prestige, or level of responsibility.
- Interpersonal relationships: socializing, spending time with family and friends.
- Personal growth: through education, religion, or other self-improvement efforts.
- Leisure: time to pursue and enjoy travel, sports, and hobbies.
- Material success: attaining some degree of financial independence and security (owning a home, a car, a stereo system, providing your children's education).

Most people would agree that the best way to seek success is through a balanced approach, one that takes all your interests into consideration. There's also a need to think about timing. Obviously, you can't achieve everything at once. It's a building process. And half of the fun in success is enjoying your achievements along the way. As you reflect on what a successful career means to you, jot down some notes. They'll be useful as you move into the next section, which outlines how you can identify the goals that you want to pursue as your stepping-stones to success.

## GOALS

The concept of setting goals has been around for quite a while. Socrates once said, "If you don't know which port you're sailing to, any wind is favorable." In this instance, he was talking about charting a course—charting "goals" to get from point A to point B.

Goals, in careers as in sports, are like game plans. They are your road map for achieving results. They help you channel your efforts, they designate what is important and meaningful to you, and they help you to make the best use of your time.

Established goals are the basis for any successful career. The best way to begin is to identify some of them, write them down, and set a preliminary timetable.

Recall the wise saying, "A goal not written down is only a wish." But remember, this is your first attempt. Just let your mind flow; you can redefine and relist your goals at any time. Also, don't limit goals to the near future. Think a bit farther than your next assignment or the next promotion.

Once you've identified your goals, ask yourself whether they are realistic and achievable. If they're not realistic, they're fantasies. For example, most of us would agree that being a commander of an Air Force submarine isn't exactly realistic. Nor would it be realistic to make the rank of chief master sergeant or colonel in less than five years of active duty. Also ask yourself whether your goals are compatible with the mission of your present organization and, in general, with the mission of the Air Force.

Let's start now:

| **Immediate Goals** (next twelve months) | **Intermediate Goals** (one to five years) | **Long-Range Goals** (five years plus) |
| --- | --- | --- |
| _____ | _____ | _____ |
| _____ | _____ | _____ |
| _____ | _____ | _____ |
| _____ | _____ | _____ |
| _____ | _____ | _____ |
| _____ | _____ | _____ |
| _____ | _____ | _____ |

**Some Ideas If You're Drawing a Blank.** More ideas for goals will come to you as you progress through this book. But if you're drawing a blank right now, think about some of the following general themes.

- Establish a professional reputation in your duty section.
- Meet or exceed standards of dress and appearance.
- Get outstanding performance reports.
- Get a high rating on your next inspection.
- Be promoted to _____ by _____.
- Receive an award or decoration for your efforts during this tour.
- Complete a university degree.
- Complete a Professional Military Education (PME) course (Airman Leadership School, NCO Academy, Senior NCO Academy).
- Narrow down the options for your next assignment and apply for it.
- Spend time with family and friends. Pursue mutual interests for leisure, hobbies, sports, or travel.
- Develop a financial plan tailored to your needs, either short-term (a new car) or long-term (a home, children's education).

**The best way to start defining your goals is to make a written list.**

**Achieving the Goals You've Set.** Now that you've established some goals, let's think about some general guidelines for achieving them. Writing them down was your first major step, because it helped you identify more clearly what you want to achieve. You've taken a step beyond most of your contemporaries—they're still thinking about their careers in general terms and taking things one day at a time.

After putting them on paper, the single most important factor in achieving goals will be your personal commitment to press on and to make progress with each of them. The best way to do that is to look at each goal closely, list all the logical steps you need to take, and then set some dates for completing each step.

For example, let's look at a senior airman who receives notification in January that he will be able to test for promotion to staff sergeant in April. If promotion is one of his goals, he won't be content with just going in to take the test. He will list some logical steps and set some target dates to make sure that the primary goal of promotion is achieved. This airman's road map to success might look something like this:

Promotion to Staff Sergeant:

1. Review promotion criteria (read the directive): January.
2. Understand the points system under the Weighted Airman Promotion System (WAPS), compute the factors that are known to me (time-in-service, time-in-grade, awards and decorations, and performance reports): January.
3. Find out what the promotion cutoff score was in my specialty for the last promotion cycle. This will tell me the approximate score I need on both the Promotion Fitness Examination (PFE) and the Specialty Knowledge Examination (SKT): January.
4. Obtain study materials: January.
5. Study PFE: January–February.
6. Study SKT: February–March.
7. Final review to avoid cramming: late March–early April.
8. Take test: April.

**Obstacles to Success.** Four main obstacles can prevent you from achieving the goals you've set for yourself:

1. "I never have enough time." This is probably the most common reason for not pursuing goals. If you find yourself using this excuse, take a good look at your daily schedule and see where all the time is going. You can map out your day, hour by hour, or you can look at it in a broader context.

| | | | |
|---|---|---|---|
| Time at work: | 10 hours × 5 days × 52 weeks | = | 2,600 hours |
| Time at sleep: | 8 hours × 7 days × 52 weeks | = | 2,912 |
| | | | ——— |
| | | | 5,512 |
| Credit for 30 duty days (annual leave) | | | –300 |
| | | | ——— |
| | | | 5,212 |
| Credit for 10 duty days (holidays) | | | –100 |
| | | | ——— |
| | | | 5,112 hours |

So, approximately 5,112 hours each year (the equivalent of 213 days) is committed to work and sleep. That's approximately 58 percent of your time. And the other 42 percent (the equivalent of 152 days) is committed to . . . what?

Many will be quick to protest, "But the Air Force is a twenty-four-hour-a-day job." It's a twenty-four-hour-a-day *responsibility,* true, but not many USAF people work twenty-four-hour shifts consistently, day after day. If you've been having problems traceable to a lack of time, take a look at where you're spending it. You'll probably be surprised at how much time you actually have at your disposal.

2. Not keeping your options open can be another obstacle. Many people who join the USAF aren't initially sure if they are going to make the service a

career, so they avoid many programs because they're planning to leave after the initial term of service. But plans do change. Most of those who decide to make the Air Force a career make the decision within the final six months.

3. Peer pressure can also have an effect on achieving goals—sometimes good, sometimes not so good. It's important to be able to tell the difference. Friends can exert a major influence on your goals, even when their own goals are different.

4. Last but not least, think about the timing required to achieve your goals and the consequences of what may happen if you get too far off track. Think of your career as a journey through life. Life offers everyone a certain amount of years. So does an Air Force career, usually thirty at the most. Let's look at a couple of examples that illustrate how poor timing and getting off track can have an adverse effect on a career:

- Airman Jones joined the Air Force. Like his father, he wanted to make it a career. He didn't do well in technical training school and had to retrain into a less desirable career field. He was frustrated and decided to go absent without leave (AWOL). He came back and received nonjudicial punishment, an Article 15, from his commander. As a result, he lost a stripe. Then he got in with the wrong crowd and started using drugs. His commander decided that his behavior was incompatible with Air Force standards. Airman Jones was separated from the USAF on a bad-conduct discharge. In this case, Airman Jones's goals weren't consistent with those of the Air Force; he was too far off track.

- Staff Sergeant Smith was also career-minded; she set her sights on making chief master sergeant. But she never really gave much thought to planning her career; she just took each day as it came. She didn't study for promotion; she didn't make any self-improvement efforts; she didn't know who wrote her performance report. She finally made technical sergeant after eighteen years. Then she started to take a closer look at her career. It took her another four years to make master sergeant, but now it was too late to make chief. She had reached her high year of tenure, and now her retirement was mandatory. In this case, Sergeant Smith failed to make chief master sergeant because of the lack of proper timing; she had a general goal in mind, but her overall commitment was too little, too late.

**The Air Force Mentoring Program.** As a part of your goal setting program, it can be beneficial to seek the counsel, guidance, and assistance from other experienced Air Force members. Air Force Instruction (AFI) 36-3401, *Air Force Mentoring,* provides information and policy to help create a climate of cultural change and personal growth—one where officers, NCOs, and civilians can pass on the principles, traditions, shared values, and lessons of the Air Force profession.

A mentor is a positive role model, trusted counselor, or guide (usually a supervisor or other person in an airman's unit or chain of command) who helps another person develop both personally and professionally. Mentoring is further defined as a year-round process that goes beyond performance feedback sessions, career guidance, and core values. Under the policy, mentors are to teach airmen about the Air Force history and heritage, its air and space power doctrine, its strategic vision, and its contribution to joint war fighting. They relate this, based on their background and experience, by also speaking to their personnel about important career development initiatives. These include:

- Pursuing the benefits of professional military education and continuing education classes.
- Joining professional associations so the person being mentored can learn job skills and meet other people in their fields.
- Understanding the promotion system and ways in which the person being mentored can understand that he or she has had a successful career.
- Recommending people for awards and decorations, when appropriate.

In recognition of the importance of the Air Force mentoring program, the Air Force developed a guide to assist Air Force leaders in mentoring on air and space power. The guide offers a "menu" of air and space topics for use in developing mentoring sessions. Copies of the mentoring guide and essays may be obtained through the Air University Press at (334) 953-2773.

**Reviewing and Updating Your Goals.** From time to time you'll want to review your goals to see if you're making progress and to add new ones. When is the right time to do this? Any time is fine, really, but there are three occasions that usually stimulate a lot of thought: after you've been selected for promotion; after you've changed jobs or assignments; and in January, when most people are making resolutions for the new year or reviewing their taxes.

Conducting your review annually, in a specific month, is probably best. That way, you'll make sure to take a fresh look at your goals at least once a year. And that's important for planning purposes.

Sometimes the only way to know how far there is to go is to look back and see how far you've come. Right now, you're at the crossroads—of the past, the present, and the future.

# 15

# Career Progression Routes

Your career progression will depend on the efforts you make to develop or improve proficiency in your Air Force Specialty (AFS). This chapter will explain the Air Force Military Personnel Classification System and the criteria for the award of different skill levels. It will also tell you what kind of jobs the Air Force offers and the ways to apply for retraining.

## THE AIR FORCE MILITARY PERSONNEL CLASSIFICATION SYSTEM

The classification system identifies the duties for all positions essential to accomplishing the mission of the U.S. Air Force. It is also used to accurately identify the abilities of each individual and match them to the qualifications of the position. These positions are functionally grouped into Air Force Specialties (AFSs) based on skills and qualifications.

**Air Force Specialty Codes.** Each AFS has a title, a specialty description, and a code number known as an Air Force Specialty Code (AFSC). The specialty codes can be referred to in three different ways:

1. A Primary Air Force Specialty Code (PAFSC) shows which specialty an airman is most qualified in. It is used because some airmen are qualified to perform in more than one specialty (for example, as a medic and as an information management specialist).
2. A Duty Air Force Specialty Code (DAFSC) is used to link an airman to a specific authorized manning document position that he or she is assigned to. It does not necessarily correspond with the airman's qualification level.
3. A Control Air Force Specialty Code (CAFSC) is used to make assignments; it ensures an equitable distribution of airmen by grade and skill level against established manning requirements, and it also helps identify and control training requirements.

*The Evolution of Air Force Specialty Codes.* On November 1, 1993, Air Force Specialty Codes were converted to a new alphanumeric formula. The new

AFSCs were designed to match the restructured Air Force and to align career fields that became fragmented over the years. Many of the older original AFSCs were established in and have been in place since 1951, when the Air Force used many of the old Army military occupational specialty (MOS) codes. The new system was designed to accommodate a smaller force. By removing some AFSCs and combining others, it reduced the number of narrowly trained specialists and relied more on generalists who can be assigned to a broader range of duties and career-broadening opportunities.

### Figuring Out the New Codes.
- The first digit of the new enlisted AFSCs shows the career grouping.
- The second character is a letter that identifies the career field.
- The third character shows a career field subdivision.
- The fourth character marks the airman's level of qualification:

|   |   |
|---|---|
| 1 | helper |
| 3 | apprentice |
| 5 | journeyman |
| 7 | craftsman |
| 9 | superintendent |
| 0 | chief enlisted manager |

- The fifth character notes the airman's specialty.

The following is an example of AFSC 1A571, which is used to classify one of the levels of the Airborne Radar Systems Craftsman career field.

| Career Grouping | Career Field | Career Field Subdivision | Skill Level | Specific AFSC |
|---|---|---|---|---|
| 1 | A | 5 | 7 | 1 |
| Operations | Aircrew Operations | Airborne Systems | Craftsman | Computer and Radar |

**Proficiency Skill Levels.** Proficiency skill levels are awarded as codes for Air Force Specialties (AFSs), Special Duty Identifiers (SDIs), and Chief Enlisted Managers (CEMs). They come at intervals during airmen's careers based on their grade, time requirements, performance within their career field, completion of training requirements, and supervisor's recommendation. Generally, it works this way:

1. The 1 skill level designates initial entry into an Air Force specialty.
2. The 3 skill level is awarded to those who qualify as bypass specialists, complete a formal technical training course, or complete 3-level upgrade training on the job.
3. The 5 skill level is awarded for satisfactorily performing on 5-level upgrade training and passing 5-level career development courses. Most airmen who

complete a formal technical training course are entered into 5-level training at their first permanent duty station.

4. The 7 skill level is awarded for satisfactorily performing on 7-level upgrade training and passing the 7-level career development course for the appropriate specialty. Those promoted to the grade of staff sergeant are entered into upgrade training for the 7 level.

5. The 9 skill level is awarded to master sergeants and senior master sergeants who are satisfactorily performing in their AFSCs. In some cases, completion of the Senior NCO Academy is a prerequisite for the award of the 9 level.

6. The Chief Enlisted Manager (CEM) codes identify all chief master sergeant positions in the airman classification structure. These codes are awarded to chief master sergeants (or selectees) who already possess a 9-level AFSC. These codes identify personnel who, through extensive experience and training, have demonstrated the leadership and management ability to effectively control a wide range of programs and activities.

7. Special Duty Identifiers (SDIs) are awarded based on satisfactory performance and the date entered into the special duty.

## THE AIRMAN CLASSIFICATION STRUCTURE: "WHERE THE JOBS ARE"

The Air Force divides its AFSCs (enlisted jobs) into the several categories: Operations, Maintenance & Logistics, Support, Medical & Dental, Legal & Chaplain, Finance & Contracting, Special Investigations, and Special Duty Assignments.

### Operations

1A—Aircrew Operations
1C—Command & Control Systems Operations
1N—Intelligence
1T—Aircrew Protection
1S—Safety
1W—Weather

### Maintenance & Logistics

2A—Manned Aerospace Maintenance
2E—Communications & Electronics
2F—Fuels
2G—Logistics Plans
2M—Missile & Space Systems Maintenance
2P—Precision Measurement Equipment Laboratory
2R—Maintenance Management Systems
2S—Supply
2T—Transportation & Vehicle Maintenance
2W—Munitions & Weapons

## Support

3A—Information Management
3C—Communications & Computer Systems
3H—Historian
3M—Services
3N—Public Affairs
3P—Security Forces (Military Police)
3E—Civil Engineering
3S—Mission Support
3U—Manpower
3V—Visual Information

## Medical & Dental

4X—Medical
4Y—Dental

## Legal & Chaplain

5J—Paralegal
5R—Chaplain Assistant

## Finance & Contracting

6C—Contracting
6F—Financial

## Special Investigations

7S—Special Investigations (OSI)

## Special Duty Assignments

Special Duty Assignments are usually jobs that a member performs temporarily, working outside of their normal AFSC. When the special duty tour is completed, members usually return to their primary AFSC (enlisted job). Examples would be recruiter, first sergeant, or military training instructor.

8X—Special Duty Identifiers
9X—Special Reporting Identifiers

Within these categories, AFSCs are further assigned to "career fields." A career field may have one AFSC assigned to it, or it may have several. AFSCs with similar functions are grouped together in the same career field. During the course of their Air Force careers, airmen sometimes switch jobs and receive multiple AFSCs to denote training in multiple specialties. A Primary AFSC (PAFSC) is the designation for the specialty in which the individual possesses the highest skill level. The Duty AFSC (DAFSC) reflects the actual manpower position the airman is assigned to. The Control AFSC (CAFSC) is a management tool to make assignments, assist in determining training requirements, and consider individuals for promotion. Often an enlisted airman's PAFSC will reflect a higher skill level than his or her CAFSC since the CAFSC skill level is tied to rank while the PAFSC skill level is tied to performance and education.

The "normal" situation for most airmen is for the PAFSC, DAFSC, and CAFSC to be the same; however, there are situations (retraining, special duties, Air Force-level changes, and other situations either within or beyond an airman's control) when the three will differ. Additionally, Airmen retraining into other specialties may acquire one or more secondary AFSCs.

The following is a more complete list of career fields as of October 2006.

| AFSC | Enlisted Career Fields | # Personnel Assigned |
|---|---|---|
| 1A0X1 | In-Flight Refueling | 789 |
| 1A1X1 | Flight Engineer | 1,537 |
| 1A2X1 | Loadmaster | 2,172 |
| 1A3X1 | Airborne Communications & Electronic Systems | 971 |
| 1A4X1 | Airborne Battle Management | 891 |
| 1A5X1 | Airborne Missions Systems | 376 |
| 1A6X1 | Flight Attendant | 204 |
| 1A7X1 | Aerial Gunner | 378 |
| 1A8X1 | Airborne Cryptologic Linguist | 1,038 |
| 1C0X2 | Operations Resource Management | 1,543 |
| 1C1X1 | Air Traffic Control | 3,117 |
| 1C2X1 | Combat Control | 450 |
| 1C3X1 | Command Post | 2,195 |
| 1C4X1 | Tactical Air Command & Control | 1,034 |
| 1C5X1 | Aerospace Control & Warning Systems | 1,354 |
| 1C6X1 | Space Systems Operations | 958 |
| 1N0X1 | Intelligence Applications | 2,606 |
| 1N1X1 | Imagery Analysis | 1,312 |
| 1N2X1 | Communications Signals Intelligence Production | 1,403 |
| 1N3XX | Linguist | 2,604 |
| 1N4X1 | Network Intelligence Analysis | 1,614 |
| 1N5X1 | Electronic Signals Intelligence Exploitation | 858 |
| 1N6X1 | Electronic System Security Assessment | 370 |
| 1S0X1 | Safety | 353 |
| 1T0X1 | Survival, Evasion, Resistance & Escape Operations | 490 |
| 1T1X1 | Aircrew Life Support | 1,569 |
| 1T2X1 | Pararescue | 378 |
| 1W0X1 | Weather | 2,384 |
| 2A0X1 | Avionics Test Stations & Components | 2,382 |

| AFSC | Enlisted Career Fields | # Personnel Assigned |
|------|------------------------|----------------------|
| 2A3X1 | A-10, F-15, U-2 Avionic Systems | 1,744 |
| 2A3X2 | F-16, F-117, FQ-1, CV-22 Avionic Systems | 1,945 |
| 2A3X3 | Tactical Aircraft Maintenance | 9,692 |
| 2A5X1 | Aerospace Maintenance | 10,503 |
| 2A5X2 | Helicopter Maintenance | 822 |
| 2A5X3 | Integrated Avionics Systems | 5,953 |
| 2A6X1 | Aerospace Propulsion | 6,003 |
| 2A6X2 | Aerospace Ground Equipment | 4,182 |
| 2A6X3 | Aircrew Egress Systems | 945 |
| 2A6X4 | Aircraft Fuel Systems | 1,847 |
| 2A6X5 | Aircraft Hydraulic Systems | 2,079 |
| 2A6X6 | Aircraft Electrical & Environmental Systems | 3,887 |
| 2A7X1 | Aircraft Metals Technology | 778 |
| 2A7X2 | Nondestructive Inspection | 702 |
| 2A7X3 | Aircraft Structural Maintenance | 3,027 |
| 2A7X4 | Survival Equipment | 734 |
| 2E0X1 | Ground Radar Systems | 806 |
| 2E1X1 | Satellite, Wideband & Telemetry Systems | 2,364 |
| 2E1X2 | Meteorological & Navigation Systems | 629 |
| 2E1X3 | Ground Radio Communications | 2,380 |
| 2E1X4 | Visual Imagery & Intrusion Detection Systems | 493 |
| 2E2X1 | Communication, Network, Switching & Crypto Systems | 2,633 |
| 2E6X2 | Communication Cable & Antenna Systems | 553 |
| 2E6X3 | Telephone Systems | 1,281 |
| 2F0X1 | Fuels | 4,059 |
| 2G0X1 | Logistics | 726 |
| 2M0X1 | Missile & Space Systems Electronics Maintenance | 1,060 |
| 2M0X2 | Missile & Space Systems Maintenance | 716 |
| 2M0X3 | Missile & Space Facilities | 487 |
| 2P0X1 | Precision Measurement Equipment Laboratory | 836 |
| 2R0X1 | Maintenance Management Analyst | 630 |
| 2R1X1 | Maintenance Production | 840 |
| 2S0X1 | Supply Management | 7,461 |
| 2S0X2 | Supply Systems Analyst | 405 |
| 2T0X1 | Traffic Management | 1,637 |
| 2T1X1 | Vehicle Operations | 2,349 |
| 2T2X1 | Air Transportation | 4,673 |
| 2T3X1 | Special Purpose Vehicle & Equipment Maintenance | 1,747 |
| 2T3X2 | Special Vehicle Maintenance | 741 |
| 2T3X5 | Vehicle Body Maintenance | 185 |
| 2T3X7 | Vehicle Management & Analysis | 392 |

| AFSC | Enlisted Career Fields | # Personnel Assigned |
|------|------------------------|----------------------|
| 2W0X1 | Munitions Systems | 6,869 |
| 2W1X1 | Aircraft Armament Systems | 7,523 |
| 2W2X1 | Nuclear Weapons | 827 |
| 3A0X1 | Information Management | 8,387 |
| 3C0X1 | Communication-Computer Systems Operations | 8,545 |
| 3C0X2 | Communication-Computer Systems Programming | 1,343 |
| 3C1X1 | Radio Communications Systems | 576 |
| 3C1X2 | Electromagnetic Spectrum Management | 82 |
| 3C2X1 | Communication-Computer Systems Control | 2,653 |
| 3C3X1 | Communication-Computer Systems Planning & Implementation | 611 |
| 3E0X1 | Electrical | 1,683 |
| 3E0X2 | Electrical Power Production | 1,531 |
| 3E1X1 | Heating, Ventilation, AC, Refrigeration | 1,771 |
| 3E2X1 | Pavement & Construction Equipment | 1,706 |
| 3E3X1 | Structural | 1,723 |
| 3E4X1 | Utilities Systems | 1,427 |
| 3E4X2 | Liquid Fuel Systems Maintenance | 312 |
| 3E4X3 | Environmental Controls | 232 |
| 3E5X1 | Engineering | 919 |
| 3E6X1 | Operations Management | 530 |
| 3E7X1 | Fire Protection | 3,621 |
| 3E8X1 | Explosive Ordnance Disposal | 1,271 |
| 3E9X1 | Readiness | 803 |
| 3H0X1 | Historian | 70 |
| 3M0X1 | Services | 3,958 |
| 3N0X1 | Public Affairs | 409 |
| 3N0X2 | Radio & Television Broadcasting | 183 |
| 3N1X1 | Regional Band | 519 |
| 3N2X1 | Premier Band | 261 |
| 3P0X1 | Security Forces | 23,705 |
| 3S0X1 | Personnel | 5,889 |
| 3S1X1 | Military Equal Opportunity | 220 |
| 3S2X1 | Education & Training | 1,148 |
| V0X1 | Visual Information | 444 |
| 3V0X2 | Still Photographic | 546 |
| 3V0X3 | Visual Information Production- Documentation | 257 |
| 4A0X1 | Health Services Management | 3,009 |
| 4A1X1 | Medical Materiel | 1,067 |
| 4A2X1 | Biomedical Equipment | 568 |
| 4B0X1 | Bioenvironmental Engineering | 829 |

| AFSC | Enlisted Career Fields | # Personnel Assigned |
|------|------------------------|----------------------|
| 4C0X1 | Mental Health Service | 637 |
| 4D0X1 | Diet Therapy | 392 |
| 4E0X1 | Public Health | 928 |
| 4H0X1 | Cardiopulmonary Laboratory | 305 |
| 4J0X2 | Physical Medicine | 290 |
| 4M0X1 | Aerospace Physiology | 332 |
| 4N0X1 | Medical Service | 6,187 |
| 4N1X1 | Surgical Service | 798 |
| 4P0X1 | Pharmacy | 978 |
| 4R0X1 | Diagnostic Imaging | 898 |
| 4T0X1 | Medical Laboratory | 1,251 |
| 4T0X2 | Histopathology | 82 |
| 4T0X3 | Cytotechnology | 26 |
| 4V0X1 | Optometry | 287 |
| 4Y0X1 | Dental Assistant | 1,975 |
| 4Y0X2 | Dental Laboratory | 443 |
| 5J0X1 | Paralegal | 936 |
| 5R0X1 | Chaplain Assistant | 442 |
| 6C0X1 | Contracting | 1,297 |
| 6F0X1 | Financial Management & Comptroller | 2,950 |
| 7S0X1 | Special Investigations | 884 |
| 8A1X0 | Career Assistance Advisor | 87 |
| 8A2X0 | Enlisted Aide | 85 |
| 8B0X0 | Military Training Instructor | 518 |
| 8B1X0 | Military Training Leader | 356 |
| 8B2X0 | Academic Training Military NCO | 90 |
| 8C0X0 | Family Support Center | 160 |
| 8D0X0 | Linguist Debriefer | 38 |
| 8F0X0 | First Sergeant | 1,270 |
| 8G0X0 | USAF Honor Guard | 250 |
| 8J0X0 | Correctional Custody Supervisor | 5 |
| 8M0X0 | Postal Specialist | 615 |
| 8P0X0 | Courier | 88 |
| 8P1X0 | Defense Attaché' Specialist | 124 |
| 8RXX0 | Recruiter | 2,518 |
| 8S0X0 | Missile Facility Manager | 207 |
| 8T0X0 | Professional Military Education Instructor | 651 |
| 9C0X0 | Chief Master Sergeant of the Air Force | 1 |
| 9D0X0 | Dormitory Manager | 298 |
| 9E0X0 | Senior Enlisted Advisor | 133 |
| 9F0X0 | First Term Airmen Center | 79 |

| AFSC | Enlisted Career Fields | # Personnel Assigned |
|------|------------------------|----------------------|
| 9G1X0 | Group Superintendent | 240 |
| 9J0X0 | Prisoner | 426 |
| 9L0X0 | Interpreter/Translator | 65 |
| 9P0X0 | Patient | 17 |
| 9S1X0 | Technical Applications Specialist | 428 |
| 9T0X0 | Basic Trainee | 7,081 |
| 9T1X0 | Officer Trainee | 81 |
| 9T2X0 | Pre-Cadet Assignee | 244 |

**Special Experience Identifiers (SEIs).** SEIs identify special experience and training that are not otherwise identified by AFSC or other codes within the military personnel data system (MilPDS). These codes do the following: identify experience or training that is critical to individuals and the jobs they perform when no other identification is appropriate or available. They permit rapid identification of a resource already qualified to meet unique circumstances, contingency requirements, or management needs, and provide a means to track individuals and identify positions requiring or providing unique experience or training that otherwise would be lost. SEIs are tied to the assignment process and are used to better distribute personnel and optimize the job-and-person match as much as possible.

Most SEI codes are composed of three numeric characters, although three alphanumeric characters can be used for some AFSCs when authorized to do so by the Air Intelligence Agency (AIA). The individual characters within these codes have no specific meaning. Most SEIs are authorized for award with specific AFSCs; some are authorized with any AFSC. The SEIs are functionally grouped by category, such as Civil Engineering, Contracting, Communications, Communications-Electronics, Weather, Security, Medical, Aircraft Maintenance and Weapons Systems (such as Engines and Avionics), Missiles and Space Operations, and Command and Control Systems.

| SEI Code | Title |
|----------|-------|
| 004 | Orderly Room/Unit Administration |
| 009 | Wholesale Logistics Experience |
| 014 | AFOSI Technical Services |
| 031 | Crime Prevention/Resources Protection |
| 032 | Budget Experience |
| 039 | Aviation Fuels Monitor |
| 040 | Aviation Fuels Accounting |

| SEI Code | Title |
|----------|-------|
| 045 | Tactical Air Control System Direct Air Support Center or Air Support Operations Center (TACS DASC/ASOC) |
| 046 | Tactical Air Control System (TACS) Airborne Battlefield Command and Control Center |
| 048 | Joint Operations Planning System Automated Data Processing (JOPS ADP) End User |
| 053 | Ground Control Approach |
| 056 | Control Tower |
| 058 | Atmospheric Research Equipment |
| 064 | Combat Crew Training |
| 065 | Central Flight Instructor Course Instructor |
| 073 | KC-135 Boom Operator |
| 084 | Aircraft Flight Test |
| 090 | Tanker Airlift Control Element (TALCE) |
| 095 | Operational Test and Evaluation (OT&E) |
| 153 | Contract Administration |
| 187 | National Military Command Center Communications– Electronics Systems Maintenance |
| 239 | Combat Crew Communications |
| 256 | Airborne Command Post |
| 297 | Personnel Control Team (PCT) Member |
| 301 | Air National Guard Readiness Center (ANGRC) |
| 305 | NCO Preparatory Course Instructor |
| 306 | Special Operations Force |
| 321 | Security Police Investigator |
| 326 | Red Horse Experience |
| 328 | Air Base Survivability (ABS) |
| 332 | Photojournalist |
| 348 | Safety Education Program |
| 350 | Airspace Management |
| 372 | Additional Duty Social Actions NCO |
| 475 | Substance Abuse Certification |
| 501 | A-10 |
| 503 | KC-10 |
| 506 | F-117 |
| 510 | U-2 |
| 513 | AC-130H/U, Spectre Gunship |
| 514 | HC-130 |
| 525 | Predator, Unmanned Aerial Vehicle (UAV) |
| 533 | F-15 |
| 535 | F-16 |

| SEI Code | Title |
|---|---|
| 545 | C-5 |
| 546 | C-17 |
| 547 | C-12 |
| 550 | C-141 |
| 569 | E-3A/B (AWACS) |
| 596 | B-2 |
| 677 | Air Force Satellite Communications Systems |
| 809 | Missile Electronic Equipment Maintenance |
| 836 | Munitions Inspector |
| 900 | Combat Airspace Manager |
| 916 | Strategic Defense Radar Systems Evaluator |
| 927 | Ballistic Missile Early Warning System (BMEWS)—Mechanical |
| 928 | Ballistic Missile Early Warning System (BMEWS)—Phased Array |
| 942 | 484L Presidential Aircraft Support System |
| 970 | Special Tactics |
| 979 | Space Defense Operations Center (SPADOC) |
| 986 | Sea Launched Ballistic Missile (SLBM) Phased-Array Warning System (PAVE PAWS) |
| 990 | Space Surveillance Center |
| 991 | Air Force Space Operations Center |
| 992 | Space Command Center |
| 993 | Global Positioning System |
| 994 | Deep Space Tracking System |
| 996 | Defense Support Program/Satellite Control Network |

## Reporting Identifiers

| Identifier | Title |
|---|---|
| 9A000 | Enlisted Airman Awaiting Retraining—Disqualified for Reasons Beyond Control |
| 9A100 | Enlisted Airman Awaiting Retraining—Disqualified for Reasons Within Control |
| 9A200 | Enlisted Airman Awaiting Discharge, Sep, Retire for Reasons Within Their Control |
| 9A300 | Enlisted Airman Awaiting Discharge, Sep, Retire for Reasons Beyond Their Control |

| Identifier | Title |
|---|---|
| 9C000 | Chief Master Sergeant of the Air Force |
| 9D000 | Dormitory Manager |
| 9E000 | Senior Enlisted Advisor |
| 9F000 | First Term Airmen Center |
| 9J000 | Prisoner |
| 9L000 | Interpreter/Translator |
| 9P000 | Patient |
| 9R000 | Civil Air Patrol (CAP)—USAF Reserve Assistant NCOs |
| 9S100 | Technical Applications Specialist |
| 9T000 | Basic Enlisted Airman |
| 9T100 | Officer Trainee |
| 9T200 | Pre-cadet Assignee |
| 9U000 | Enlisted Airman Ineligible for Local Utilization |
| 9U100 | Unallotted Enlisted Authorization |

## Air Force Specialty Code Prefixes

| Prefix | Title |
|---|---|
| A | Development Craftsman |
| C | Flying Crew Chief |
| F | F-22 |
| G | Automated Systems Programming Craftsman |
| J | Parachutist |
| K | Aircrew Instructor |
| N | Network Systems Administration |
| Q | Aircrew Standardization/Flight Examiner |
| R | Contingency/War Planner |
| T | Formal Training Instructor |
| U | Information Operations |
| V | Automated Functional Applications Analyst/Monitor |
| X | Aircrew |

## RETRAINING OPPORTUNITIES

Airmen may retrain from one career field to another on either a voluntary or selective basis. The voluntary method is preferred because Air Force requirements and individual career goals are satisfied at the same time. The selective method is used primarily when there is a shortage of personnel in a specific career field and a surplus in another; personnel are then "selected" to retrain. Shortages frequently occur when a new weapons system becomes operational, when airmen become disqualified or are not able to work in their present career field, and during the normal process of separations, discharges, and retirements.

In most cases, first-term airmen are not eligible to retrain until they have completed a specified period of their first enlistment. Four-year enlistees must complete a minimum of thirty-six months before applying for retraining. Six-year enlistees must complete a minimum of sixty months. Once they are eligible, most airmen who wish to retrain in another career field apply under the CAREERS (Career Airman Reenlistment Reservation System) program. Second-term and career airmen can also ask to retrain into another field. Here, too, approval depends largely on the manning levels in the present and prospective fields. Periodically, airmen from overmanned fields are sought by the Air Force Personnel Center (AFPC) to retrain voluntarily into skills with shortages. If voluntary goals are not met, then selective retraining is initiated.

Force shaping, or downsizing, is a move to recapitalize and modernize our force while staying within budget constraints. The outlook is that thousands of airmen will be cut from the ranks. The total force numbers will continue to be carefully considered with respect to politics, budget, manpower, and global military necessity.

The best way to find out about current retraining opportunities is to see your unit career advisor or the base career advisor. You can also stop by the Military Personnel Section (MPS) and visit the customer service branch or the classification and training unit. They regularly receive from AFPC the USAF Retraining Advisory, an up-to-date list of all AFSCs showing retraining requirements and overage conditions.

## SOURCES OF ADDITIONAL INFORMATION

Air Force Instruction 36-2101, *Classifying Military Personnel*

Air Force Instruction 36-2626, *Airman Retraining Program.*

Consult your unit career advisor or the base career advisor. When discussing career fields you are interested in, be sure to read current duty descriptions. Career fields are redesignated and renumbered from time to time based on new weapons systems and the needs of the Air Force.

The list of current Air Force Specialty Codes is always changing. New systems are coming on line, old systems are being retired, and new organizational structures are evolving. For the current list of AFSCs, consult the Classification and Training section at your MPS.

# 16

# Training and Education

*Receive instruction and be wise.*
—Ancient proverb

Whether you pursue a career in the U.S. Air Force or venture out into the civilian community, training and education will play a major role in determining your future. It has often been said that who we are today is a result of our preparation in the past. Within the USAF, there are many avenues to training, education, and experience—some on duty, some off duty. Some airmen decide not to take full advantage of these programs because they will be leaving the USAF to pursue their education. This may be wise if your goals are highly specialized. But in most cases, it's more advantageous and economical to continue your education while in the Air Force.

## ENLISTED EDUCATION AND TRAINING
Enlisted Education and Training (E&T) prepares airmen to perform their jobs within the Air Force and an assigned Air Force specialty (AFS). Its goals are to develop military professional skills through professional military education (PME) and to qualify and upgrade airmen in each skill level of an AFS. These goals are achieved by pursuing a mix of formal (classroom) and informal (on-the-job) training.

**Formal Training Program.** Generally, formal training is provided in one of three ways:

1. Air Education and Training Command (AETC) operates *Technical Training Centers (TTCs)* to teach airmen and noncommissioned officers basic skills needed in their specialties. Some courses are short, from four to six weeks; others are six or eight months. Attendance is in-residence, usually after basic training or when retraining is approved. At graduation, personnel are usually awarded a 3 skill level designation and then reassigned to a permanent duty station.

2. Specialized formal training is also provided to experienced personnel, who usually have a 5 skill level or higher. There are formal in-resident Air Education and Training Command (AETC) courses, special factory training by a contractor (for example, General Dynamics or McDonnel Douglas), or special training by AETC mobile training teams at the operating unit's location. Information about these programs is outlined in Air Force Catalog 36-2223, *USAF Formal Schools Catalog.*
3. *Field Training Detachment (FTD) courses* are on-site training conducted at base level. These courses use a combination of classroom lectures and hands-on work with equipment. They are primarily for aircraft maintenance personnel and are principally used when there is a change of weapons systems on the base.

**On-the-Job Training Programs.** On-the-job training, most frequently referred to by the familiar acronym OJT, is the most economical way to train personnel. The first phase of the Air Force dual-channel OJT is career knowledge training, which uses guided study of career development courses (CDCs). CDCs are printed texts for each Air Force specialty, written by noncommissioned officers who have broad experience within the specialty. Other reference materials may also be used for specific subjects. In the second phase, job qualification training, trainees, working under the supervision of a trainer, gain hands-on experience in a work environment.

Air Force Form 623, "On-the-Job Training Record," is used to determine an individual's qualifications, identify training needs, and document progress. One is maintained for each airman in grades airman basic through technical sergeant, and for master sergeant through chief master sergeant if they are in a retraining status. In appearance, it looks like a file folder, with fasteners to hold status updates. One of the most important documents in the OJT training record is an Air Force publication known as the Specialty Training Standard (STS). Each specialty has one; it outlines what a trainee is expected to be able to do for that particular job. Once inserted in the training record, the STS is called a job qualification standard (JQS) and is used to record training completed for each task.

To ensure the effectiveness of OJT programs, specific responsibilities have been established. Commanders have the overall responsibility for effective programs. To assist them, the Military Personnel Section (MPS) has an OJT manager who plans, organizes, and directs the overall program for the base. The base OJT manager works closely with OJT managers from each unit (usually at the squadron level). In turn, unit OJT managers advise their immediate commanders and work closely with supervisors, trainers, and trainees. Supervisors select qualified trainers who plan, conduct, and evaluate training. Each trainee is responsible for learning the required skills and attaining appropriate proficiency levels.

The overall success of an OJT program is usually traceable to a concerted team effort. Each individual charged with a responsibility is actively involved and

# Enlisted Education and Training Path

| EDUCATION AND TNG REQUIREMENTS | AVG SEW-ON TIME |
|---|---|

- BASIC MILITARY TRAINING SCHOOL  6 MONTHS

- APPRENTICE TECH SCHOOL = 3 SKILL LEVEL  16 MONTHS

- UPGRADE TO JOURNEYMAN = 5 SKILL LEVEL  36 MONTHS
    - 6 MONTHS DUTY POSITION/APPRENTICE IS REQUIRED BEFORE ENTERING JOURNEYMAN TRAINING
    - MINIMUM 12 MONTHS ON-THE-JOB TRAINING (OJT)
    - COMPLETE APPROPRIATE CDC IF/WHEN AVAILABLE
    - SRA SEW-ON
    - (INTERIM: ALL OF ABOVE)

- AIRMAN LEADERSHIP SCHOOL (ALS)  7.5 YEARS AVERAGE
    - MUST BE A SRA WITH 48 MONTHS TIME IN SERVICE, OR BE A SSGT SELECTEE
    - RESIDENT GRADUATION IS A PREREQUISITE FOR SSGT SEW-ON

- UPGRADE TO CRAFTSMAN = 7 SKILL LEVEL  12.5 YEARS AVERAGE
    - MINIMUM RANK OF SSGT
    - 18 MONTHS OJT
    - FORMAL ADVANCED SKILL TRAINING (TECHNICAL SCHOOL)
    - (INTERIM: UNTIL 7-LEVEL SCHOOLS ARE AVAILABLE, MINIMUM RANK OF SSGT WITH 18 MONTHS OJT)
    - MUST BE 7-LEVEL TO SEW ON TSGT

- NONCOMMISSIONED OFFICER ACADEMY (NCOA)  16 YEARS AVERAGE
    - MUST BE A TSGT OR TSGT SELECTEE*
    - RESIDENT GRADUATION IS A PREREQUISITE FOR MSGT SEW-ON

- USAF SENIOR NCO ACADEMY (SNCOA) 19.2 YEARS AVERAGE
    - MUST BE A SMSGT OR SMSGT SELECTEE*
    - RESIDENT GRADUATION IS A PREREQUISITE FOR CMSGT SEW-ON

- UPGRADE TO SUPERINTENDENT = 9 SKILL LEVEL 21.5 YEARS AVERAGE
    - MINIMUM RANK OF SMSGT
    - MUST BE A RESIDENT SNCOA GRADUATE*
    - (INTERIM: AT SMSGT SEW-ON)

* ACTIVE DUTY ONLY

committed. Collectively, all recognize that quality training programs will have a positive effect on quality of work and ultimately on their unit's mission.

## PROFESSIONAL MILITARY EDUCATION (PME)

PME is provided to members of the enlisted force based on grade, time-in-service, and supervisory duties. Enlisted PME attempts to broaden enlisted members' perspectives beyond the skills of their Air Force specialties in order to increase their knowledge of military studies, communication skills, quality force issues, leadership, and supervisory techniques. The in-resident enlisted PME program consists of three courses, each designed for personnel with a particular grade and experience level.

### Airman Leadership School (ALS)

ALS prepares senior airmen (SrA) to assume supervisory duties. The four-and-a-half-week course offers instruction and practice in leadership and followership, written and oral communication skills, and military citizenship in the Air Force. Students learn to appreciate their role as military supervisors and how they contribute to the overall goals and mission of the Air Force. The major commands establish selection procedures to ensure that SrA who have the growth potential and ability to become effective leaders and supervisors attend this course. This entry-level enlisted PME program is available to SrA after reaching forty-eight months of total active federal military service (TAFMS) or after being selected for promotion to staff sergeant (SSgt). ALS completion is required before assuming the rank of staff sergeant. Graduates of the ALS are authorized to wear the NCO PME Ribbon.

### The Noncommissioned Officers Academy (NCOA)

NCOA is a six-week course to further broaden the leadership and management skills of staff sergeants and technical sergeants. As in ALS, the major commands establish selection procedures. Graduates earn the right to wear the NCO PME Ribbon. They who have graduated from ALS courses are authorized to add a bronze oak leaf cluster to the basic ribbon. NCOA completion is required before assuming the grade of master sergeant (MSgt).

### Senior Noncommissioned Officers Academy (SNCOA)

SNCOA is the highest level of PME available to NCOs. This seven-week course is conducted by Air University at the Gunter Annex of Maxwell AFB, Alabama. The course provides the education necessary for senior NCOs to become more effective leaders and managers during peacetime, as well as times of crisis or conflict. The course includes communicative skills, international relations, national objectives, employment of military force in achieving Air Force objectives, the Air Force role in force application, management, and the effective use of human resources. The course also looks at the individual and the work environment, management concepts and theories, analytical decision making, managerial styles, methods of improving workers' performance, and the application of quality principles. Each year the Air Force Personnel Center (AFPC) identifies master sergeants and senior master sergeant selectees to attend the course. Chief master sergeants (CMSgts) and CMSgt selectees may also volunteer to attend. Graduates earn the right to wear the NCO PME Ribbon and clusters, when appropriate. SNCOA completion is required before assuming the grade of chief master sergeant.

Although some PME requirements may be fulfilled by correspondence, in-residence attendance is more desirable. There are fewer distractions and the learning experience is much more complete because of the formal presentations, feedback, and interaction with other attendees. There is a lot of competition for these courses; the key to being selected is to know and meet the selection criteria in Air Force Instruction 36-2301, *Professional Military Education.* It is also wise to let the decision makers—your supervisors, first sergeant, command chief master sergeant, and commander—know that you really want to attend in-residence.

You can obtain more information about enrolling in a PME correspondence course by contacting the base education office. Enrolling early in your career will broaden your professional knowledge. It is also a positive step that shows initiative. Many successful supervisors view such enrollment as an indication that a person has taken a deeper level of interest in his or her USAF career.

## OFF-DUTY EDUCATION PROGRAMS

Off-duty education services are provided worldwide to all personnel, and usually to dependents also. The focal point on each base is the base education center. These centers also support smaller geographically separated units within their areas of responsibility. The staff usually includes an education services officer, education specialists, guidance counselors, and in some cases, registrars representing colleges and universities. The primary programs include the following:

- *Extension Course Institute (ECI)* voluntary nonresident study courses are offered in three major categories—Career Development Courses (CDCs), Professional Military Education (PME), and specialized courses. Airmen often order CDCs through the education center so that they can get current materials to study for promotion or to pursue an interest in another Air Force Specialty.
- *The Community College of the Air Force (CCAF)* program provides a way for enlisted members to earn an associate in applied science degree in one of more than seventy fields. Each field is directly related to Air Force Specialties in five career areas: aircraft and missile maintenance, electronics and telecommunications, management and logistics, medical, and public and support services. CCAF is accredited by the Commission on Colleges of the Southern Association of Colleges and Schools. Course credits may be gained through an evaluation of military experience, by completing military courses (technical training schools, PME, OJT), or by completing civilian

education programs. This program is a big plus for many airmen because they find that half of their degree requirements can be satisfied by military training they have already completed. For more information, contact your base education office or log onto www.au.af.mil/au/ccaf.

- *Off-duty classes* are offered on base and in surrounding communities by over four hundred accredited colleges and universities. Courses cover a very wide spectrum, leading to a range of degrees: technical certificates, associate degrees (two years), bachelor of arts or science degrees (four years), and graduate degrees, including master's and doctorate programs. In overseas areas, U.S. institutions provide services under contract. Participation in host-nation institutions is also possible. At some locations, courses are provided throughout the day to accommodate personnel on different work shifts.

- *College credit by examination* is available through two programs: the College-Level Examination Program (CLEP) and the Defense Activity for Non-Traditional Education Support (DANTES). Up to sixty hours of college credit may be obtained through these tests, and there is no charge for military personnel.

- *Admissions examinations* for undergraduates can sometimes be scheduled for the American College Testing (ACT) Assessment Program and the Scholastic Aptitude Test (SAT). Graduate admissions tests include the Graduate Record Examination (GRE), the Graduate Management Admissions Test (GMAT), and the Law School Admissions Test (LSAT).

- *The Bootstrap Program* allows airmen who are within four months to one year of completing a college degree to finish the degree at a college or university. When these requests are approved, the airman is placed in a permissive temporary duty (TDY) status. When the degree work is completed, the airman incurs an active-duty service commitment equal to three times the length of the TDY.

- *Education centers* also serve as focal points for information on airman commissioning programs. These are described in chapter 22, "Commissioning Opportunities."

**Funding Off-Duty Education.** While most of the services provided by the education office are furnished at no expense to the military member, there are instances where fees and charges apply, primarily to cover tuition expenses for courses offered by colleges and universities. Several programs provide funding assistance for those who qualify.

*The Air Force Tuition Assistance (TA) Program.* The Air Force Tuition Assistance Program represents the Air Force's commitment to the professional and personal development of its members. Under it, the Air Force will pay 100 percent of the tuition fee for all active-duty military personnel. This is a very popular program. The cost of books and supplies and other fees are not included, however. To receive tuition assistance, obtain Air Force Form 1227, "Authority for Tuition

Assistance—Education Services Program," from the education office. After you fill it out, you and your supervisor must sign the form; return it to the education office before the end of the course registration period.

*Veterans Assistance.* There are three different veterans education assistance programs. The program you qualify for depends on the date that you entered active military service.

The *Vietnam-Era GI Bill,* also referred to as "the old GI Bill," applies to those who came on active duty prior to January 1, 1977. Under this program, the full cost of the tuition fee could be paid. Entitlement to these benefits expired on December 31, 1989. However, one of the provisions of the Montgomery GI Bill (also referred to as "the new GI Bill") is a conversion feature that applies only to Vietnam-Era GI Bill eligibles who were on active duty on October 19, 1984, and had served for three consecutive years starting on July 1, 1985. This conversion process, in most cases, provides a greater monthly benefit over a reduced period of time, especially for those who never used any of their old GI Bill entitlements. Under some circumstances, such as a disability or prisoner-of-war or missing-in-action (POW/MIA) status, the time limits for using entitlements may be extended.

The *Veteran Educational Assistance Program (VEAP)* was established in 1977 as a replacement for the Vietnam-Era GI Bill. Participation under this program was optional. For every dollar invested by a military member, the government contributed $2. This program was canceled on April 1, 1987. The cancellation stops enrollment of new personnel but does not affect entitlements to members who had previously participated.

The *Montgomery GI Bill (MGIB)* affects those who entered active duty after June 30, 1985. Enrollment is voluntary. This program, like VEAP, is a pay reduction program. When a servicemember's pay is reduced by $100 for twelve consecutive months, the Department of Veterans Affairs (VA) provides a generous educational benefit. If you use "regular" MGIB while on active duty, VA will pay you whichever is less: the monthly rate based on tuition and fees for your course(s), or your maximum monthly MGIB rate (basic rate plus any increases for which you may qualify). The basic monthly rates increase on October 1 each year with the Consumer Price Index increase. They may increase at other times by an act of Congress. You can use these benefits while you are in the service after two years of continuous active-duty service. MGIB benefits expire ten years after separation or retirement. Go to your local education office or www.gibill.va.gov for more information.

The Post-9/11 GI Bill provides financial support for education and housing to individuals with at least 90 days of aggregate service on or after September 11, 2001, or individuals discharged with a service-connected disability after 30 days. You must have received an honorable discharge to be eligible for the Post-9/11 GI Bill. The Post-9/11 GI Bill also offers some servicemembers the opportunity to transfer their GI Bill to dependents.

*Scholarships, student loans,* and *partial grants* are often available from federal, state, and private sources, based on individual circumstances, including financial need, academic success, and veteran's survivor and dependent status. For specific information about the options in your area, contact your base education center.

## SUCCEEDING IN ADULT EDUCATION

Most airmen are successful in adult education programs; they attain B grades or higher. There aren't many failures. Unlike high school, attendance isn't mandatory; those who don't want to participate don't have to. Those who do attend learn more efficiently because they have stronger practical reasons for enrolling. Their motivation is self-initiated. They're setting their own goals and preparing for the future. Some attend to become more fully qualified in their present job. Some have decided to broaden into another career. Others enjoy the educational environment and the opportunity to gain knowledge and mix with people who share similar interests. Whatever the reason, they all have one thing in common: They're there because they want to be.

They also bring practical experience to the classroom. Most have had a break from the educational process, and they know that life is much more than textbooks. This provides a frame of reference for the information they are being taught. They know what's important and how they intend to use it.

Right now you're at the crossroads of the past, the present, and the future. Past is past, but the future depends on the present. If you're even vaguely interested in pursuing your education, the best thing to do is to go to the education center. Take a look at what they have to offer. Talk to a counselor, registrar, or education specialist. Enroll in a course that will be interesting but not overwhelming. After you've made a start, move at your own speed in a direction of your choice. Most airmen agree that the first step is the hardest one. After that, it's all downhill. Momentum seems to build with interest in the subject matter, interaction with other students, and the anticipation of completing degree requirements.

One word of caution: Always remember that your value to the Air Force is based primarily on how well you perform in your *present* job. You do want to broaden your horizons, but you don't want to ignore your regular duty performance.

## SOURCES OF ADDITIONAL INFORMATION

Air Force Instruction 36-2201, *Air Force Training Program.*
Air Force Instruction 36-2301, *Developmental Education.*
Air Force Instruction 36-2306, *Voluntary Education Program.*
Air Force Pamphlet 36-2241, *Professional Development Guide.*
Air Force Policy Directive 36-22, *Air Force Military Training.* www.gibill.va.gov.

# 17

# Performance Reports

**THE ENLISTED EVALUATION SYSTEM (EES)**
The Enlisted Evaluation System used by the U.S. Air Force today was first implemented on May 1, 1989. Today's EES is the result of enlisted and officer concerns about the prior Airman Performance Report (APR), which the Air Force had used for over twenty years to evaluate enlisted duty performance.

There are four terms used in this chapter that you should be familiar with: *ratee, rater, indorser,* and *evaluators.* A *ratee* is the servicemember who is being rated on an enlisted performance report or a performance feedback worksheet. A *rater* is a person who writes enlisted performance reports or performance feedback worksheets. The rater is usually the ratee's immediate supervisor (E-4 and above). An *indorser* is usually the rater's rater or another person in the ratee's chain of command. Raters and indorsers are referred to as *evaluators.*

**Major Features of the EES.** The EES includes the following features:
- Formal feedback sessions are mandatory for technical sergeants and below and highly encouraged for master sergeants and above.
- Enlisted Performance Reports (EPRs) are no longer required for most airmen basic, airmen, and airmen first class with less than twenty months' total active federal military service (TAFMS).
- EPR indorsements for technical sergeants and below are capped at the rater's rater.
- The highest final voluntary indorsement on EPRs for master sergeants through chief master sergeants is the senior rater (usually the wing commander or equivalent).
- The first field-grade officer in the rating chain may close out the EPR.
- A new regulation was issued to outline the changes in policy and to prescribe new forms with revised rating scales.

**Benefits for Air Force Members.** The current EES offers three benefits for Air Force members:

1. The performance feedback program increases communication at all levels. Ratees know what their supervisors expect, what their own strengths and weaknesses are, and how to improve.
2. The involvement of senior NCOs and others who are in the immediate supervisory chain is increased. Raters are closer to their ratees and will have direct knowledge of duty performance.
3. The job of producing evaluation reports is made easier with fewer and simpler forms, fewer evaluators, and less need to send reports with justification to higher headquarters. This, in turn, gives supervisors more time to work on their unit's mission.

## THE PERFORMANCE FEEDBACK PROGRAM

Performance feedback is a formal written communication between the ratee and the rater about the ratee's responsibilities and duty performance. It consists of the rater filling out a simple, handwritten form followed by a face-to-face discussion between the rater and the ratee. The original copy of the form is given to the ratee. Raters may keep copies of the form for their own records, for future feedback sessions, and for preparation of performance reports.

The rater must provide performance feedback. He or she is usually responsible for the total job effort and is in the best position to observe the ratee's duty performance on a day-to-day basis. Raters normally have the knowledge and experience necessary to discuss the Air Force's expectations regarding general military factors and the opportunities for maintaining proficiency in one's Air Force Specialty (AFS).

Performance feedback is mandatory for the grades of technical sergeant (TSgt) and below. It is optional, but strongly encouraged, for the grades of master sergeant (MSgt) through chief master sergeant (CMSgt).

**Scheduling Performance Feedback Sessions.** Performance feedback sessions are scheduled at periodic intervals.

- Initial feedback sessions should be held within 60 days after a ratee is assigned a rating official. The new rater should use this session with the ratee to clearly define his or her performance expectations for the upcoming period.
- Follow-up feedback sessions are due approximately 180 days after the initial feedback session. At this time, the rater should discuss performance during the past period of supervision and provide direction and expectations for the future. Follow-up sessions are also provided within 30 days after the completion of an EPR, during which the rater should discuss the performance recorded on the EPR and provide direction and expectations for the new rating period.
- Midcourse feedback sessions for airmen who receive EPRs should be held midway between the date supervision began and the projected EPR close-

## When to Prepare PFWs

| R U L E | A | B | C |
|---------|---|---|---|
|   | If the ratee is | and | then a feedback session is required and must be conducted |
| 1 | a CMSgt or below | has not had an initial feedback session with the current rater | within 60 days of the date supervision began. |
| 2 | an AB, Amn, or A1C (with less than 20 months of TAFMS) | has had an initial feedback session with the current rater | every 180 days or until the rater writes an EPR. |
| 3 | an AB, Amn, or A1C (with 20 or more months of TAFMS) or a SrA through CMSgt | has had an initial feedback session with the current rater | midway between the time supervision began and the planned EPR closeout date (notes 1 and 2). |
| 4 | a CMSgt or below | has had an EPR written without a change of rater | within 60 days after closeout of the EPR. |
| 5 | an AB through CMSgt | requests a feedback session | within 30 days of the request if at least 60 days have passed since the last feedback session. |
| 6 | an AB through CMSgt | the rater determines there is a need for a feedback session | as the rater determines. |

*Notes:*
1. If the ratee is due an annual EPR and the period of supervision is less than 150 days, the rater conducts the feedback session approximately 60 days before the projected EPR closeout date.
2. If the ratee is getting a change of rating official (CRO) EPR and time permits, the rater will hold a feedback session within 60 days, but not later than 30 days of the EPR closeout date.

out date. Such a session will focus on how well the ratee is performing and meeting the expectations and direction established in the initial feedback session. The purpose is to provide the ratee a performance progress report and the opportunity to improve that performance, if necessary, before the EPR is written.

These sessions are scheduled based on the following criteria, as noted in Air Force Instruction 36-2403, *The Enlisted Evaluation System.*

**Performance Feedback Worksheets (PFWs).** Two formats are used to record performance feedback:

- AF Form 931, "Airman Performance Feedback Worksheet," is used when the ratee is in the grade of airman basic through technical sergeant.
- AF Form 932, "NCO Performance Feedback Worksheet," is used when the ratee is in the grade of master sergeant through chief master sergeant.

The accompanying illustrations are copies of the forms used for performance feedback. Section IV differs between the forms because personnel are evaluated in different areas as they assume positions of increased grade and responsibility.

*Section I* is for personal information such as the ratee's name, grade, and unit to which assigned.

*Section II* indicates the type of feedback being conducted, that is, initial, midterm, follow-up, ratee requested, or rater directed.

*Section III* is for listing the major job-specific duties for which the ratee is responsible. The space provided is adequate in most instances. If additional space is needed, continue in *Section V*, Comments.

*Section IV* is for performance feedback. This section incorporates both primary factors and general military factors into one major category. Primary factors are AFS related, and the rater's feedback is generally based on what occurs in the work environment. General military factors focus on characteristics considered essential to military order, image, and tradition. Performance feedback encompasses both of these factors to emphasize how the ratee performs his or her particular job and how the ratee upholds and supports the long-established military traditions, customs, standards, and institutional values. Both are essential considerations in determining overall duty performance.

The rater also has space to add additional factors. Usually, these factors are unique to special duties and locations or may not have been adequately covered in the primary duty or general military factors. Each subheading lists some behaviors that must be evaluated and scored by placing an "X" on the scale in the position that most accurately identifies the ratee's performance. Areas marked to the far left of the sliding scale indicate the ratee needs to work extra hard in these areas. Areas marked to the far right indicate the member is performing quite well and needs to either maintain or slightly improve. Any area marked in between requires discussion to explain its exact meaning to the ratee. Remember, the form is just a tool to help guide the session and facilitate communication between the rater and the ratee. The most important objective is for the ratee to clearly understand the rater's position regarding performance and what direction to take if performance improvement is needed. Space is also provided to explain ideas and to give examples of behaviors noted.

The PFW is not an official record of performance; it is a private communication between the rater and the ratee. In preparing the PFW, the rater prepares and signs it in his or her own handwriting. Typing the form using word-processing equipment is prohibited.

The PFW is designed to assist the ratee in improving his or her performance. As such, the ratee may use the form as he or she chooses. The rater who prepares the PFW may keep a copy of the worksheet for personal use to assist in preparing the next EPR, if applicable, and subsequent feedback sessions. However, the PFW may not be shown to any other individual or used in any personnel actions unless the ratee first introduces it or unless the ratee alleges that the rater did not hold a required feedback session.

Raters should conduct feedback sessions face-to-face. Telephone sessions are conducted only in unusual circumstances, such as when there is a geographical separation and a trip for a face-to-face session is not practical.

## PERFORMANCE FEEDBACK WORKSHEET (AB thru TSGT)

**I. PERSONAL INFORMATION**

| NAME | | | GRADE | | UNIT | |
|---|---|---|---|---|---|---|
| FALISHA A. CARMAN | | | SSgt | | AFOMS/PD | |

| II. TYPES OF FEEDBACK: | INITIAL | MID-TERM | FOLLOW-UP | RATEE REQUESTED | RATER DIRECTED |
|---|---|---|---|---|---|
| | | | | | |

**III. PRIMARY DUTIES**

*Outline specific duties (specialty or assignment).*
*These entries include the most important duties and*
*correspond to the job reflected on the EPR.*

**V. COMMENTS**

*Place a mark on the scale for each behavior that applies. If a particular behavior is not applicable to what the ratee does, write "NA."*

**IV. PERFORMANCE FEEDBACK**

*In Section V, write factual, helpful performance feedback so ratees can improve their duty performance or define their professional development goals. Comments on performance should relate to the placement of the marks in Section IV.*

| | needs significant improvement | needs little or no improvement |
|---|---|---|

**1. PERFORMANCE OF ASSIGNED DUTIES**
- Quality of Work
- Quantity of Work
- Timeliness of Work

**2. KNOWLEDGE OF PRIMARY DUTIES**
- Technical Expertise
- Knowledge of Related Areas
- Applies Knowledge to Duties

**3. COMPLIANCE WITH STANDARDS**
- Dress and Appearance
- Weight
- Fitness
- Customs & Courtesies

**4. CONDUCT/BEHAVIOR ON/OFF DUTY**
- Financial Responsibility
- Support for Organizational Activities
- Respect for Authority
- Maintenance of Government Quarters/Facilities

**5. SUPERVISION/LEADERSHIP**
- Sets and Enforces Standards
- Initiative
- Self Confidence
- Provides Guidance/Feedback
- Fosters Teamwork

**6. INDIVIDUAL TRAINING REQUIREMENTS**
- Upgrade (OJT/CDC)
- Professional Military Education
- Proficiency/Qualification
- Contingency/Mobility/Other

**7. COMMUNICATION SKILLS**
- Verbal
- Written

**8. ADDITIONAL FACTORS TO CONSIDER (i.e., Safety, Security, Human Relations)**

AF FORM 931, 20000101 (EF-V1)                    PREVIOUS EDITION IS OBSOLETE.

**AF Form 931, Performance Feedback Worksheet (AB thru TSgt) (Front)**

**VI. STRENGTHS, SUGGESTED GOALS, AND ADDITIONAL COMMENTS** *(Enlisted Professional Development: EES, Assignments, PME, Mentoring, Career Advice, etc.)*

*Section VI provides space to continue feedback or to help individuals understand their strengths and possible plans for the future. It is also used to continue comments from the front of the form ( Section V).*

| RATEE SIGNATURE | RATER SIGNATURE | DATE |
|---|---|---|
| *Falisha A. Carman* | *Joan A. Smith* | 1 Jul 2011 |

AF FORM 931, 20000101 *(REVERSE) (EF-V1)*

**AF Form 931, Performance Feedback Worksheet (AB thru TSgt) (Reverse)**

## PERFORMANCE FEEDBACK WORKSHEET *(MSGT thru CMSGT)*

### I. PERSONAL INFORMATION

| NAME | GRADE | UNIT | |
|---|---|---|---|
| *HORACE CARTER* | *MSgt* | *AFPC* | |

| II. TYPES OF FEEDBACK: | INITIAL | MID-TERM | FOLLOW-UP | RATEE REQUESTED | RATER DIRECTED |
|---|---|---|---|---|---|

| III. PRIMARY DUTIES | V. COMMENTS |
|---|---|
| *Outline specific duties ( specialty or assignment).* | *Place a mark on the scale for each behavior that applies. If a particular behavior is not applicable to what the ratee does, write "NA."* |
| *These entries include the most important duties and correspond to the job* | |
| *reflected on the EPR.* | |

### IV. PERFORMANCE FEEDBACK

*In Section V, write factual, helpful performance feedback so ratees can improve their duty performance or define their professional development goals. Comments on performance should relate to the placement of the marks in Section IV.*

|  | needs significant improvement | needs little or no improvement |
|---|---|---|
| **1. DUTY PERFORMANCE** | | |
| Quality of Work | ◄─────────────────► | |
| Quantity of Work | ◄─────────────────► | |
| Timeliness of Work | ◄─────────────────► | |
| **2. JOB KNOWLEDGE** | | |
| Technical Expertise | ◄─────────────────► | |
| Able to apply to job | ◄─────────────────► | |
| **3. LEADERSHIP** | | |
| Motivates peers and subordinates | ◄─────────────────► | |
| Maintains discipline | ◄─────────────────► | |
| Sets and enforces standards | ◄─────────────────► | |
| Evaluates | ◄─────────────────► | |
| Plans and organizes work | ◄─────────────────► | |
| Fosters team work | ◄─────────────────► | |
| **4. MANAGERIAL SKILLS** | | |
| Time | ◄─────────────────► | |
| Resources | ◄─────────────────► | |
| **5. JUDGMENT** | | |
| Evaluates situations | ◄─────────────────► | |
| Reaches logical conclusions | ◄─────────────────► | |
| **6. PROFESSIONAL QUALITIES** | | |
| Dedication and preservation of military values | ◄─────────────────► | |
| Integrity | ◄─────────────────► | |
| Loyalty | ◄─────────────────► | |
| **7. COMMUNICATION SKILLS** | | |
| Organizes ideas | ◄─────────────────► | |
| Expresses ideas | ◄─────────────────► | |
| **8. ADDITIONAL FACTORS** *(e.g., Safety, Security, Human Relations)* | | |
| | ◄─────────────────► | |
| | ◄─────────────────► | |
| | ◄─────────────────► | |
| | ◄─────────────────► | |

AF FORM 932, 20000101 *(EF-V1)*          PREVIOUS EDITION IS OBSOLETE.

**AF Form 932, Performance Feedback Worksheet (MSgt thru CMSgt) (Front)**

**VI. STRENGTHS, SUGGESTED GOALS, AND ADDITIONAL COMMENTS** *(Enlisted Professional Development: EES, Assignments, PME, Mentoring, Career Advice, etc.)*

*Section VI provides space to continue feedback or to help individuals understand their strengths and possible plans for the future. Also use it to continue the comments from the front of the form.*

| RATEE SIGNATURE | RATER SIGNATURE | DATE |
|---|---|---|
| *Horace Carter* | *John B. Jones* | 1 Jul 2011 |

AF FORM 932, 20000101 *(REVERSE) (EF-V1)*

**AF Form 932, Performance Feedback Worksheet (MSgt thru CMSgt) (Reverse)**

Since the rater may not introduce the PFW in any proceedings unless the ratee introduces it first, a feedback session that includes discussion of performance, behavior, or conduct that may result in further administrative or judicial action should be recorded on other appropriate forms (e.g., AF Form 174, "Record of Individual Counseling").

**Performance Feedback Sessions.** To prepare for a feedback session, the rater needs to do the following:

1. *Select a time and place.* Sessions should be scheduled in advance so that the rater and the ratee have sufficient preparation time. The place selected should provide a relaxed atmosphere so that both parties can talk comfortably. It should be properly lit, ventilated, and relatively free from distractions and interruptions. The amount of time allowed for a session may vary depending on the needs of the rater and the ratee and the depth of topics to be discussed. As a general rule, sessions will usually be thirty to sixty minutes in duration.

2. *Set an agenda.* This includes a basic outline of topics and the sequence in which they will be discussed.

3. *Plan to discuss strengths and accomplishments* as well as areas that need improvement.

4. *Anticipate pitfalls and plan to avoid them.* When providing feedback, the role of the rater should be that of a coach or a helper, not one of a critic or a superior who has no faults. Some of the pitfalls that the rater should be aware of and try to avoid are as follows:
   - A reluctance to provide or receive feedback.
   - Inadequate planning.
   - Personal bias or stereotyping.
   - Focusing on the person instead of the behavior.
   - Drawing or jumping to conclusions based on limited observations or poor recall.
   - Rating performance as outstanding when it is not.
   - Telling an individual that he or she is the "best" when the individual is not.
   - Giving favorable ratings to an individual who is well liked or unfavorable ratings to an individual who is not.
   - Loss of emotional control.

5. *Prepare the feedback form,* except for the rater's signature and the date, prior to the session.

During the feedback session, the rater should do the following:

1. *Open in a friendly, relaxed manner.* Be sincere and brief and explain the purpose of the session. The approach should be based on accepted standards and the needs of the Air Force. Seek ideas and opinions from the ratee.

2. *Be a good listener.* Pay full attention to what is being said, and if necessary, rephrase your statements or ask direct questions to clarify areas that are

ambiguous. It is also important to be attuned to nonverbal communication, such as eye contact, posture, head nods, and facial expressions.

3. *Consider referrals to agencies that can provide "specialized" assistance,* if potential problems surface during the session that are beyond the scope of performance feedback. For example, assistance is available from chaplains (religious, marital, personal), medical personnel (physical, mental), the Family Support Center, Family Services, the AF Aid Society, the legal office, EOT (equal opportunity and treatment) programs, and the American Red Cross.

4. *Keep the discussion positive and on track.* Give feedback in a manner that communicates acceptance of the ratee as a worthwhile person. Avoid loaded terms that may produce emotional reactions and heightened defenses.

5. *Summarize.* Before the session ends, the rater should take a few moments to review and summarize the key items discussed and to reinforce the goals for the next observation period. A good method of summarizing is to ask the ratee for comments on the discussion to make sure that he or she understands the results of the session. It is important to end on a positive, encouraging, and forward-looking note. One way to do so is to briefly discuss a road map of goals and priorities that the ratee can use for achieving future successes.

6. *In closing, sign and date the performance feedback worksheet and give the original copy to the ratee.*

**Program Controls and Responsibilities.** A variety of responsibilities are assigned at different levels to assure that the spirit and intent of the performance feedback program are met.

The Military Personnel Section (MPS) provides PFW notices to raters and ratees. It also provides the unit with a list of airmen who do not receive EPRs but are due a scheduled feedback session.

Unit commanders administer the performance feedback program for their personnel. In doing so, they periodically canvass raters and ratees to ensure that feedback is being accomplished; review the signed PFW notices on airmen who did not receive EPRs; and consider disciplining and removing from supervisory positions raters who fail to conduct documented feedback sessions.

Each rater's rater is responsible for being familiar with the subordinate's duty performance; periodically querying subordinates to ensure that raters are accomplishing feedback sessions; conducting performance feedback sessions when a subordinate rater is not available because of unusual circumstances or when assuming the subordinate rater's responsibilities; and signing the PFW notice and returning it for the unit commander's review in cases where a ratee does not receive EPRs.

The rater prepares, schedules, and conducts feedback sessions; plans sessions to avoid conflicts with TDY, leave, change of raters, and so forth; provides realistic, uninflated feedback to help the ratee improve duty performance and behavior; conducts feedback to help the ratee improve duty performance and behavior; conducts feedback sessions within thirty days of a ratee's request (*Note:* Raters are not required to conduct more than one documented feedback session per sixty-day period; however, they may do so at their discretion); and signs the PFW notice on airmen who do not receive EPRs and returns it to the unit for review by the commander, who destroys the PFW notice after he or she determines that the feedback session has taken place.

The ratee notifies the rater and, if necessary, the rater's rater when a required feedback session does not take place, and may request additional feedback sessions.

## ENLISTED PERFORMANCE REPORTS (EPRs)
In the majority of cases, Enlisted Performance Reports are prepared for ratees who have twenty or more months of total active federal military service (TAFMS) and have not had a report for at least a year. HQ USAF or a commander can order an EPR in eleven other instances, primarily in cases where there is a change of rater, unsatisfactory performance or conduct, a discharge action, or interruptions in supervision caused by a change of duty status (e.g., extended temporary duty, missing in action, permanent change of station).

The Enlisted Performance Report is probably the single most important document in your personnel record. The EPR provides the Air Force with information on your duty performance and your potential for increased responsibility. When used with other information, it provides a basis for selective retention, promotions, assignments, and retraining.

Three standard forms are prescribed for recording performance:
- AF Form 910, "Enlisted Performance Report (AB thru TSGT)" is used for technical sergeant, staff sergeant, senior airman, airman first class, airman, and airman basic.
- AF Form 911, "Senior Enlisted Performance Report (MSGT thru CMSGT)" is used for master sergeant, senior master sergeant, and chief master sergeant.
- AF Form 77, "Supplemental Evaluation Sheet," is used as a letter of evaluation (LOE), continuation sheet for referral reports, commander's comments or an additional evaluator's indorsement, and Air Force advisor reviews. The same form is used for all grades.

See accompanying illustrations of the forms used. You will see that some sections in the Enlisted Performance Reports (AFForms 910 and 911) differ; personnel are evaluated in different areas as they assume positions of increased grade and responsibility.

**How a Performance Report Is Prepared.** When a performance report is due, the Military Personnel Section (MPS) sends a computer product (commonly referred to as an EPR notice or an EPR shell) to the member's unit of assignment. The rater is encouraged to review this notice with the ratee to ensure that all the information is accurate. The rater then completes the form.

*Section I: "Ratee Identification Data."* All information for this section is provided on the computer product (the EPR notice or shell).

*Section II: "Job Description."* The duty title used should be the one noted on the EPR notice. Since the personnel data system has space limitations, the duty titles on some EPR notices may be abbreviated. These computer abbreviations may be used, but if the entries are not clear they should be spelled out. Under "Key Duties, Tasks, and Responsibilities," a clear description of the ratee's duties should be entered. The description should note the nature of the tasks the ratee performs, the degree of assignment selectivity involved, the scope and level of responsibility, dollar value of projects managed, number of people supervised, and so forth. Additional duties during the reporting period may also be included if they influence the ratings and comments. Jargon and acronyms that obscure rather than clarify the meaning should be avoided.

*Section III: "Performance Assessment."* For each item in Section III, the rater places an "X" in the block that accurately describes the ratee's performance. Additional evaluators review reports to ensure the ratings accurately describe the ratee's performance and that comments are compatible with and support the ratings. Evaluators must return reports with unsupported statements to the rater for additional information or rating reconsideration. Additional evaluators can show disagreement with the rating by marking "non-concur" and making specific comments regarding the exact standards and/or comments with which they disagree.

*Section IV: "Rater Information."* Enter rater identification as of the closeout date. The forms have digital signature and auto-date capability. In the unlikely circumstance that digital signatures cannot be used, sign in reproducible black or blue ink. Do not sign before the closeout date (only on or after). The rater assessment and feedback block will be locked and additional rater signature capability unlocked with the rater's digital signature.

*Section V: "Overall Performance Assessment."* Consider the ratee's readiness for increased rank and responsibility and how he or she compares to others in the same grade and AFSC. The rater places an "X" in the block that best describes the ratee's promotion potential. Raters must not rate people with strong performance records and potential the same as average or weak performers.

*Feedback Certification.* Raters certify performance feedback in this area by entering the date when the most recent feedback was provided. Enter date as DD MMM YYYY. If feedback was not accomplished, state the reason why. If feedback was not required, enter "N/A." Complete this section before the rater digitally signs the form. Do not use the date feedback was provided in conjunction with completion of the evaluation.

## ENLISTED PERFORMANCE REPORT *(AB thru TSgt)*

**I. RATEE IDENTIFICATION DATA** *(Refer to AFI 36-2406 for instructions on completing this form)*

| 1. NAME *(Last, First, Middle Initial)* | 2. SSN | 3. GRADE | 4. DAFSC |
|---|---|---|---|

| 5. ORGANIZATION, COMMAND, LOCATION, AND COMPONENT | 6. PAS CODE | 7. SRID |
|---|---|---|

| 8. PERIOD OF REPORT  From:                    Thru: | 9. NO. DAYS SUPERVISION | 10. REASON FOR REPORT |
|---|---|---|

**II. JOB DESCRIPTION**

| 1. DUTY TITLE | 2. SIGNIFICANT ADDITIONAL DUTY(S) |
|---|---|

3. KEY DUTIES, TASKS, AND RESPONSIBILITIES      *(Limit text to 4 lines)*

**III. PERFORMANCE ASSESSMENT**

1. PRIMARY/ADDITIONAL DUTIES *(For SSgt/TSgt also consider Supervisory, Leadership and Technical Abilities)*

Consider Adapting, Learning, Quality, Timeliness, Professional Growth and Communication Skills    *(Limit text to 4 lines)*

☐ Does Not Meet    ☐ Meets    ☐ Above Average    ☐ Clearly Exceeds

2. STANDARDS, CONDUCT, CHARACTER & MILITARY BEARING *(For SSgt/TSgt also consider Enforcement of Standards and Customs & Courtesies)*

Consider Dress & Appearance, Personal/Professional Conduct On/Off Duty   *(Limit text to 2 lines)*

☐ Does Not Meet    ☐ Meets    ☐ Above Average    ☐ Clearly Exceeds

3. FITNESS *(Maintains Air Force Physical Fitness Standards)* *(For referrals, limit text to 1 line)*

☐ Does Not Meet    ☐ Meets    ☐ Exempt

4. TRAINING REQUIREMENTS *(For SSgt/TSgt also consider PME, Off-duty Education, Technical Growth, Upgrade Training)* Consider Upgrade, Ancillary, OJT and Readiness *(Limit text to 2 lines)*

☐ Does Not Meet    ☐ Meets    ☐ Above Average    ☐ Clearly Exceeds

5. TEAMWORK/FOLLOWERSHIP *(For SSgt/TSgt also consider Leadership, Team Accomplishments, Recognition/Reward Others)* Consider Team Building, Support of Team, Followership *(Limit text to 2 lines)*

☐ Does Not Meet    ☐ Meets    ☐ Above Average    ☐ Clearly Exceeds

6. OTHER COMMENTS *(Consider Promotion, Future Duty/Assignment/Education Recommendations and Safety, Security & Human Relations)* *(Limit text to 2 lines)*

**IV. RATER INFORMATION**

| NAME, GRADE, BR OF SVC, ORGN, COMMAND AND LOCATION | DUTY TITLE | | DATE |
|---|---|---|---|
|  | SSN | SIGNATURE |  |

**AF FORM 910, 20070625**          PREVIOUS EDITIONS ARE OBSOLETE          PRIVACY ACT INFORMATION: The information in this form is FOR OFFICIAL USE ONLY. Protect IAW the Privacy Act of 1974.

**Sample AF Form 910, Enlisted Performance Report (Front)**

| V. OVERALL PERFORMANCE ASSESSMENT | | | RATEE NAME: | | | |
|---|---|---|---|---|---|---|
| Overall Performance During Reporting Period | | | | | | |
| ASSESSMENT | POOR (1) | NEEDS IMPROVEMENT (2) | AVERAGE (3) | ABOVE AVERAGE (4) | TRULY AMONG THE BEST (5) |
| RATER'S ASSESSMENT | ☐ | ☐ | ☐ | ☐ | ☐ |
| ADDITIONAL RATER'S ASSESSMENT | ☐ | ☐ | ☐ | ☐ | ☐ |

Last feedback was performed on: _____   If feedback was not accomplished in accordance with AFI 36-2406, state the reason.

| VI. ADDITIONAL RATER'S COMMENTS *(Limit text to 3 lines)* | ☐ CONCUR | ☐ NON-CONCUR |
|---|---|---|

| NAME, GRADE, BR OF SVC, ORGN, COMMAND AND LOCATION | DUTY TITLE | | DATE |
|---|---|---|---|
| | SSN | SIGNATURE | |

| VII. FUNCTIONAL EXAMINER/AIR FORCE ADVISOR *(Indicate applicable review by marking the appropriate box.)* | ☐ FUNCTIONAL EXAMINER | ☐ AIR FORCE ADVISOR |
|---|---|---|

| NAME, GRADE, BR OF SVC, ORGN, COMMAND AND LOCATION | DUTY TITLE | | DATE |
|---|---|---|---|
| | SSN | SIGNATURE | |

| VIII. UNIT COMMANDER/CIVILIAN DIRECTOR/OTHER AUTHORIZED REVIEWER | ☐ CONCUR | ☐ NON-CONCUR |
|---|---|---|

| NAME, GRADE, BR OF SVC, ORGN, COMMAND AND LOCATION | DUTY TITLE | | DATE |
|---|---|---|---|
| | SSN | SIGNATURE | |

**IX. RATEE'S ACKNOWLEDGEMENT**

I understand my signature does not consitute agreement or disagreement. I acknowledge all required feedback was accomplished during the reporting period and upon receipt of this report.

| SIGNATURE | DATE |
|---|---|

**INSTRUCTIONS**

*Complete this report IAW AFI 36-2406. Reports written by Colonels or civilians (GS-15 or higher, or Supervisory Pay Band 3), do not require an additional rater; however, endorsement by the rater's rater is permitted unless the report is written by a senior rater or the Chief Master Sergeant of the Air Force. When the rater's rater is not at least a MSgt or civilian (GS-07 or higher, or Supervisory Pay Band 1), the additional rater is the next official in the rating chain meeting grade requirements. An overall rating of 2 or negative comments require the EPR to be referred IAW AFI 36-2406. Rationale for any additional evaluator nonconcurring with an overall rating must be included. Section VIII Reviewer nonconcurrence must be included on an AF Form 77, Letter of Evaluation. If ratee is deployed, provide copy and feedback via e-mail/telecon.*

**PRIVACY ACT STATEMENT**

AUTHORITY: *Title 10 United States Code, Section 8013 and Secretary of the Air Force and Executive Order 9397, 22 November 1943.*

PURPOSE: *Information is needed for verification of the individual's name and Social Security Number (SSN) as captured on the form at the time of rating.*

ROUTINE USES: *None.* RATIONALE: *This information will not be disclosed outside DoD channels.*

DISCLOSURE: *Disclosure is mandatory; SSN is used for positive identification.*

| AF FORM 910, 20070625 | PREVIOUS EDITIONS ARE OBSOLETE | PRIVACY ACT INFORMATION: The information In this form is FOR OFFICIAL USE ONLY. Protect IAW the Privacy Act of 1974. |
|---|---|---|

**Sample AF Form 910, Enlisted Performance Report (Reverse)**

| ENLISTED PERFORMANCE REPORT *(MSgt thru CMSgt)* | | | |
|---|---|---|---|

**I. RATEE IDENTIFICATION DATA** *(Refer to AFI 36-2406 for instructions on completing this form)*

| 1. NAME *(Last, First, Middle Initial)* | 2. SSN | 3. GRADE | 4. DAFSC |
|---|---|---|---|

| 5. ORGANIZATION, COMMAND, LOCATION, AND COMPONENT | 6. PAS CODE | 7. SRID |
|---|---|---|

| 8. PERIOD OF REPORT<br>From:                                    Thru: | 9. NO. DAYS SUPERVISION | 10. REASON FOR REPORT |
|---|---|---|

**II. JOB DESCRIPTION**

| 1. DUTY TITLE | 2. SIGNIFICANT ADDITIONAL DUTY(S) |
|---|---|

3. KEY DUTIES, TASKS, AND RESPONSIBILITIES    *(Limit text to 4 lines)*

**III. PERFORMANCE ASSESSMENT**

**1. PRIMARY DUTIES**

Consider Quality, Quantity, Timeliness, Technical Knowledge, Leading, Managing and Supervising  *(Limit text to 4 lines)*

☐ Does Not Meet    ☐ Meets    ☐ Above Average    ☐ Clearly Exceeds

**2. STANDARDS: ENFORCEMENT AND PERSONAL ADHERENCE, CONDUCT, CHARACTER, MILITARY BEARING & CUSTOMS AND COURTESIES**

Consider Dress & Appearance, Personal/Professional Conduct On/Off Duty  *(Limit text to 2 lines)*

☐ Does Not Meet    ☐ Meets    ☐ Above Average    ☐ Clearly Exceeds

**3. FITNESS** (Maintains Air Force Physical Fitness Standards)  *(For referrals, limit text to 1 line)*

☐ Does Not Meet    ☐ Meets    ☐ Exempt

**4. RESOURCE MANAGEMENT AND DECISION MAKING**

Consider Efficiency, Judgment, Setting and Meeting Goals  *(Limit text to 2 lines)*

☐ Does Not Meet    ☐ Meets    ☐ Above Average    ☐ Clearly Exceeds

**5. TRAINING, EDUCATION, OFF-DUTY EDUCATION, PME, PROFESSIONAL ENHANCEMENT AND COMMUNICATION**

Consider Providing, Supporting and Personal Growth  *(Limit text to 2 lines)*

☐ Does Not Meet    ☐ Meets    ☐ Above Average    ☐ Clearly Exceeds

**6. LEADERSHIP/TEAM BUILDING/FOLLOWERSHIP/MENTORSHIP**

Consider Team Accomplishments, Leveraging Personal Experiences and Community Support, Recognition/Reward for Others   *(Limit text to 2 lines)*

☐ Does Not Meet    ☐ Meets    ☐ Above Average    ☐ Clearly Exceeds

**7. OTHER COMMENTS**  (Consider Promotion, Future Duty/Assignment/Education Recommendations, Safety, Security & Human Relations)   *(Limit text to 2 lines)*

**IV. RATER INFORMATION**

| NAME, GRADE, BR OF SVC, ORGN, COMMAND AND LOCATION | DUTY TITLE | | DATE |
|---|---|---|---|
|  | SSN | SIGNATURE |  |

AF FORM 911, 20070625          PREVIOUS EDITIONS ARE OBSOLETE          PRIVACY ACT INFORMATION: The information in this form is FOR OFFICIAL USE ONLY. Protect IAW the Privacy Act of 1974.

**Sample AF Form 911, Senior Enlisted Performance Report (Front)**

| V. OVERALL PERFORMANCE ASSESSMENT Overall Performance During Reporting Period | | | RATEE NAME: | | |
|---|---|---|---|---|---|
| ASSESSMENT | POOR (1) | NEEDS IMPROVEMENT (2) | AVERAGE (3) | ABOVE AVERAGE (4) | TRULY AMONG THE BEST (5) |
| RATER'S ASSESSMENT | ☐ | ☐ | ☐ | ☐ | ☐ |
| ADDITIONAL RATER'S ASSESSMENT | ☐ | ☐ | ☐ | ☐ | ☐ |

Last feedback was performed on: _____   If feedback was not accomplished in accordance with AFI 36-2406, state the reason.

**VI. ADDITIONAL RATER'S COMMENTS** *(Limit text to 3 lines)*     ☐ CONCUR     ☐ NON-CONCUR

| NAME, GRADE, BR OF SVC, ORGN, COMMAND AND LOCATION | DUTY TITLE | | DATE |
|---|---|---|---|
| | SSN | SIGNATURE | |

**VII. REVIEWER'S COMMENTS** *(Limit text to 3 lines)*     ☐ CONCUR     ☐ NON-CONCUR

| NAME, GRADE, BR OF SVC, ORGN, COMMAND AND LOCATION | DUTY TITLE | | DATE |
|---|---|---|---|
| | SSN | SIGNATURE | |

| VIII. FINAL EVALUATORS POSITION | IX. TIME-IN-GRADE ELIGIBLE |
|---|---|
| ☐ SENIOR RATER | N/A for CMSgt or CMSgt Selectee |
| ☐ SENIOR RATER'S DEPUTY | ☐ N/A |
| ☐ INTERMEDIATE LEVEL | ☐ YES |
| ☐ LOWER LEVEL | ☐ NO |

**X. FUNCTIONAL EXAMINER/AIR FORCE ADVISOR**
*(Indicate applicable review by marking the appropriate box)*     ☐ FUNCTIONAL EXAMINER     ☐ AIR FORCE ADVISOR

| NAME, GRADE, BR OF SVC, ORGN, COMMAND AND LOCATION | DUTY TITLE | | DATE |
|---|---|---|---|
| | SSN | SIGNATURE | |

**XI. UNIT COMMANDER/CIVILIAN DIRECTOR/OTHER AUTHORIZED REVIEWER**     ☐ CONCUR     ☐ NON-CONCUR

| NAME, GRADE, BR OF SVC, ORGN, COMMAND AND LOCATION | DUTY TITLE | | DATE |
|---|---|---|---|
| | SSN | SIGNATURE | |

**XII. RATEE'S ACKNOWLEDGEMENT**

I understand my signature does not constitute agreement or disagreement. I acknowledge all required feedback was accomplished during the reporting period and upon receipt of this report.

| SIGNATURE | DATE |
|---|---|
| | |

**PRIVACY ACT STATEMENT**
AUTHORITY: Title 10, United States Code, Section 8013 and Executive Order 9397, 22 November 1943.
PURPOSE: Information is needed for verification of the individual's name and Social Security Number (SSN) as captured on the form at the time of the rating.
ROUTINE USES: None. RATIONALE: This information will not be disclosed outside DoD channels.
DISCLOSURE: Disclosure is mandatory; SSN is used for positive identification.

AF FORM 911, 20070625     PREVIOUS EDITIONS ARE OBSOLETE     PRIVACY ACT INFORMATION: The information in this form is FOR OFFICIAL USE ONLY. Protect IAW the Privacy Act of 1974.

**Sample AF Form 911, Senior Enlisted Performance Report (Reverse)**

*Section VI: "Additional Rater's Comments."* Use this section to support the rating decision and comment on the ratee's overall performance and performance-based potential as compared to others in the same grade. When agreeing with the report, mark the "concur" block. Use bullet format to provide comments that add meaning and are compatible with the rating in Section VI. Do not repeat comments provided in the previous section. The additional rater must be the rater's rater unless he or she does not meet grade requirements. The rater and additional rater should discuss disagreements, if any, when preparing reports. Prior evaluators are first given an opportunity to change the evaluation. However, they should not change the evaluation just to satisfy the evaluator who disagrees. If, after discussion, the disagreement remains, the disagreeing evaluator marks the "non-concur" block and comments on each item with which he or she disagrees.

*Additional Rater Identification.* Additional raters may be assigned after the closeout date. For evaluators assigned on or before the closeout date, enter identification data as of the closeout; for evaluators subsequently assigned, enter identification data as of the signature date. The forms have digital signature and auto-date capability. In the unlikely circumstance that digital signatures cannot be used, sign in reproducible black or blue ink. Do not sign before the closeout date (only on or after). The additional rater assessment block will be locked with the additional rater's signature. On the AF Form 911, the reviewer's block will also be unlocked with the additional rater's digital signature.

*AF Form 910, Section VII, and AF Form 911, Section X, Functional Examiner/Air Force Advisor.* When the final evaluator on an EPR is not an Air Force officer or Department of the Air Force official, an Air Force advisor will be designated to advise raters on matters pertaining to Air Force performance reports. For EPRs on TSgts and below, the Air Force advisor will be a MSgt or above. For EPRs on MSgt through CMSgt, the Air Force advisor will be a Major or above. The Air Force advisor will not change any statement or rating on the performance report. The advisor may use the AF Form 77 to provide clarification regarding ratee duty performance, according to AFI 36-2406, and attach it to the performance report. An Air Force advisor must have, or be able to obtain, knowledge of the ratee, be higher in grade than the ratee, and when feasible, be equal to or higher in grade than the final evaluator.

*AF Form 911, Section VII, Reviewer's Comments.* Do not use Section VII if Section VI is not completed. If the additional rater is the final evaluator, enter "This section not used." If used, this section must contain comments in bullet format. The reviewer will mark the "concur" or "non-concur" block, and make appropriate comments (if applicable). Senior raters may endorse EPRs:

• To differentiate between individuals with similar performance records as both ratings and endorsement levels influence those using the AF Form 911 to make personnel decisions.

• To meet the minimum grade requirement to close out the report.

• When the ratee meets the TIG requirements for promotion.

• When the ratee is a CMSgt or a CMSgt-selectee.

*AF Form 910, Section VIII, and AF Form 911, Section XI, Commander's Review.* In the commander's review (Section VIII, AF Form 910, and Section XI, AF Form 911), the unit or squadron section commander influences report quality, removes exaggerations, identifies inflated ratings, and provides information to evaluators for finalizing reports. If the commander agrees with the report, he or she marks the "concur" block and digitally signs in the space provided. Comments should not be provided unless the commander disagrees with a previous evaluator, refers the report, or is named as the evaluator in the referral memorandum. If the commander disagrees with the report, he or she provides reasons for disagreement on AF Form 77. Commanders who are part of the rating chain will fill out and sign both the commander's review section and the appropriate evaluator's section, meaning they will sign the report twice. The two signatures serve separate purposes, one as an evaluator regarding duty performance, and one as a commander regarding quality review. Enlisted personnel authorized to perform the commander's review must include the words "Commander," "Commandant," or "Detachment/Flight Chief" in the signature block.

*AF Form 911, Section VIII, Final Evaluators Position.* The final evaluator completes Section VIII by placing an "X" in the appropriate block for the level of endorsement.

*AF Form 911, Section IX, Time-in-Grade (TIG) Eligible.* Section IX pertains to TIG eligibility for senior rater endorsement—not the ratee's actual promotion eligibility as of the closeout date. Using information extracted from the EPR notice, the rater completes Section IX before forwarding the EPR for additional endorsement. TIG does not apply to CMSgts, CMSgtselectees, or reservists. SMSgt-selectees are not eligible for senior rater endorsement because they are not eligible for TIG for the next promotion cycle. AFI 36-2406 explains TIG eligibility.

*AF Form 910, Section IX, and AF Form 911, Section XII, Ratee's Acknowledgement.* The rater is required to conduct face-to-face feedback in conjunction with issuing the evaluation. The EPR serves as the feedback form. Do not use a PFW.

***Other Considerations.*** Enlisted Performance Reports, attachments to reports, referral letters, or indorsements to a referral letter should never contain classified information. If an entry would result in the release of classified material, the word *classified* must be used in place of the entry.

All marks (Xs) and signatures must be made only in black or dark blue ink. Most organizations prefer black, as other colors do not reproduce well on office copiers.

A referral report is an EPR that contains a "Does Not Meet Standards" in any block in Section III, or in which the ratee receives a "Poor" (overall rating "1") or "Needs Improvement" (overall rating "2") in Section V. Also, an EPR must be referred if it includes comments that are derogatory in nature or imply or refer to behavior that does not meet minimum acceptable standards of personal conduct, character, or integrity. The rater should ensure consistency among performance factors, ratings, and comments.

An evaluator whose ratings or comments cause a report to become a referral report must give the ratee a chance to comment on the report. Although a report may be referred several times during processing, an evaluator will not normally refer the report more than once. This, however, does not include reports referred again to allow the ratee the opportunity to rebut a report that, after initial referral, was corrected or changed before becoming a matter of record. Additionally, a report will be referred more than once when a subsequent evaluator gives additional referral ratings or comments. Referral procedures are established to allow the ratee to respond to items that make a report referral before it becomes a matter of record.

## WHEN YOU PREPARE REPORTS

You can think about performance reports from two perspectives: the ones written on you and the ones you write on airmen you supervise. When you are doing the writing, make sure you know the difference between a poor EPR and a good one.

**Poorly Written Reports.** Poorly prepared performance reports can have an adverse effect on people's promotions and assignments. What makes a poor EPR? There are three common problem areas, all related to the written comments on the reverse side of the form:

1. *The contents are weak.* Facts and *specific* achievements are in short supply. Statements are much too general and are routinely filled with flowery adjectives. Some raters compile a report by extracting general statements from previous reports they've written—often referred to as the cut-and-paste method. They feel that if it was accepted before, it probably will be again.

2. *The writing itself is poor.* Sentences are long and rambling. Imprecise words are used. For example, saying someone is "aware of" or "accepts" a responsibility can leave doubt about whether the individual actively pursues or supports the responsibility. Or, raters may say that an airman has "ability" or "capability," but they may not say *how* or *to what extent* an airman uses it. Undefined abbreviations can confuse someone from another career field (for example, a promotion board member from another Air Force Specialty).

3. *Insufficient quality-control procedures are used.* Some raters have low standards: "It's just another piece of paper." Some supervisors don't return poor products for rework, either because they don't want to offend the writer or because they're behind and don't want the report to be late. Some reports have obvious errors and omissions (for example, not mentioning a specific achievement or award). By all means watch out for typographical errors, which detract from the overall effectiveness of the report. Sometimes they can even damage the credibility of the person being discussed. For example, imagine an NCO who "works programs with command

impact with *out* [should be *our*] maintenance contemporaries at the major command level."

**Well-Written Reports.** Having high marks on the front side of the report is where the rating starts. In today's Air Force a great number of airmen get good ratings—a commendable achievement. At the same time, it's important to look closely at the written comments on the reverse side. What's said there will have the greatest overall impact, especially for placement in key positions and promotions to the senior grades.

To provide a well-written and comprehensive report, the first thing you need to do is organize your information. Start by reflecting on the individual's duty description, but do not simply recopy it. Tell how the individual performed and cite specific examples to support your views. Think about personnel (supported or supervised), special projects, innovative techniques, plans, inspection results, aircraft, deployments and exercises, weapons, equipment (acquired or operated), sorties, and resources (value in dollar amounts). Define the scope of the programs implemented and the positive effect on the Air Force mission.

Use direct quotes: The Inspector General stated, "Management of this function was the best observed in the command during the most recent two-year period." Numbers provide depth to your descriptions: "She was responsible for a $2.3 million annual budget." "During January and February, his crew processed sixteen J-79 jet engines and obtained a 97 percent utilization rate."

List exercises and deployments the individual supported: name, location, and level (unit, wing, major command, or joint service). For example, "Sergeant Jones was personally selected to support OPERATION VALIANT, a joint exercise that involved forces from six allied nations." Note any new procedures or innovative techniques the individual developed that have potential for use at other locations. "Sergeant Smith designed a fuel-saving device for use on the ZX aircraft. Its use was approved by headquarters and its implementation resulted in savings of $4.1 million annually at six other bases."

Describe positive aspects of the individual's performance that deserve special note. Some themes you may wish to expand on include the following:

Ability to perform (under pressure or competitive conditions)
Appearance and image
Communicative skills (writing and speaking)
Dependability (reliability and integrity)
Initiative and willingness to accept responsibility
Instructing or training (ability to convey complex tasks)
Judgment and common sense (ability to make sound decisions)
Leadership (sets the example for others to follow)
Loyalty (to mission, commander, peers, subordinates)
Organizational ability (attention to detail)
Self-confidence and pride in work
Tact and diplomacy
Team player (inspires respect and confidence in others)
Technical expertise and competence in career field

If you note recommended improvement areas, clearly specify whether references are to serious deficiencies, faults, bad habits, or occasional tendencies. Indicate what progress, if any, has occurred before preparing the report: "This subject has been discussed with him and a marked improvement noted." Comment on any special training or courses of instruction that the ratee completed or actively participated in. Indicate whether participation was in-residence or by correspondence. Also note off-duty education, such as college courses or the Community College of the Air Force. Emphasize progress being made, not merely enrollment in a course. These comments reflect initiative and are viewed very favorably, especially by promotion boards selecting personnel for senior grades.

If applicable, comment on the manner in which the ratee discharges his or her on-the-job (OJT) training responsibilities, whether as an OJT supervisor, trainer, or trainee.

Recommendation for suggested assignments should be consistent with the individual's AFSC, experience, and performance; it should also be timed appropriately, based on the person's grade. This section is especially important for staff sergeants and above because their records are often reviewed at new duty locations; it could determine whether they are selected to be a shop chief, branch chief, or policy maker at an intermediate headquarters or a major command. This section is also used to recommend personnel for specific special-duty assignments: "Sergeant Doe is exceptionally well qualified to serve as a military training instructor (MTI)."

**The Writing Phase.** After you have gathered all the information, it's time to move into the writing phase. The goal is to put together an accurate, factual, and effective product. One of the recommended ways to do this is to use the "decorated cake approach." The "cake" consists of *specific* facts, achievements, and comments about the ratee. "Icing" consists of commonly used "one-liners" with lots of adjectives and adverbs. Too much "icing" can do more harm than good. When you write the report, make the cake first, then apply the icing. You can also look at it from another angle: Eliminate the icing and see how much cake is left.

Your first draft might look something like this:

> SSgt Marvel is an outstanding noncommissioned officer and maintenance specialist whose organization, planning, and steadfastness during critical situations have been a key factor in the accomplishment of the squadron mission. Regardless of the tasking, his performance has been consistently superior. This NCO has had a significant impact on all areas of the unit from unit administration to daily maintenance. He completed a staff study that identified deficiencies in aircrew scheduling. He has consistently increased effectiveness and significantly improved overall unit operations. SSgt Marvel always strives to improve his professional qualities and recently completed 40 percent of the off-duty education requirements for a bachelor's degree.

Now here it is without the icing:

SSgt Marvel completed a staff study that identified deficiencies in air-crew scheduling and recently completed 40 percent of the off-duty education requirements for a bachelor's degree.

Here's a rule of thumb: If you can change the person's duty title (for example, from aircraft maintenance specialist to medic) and the report still makes sense, it probably needs to be rewritten.

## PLANNING AHEAD: FOUR FINAL TIPS

1. Always know when your next report is due. If you write reports on other airmen, you should know when theirs are due too.
2. Keep track of accomplishments—yours and theirs. When the time for a report comes, your supervisor may ask for input, and you may want to ask the airmen you supervise for input. A short handwritten note, including such items as primary achievements, additional duties, educational accomplishments, off-duty activities, complimentary reports, or special recognition, is sufficient.
3. Take time to write. Get your thoughts on paper, then revise, edit, and rewrite until you are pleased with the product. As a general rule, you should spend as much time on someone else's report as you would like your rater to spend on yours. You should also allow processing time for temporary duty assignments, leave, and indorsements.
4. Submit reports on time. This keeps everyone in the rating chain happy. Late reports can be an administrative headache and a source of embarrassment to the unit concerned. In extreme cases, they can result in missed or unwarranted promotions.

## SOURCES OF ADDITIONAL INFORMATION

Air Force Instruction 36-2406, *Officer and Enlisted Evaluation Systems.* This directive establishes Air Force policy for enlisted and officer personnel who are on active duty in the USAF and in the USAF Reserve (USAFR). It applies to all major commands (MAJCOMs), field operating agencies (FOAs), direct reporting units (DRUs), and other activities of the Air Force. It does not apply to the Air National Guard. It tells how to implement the spirit and intent of the evaluation programs and includes guidance about new forms and rating criteria.

AFPAM 36-2241V1, *Professional Development Guide.*

Personnel in your immediate chain of command (your supervisor and your unit's EPR monitor, first sergeant, and commander) can provide the best information about submission times and levels of indorsements.

# 18

# Promotion Systems

News travels fast when promotion time comes around. Sometimes it's good news:
"I got my promotion line number!"
"Congratulations!"
"The commander and first sergeant came around to give me my new set of stripes!"
"When's the party?"

Sometimes it's not so good:
"I got passed over again."
"It's the system, you know; it's just not fair."
"Bob's not saying very much; he must not have made it."
"The test asked questions about things I haven't even heard about in my career field."

Everyone wants to be promoted. There are many benefits, some big, some small. To many people promotion means a sense of self-satisfaction and achievements. To others it can mean increased opportunity or responsibility. And, of course, it also means extra dollars and cents, which can always be put to good use.

## USAF PROMOTION POLICY
Promotions are conducted every year, based on the need to fill USAF requirements for specific grades within the ceilings. Promotions fill "grade vacancies" caused by changes in the status of other airmen, for reasons such as discharges, separations, retirements, demotions, deaths, and alterations to the annual grade ceilings. Promotions to the grades of senior airman through chief master sergeant are affected each fiscal year by monetary and statutory constraints. By law, the top two enlisted grades for chief master sergeant and senior master sergeant are limited to 1 and 2 percent, respectively, of the total number authorized for the enlisted force. Promotions to airman and airman first class are not limited by grade ceilings; personnel are promoted when they meet basic eligibility requirements.

With grade ceilings in mind, the Air Force determines how many airmen can be promoted each fiscal year. Then it's a matter of selecting those who have demonstrated outstanding performance and potential for handling increased responsibility. The selection process differs by grade. Selection for promotion to airman, airman first class, and senior airman is done on a fully qualified basis (completion of time-in-service or time-in-grade requirements, completion of training requirements, and recommendation by the airman's unit commander). Competition for promotion to staff sergeant, technical sergeant, and master sergeant falls under two different programs: the Weighted Airman Promotion System (WAPS) and the Stripes for Exceptional Performers (STEP) program. The promotion system for the top two enlisted grades, senior master sergeant and chief master sergeant, has two phases: the first is a review of weighted factors similar to the WAPS program, and the second is a score awarded by a central evaluation board at the Air Force Manpower Personnel Center (AFMPC) after a review of the candidate's promotion folder.

## PROMOTION TO AIRMAN AND AIRMAN FIRST CLASS

Air Force members are promoted to airman (Amn) and airman first class (A1C) on a noncompetitive basis as long as they are eligible, fully qualified, and recommended by their unit commander. As a general rule, an airman basic (AB) must have six months' time-in-grade (TIG) and time-in-service (TIS) to be eligible for promotion to airman. An airman must have ten months' TIG to be eligible for promotion to airman first class. An exception occurs when a member's enlistment agreement guarantees a promotion to airman or airman first class; in this case the promotion becomes effective the day after graduation from basic military training.

## PROMOTION TO SENIOR AIRMAN

Promotion to senior airman (SrA) depends on vacant positions caused by promotions, separations, discharges, and so on. AFMPC then computes the number of openings and establishes a promotion quota, then announces a date of rank (DOR) limit for all airmen first class. Those who meet the DOR cutoff are promoted on a fully qualified basis on the first day of the next month as long as they meet the following eligibility conditions: a 5 skill level (or a 3 level when no 5 level exists in their AFSC); either thirty-six months TIS and twenty months TIG or twenty-eight months TIG, whichever occurs first; and recommendation by the promotion authority.

An airman first class can also compete for early advancement to senior airman under the Below-the-Zone (BTZ) Promotion Program. This opportunity comes only once, usually six months before normal promotion time. To compete for a BTZ promotion, airmen must first meet all the eligibility criteria for normal promotion. They compete with other nominees in either a unit (if the unit has a large number of nominees) or a central base selection board (for smaller units with fewer numbers of nominees). In selecting those for BTZ promotion, commanders and board members will consider recommendations from supervisors, past performance reports, and supplementary data.

The emphasis will be on promoting top-quality personnel who have clearly demonstrated potential for assuming increased grade and responsibility. If the selection boards feel the quality is not there, they are not required to promote those nominated just to meet the full quota. In some cases, nominees are required to personally meet a formal selection board similar to that described in chapter 10, "Awards, Decorations, and Recognition Programs." This process is preferred by many selection board members because it permits personal observation and avoids the promoting of personnel sight unseen.

## PROMOTIONS TO THE GRADES OF STAFF SERGEANT THROUGH MASTER SERGEANT

Airmen are promoted to the grades of staff sergeant (SSgt) through master sergeant (MSgt) under one of two programs: the Weighted Airman Promotion System (WAPS) or the Stripes for Exceptional Performers (STEP) program. Both programs evolved out of the need for an equitable, objective, and readily understood promotion system that provides feedback to those concerned.

In the WAPS program, each eligible person receives a scorecard explaining how they fared in each weighted area. In the STEP program, only a very small number of nominees are selected for promotion. The authority to grant these stripes is restricted to senior Air Force officers who command large organizations. They base their decisions on recommendations forwarded through the chain of command. In every case those nominated must have clearly demonstrated that their performance was consistently outstanding and of a magnitude warranting immediate promotion to the next highest grade.

As noted in chapter 16, Airman Leadership School and NCO Academy attendance are necessary for promotion to NCO ranks.

## THE WEIGHTED AIRMAN PROMOTION SYSTEM (WAPS)

WAPS is the primary program used to select airmen for promotion to the grades of staff sergeant, technical sergeant, and master sergeant. The system gives credit and scores to six weighted factors:

1. A Specialty Knowledge Test (SKT) for the career field.
2. A Promotion Fitness Examination (PFE), which tests general Air Force knowledge.
3. Credit for time-in-service (TIS).
4. Credit for time-in-grade (TIG).
5. Credit for decorations awarded.
6. A numerical score for the average ratings received on performance reports.

Analysis of these six weighted factors helps in selecting the airmen who have demonstrated potential for increased responsibility, consistent with grade ceilings and budget limitations.

The number of promotions to any grade is based on the total Air Force vacancies in that grade. You will compete for worldwide vacancies with all other airmen

## TIS and TIG Requirements, Promotion Eligibility Cutoff Dates, and Test Cycles for Promotion to Amn Through CMSgt

| L I N E | A | B | C | D | E |
|---|---|---|---|---|---|
| | Grade | TIS | TIG | PECD | Test Cycle |
| 1 | Amn | — | 6 months | NA | NA |
| 2 | A1C | — | 10 months | NA | NA |
| 3 | SrA | 36 months | 20 months or 28 months | NA | NA |
| 4 | SSgt | 3 years | 6 months | 31 Mar | Apr–Jun |
| 5 | TSgt | 5 years | 23 months | 31 Dec | Jan–Mar |
| 6 | MSgt | 8 years | 24 months | 31 Dec | Jan–Mar |
| 7 | SMSgt | 11 years | 20 months | 30 Sep | Oct |
| 8 | CMSgt | 14 years | 21 months | 31 Jul | Aug |

who have the same grade and Control Air Force Specialty Code (CAFSC). This ensures equitable consideration by career field, since each career field receives the same percentage promotion quota. For example, if 10 percent of all airmen can be promoted to the next higher grade, then at least 10 percent of the airmen eligible in every CAFSC will be promoted. If two thousand security police airmen are eligible and the promotion rate is 10 percent, then two hundred will be promoted. If it is a smaller career field of only one hundred eligible airmen (such as radiologists from medical facilities), then ten airmen will be promoted.

Once the Air Force determines how many will be promoted in each career field, a promotion cutoff score is set. This is determined by the score of the last promotee; for example, if two hundred security police personnel are selected for promotion, the top two hundred with the highest scores will be promoted and the score of the airman who placed two hundredth amongst the selectees will be used as a cutoff. In case of tie scores, everyone with the same cutoff score will be promoted, even if it means promoting slightly more than the selection percentage. When the promotion list is released, everyone (selectees and nonselectees) gets a score notice that explains strong and weak areas and relative standings (for example: total number eligible in your AFSC, two thousand; your standing among other selectees, two hundred).

# Minimum Eligibility Requirements for Promotion (Note 1)

| | A | B | C | D | E | F |
|---|---|---|---|---|---|---|
| **R** **U** **L** **E** | If promotion is to the grade of (note 2) | and the PAFSC as of PECD is at the | and time in current grade computed on the first day of the month before the promotions are normally made in the cycle is | and the TAFMS on the first day of the last month of the promotion cycle is (note 3) | and the member has | then |
| **1** | SrA | 3 level (note 4) | not applicable | 1 year | | the airman is eligible for promotion if recommended, in writing, by the promotion authority. He or she must serve on active duty in enlisted status as of the PECD, serve in continuous active duty until the effective date of promotion, and not in a condition listed in AFI 36-2502, table 1.1, *Determining Ineligibility for Promotion*, on or after the PECD. The individual must be in Promotion Eligibility Status (PES) code X on effective date of promotion (note 6). |
| **2** | SSgt | 5 level (note 4) | 6 months ⋅ | 3 years | | |
| **3** | TSgt | 7 level (note 4) | 23 months effective Cycle 95A6 | 5 years | | |
| **4** | MSgt | 7 level | 24 months | 8 years | | |
| **5** | SMSgt | 7 level (note 4) | 20 months | 11 years | 8 years cumulative enlisted service (TEMSD) creditable for basic pay (note 5) | |
| **6** | CMSgt | 9 level (note 4) | 21 months | 14 years | 10 years cumulative enlisted service (TEMSD) creditable for basic pay (note 5) | |

*Notes:*

1. Use this table to determine standard minimum eligibility requirements for promotion consideration. HQ USAF may announce additional eligibility requirements. The individual must serve on enlisted active duty and have continuous active duty as of promotion eligibility cutoff date (PECD).

2. The high year of tenure policy applicable as of PECD may affect promotion eligibility in grades SrA and above.

3. Use years of satisfactory service for retirement in place of TAFMSD to determine promotion eligibility for Air National Guard and Air Force Reserve airmen ordered to active duty under a mobilization. Mobilized airmen are eligible for any cycle that has a PECD at least 60 calendar days after mobilization. For promotion to SrA an airman must serve on active duty at least 60 calendar days before the effective date promotion incrementing starts for that cycle.

4. Airmen must meet skill level requirements by the effective date of promotion for SrA. Airmen must meet skill level requirements by the PECD for SSgt. SSgts test and compete for promotion to TSgt if they have a 5-skill level as of PECD; however, they must have a 7-skill level before promotion. MSgts and SMSgts must meet minimum skill level requirements listed above. In some cases, commanders may waive this to allow them to compete for promotion.

5. Service in a commissioned, warrant, or flight officer status is creditable for pay. Such service does not count for this requirement (38 Comptroller General 598). You may consider a promotion for airmen who meet this requirement on the first day of the last month promotions are normally made in the cycle. Actual promotion does not occur earlier than the first day of the month following the month the airman completes the required enlisted service. This applies if the selectee had a sequence number in an earlier promotion increment; however, if the airman meets the required enlisted service on the first day of the month, the DOR and effective date is that date.

6. If a TDY student meets the requirements of this table but does not maintain satisfactory proficiency, the MPF that services the airman's TDY unit tells the MPF servicing the airman's unit of assignment.

**How Will You Measure Up?** The best way to start preparing for a WAPS testing cycle is to compute the weighted factors that you already know—your time-in-service (TIS), time-in-grade (TIG), decorations, and performance reports. Then you need to get the promotion cutoff score used for your AFSC's last promotion cycle. It can be obtained from one of your contemporaries who tested during the last cycle or from the promotion and testing branch of your Military Personnel Section (MPS). Subtracting the four factors you already know from the cutoff score will give you the approximate total score you will need on your SKT and PFE tests. Divide this number by two, and you'll know approximately what scores to aim for on each test. Remember that promotion cutoff scores will change slightly from cycle to cycle, so the figures will not be absolute, but they will be close enough for now. Fill in the accompanying computation sheet to see how you stand.

---

### WEIGHTED AIRMAN PROMOTION SYSTEM (WAPS)
### POINTS COMPUTATION SHEET

| | Maximum points obtainable | Your projected score |
|---|---|---|
| Specialty Knowledge Test (SKT) score | 100 | _____ |
| Promotion Fitness Examination (PFE) score | 100 | _____ |
| Time-in-service (TIS) score (see note 1) | 40 | _____ |
| Time-in-grade (TIG) score (see note 2) | 60 | _____ |
| Decorations score (see note 3) | 25 | _____ |
| Performance report score (see note 4) | 135 | |
| Maximum total score | 460 | _____ |

*Note 1:* Two points are awarded for each year of total active federal military service (TAFMS) up to twenty years. Your points are computed up to the last day of the promotion cycle. One-sixth of a point is credited for each month; fifteen days or more is counted as a month, fourteen days or less is not counted.

*Note 2:* One-half of a point is awarded for each month you have held your current grade, not to exceed ten years. Compute your score up to the first day of the last month of the promotion cycle. Fifteen days or more is counted as a month, fourteen days or less is not counted.

*Note 3:* Specific point values are assigned based on the decoration's order of precedence, as follows: fifteen points: Medal of Honor; eleven points: Air Force Cross, Navy Cross, and Distinguished Service Cross; nine points: Defense Distinguished Service Medal, Distinguished Service Medal, and Silver Star; seven points: Legion of Merit, Defense Superior Service Medal, and Distinguished Flying Cross; five points: Airman's Medal, Soldier's Medal, Navy-Marine Corps Medal, Coast Guard Medal, Bronze Star Medal, Defense Meritorious Service Medal, Meritorious Service Medal, and Purple Heart; three points: Air Medal, Air Force Commendation Medal, Army Commendation Medal, Navy Commendation Medal, Joint Service Commendation Medal, and Coast Guard Commendation Medal; one point: Navy Achievement Medal, Coast Guard Achievement Medal, and Air Force Achievement Medal.

*Note 4:* Due to the introduction of the new Enlisted Performance Report (EPR), the procedure for computing performance report points under the WAPS program has changed. Computations are now based on a time-weighting system that places more emphasis on recent duty performance. Scores are based on performance reports that have closed out within five years preceding the promotion eligibility cutoff date (PECD). Not more than ten of the most recent reports may be used. The overall evaluation for each performance report is multiplied by one of ten time-weighting factors (the most recent report has a factor of 50, the second most recent report has a factor of 45, and so forth in descending order in increments of five points per report). The subtotal for each report is then multiplied by an EPR multiplier of 27 or an APR multiplier of 15. That product, in turn, results in an EPR or APR performance value. These performance values are added together and then divided by the total number of time weighting factors. The answer is the performance score. The highest attainable score is 135.

**Computing Your Performance Report Score.** The following is an example for a servicemember who had five performance reports considered.

| EPR/APR Ratings (most recent first) | × | Time-Weighting Factor | = | Subtotal | × | EPR/APR Multiplier (EPR = 27) (APR = 15) | = | EPR/APR Performance Value |
|---|---|---|---|---|---|---|---|---|
| 4 (EPR) | × | 50 | = | 200 | × | 27 | = | 5,400 |
| 4 (EPR) | × | 45 | = | 180 | × | 27 | = | 4,860 |
| 9 (EPR) | × | 40 | = | 360 | × | 15 | = | 5,400 |
| 9 (EPR) | × | 35 | = | 315 | × | 15 | = | 4,725 |
| 4 (EPR) | × | 30 | = | 240 | × | 15 | = | 3,600 |
| — | × | 25 | | | | | | |
| — | × | 20 | | | | | | |
| — | × | 15 | | | | | | |
| — | × | 10 | | | | | | |
| — | × | 5 | | | | | | |
| | | 200* | | | | | | 23,985 |

(*Total only the time-weighting factors for the number of reports used.)

The total sum of performance values (23,985) divided by the total time weighting factors (200) equals a performance score of 119.91.

To compute your performance report score for WAPS, fill in the blanks on the following format.

| EPR/APR Ratings (most recent first) | × | Time-Weighting Factor | = | Subtotal | × | EPR/APR Multiplier (EPR = 27) (APR = 15) | = | EPR/APR Performance Value |
|---|---|---|---|---|---|---|---|---|
| _____ | × | 50 | = | _____ | × | _____ | = | _____ |
| _____ | × | 45 | = | _____ | × | _____ | = | _____ |
| _____ | × | 40 | = | _____ | × | _____ | = | _____ |
| _____ | × | 35 | = | _____ | × | _____ | = | _____ |
| _____ | × | 30 | = | _____ | × | _____ | = | _____ |
| _____ | × | 25 | = | _____ | × | _____ | = | _____ |
| _____ | × | 20 | = | _____ | × | _____ | = | _____ |
| _____ | × | 15 | = | _____ | × | _____ | = | _____ |
| _____ | × | 10 | = | _____ | × | _____ | = | _____ |
| _____ | × | 5 | = | _____ | × | _____ | = | _____ |

The total sum of performance values (_____) divided by the total time weighting factors (_____) equals a performance score of _____.

**Analyzing a Sample WAPS Computation Sheet.** Let's imagine that SrA Jim E. Bent is getting ready to test for staff sergeant under the WAPS program. Jim would start listing the data he knows.

**Time-in-service (TIS) score**:
(7 years = 84 months × $\frac{1}{6}$ point per month)  14.00  points
**Time-in-grade (TIG) score**:
(3 years and 6 months = 42 months × $\frac{1}{2}$ point per month)  21.00
**Decorations score**:
(One Air Force Achievement Medal = 1 point)  1.00
**Performance score**:
(4-EPR, 4-EPR, 9-APR, 9-APR, 8-APR)  119.92

**Jim's total score without the SKT and PFE**:  155.92  points

Jim's next step is to find out the cutoff selection score for promotion to staff sergeant in his career field during the last promotion cycle. He reviews his shop-mate's score notice and finds that the promotion cutoff was 297.50.

Now Jim subtracts his raw score of 155.92 from 297.50. This leaves 141.58, the approximate total score that Jim must try to achieve for his SKT and PFE tests together. Carrying this one step further, Jim can divide 141.58 by two tests and see that he needs to score at least a 70.79 on each. He can also see that if he gets a maximum score of 100 on one test, he will need a 41.58 score on the other.

**Preparing for Your WAPS Test.** As you prepare to take your WAPS test, there are six areas you need to concentrate your efforts on.

1. Know the criteria; learn how the WAPS program works and what will be covered on your PFE and SKT tests. The best way to start is to review the WAPS catalog, which lists the publications used by test writers to develop promotion tests for the current year. The WAPS catalog is available on the Air Force Personnel Center's web site at *www.afpc.randolph.af.mil/testing/wapsca0.htm*. The primary reason for the change to a web site catalog is speed—airmen can access information as soon as it is available. With it, you can quickly identify the Career Development Course (CDC), directives, and technical orders used to write your SKT. You can also eliminate items that will not appear on the test. The Promotion Fitness Examination (PFE) test is largely derived from Air Force Pamphlet 36-2241, Volume 1, *Professional Development Guide.*

2. Set up a study schedule. Have a specific time and place to study. Consider temperature, ventilation, lighting, table, desk, and chair; be organized; have all your study materials ready. Avoid distractions: TV, radio, stereo, and other interruptions, such as people and pets.

   Break the information down into smaller units; it will be easier to study. Establish a timetable based on your test date. Preparing properly usually takes a minimum of three months. You will need enough time to read all the material and plan an overall review. Allow at least one day to read each of the twenty chapters in the PFE study guide and each chapter in the CDCs. After this, you should allow at least two weeks for an overall review. Review the important areas, consolidate your notes, and get assistance for subjects that you do not fully understand. The week before you take the test should be a time to relax and program your memory. If you are still doing some of the initial reading during this final week, it's probably too late to score high.

3. Develop good reading habits. You have to be able to read for understanding. Moving your eyes over a written page is looking, not reading. Looking at the pages of a CDC book but thinking of something else won't raise your scores on the next test.

   Skimming the content of a chapter before you read can be useful. It lets you know what to expect and keys you into interrelationships of ideas. As you read, look for facts (descriptions, events, systems, people) and work to integrate these facts into concepts, principles, and ideas. Remember, you won't be able to integrate concepts if you missed some of the facts. If you're not able to explain a concept in your own words, it may be a sign that you don't fully understand it.

   Monitor what you read. Get into the habit of catching your mind as soon as it wanders off the material. Did you ever get to the bottom of a page, realize your mind was on something else, and say to yourself, "I don't remember a thing I read"? In cases like this, if you go on to the next page you're doing yourself a disservice. If you can't get into it, stop. There will be times when you are fatigued or preoccupied, and attempting to study further seems impossible. Take a break. But if you find yourself taking too many breaks or not sticking to your study schedule, ask yourself a very basic question: "Do I really want to get promoted this time?"

4. Designate what's important and program your memory. Plan for two levels: memorizing (the ability to recall facts) and understanding (grasping the meaning without necessarily recalling exact facts and definitions).

   Recognize that memory is limited. Start programming your memory when you first start to study. Avoid cramming; don't go over material too quickly. If your mind isn't organized as the material goes in, it won't be organized when the material comes out (for the test). Form mental images to help remember key facts. Use key words or phrases, such as ROB—red, orange, blue—for parts of components or electrical wiring. Use numbers in larger units; 7642 may be easier to commit to memory as 76-42 than as 7-6-4-2).

   Designate what's important during your reading by underlining or highlighting significant material. It's quick, easy to do, and will help reduce the amount of material to be restudied. Do it after you understand the passage you've read. Oftentimes key words or key phrases in a sentence will suffice. Don't overdo it; 20 to 50 percent is enough. Remember, you're trying to designate what's important. After you've read everything for the first time, go back and review the items you've underlined or highlighted. Identify what you know is of primary importance or requires more attention for concepts you may not fully understand with notes in margins, asterisks, and so on.

As a final step, take notes to reduce the amount of material to study for your final review. Use a spiral notebook (loose pages tend to get lost). Keep your notes simple, not more than a page per chapter, and only key words and phrases. These notes will be your key study material as you get closer to your test date.

5. Don't worry! Anxiety is basically a response to a perceived threat. The key to doing well is to know the material; "overlearn" it beyond the point at which you first feel you have mastered it. Before your testing date, do practice tests and volume review exercises (VREs), and study questions within your career development courses (CDCs) that come after each study module (001, 002, and so on). The night before the test, go over your review notes. Then hit the sack at the regular time. You've gone through a lot of careful preparation over the past few months. Get a good night's sleep so you will be rested and alert during the test.

6. Taking the test: First and foremost, make sure you are present to take the test at the time and date you've been scheduled for. If you are not, you could be identified as a "no-show" and rendered ineligible for consideration during the promotion cycle.

When you go in to take the test, it's normal to be a bit apprehensive and nervous. Forget about the other people in the room; relax and concentrate on the test. After all, you haven't crammed; you've studied and you know the material. Carefully follow the test officer's instructions. Resist the temptation to rush, but don't waste time.

Always read the full question carefully; look for the main point, principle, or theme. Look for the subject of the question and the basis for the decision (best, most, least). Then read all the answers. Several of the answers may sound partially right. You're looking for the *most correct* one. Watch out for key words like *succeeded, successor, preceded, predecessor* (what comes after or what comes before). Look for negatives (which of the following *never*) and positives (which of the following *always*). If you're having difficulty with a question, eliminate answers you know are wrong or reverse the question. "When is an NCO not in compliance with dress and appearance standards" can be changed to "When is an NCO always in compliance with dress and appearance standards?" Rearranging a question may help jog your memory for the answer by thinking about it from a different perspective. Reduce the number of possible answers by working the answers backward. Find the worst answer and eliminate it; try to find the better of two answers, not the best of four.

Your first impression is usually your best bet. If you're unsure about your answer, avoid changing it. Ask NCO Academy graduates about their tests; ask how many of their answers would have been correct had they not changed their first impressions. If you cannot solve a question after a reasonable length of time, eliminate responses you know are wrong, mark an answer, and don't waste any more time. In advance, select one column for all guesses, such as column C. Don't vary; you'll get some right every test. If you wander about in your guessing, it's doubtful that you'll get many right.

During the test, constantly compare question numbers with answer numbers. You don't want to get out of sequence and transfer your answers to the incorrect space. When you finish the test, check to see that all the questions on the answer sheet have been marked. Random check a few to ensure they were answered in the correct sequence (question 74, answer sheet 74).

7. After you've completed the test, you can hand in your materials, breathe a sigh of relief, and depart. When you return to your duty section, do not discuss the content of either test. That is prohibited by regulation and could require an investigation for test compromise. It could also affect your selection because your contemporaries in your duty section may not have tested yet and they are some of your competition for the same stripes.

In summary, the WAPS is a very good program in many ways. The selection criteria are known to all concerned. The scoresheet provides feedback and lets you know which areas require improvement. Also, the testing process requires study. This has an added benefit of enhancing your knowledge of the Air Force and your proficiency in your career field. Each of these tests was written by a select group of senior noncommissioned officers drawn from the major commands and from almost every career field in the USAF.

The primary emphasis in this chapter has been on testing, since these results make up almost half the total WAPS score. Doing well on the tests is the prime factor in getting promoted rapidly. Those who do not study must wait for points to accrue in other areas, primarily time-in-service (two points a year) and time-in-grade (six points a year). That could delay promotions by several years.

## THE STRIPES FOR EXCEPTIONAL PERFORMERS (STEP) PROGRAM
STEP is much smaller in scope than the WAPS program. It was established as a means to provide immediate on-the-spot promotion to the grades of staff sergeant, technical sergeant, and master sergeant. It allows major command commanders, commanders of separate operating agencies (SOAs), and senior Air Force officers

in organizations with large enlisted populations to promote those whose performance has clearly been exceptional and of a magnitude that warrants immediate advancement to a position of increased grade and responsibility.

STEP promotions are made once or twice each year. Numerical quotas are allocated to each agency that has been delegated STEP selection authority by HQ USAF. These agencies establish their own selection criteria. In general, selections are based on a review of a recommendation from the nominee's supervisor or commander and the nominee's last five performance reports.

To be eligible for consideration, nominees must meet the following time-in-service requirements: for promotion to staff sergeant, three years; to technical sergeant, five years; to master sergeant, eight years. There are no time-in-grade requirements; however, the military member concerned can receive only one promotion under any promotion program within a twelve-month period.

## PROMOTION TO SENIOR MASTER SERGEANT AND
## CHIEF MASTER SERGEANT

Promotion to the top two enlisted grades is very competitive; your performance over many years will be considered. It's a two-phase process. Phase 1 consists of a weighted score, computed like the WAPS score. The total score possible is 360 points. The six individual factors considered and the maximum scores for each are as follows:

1. The USAF Supervisory Examination (USAFSE): 100 points (based on the percent of correct answers).
2. Performance report score: 135 points (computed the same way as under the WAPS program).
3. Professional Military Education (PME): 15 points for the Command NCO Academy; the method of completion, whether in-residence or by correspondence, has no bearing on the point value. (*Note:* Beginning with the CMSgt 90S9 promotion cycle, the 20 points for the Senior NCO Academy have been deleted for both CMSgt and SMSgt promotions. The Senior NCO Academy will reflect on your selection brief, and the Central Selection Board will consider it.)
4. Decorations score: 25 points (based on the decoration's order of precedence, the same way as under the WAPS program).
5. Time-in-grade (TIG) score: 60 points (computed as one-half point for each month in current grade, based on the individual's date of rank, up to a period of 10 years, computed as of the first day of the last month of the promotion cycle).
6. Time-in-service (TIS) score: 25 points (based on one-twelfth point for each month of total active federal military service [TAFMS], up to 25 years, computed as of the last day of the promotion cycle).

Phase 2 is conducted by a Central Promotion Evaluation Board (CPEB) at the Air Force Personnel Center (AFPC). It entails scoring each member's promotion selection folder using the whole-person concept, which considers the member's performance over a period of years. The factors evaluated are duty performance, level of responsibility, breadth of experience, leadership, professional competence, awards and decorations, and education. The results of the Phase 1 board score (the weighted factors) are not reviewed as part of the Phase 2 evaluation.

All the airmen competing for promotion in a single Air Force Specialty Code (AFSC) or Special Duty Identifier (SDI) are considered by the same panel, which consists of two colonels and one chief master sergeant. Each member of the panel reviews every selection folder and evaluates each candidate's potential for increased grade and responsibility. Individually, they assign a numerical score using a rating scale of 6 through 10 in half-point increments. The three scores are added together and multiplied by 15, and the result is the candidate's Phase 2 board score. The highest possible board score for this phase is 450 points.

The final selection is based on the combined scores for Phase 1 and Phase 2 (the maximum number of points obtainable is 810). Candidates are rank-ordered in order of merit within each career field, and a promotion cutoff score is set based on the allocation quota. Candidates with the highest number of points are selected for promotion. As in the WAPS program, all airmen with a tie score at the cutoff point are selected for promotion.

After the promotion list is released, all master sergeants and senior master sergeants who were considered will receive a senior NCO promotion score notice showing their promotion status, points for weighted factors, total weighted score, board score, relative standing, and groupings by board scores of selectees and non-selectees. If errors are detected on the score notice, supplemental consideration may be requested.

## ONE FINAL NOTE

Traditionally, the airmen who have obtained timely promotions have a record of outstanding performance and have made the effort to research requirements, ask questions, and seek out answers *before* the promotion cycle.

## SOURCES OF ADDITIONAL INFORMATION

Air Force Instruction 36-2502, *Airman Promotion/Demotion Program.*
Air Force Pamphlet 36-2241, *Professional Development Guide.*

# 19

# How to Get the "Right" Assignments

The word *assignments* is close to the hearts of almost everyone in the U.S. Air Force. Sometimes it brings smiles, sometimes frowns. It refers to the location (an Air Force base or station) and organization (wing, group, squadron, special activity) where you will live and perform your duties. To get the assignments you're interested in, it helps to understand how the system works.

After you've received your initial training in your designated career field, you will be awarded a skill level in your Air Force Specialty (AFS). Your assignment will then be determined based on the number of people in your specialty, by rank and skill level, needed to meet mission requirements at each base or operating location. That number is based on the assigned strengths (how many airmen are required to perform the mission). If there is a shortage of personnel, the assignment system identifies a vacancy and names an airman to fill that vacancy. When an airman is permanently assigned (or reassigned) to a new location, that is referred to as a permanent-change-of-station (PCS) move.

The Air Force Personnel Center (AFPC) at Randolph AFB, Texas, is the agency responsible for determining PCS assignments. The major commands (MAJCOMs) can also initiate some types of assignments, with the review and approval of the AFPC. Computer programs help identify personnel to fill positions for assignments to and from overseas and from technical training schools. The balance of requirements are usually processed manually as requirements become known.

Many considerations are taken into account when an airman is selected for an assignment: an airman's status (volunteer or nonvolunteer), retainability (how much time remains on the term of enlistment), eligibility requirements, and past assignment history. Individual preferences are weighed against the mission requirements of the Air Force. Moving costs are scrutinized with a view toward meeting the manning needs of each organization in the most cost-effective manner. Humanitarian requests—to help a military member alleviate a serious personal problem or hardship—are reviewed on a case-by-case basis. Equal opportunity is also of prime concern. Air Force assignments are made without regard to color, race, religion, national origin, ethnic background, age, or sex, except where limitations are set by law, living facilities, or physical capabilities.

## FORECASTING FOR YOUR ASSIGNMENTS

The Military Personnel Section (MPS) is the focal point at base level for all assignment actions. Within the MPS, two offices can help you with questions concerning assignments. The customer service branch helps with general inquiries, and the assignments branch deals more with specific issues and provides personal counseling when required.

The key to your assignment future is Air Force Form 392, "Airman Assignment Preference Statement." It's used by all airmen, airman basic through senior master sergeant, to list their preferences for U.S., overseas, and AFPC-Controlled Special Duty Assignments. From this form, the places you would like to go are put into the Air Force personnel computer. Afterward, it's kept in your official personnel records until you change your preferences by completing another AF Form 392. The computer is used to match persons with places. So it's very important that you carefully review all your options and be as specific as possible when filling out this form.

The Air Force is transitioning to an electronic process, but still uses AF Form 392. SMSgt and below use the AF Form 392 during basic training. After that, you can change your assignment preferences or volunteer for overseas duty at almost any time. For the most part, the opportunity will be brought to your attention by the personnel specialists during annual record reviews, on arrival at a new duty station, or during overseas returnee counseling.

As you can see from the accompanying illustration, there are five major sections to the form. Filling out the form in the most advantageous way will help you get where you want to go—or close to it.

The introductory information is self-explanatory: name, grade, Social Security account number, organization, and duty telephone.

Section 1 is for listing your overseas preferences. If you do not wish to be an overseas volunteer, enter "none" in the first preference block. This is not your best option. By entering "none" you are telling the personnel system that you are a nonvolunteer for every overseas assignment (because you haven't listed any specific country that you have a preference for). If their list of volunteers has been exhausted, they will turn to the list of eligible people who are nonvolunteers. Bottom line: If you are eligible for an overseas assignment you can be sent almost anywhere, even if you did enter "none."

You can use all eight blocks listing individual countries or worldwide preferences. This is a good option if there are eight countries that you really want to be assigned to. But one very important point to remember is that the eight blocks do not represent first, second, and third choice; all preferences are considered equally for assignment purposes, in no specific order.

## AIRMAN ASSIGNMENT PREFERENCE STATEMENT

*AUTHORITY: 10 USC 8012; 44 USC 3101; and EO 9397.*
*PRINCIPAL PURPOSES: Allows airman to indicate geographic preferences for CONUS assignment, volunteer status for oversea duty, homebasing/follow-on volunteer status for special duty volunteer status.*
*ROUTINE USES: Used as a source document for data entered into the Advanced Personnel Data System. Data used in assignment selection at MAJCOMs and AFMPC. The SSAN is used for identification.*
*DISCLOSURE IS VOLUNTARY: If the information is not provided, assignment selections are made without regard to member's preferences.*

| NAME *(Last, First, Middle Initial)* | GRADE | SSAN | ORGANIZATION | DUTY TELEPHONE |
|---|---|---|---|---|
| MARSHALL, JOHN, V. | SrA | 000-00-0000 | 000 Headquarters Squadron | EXT: 1234 |

**I.** 

**OVERSEA PREFERENCE**

OVERSEA VOLUNTEER STATUS CODES
A - COT to Long *(standard tour)*
B - COT to Long *(extended tour)*
C - COT to Short *(standard tour)*
N - Non-CONUS Resident to Home Area

1 - CONUS to Long *(standard tour)*
2 - CONUS to Long *(extended tour)*
3 - CONUS to Short *(standard tour)*

Enter up to eight country, or "worldwide" preferences in any combination. Enter separate status code from the list at right for each preference. If you do not wish to be an oversea volunteer, enter "none" in 1st preference block. See Note 1 on reverse.

| | 1ST | 2ND | 3RD | 4TH | 5TH | 6TH | 7TH | 8TH |
|---|---|---|---|---|---|---|---|---|
| COUNTRY | SPAIN | ENGLAND | ITALY | JAPAN | KOREA | PHILIP-PINES | AZORES | HAWAII |
| VOLUNTEER STATUS | 2 | 1 | 1 | 1 | 3 | 1 | 1 | N |

**II.**

**CONUS PREFERENCE**

Enter up to eight bases, locales, states, or areas in any combination. If you have no preference, enter "None" in 1st preference block. See Note 2.

| | 1ST | 2ND | 3RD | 4TH | 5TH | 6TH | 7TH | 8TH |
|---|---|---|---|---|---|---|---|---|
| BASE/LOCALE/STATE/AREA | Base BP | Base BT | Base CD | Base CN | State (CA) Code: 06 | State (NY) Code: 32 | Locale M6 | Area 5 |

**III.**

**AFPC-CONTROLLED SPECIAL DUTY ASSIGNMENT VOLUNTEER STATUS**

If you wish to volunteer for an AFPC-Controlled Special Duty Assignment, indicate the specific type of duty and up to three geographical preferences *(Oversea country, CONUS state, or "World-wide".)* Otherwise enter "None" in Type Duty block. See Note 3.

| TYPE DUTY | | 1ST | 2ND | 3RD |
|---|---|---|---|---|
| POSTAL SPECIALIST | GEOGRAPHICAL PREFERENCES | SPAIN | ENGLAND | ITALY |

**IV.**

**CERTIFICATION**

I have read and understand the applicable items on the front and back of this form. I am a volunteer for any oversea location listed in Section I and/or duty listed in Section III.

| DATE | SIGNATURE OF AIRMAN | CBPO USE ONLY | |
|---|---|---|---|
| | | DATE OF BLMPS UPDATE | INITIALS |
| 15 SEP 2011 | | | |

**V.**

**COMMANDER'S CERTIFICATION**
*(To be completed for members who volunteer for AFPC-Controlled Special Duty Assignments)*

I have personally interviewed the applicant for the type of assignment for which he or she has applied, considering his or her judgement, emotional stability, moral character, financial encumbrances, and other pertinent information.

| | DATE | SIGNATURE OF COMMANDER |
|---|---|---|
| ☒ RECOMMENDED ☐ NOT RECOMMENDED *(Justify and return to individual)* | 1 OCT 2011 | *James A. Doe,* Lt Colonel, USAF |

AF FORM 392 OCT 82    PREVIOUS EDITION WILL BE USED.

GPO : 1986 O - 499-341

## Air Force Form 392, Airman Assignment Preference Statement

Under each country you should put an overseas status code; codes help determine your position on the waiting list for each country. Codes 1, 2, and 3 are for people who want to go from the continental United States (CONUS) to an overseas tour (*long* or *short* refers to the length of a tour; long is eighteen months or more, short is less than eighteen months). Codes A, B, and C are for people who are presently overseas and would like to be assigned to another base overseas. This is known as a request for a consecutive overseas tour (COT). Code N may only be used by non-CONUS residents applying for assignment to their home of record. A non-CONUS resident is an airman whose official home of record is Alaska, Hawaii, the territories of the Virgin Islands, Guam, American Samoa, Trust Territory of the Pacific Islands, the Commonwealth of Puerto Rico, and the Canal Zone (for those who enlisted prior to 1 October 1979).

Or you can list only a few specific countries that you want to be assigned to and list your volunteer status codes under each preference. For example, you might put England in block 1, Germany in block 2, and then put "none" in blocks 3 through 8. This is a good option if you want to list a few countries but not overvolunteer.

In Section 2 you list your CONUS preferences. You can list codes for up to eight bases, locales, states, or areas. The codes are listed in Air Force Instruction 36-2110.

*Base* and *state* are self-explanatory. A *locale* is defined as a grouping of major installations and bases in the same general area. For example, the southern California locale is Locale Code M6. The places you could be assigned to under that code include Edwards AFB, El Centro NAS, Hawes CCM, Los Angeles AFB, March AFB, Ontario CTY, and Vandenberg AFB, in California; and Hawthorne RBS, Indian Springs AAF, Lake Mead Base AIN, Las Vegas CTY, Nellis AFB, and Pittman ADM in Nevada (a total of thirteen locations). An *area* consists of several states in the same general region. For example, Area 5 includes all the major installations and bases in Arizona, California, Colorado, Nevada, New Mexico, and Utah.

When you list your CONUS preferences, there are two major points to remember. Your preferences will be considered in the order you list them. Also, it's best to list choices from each category rather than to select only eight specific bases. For example, if you wanted to go to specific bases in southern California it would be best to list the bases in blocks 1 through 4, the states of California and Nevada in blocks 5 and 6, the code M6 for the southern California locale in block 7, and the code for Area 5 in block 8. That way, you will be considered against the requirements at all the bases named and within that locale or area. It means you've multiplied your options. Instead of limiting yourself to eight specific bases, you've established your preferences (in a priority sequence) for approximately sixty locations in a geographical area of your choice.

Section 3 is to be completed if you wish to volunteer for an AFPC-Controlled Special Duty Assignment. More information about this is provided later in this chapter. If you are interested in this type of duty, you will be considered a volunteer to serve only at the overseas country listed.

Section 4 is for your certification: date and signature.

Section 5 is for your commander's certification if you have volunteered for an AFPC-Controlled Special Duty Assignment. He or she will either recommend or not recommend approval.

On a final note, there is one major consideration that you should always remember when filling out your AF Form 392. Think about your Air Force Specialty, and make sure the place you want to go to has openings for your career field. For example, an air traffic controller would not want to select a small Air Force station without a runway, a mental health technician would not want to select a small base whose hospital did not have a mental health clinic, and an aircraft maintenance specialist who works on the F-16 would not want to volunteer for an assignment to a remote communications site that doesn't have any assigned aircraft. Bottom line: Make the most of your form; put a valid preference in each block.

## YOUR FIRST ASSIGNMENT

Assignments for airmen from basic military training school and technical training school are based on the preferences made on their AF Form 392 and the manning needs of the Air Force at the time of their projected graduation date. If airmen do not successfully complete training courses, they are evaluated to see if they should be allowed to remain in the USAF. Some are discharged. Others are allowed to apply for retraining, in which case up to six Air Force Specialty Code (AFSC) preferences that these airmen are qualified for are sent through personnel channels. If retraining is approved, the airmen are sent either to another technical training school or on a directed duty assignment (DDA) straight to their first base, where they are entered into on-the-job training (OJT).

The Pipeline Student Airman Swap Program was established to let airmen exchange assignments with each other. To do so, they must have the same AFSC, be projected graduates of the same course, and be of similar rank. Swap requests must be submitted to the personnel office not later than three workdays after you are first advised of your initial assignment. You will be advised if there are other general criteria that must be met. Overall it's a very good program, especially for two airmen who want to have each other's assignments.

## TEMPORARY DUTY ASSIGNMENTS

Temporary duty assignments (TDY) can be scheduled after you've been assigned to your permanent base. They are used primarily when a member's presence is required at another location for training purposes, exercises, or manning assistance. The length of time can vary; it's usually 30 days or less but can be scheduled for up to 179 days if no training is involved. TDY is based on military necessity balanced with a view toward keeping costs, personnel moves, and family separation at minimum levels.

## OVERSEAS ASSIGNMENTS

Overseas assignments can be scheduled at any time during your career after you complete your initial training. Airmen are selected for these tours based on grade and skill level within each Air Force specialty. A lot also depends on what the Air Force calls your "vulnerability" for an overseas tour, which takes into account your volunteer status and past overseas assignment history. From this information, they place each airman in a priority list to ensure the equitable distribution of assignments. Basically, your last overseas return date, number of overseas tours, and the amount of time you have been on your present base are looked at in determining who is the most eligible to fill an overseas tour requirement. Ideally, everyone will go on at least one overseas tour (long or short) before someone is selected involuntarily to go on a second overseas tour.

The types of tours vary. There are long tours, served with or without dependents, ranging from eighteen to forty-eight months. There are short tours, less than eighteen months, usually served without dependents. At some locations, you are given the option to stay longer. This is called a voluntary extension of overseas tour. In many cases, this can be beneficial to both you and the Air Force. Many families enjoy life overseas; it affords the opportunity to travel, save money, pursue educational goals, and enjoy family life at one location. It's advantageous to the Air Force because fewer PCS moves are required, so costs are lowered, and because of the increased continuity of operation in the overseas unit. Requests for extensions are reviewed on a case-by-case basis, and recommendations for approval or disapproval are made by the member's immediate commander.

There is a wide range of overseas locations you may be eligible to be assigned to. Some of the countries with large contingents of U.S. Armed Forces include the Azores (Portugal), Germany, Guam, Iceland, Italy, Japan, Korea, Okinawa (Japan), Turkey, and the United Kingdom.

To be eligible for an overseas assignment, you must have, or be able to obtain, the retainability for the tour for which you are volunteering. For example, if you have a high year of tenure (HYT) restriction that is twenty-eight months away and you volunteer for a thirty-six-month tour, you won't get selected because you cannot obtain the full thirty-six months of retainability for the assignment. If you are a second-term or career airmen (not a first-termer), and are selected and then decline to get the required retainability, your assignment will be canceled and you will be required to separate or retire on your current date of separation. If you do decline an assignment or have one canceled because of your unwillingness to obtain sufficient retainability, you will be ineligible for other assignments, except those for which you have the needed retainability. You can volunteer for overseas tours at your Commander's Support Staff (CSS) or MPS by completing Air Force Form 392 or through PC III.

To find out how to apply for overseas duty, see "Forecasting for Your Assignments," above.

## SPECIAL DUTY ASSIGNMENTS

Special Duty Assignments (SDAs) are one of the Air Force's best-kept secrets. They're not really secrets, actually; it's just that thousands of positions are available, but their existence and the procedures for applying for them are not common knowledge.

Why would you apply for SDAs? For the prestige and challenge, perhaps. You'll have the opportunity to be a member of an organization with a well-known and highly visible mission. You'll also be able to work with other high-caliber personnel.

SDAs also offer enhanced promotion opportunity. Positions such as these indicate that a person is capable of increased responsibility in a position of special trust and confidence. SDAs also mean a controlled tour of duty. Most assignments are for a specific period of time (two, three, or four years, sometimes with an option to stay longer), which offers stability. Your future becomes much more predictable and you can plan for other commitments (family, education, purchasing a home). And of course, they provide the opportunity to travel extensively, especially overseas, where some of the assignments are in major cities like London, Tokyo, Rome, or Paris.

The following pages will give examples of some of the Special Duty Assignments available. Each position has a list of eligibility and ineligibility criteria, all of which may not be listed here. Our primary concern for now is to bring this information to your attention and to stimulate some interest. If you're interested in applying for a Special Duty Assignment, you should visit your Military Personnel Section (MPS) and ask to speak to someone who works in either the customer service branch or the assignments branch. All the criteria for applying for these positions are located in Air Force Instruction 36-2110, *Assignments*.

**General Information.** In general, the Air Force has a number of special positions that require uniquely qualified personnel. Those selected must have outstanding records of performance, and there must be no unfavorable comments about their personal qualities (conduct, working relations, job knowledge, or personal appearance). In most cases, these positions are filled by volunteers. They are selected in one of two ways.

Some Special Duty Assignments are controlled directly by the responsible organization or major command (such as Air Combat Command, Air Education and Training Command, or Air Mobility Command), which can select applicants from their own bases or ask the Air Force Personnel Center (HQ AFPC) for assistance if they do not have enough applicants on file.

The other category is AFPC-Controlled Special Duty Assignments. If you volunteer for this kind of duty, you can indicate the type of duty you want and two preferences for the country or state you'd like to be assigned to. Consideration will be given to these two preferences, but ultimately, military requirements will determine the activity to which you will be assigned.

**Major Command and Organization-Controlled Special Duty Assignments**

1. Air Mobility Command (AMC) Flight and Ground School Enlisted Instructors:
   C-17, KC-135, or C-5 instructor duty at Altus AFB, Oklahoma
   Helicopter or C-130 instructor duty at Kirtland AFB, New Mexico
   C-130 instructor duty at Little Rock AFB, Arkansas
2. Air Education and Training Command (AETC) Technical Instructor for Medical Training.
3. Air Education and Training Command (AETC) Military Training Instructors (MTIs) and Student Training Advisors (STAs): Applicants for MTI duty are assigned only to the Basic Military Training School at Lackland AFB, Texas. Applicants for STA duty must be staff sergeants or above with over four years of service. They may request assignment to training centers at the following bases: Keesler AFB, Mississippi; Lackland ABF, Texas; and Sheppard AFB, Texas.
4. NCO Professional Military Education (PME) Instructor Duty: Airmen in any AFSC may apply.
5. Air Education and Training Command (AETC) Survival Training Instructor: Career airmen and nonprior-service airmen attending Basic Military Training are eligible regardless of AFSC.
6. Air Force Reserve Officer Training Corps (AFROTC): Those selected are assigned to U.S. colleges and universities. They counsel cadets on personal and administrative matters, prepare personnel records for newly commissioned officers, serve as assistants to instructors, and assist on field trips and various other cadet activities.
7. Recruiting Duty: Airmen in grades staff sergeant (with four or more years' TAFMS and career-committed) through master sergeant (with sixteen years' TAFMS or less) may apply regardless of their AFSC. Waivers for lower grades can be considered on an individual basis. Those selected are assigned to recruiting stations in cities throughout the United States.
8. USAF Honor Guard: Personnel assigned to the honor guard represent the Air Force at public ceremonies. They are inspected by the President of the United States and other high-ranking dignitaries while performing duties at the U.S. Capitol, the White House, the Pentagon, the Tomb of the Unknowns, and other official locations. Airmen in grades airman basic through senior master sergeant are eligible to apply. Selection criteria are very stringent.
9. USAF Air Demonstration Squadron (the Thunderbirds): Airmen in over twenty maintenance and support specialties are eligible to apply. F-16 experience is desirable but not mandatory. For more information, see the Thunderbirds' web site *http://www.thunderbirds.acc.af.mil.*
10. Orientation Group, USAF: The Orientation Group, USAF, is the official Air Force exhibit unit. Its personnel conceive, design, plan, construct,

maintain, and present exhibits, displays, aircraft, and other visual aids depicting Air Force progress, activities, missions, and personnel to the public. Since they interact extensively with the public, airmen of the highest caliber and skills are needed. They are stationed out of Wright-Patterson AFB, Ohio, and usually spend a great deal of time on the road in temporary duty status for thirty-five to forty-five days at a time.

11. Air Force Office of Special Investigations (OSI): Airmen in grades senior airman through technical sergeant, regardless of AFSC, are eligible to apply for investigative duties. Personnel with a background in electronics are encouraged to apply for investigative duties with the Technical Services Division. Positions for noninvestigative duty are also available for some AFSCs at HQ AFOSI and at detachments throughout the world.

12. Medical Research Duty: Airmen, grades airman through chief master sergeant, in more than a dozen medical and support career fields may be eligible to apply for research positions at the USAF School of Aerospace Medicine, Brooks AFB, Texas, or at the 6570 Aerospace Medical Research Laboratory, Wright-Patterson AFB, Ohio.

13. Pararescue Duty: Applicants are selected for duty with the Aerospace Rescue and Recovery Service (ARRS) and must be physically qualified for aircrew duty, parachutist duty, and marine diving duties. Male airmen, airman basic through senior master sergeant, who are not older than thirty-one are eligible to apply, regardless of AFSC.

14. Aerospace Guidance and Metrology Center: Selected applicants are assigned to duty at Newark AFS, Ohio. Airmen in grades staff sergeant through chief master sergeant are eligible to apply if they are highly qualified precision measurement equipment laboratory (PMEL) technicians, if they have experience in quality control and calibration procedures, and if they possess a 7-skill level Primary Air Force Specialty Code (PAFSC) in the PMEL career fields.

15. Community College of the Air Force (CCAF): There are positions for program administrators, grades staff sergeant through senior master sergeant, in twenty-eight career fields. In these positions, selectees use the expertise gained in their Air Force Specialty to help develop and administer the CCAF degree programs related to their career field and to advise students on ways and means of completing their CCAF degree requirements. There are also staff support positions for airmen in grades senior airman through master sergeant. Those selected work in areas such as management information systems, public affairs, admissions and records, institutional research, resource management, and executive support.

16. Auditor Duty: Airmen, grades staff sergeant and technical sergeant, with less than fourteen years' active military service may apply. They must be serving on a second or later enlistment and possess one or more of the following prerequisites: a Certified Public Accountant Certificate; a minimum

of twelve college semester hours in accounting and auditing subjects; or at least three years' experience in responsible accounting positions that required the application of the principles and theory of accounting.

17. Air Education and Training Command (AETC) Non-Resident Career Development Course (CDC) Writers: Career airmen, in grades of staff sergeant and above, in all Air Force specialties may apply. They must be highly qualified within their specialties and must also have excellent writing talent. Their job is to develop and write career development courses that will be used for training other USAF airmen.

Remember, there are sixty-nine MAJCOM and organization-controlled Special Duty Assignments; we've described only seventeen. For additional information, consult Air Force Instruction 36-2110; it's well worth a look. Bear in mind that as Air Force requirements change, these assignments will change. Some may be added, some discontinued. Requirements for Air Force specialties may also change; this is especially true as some career fields are combined and the numerical designations are changed.

## AFPC-Controlled Special Duty Assignments

1. Air Force Missions (Latin America): Assignments are limited to airmen in grade staff sergeant (or selectee) and above. The airman, dependents, and close living relatives must be U.S. citizens.
2. U.S. Military Training Missions to Saudi Arabia: The airman must be a U.S. citizen. The airman and dependents must be temperamentally and socially adaptable for duty that requires daily contact with the forces of allied nations.
3. Allied Command Europe (SHAPE, NATO, and HQ EUCOM): Positions are in Belgium and Germany.
4. Defense Attaché Offices: Positions are primarily overseas in major cities and capitals. Selection criteria are very stringent. Of particular importance is the role of the family members (the important part they play in these assignments and their ability to conduct themselves in a way that creates a favorable impression of the United States, especially in their associations with foreign nationals). All applicants must be career airmen. Airmen in any AFSC are eligible to apply.
5. United Nations Command and U.S. Forces (Korea).
6. Pacific Command—Joint Services Headquarters (Hawaii).
7. Joint U.S. Military Groups (JUSMAG), Advisory and Training (Greece and Turkey).
8. Inter-American Air Force Academy (Panama): Applicant must be fluent in Spanish.
9. Air Staff Duty: Assignments are primarily in Washington, D.C., in positions at HQ USAF, the Office of the Secretary of Defense (OSD), the Joint Chiefs of Staff (JCS), and the Defense Communications Agency (DCA).

10. Air Force Inspection Agency: Assignments are at Kirtland AFB, New Mexico.
11. USAF Academy: Assignments are for permanent-party airmen in a wide range of support specialties.
12. Defense Intelligence Agency (DIA): Assignment locations vary.
13. Air Force Personnel Center (AFPC): Assignment location is Randolph AFB, Texas. Most positions are for personnel and support career fields.
14. White House Communications Agency (WHCA): The WHCA mission is to provide worldwide communications for the President of the United States at all times. Also included for support are the Vice President, the U.S. Secret Service, and others as designated by the President. Duty involves some of the most sophisticated communications-electronics equipment in existence, extensive travel throughout the world, and a six-year controlled tour in the Washington, D.C., area. Applicants are selected from communications and support career fields. Selection criteria and the subsequent screening process are very stringent.
15. Postal Specialist: Requirements exist at virtually all overseas locations. Airmen in any AFSC, grades airman first class through chief master sergeant, may apply.

For information on Special Duty Assignments not listed here, consult Air Force Instruction 36-2110. Again, bear in mind that these assignments are always subject to change consistent with Air Force mission requirements.

## PROGRAM ADDITIONS TO THE ASSIGNMENT PROCESS

The following three programs have been added to enhance your say in what type of job and location you are assigned to. You can obtain more information about these programs from your Military Personnel Section (MPS). If you have a question they cannot answer, they can send a message to your MAJCOM or HQ AFPC for a response. Up-to-date information and guidance are also distributed by way of your base newspaper, bulletin, and *Airman* magazine. The *Air Force Times* publishes EQUAL listings on a recurring basis.

**Enlisted Quarterly Assignments Listing (EQUAL).** The Enlisted Quarterly Assignments Listing system provides airmen with a listing of assignment requirements that are available for upcoming assignment cycles and tells you what is available, by AFSC and grade, at particular locations. It also allows you to make your AF Form 392, "Airman Assignment Preference Statement," a better means to align your assignment preferences to Air Force needs. Overall, the EQUAL system enhances your opportunity to get the assignments you want. It provides a clearer picture of what is available, so that you will know when and where the openings are, and it lets you prioritize those options in the sequence you desire.

**EQUAL-Plus.** EQUAL-Plus supplements EQUAL by advertising special assignments, such as joint and departmental service requirements, special duties, 1AXXX assignments, and all chief master sergeant assignments. EQUAL-Plus shows upcoming requirements, any special qualifications a person needs to be eligible for selection, the available locations, reporting instructions, and points of contact for additional information.

EQUAL-Plus also advertises MAJCOM/AFPC controlled special duties (i.e., instructor duty, recruiting duty, duty with the Thunderbirds, postal duty, Air Staff/MAJCOM positions, and defense attaché duties around the world) and short-notice overseas assignments. If you decide to volunteer for a particular ad, you must update your application via PC-III in your unit orderly room, MPS, or through the AMS web site, and submit a formal application, if required. Be sure to include the specific job/requisition number you are volunteering for. You may only volunteer for one special duty at a time. For further information applicable to overseas personnel, please refer to the counseling handout for overseas returnees which is available at your local CSS or MPS. The listing is available online and at the MPS customer service office. The listings are updated on a weekly basis and are arranged by grade and AFSC.

**Volunteer Enlisted CONUS Assignment Program (VECAP).** This program allows airmen to volunteer for any CONUS base after completing six years on the current duty location. To qualify, you must be eligible for reassignment, not have an assignment selection date, and not be assigned to a base or unit that is scheduled for closure or deactivation. Your application for this program must be supported with your unit commander's approval.

## SOURCES OF ADDITIONAL INFORMATION

Air Force Instruction 36-2110, *Assignments.*

At the Military Personnel Section (MPS), the customer service branch or the assignments branch can provide current information, answer questions, and help you process the paperwork necessary to apply for the duty desired.

Other airmen, especially your supervisor and experienced personnel in your career field, can provide information about duty locations and career progression opportunities. Most career airmen will advise you that preplanning is a must. The day you begin processing into your new base is a very good time to start thinking about your next assignment.

The Air Force Personnel Center web site, http://www.afpc.af.mil/, is an excellent source of additional information on assignments, especially the "Site Index" page.

Air Force Pamphlet 36-2241, *Professional Development Guide.*

# 20

# Going to a
# New Assignment

Reassignments to new duty stations, including overseas stations, are routine and frequent events that affect all military members and their dependents. The reassignment process begins when personnel channels officially notify you of your selection for a permanent change of station (PCS). You will receive printed copies of PCS orders that will confirm the unit and location to which you are being reassigned and the date that you must be there. The Military Personnel Section from your present base will arrange your outprocessing needs, and personnel from your next base will provide you with information to help your transfer go smoothly.

This chapter discusses what to expect in a new assignment and some hints on how to "hit the ground running" in your new assignment. For information on getting the "right" assignment and a more detailed discussion of the assignment process, see chapter 19.

## SPONSOR PROGRAMS
The virtual eSponsor program provides all-access benefits to incoming Airmen and their sponsors. The eSponsor program allows the sponsor to create an online registration and data record for the newcomer where a needs-assessment checklist requests information about spouses, children, and pets. The program was developed to create a standardized process worldwide.

Sponsor programs were designed to provide new personnel with information before their arrival, and then to help them settle in. Sponsors are from the next unit of assignment, preferably the immediate duty section, at the shop or branch level. In most cases, personnel of similar grade and status are assigned as sponsors (airmen for airmen, NCOs for NCOs, singles for singles, married personnel for married personnel, and so on). For senior personnel, sponsors may be the commander or person they are replacing.

Sponsors provide information about the mission of the organization, the military member's duty section, family needs (housing, schools, and base facilities), and any special aspects about the surrounding community (especially if it is an overseas area). Sometimes base brochures outline topics of common interest.

If the assignment is to an overseas duty location, sponsors should always provide additional information: available services, differences in electrical current, the size of quarters on and off base (especially if they are small), and the availability of parts and service facilities for American automobiles.

## ARRIVING AT A NEW LOCATION

At duty locations in the United States, new personnel usually arrive by commercial transportation or private vehicle. If possible, try to make prior arrangements to have your sponsor meet you or make reservations for temporary lodging. If prior arrangements have not been made, the base billeting office can advise you on temporary lodging. Usually it will have information for in-processing of new personnel. At most overseas locations, new personnel and their families are met at an air terminal by a base representative who arranges transportation to a central point on base, where sponsors help them obtain temporary quarters and instructions for in-processing.

**In-Processing.** In-processing consists of reporting in to the orderly room of your new unit of assignment, your duty section, and the Military Personnel Section (MPS). At the MPS, you will turn in most of the official records you brought with you and will be scheduled for a variety of appointments based on your grade and sometimes your career field.

One of the appointments will be a newcomer's orientation, a meeting that provides information for new arrivals, including spouses if they wish. It covers the unit's mission and areas of common interest, including housing, educational opportunities, and base facilities and programs. In overseas areas, other topics, such as driving, travel, and host nation sensitivities, may be included. Personnel then visit other locations on base, depending on their individual needs, collecting travel allowances, obtaining housing, arranging delivery of household goods, registering a vehicle on base, meeting training schedules, and so forth.

**Getting Permanent Living Quarters.** Three primary categories of permanent living quarters are available, and members are assigned based on marital status (married or single), grade, and number of dependents.

- Rooms in dormitories, previously referred to as barracks, are assigned to single and unaccompanied personnel by their unit of assignment or a Central Dormitory Management Office (CDMO).
- Base housing, when available, is assigned to accompanied members on a priority system, based primarily on the date of arrival and the number of bedrooms needed for dependents.

- Off-base quarters are obtained by accompanied or unaccompanied personnel when on-base quarters are not available. They are usually rented from
private owners, or can be purchased if a member prefers.

Anyone renting off-base property should be sure to read the rental agreement
carefully. It will specify the period of your lease and may include special provisions. If standard contracts are offered by the base housing office, they should be
used. They usually contain a standard military release clause that will enable you
to move out early if you are offered base housing.

Also, take time to complete an accurate inventory of the rental property. Note
the condition of the house or the apartment itself (condition of paint, windows,
fences, doors, any damage such as scratches or chips) and the condition of any
items not permanently fixed (appliances, curtains, carpets). By doing this you
reduce the possibility of being charged for damage that was not your fault. Some
housing offices have standard forms for this purpose.

Finally, when you are moving out, be sure to provide formal written notice to
the landlord or agent and to do so as early as possible, although the amount of
notice you are required to give should be specified in your contract.

**Obtaining Private Transportation.** Whatever mode of transportation you
choose (car, motorcycle, or bicycle), be sure it is safe and reliable. Sometimes bar-
gains work out satisfactorily. When they don't, the outcome can be a real source of
frustration, affecting both your health and your bank account.

## REPORTING FOR DUTY

Reporting for duty includes becoming familiar with your new unit's mission, the
personnel assigned, and the role you will be expected to assume. When you arrive,
the focal point is usually a unit orderly room. Here, newcomers are processed in
and introduced to key personnel such as the supervisor, the first sergeant, and the
commander. Afterward, individual or group meetings provide insight into the unit's
specific mission and how it complements the base or installation mission, any special policies or procedures, and some information about where you will work and
what or whom you will be responsible for (or to). Then you will go to your immediate duty section (a branch, shop, or office), where you will meet the supervisors,
peers, and subordinates you will work with. Duty assignments based on each individual's grade and experience are determined, and work schedules are established.

## SUPERVISORY POSITIONS

Experienced airmen may be placed in supervisory positions. These positions carry
a wide range of responsibilities and are subject to much discussion. What do these
roles encompass? In the words of CMSgt Donald L. Neiworth, being in a supervisory position means "understanding and being actively involved and committed to
the Air Force mission, providing leadership through example, and taking care of
your people."

**Understanding the Mission.** Initial information about the mission and your area of responsibility comes from discussions with key personnel and members of the duty section. These will usually emphasize known and projected mission requirements, projects that have been done well, and those that require attention. You'll also get information from directives that outline program requirements, inspection reports, self-inspection programs, manning documents, and reports that note observations made during staff assistance visits from higher headquarters and other base-level agencies (such as safety, training, budget, audit, and security functions).

**Providing Leadership Through Example.** Many books have been written on the subject of leadership and its importance in achieving results and making good things happen. In the USAF, supervisors provide the leadership to appropriately influence and direct people in order to accomplish the mission. The traits of successful leaders include loyalty, integrity, commitment, initiative, decisiveness, and selflessness (not placing individual comfort before the mission or the people). The most effective style is tailored to the mission, the people, and the environment. The functions of a leader include developing professional relationships, setting goals and standards, providing technical competence, maintaining channels of communication, motivating people, and identifying problems that affect job performance.

**Taking Care of Your People.** Successful supervisors must be sensitive to subordinates' motivational levels and needs if they are to have a positive effect on their performance and job satisfaction. No set of rules can anticipate or cover all the elements of motivating the people who work for you, nor is a textbook solution always the best one. In general, Air Force personnel perform at higher motivational levels when they feel that:
- They are an important part of the unit.
- A supervisor takes a personal interest in them as an individual and encourages them to use their initiative and accept additional responsibilities.
- Their grade and AFSC are fairly matched to the job they're doing.
- They have the opportunity for advancement in skill levels, positions of increased responsibility, professional military education, and promotion.
- Work activities and tasks are sensibly organized and decisions are well thought out, correct, and not constantly changing.
- Standards are applied on a consistent basis without bias, and discipline is fair and just (it's OK for it to be "hard" as long as it's fair).
- The base or installation is a good place to work and live.

**Managing Resources.** If you are in a supervisory position in your new assignment, you are likely to be responsible for managing resources. At base level, the requirements for funds, supplies, and equipment are managed by two functions: the Budget Office, a branch of the Accounting and Finance Office; and Supply. Funds for official programs are based on known and projected requirements. They are controlled by cost center managers and resource advisors on a daily, quarterly, and annual basis every financial calendar (fiscal) year, which runs from the first day of October to the last day of the following September. They, in turn, work closely with supervisors, commanders, and personnel from the Budget Office. Training classes are held periodically for those responsible for managing funds.

Supplies are obtained from Base Supply, according to the local procedures and those outlined in Air Force Manual (AFMAN) 23-110, *USAF Supply Manual.* Some are stocked by Base Supply; others must be ordered. Future requirements can often be determined by past usage rates and other known indicators, such as upcoming exercises and deployments.

Equipment requirements are controlled by the Air Force Equipment Management System, which enables the Air Force to determine needs, authorizations, accountability, and the types and quantities of equipment required to accomplish specified missions. It also provides a database for budgeting and purchasing programs. At the local level, equipment account custodians in each unit or organization identify needs, order items, and are responsible for accounting for each piece of property. They work with personnel from the base's Equipment Management Office. Orders are made on equipment allowance documents that prescribe the items and quantities required for assigned missions and functions. This system provides organizations with a ready reference to equipment selected for Air Force use. It also encourages uniformity of equipment for similar functions, for example, machine shops, print shops, and administrative offices. Procedures are outlined in AFMAN 23-110. Orientation classes are also conducted for equipment custodians.

**Maintaining Facilities.** The physical appearance of a duty section and the way it is maintained often reflect the efficient, professional, and confident spirit of an organization and its personnel. Efforts to provide the best working conditions should always be made with due consideration to the job at hand, the efficient arrangement of personnel and equipment, safety features, lighting, and temperature controls.

Improvements require careful planning and the support of supervisors and commanders. They are also dependent on available funds and the approval of other base agencies, such as the safety office and the base civil engineer. Any facility-improvement project should be carefully thought out and developed into a complete and well-harmonized plan.

**Security Requirements.** Responsibilities for security are shared by everyone in the USAF. The USAF Information Security Program is a system of administrative policies and procedures designed to identify, control, and protect certain types of information from unauthorized disclosure. The Security Police have the overall responsibility for managing this program. They, in turn, are supported by security managers who have been appointed in all units and staff agencies.

At the working level, all members should know how to control, secure, and account for classified materials; assure the adequacy of storage facilities, work areas, and operating procedures; acquire appropriate security clearances for assigned personnel; and provide a continuing security education awareness program.

Specific program information and requirements are outlined in Air Force Instruction 31-401, *Information Security Program Management.* Additional information may be prescribed at local and major command levels based on the needs of specific career fields and duty locations.

**Changing Procedures.** Newly assigned personnel or supervisors should be careful about immediately making changes. However, changes are sometimes necessary to streamline procedures and enhance the efficiency of an operation. Sometimes rapid changes are needed because of safety or funding considerations. To be effective, a change should be well thought out in advance. It should improve an existing condition and provide a benefit. It should be explained to those affected and implemented gradually. This will help facilitate acceptance and reduce resistance.

**Additional Duties.** Additional duties are those assigned to personnel in addition to the primary duties of their Air Force specialty. They include positions such as equipment or supply custodian, safety representative, historian, unit public affairs representative, training manager, suggestion monitor, resource advisor or cost center manager, advisory council member, security manager, and unit career advisor. These duties place increased demands on a supervisor's time, but they also provide many benefits. They can broaden your overall understanding about other Air Force programs and prepare you for increased responsibility. Supervisors and commanders are aware of the importance of these programs and frequently comment on them in performance reports.

## THINKING ABOUT THE FUTURE

The best time to think about future assignments is two or three months after you arrive at your new base. Future promotions and assignments are based on performance and the breadth and depth of experience within an Air Force specialty. Getting that kind of experience is not always possible if you remain at one location.

Declining productivity curves and stagnation factors are also associated with staying in one position for too long. With time, each job becomes more routine and it is difficult to remain creative, innovative, and energetic. When that happens, your productivity curve starts heading downward. Those who were there when you arrived will usually depart before you. New supervisors may not be aware of the full extent of previous achievements. If someone makes a suggestion for improving a policy or procedure, and you hear yourself saying, "But we've always done it that way," stagnation has set in.

There are two ways to broaden your experience. One is to seek a change in duty positions at the same location. The other is to seek reassignment to another base or installation by updating your Air Force Form 392, "Airman Assignment Preference Statement." This form communicates your intentions to career managers through the personnel system. When completing it, be sure to consult Air Force Instruction 36-2110, *Assignments,* and select choices that are relevant to Air Force needs at bases or locations that require your Air Force specialty. Again, see chapter 19 on getting the "right" assignment.

## SOURCES OF ADDITIONAL INFORMATION

For questions about duty section requirements, consult your supervisor, first sergeant, or commander.

# 21

# NCO Leadership

By setting goals, completing PME, and gaining expertise in a skill area, it is reasonable to expect that sharp and talented airmen will be rapidly promoted to the grade of staff sergeant and technical sergeant. In addition to technical expertise, noncommissioned officers are also leaders of other airmen. Leadership can be exerted by anyone in a variety of situations, but in the Air Force, leadership is the principal reason men and women are promoted in rank to serve as officers and noncommissioned officers.

The Air Force seeks to identify leadership potential early in an airman's career. Look, for example, at the enlisted and senior enlisted performance report forms (AF Forms 910 and 911). Both have leadership blocks that ask the rating official to comment on how well the airman sets and enforces standards, displays initiative and self-confidence, provides guidance and feedback, fosters teamwork, motivates peers and subordinates, maintains discipline, and plans and organizes work.

## THE ART OF LEADERSHIP

NCOs are both leaders and managers, but there is a distinction between leadership and management. Leadership is the art of influencing and directing people to accomplish the mission. Management is the science of calculating and using resources to achieve objectives. Air Force NCOs *lead* people and *manage* things.

Leadership is what gets things done. It's not just rules, although they are important. It's not just management, although that's important also. Rather, leadership is getting a team effort focused on common, reasonably attainable, and mission-related objectives. It's making sure that the resources are on hand for a team to attain those objectives. It's inspiring people to do more than they thought they could based on the simple but vital assumption that the Air Force is made up of bright, dedicated, and patriotic people. Promotion to a leadership rank in the Air Force won't get handed to you for just showing up. To be successful, it takes hard work, determination, a positive mental attitude, and a strong, personal desire to be a leader.

Leaders are visionaries. They are inquisitive. They view facts and ideas and see patterns and new opportunities at earlier junctures than others. They don't retreat from change. They see new alternatives and options as a challenge, not as a threat.

Leaders aren't just talkers. They have a comprehensive understanding of and an expertise in what they do, and they are able to demonstrate it. We often hear this referred to as leadership by example.

Finally, leaders live the Air Force core values of integrity, service before self, and excellence in all they do.

## THE AIR FORCE LEADERSHIP CONCEPT

Leaders in the Air Force are most effective when they keep in mind two fundamental elements—the *mission* and the *people.*

The primary task of a military organization is to perform its mission. As a leader, your primary responsibility is to lead people to carry out the unit's mission successfully. Most missions involve many tasks that must be completed if the unit is to fulfill its responsibilities. The leader defines the mission and sets priorities for its various components.

People perform the mission. They are the heart of the organization, and without their support a unit will fail. You cannot be totally successful at getting the most out of people without first knowing their capabilities and what motivates them. Your responsibilities also include the care and support of your unit's personnel. To be a successful leader, you must continually ensure that the needs of the people in your unit are met promptly and properly.

## LEADERSHIP PRINCIPLES

Leadership principles are guidelines that have been tested and proven over the years by successful leaders. The most important of these principles are discussed here.

**Know Your Job.** People will follow you if you are a competent person who has the knowledge needed to complete the mission successfully. You should have a broad view of your unit's mission, and you must make sure all members of your unit understand how their jobs relate to mission accomplishment. Just as important as your own competence is ensuring that assigned people know their responsibilities.

**Know Yourself.** Knowing your own strengths and weaknesses is important to successful leadership. You, the leader, must recognize your personal capabilities and limitations. Former Chief Master Sergeant of the Air Force Robert Gaylor put it this way: "Sure, everyone wants to be an effective leader. You can and will be if you identify your strengths, capitalize on them, and consciously strive to reduce and minimize the times you apply your style inappropriately."

Airmen like SMSgt Cris Redburn know the importance of taking time to get to know the people they work with. The extra time invested in recognizing good character, looking for potential for greater responsibility, and seeing how each person contributes to the overall mission, turns "employees" into comrades and fellow warriors for freedom. Air force leaders who know their jobs well and have a passion for excellence are true ambassadors for the U.S. Air Force and the United States of America.

**Set the Example.** You must set the standard for your unit. People will emulate your standards of personal conduct and appearance. They will observe your negative characteristics as well as your positive ones. If you are arrogant or domineering, you will get no respect, only resentment. If you violate basic standards of morality, you will invariably end up in a compromising situation. If you drink excessively or abuse drugs, you send a dangerous message. Lack of self-discipline in a leader destroys the unit's cohesion and ultimately impairs its ability to perform the mission.

**Keep Physically Fit.** When you are in good physical condition, you are better prepared for any assigned mission. Setting the right example includes supporting a unit physical fitness program and enforcing Air Force fitness standards. As a military leader, you must be a positive example of professional conduct, appearance, and physical conditioning. As General Patton aptly remarked, "You are always on parade."

**Take Care of People.** Find out what their requirements are and be sensitive to human needs. Are the people housed adequately? Are they well fed? Are there personal problems with which they need help? When people are worried about these things, they cannot focus their full attention on their jobs, and the mission suffers. If you take care of your people as well as circumstances permit, you, as leader, are in a position to earn their confidence, respect, and loyalty.

**Communicate.** Information should flow continuously throughout the organization. Communication is a two-way street. Only as an informed leader will you be able to evaluate realistically your unit's progress. You must listen to what your people have to say and always look for good ideas that can flow up the chain.

**Educate and Train.** Airmen should be properly educated and trained to do their jobs. General Douglas MacArthur observed, "In no other profession are the penalties for employing untrained personnel so appalling or so irrevocable as in the military."

**Equip.** It is also your responsibility to ensure that your subordinates are equipped properly. Just as an aircrew should never be expected to engage in combat without a well-armed aircraft, personnel should not be sent ill-equipped to the office, shop, or flight line. Your leadership responsibilities include identifying needs, securing funds, and then obtaining the necessary weapons, tools, and equipment.

**Motivate and Mentor Subordinates.** Your greatest challenge is motivating subordinates to achieve the high standards set for them. Motivation is the moving force behind successful leadership. In fact, the ability to generate enthusiasm about the mission may be the single most important factor in leadership. Recognition of the efforts people put forth is one positive way in which motivation toward mission accomplishment pays dividends. When you publicly applaud the efforts of unit personnel, you build a cohesive organization that will accomplish the mission. "Leaders should work hard at earning the respect of their subordinates," Lt. Col. Kevin Sherrick, former 97th Security Forces commander, advises, "not merely settling for commanded respect."

**Accept Responsibility.** General LeMay was once asked to provide a one-word definition of leadership. After some thought, he replied, "If I had to come up with one word to define leadership, I would say *responsibility*." As a leader, you are responsible for performing the unit's mission. If you fail, you are accountable for the consequences.

**Develop Teamwork.** As a leader, you must mold a collection of individual performers into a cohesive team that works together to accomplish the mission. The unit's mission will suffer if each person in your organization is doing his or her own thing. Teamwork comes when individuals are willing to work together in a manner that is focused on the unit's mission tasks.

**Be Flexible.** There is no one perfect leadership style. Rather, the most effective style is the one that the leader tailors to the mission, the people, and the environment. You should carefully consider the environment in which you work. Leadership methods that worked in one situation with one group may not work with the same group in a different environment. Consider the squadron that is permanently based in the United States but deploys overseas for an extended period of temporary duty. Billeting or food service difficulties, equipment or parts shortages, family separation problems, inclement weather, or other problems may occur. Any of these situations creates an entirely new environment with which you must respond as leader. Accommodate changes; be sensitive to your surroundings.

## LEADERSHIP PREPARATION

The Air Force's leadership and NCO schools are not the only way to prepare yourself to lead. Successful leaders have mentioned three things you can do every day outside the PME environment to help prepare yourself for leadership at progressive levels.

**Think About Leadership.** What would you do in a given situation, and why? If you were placed in charge of your work unit tomorrow, how would you act? Remember the principles of leadership, the Air Force core values.

**Observe Leaders in Action.** How does your boss handle a given situation? Why did a particular action succeed or fail? How does your wing commander, squadron commander, first sergeant, or supervisor lead?

**Study Leadership and the Profession of Arms.** The military has a long tradition of leadership. Read about the successful leaders in our history and how they led. The professional reading list at appendix A is a good place to start your study.

## A LEADER'S AUTHORITY AND RESPONSIBILITIES

AFI 36-2618, *Enlisted Force Structure,* contains specific responsibilities for noncommissioned officers in the Air Force. It summarizes the above concepts and principles and is worth repeating here.

**Authority.** NCOs are delegated the authority necessary to exercise leadership commensurate with their rank and assigned responsibilities. They carry out orders of those appointed over them, and they give orders in the execution of their duties.

**Responsibilities.** NCOs are expected to:
- Attain, maintain, and demonstrate NCO skill levels.
- Demonstrate and maintain Air Force standards of conduct.
- Ensure proper care of Air Force equipment and funds.
- Execute duties in a timely manner.
- Conduct individual and group training.
- Actively participate in Air Force health and safety programs.
- Actively support the Air Force's programs against discrimination and sexual harassment.
- Counsel and correct individuals regarding duty performance, professional relationships, and personal appearance.
- Mentor and assist subordinates in duty performance and professional development.

The Air Force depends on positive, effective leaders at all levels to perform its worldwide mission. Leadership is not the private domain or responsibility of our most senior officers and noncommissioned officers. It is a responsibility for which every member of the Air Force must prepare. Leaders are not born. They are educated, trained, and made—just as they are in any other profession.

# 22

# Commissioning Opportunities

While on active duty, airmen from the enlisted force have the opportunity to become commissioned officers through one of several commissioning programs. Competition for these programs is extremely keen and selection criteria are very high. Even so, it is an attainable goal, one that many enlisted personnel have achieved. It provides expanded opportunities for those who have demonstrated the potential to assume higher levels of responsibility. It also allows members to apply for a variety of specialized positions where being a commissioned officer is a prerequisite (such as rated positions for pilots and navigators).

## PRIMARY OPPORTUNITIES

There are four commissioning routes that are most commonly pursued.

**USAF Officer Training School (OTS).** The OTS program provides an opportunity for enlisted members with a baccalaureate or higher degree from an accredited college or university, completed either before entry in active service or during off-duty education programs while serving on active duty. To be eligible, applicants must demonstrate outstanding potential for commissioning and be recommended by their commander; be a U.S. citizen; achieve favorable scores on the Air Force Officer Qualification Test (AFOQT); be physically qualified; and be commissioned before the age of thirty for nonflying duties or twenty-seven and a half for flying training. There are no marital restrictions. For further information, contact the Military Personnel Flight (MPF) at your base.

**Airmen Education and Commissioning Program (AECP).** This program provides the opportunity for career-minded airmen with a college background to complete a baccalaureate degree in selected technical fields, such as engineering, meteorology, or computer sciences. To apply for the program, airmen must have completed at least forty-five semester hours, including six in calculus and analytic geometry and, in some cases, one course in physics or chemistry (with laboratory experience). Those selected are allowed up to thirty-six months to complete their degree requirements while attending a civilian college or university; tuition costs are paid by the Air Force. After graduation, those selected are enrolled in Officer Training School. To be eligible, applicants must meet the criteria listed above; demonstrate outstanding potential for commissioning and be recommended by their commander; be a U.S. citizen; be physically qualified; achieve favorable scores on the Air Force Officer Qualification Test (AFOQT); have at least one year on active duty as an enlisted member (if serving at an overseas location, members must complete at least one-half of their overseas tour before being entered into this program); and meet age requirements similar to those for the OTS program. There are no marital restrictions.

**Air Force Reserve Officer Training Corps (AFROTC).** The Airman Scholarship and Commissioning Program (AFROTC-ASCP) establishes procedures for active-duty airmen to receive AFROTC scholarships and attend the college or university of their choice in a four-year AFROTC program. Those selected are subsequently discharged from active duty and enlisted in the Air Force Reserve. Upon completion of their degree and AFROTC requirements, airmen are commissioned as officers in the Air Force, with active-duty service commitments of four years or longer, depending on the scholarship awarded and the career field they are entered into. To be eligible, airmen must meet the criteria noted above; demonstrate outstanding potential and be recommended by their commander; be a U.S. citizen; be physically qualified; achieve favorable scores on the Air Force Officer Qualification Test (AFOQT); have an academic eligibility letter from AFROTC; and be under age twenty-nine as of June 30 of the calendar year in which they would be eligible for appointment as a commissioned officer. There are no marital restrictions.

**The Air Force Academy and Air Force Academy Preparatory School.** These programs offer opportunities to attend the U.S. Air Force Academy in Colorado Springs, Colorado, graduate with a bachelor of science degree, and be commissioned as an officer in the Regular Air Force. Selection processes are extremely competitive and attract the highest caliber of candidates from every part of the nation.

Vacancies are available for airmen serving on active duty and for those serving in the Air Force Reserve and the Air National Guard. Prospective candidates must apply through their unit commander, who processes the application and forwards it to the Director of Cadet Admissions for a determination of eligibility. Before airmen apply, they must meet the following basic eligibility criteria: be at least seventeen years of age and not have passed their twenty-second birthday as of July 1 in their year of entry into the Academy program; meet physical requirements; be a U.S. citizen; be unmarried; and not have a legal obligation to support a child or children or any other person.

The Air Force Academy Preparatory School was established for those who require additional instruction to improve their performance on Academy entrance examinations and to help them prepare for Academy courses. It is open to civilian candidates, as well as military personnel on active duty in the USAF and airmen serving in the Air Force Reserve and the Air National Guard. Prospective candidates must apply through their unit commander, who will review the application and forward it along with a statement of recommendation to the Cadet Admissions Office at the Academy. Academic terms at the Preparatory School usually last for ten months; members are then enrolled as cadets in the formal Academy course. To apply, airmen must meet the following basic eligibility criteria: be at least seventeen years of age and not over twenty-one years old as of July 1 in the year they would be admitted to the Preparatory School; meet physical requirements; be a U.S. citizen; be unmarried; and have no dependent children.

For additional information on the two programs, consult your base's Academy Project Officer, or write to the Cadet Admissions Office, U.S. Air Force Academy, Colorado Springs, CO 80840.

## OTHER COMMISSIONING OPPORTUNITIES

**Air Force Reserve Officer Training Corps (AFROTC).** The AFROTC offers a Professional Officer Course (POC) Early Release Program for airmen on active duty. You must request voluntary separation to enter an AFROTC program at an accredited college or university. Those who apply must be able to complete all degree and commissioning requirements within two academic years. Normally, selectees must complete all requirements and be commissioned before they turn thirty. For outstanding and deserving airmen, the Air Force Personnel Center (AFPC) may extend this age restriction to thirty-five.

**Leaders Encouraging Airman Development (LEAD).** This program offers two avenues for commissioning for active-duty enlisted personnel. The first allows wing commanders to nominate airmen who are younger than twenty-one before July 1 to attend the Preparatory School at the USAF Academy. The second allows major command commanders to select airmen to receive two- to four-year scholarships at AFROTC-offering universities. This latter program is allowed to offer fifty scholarships annually. Applicants must be career airmen with less than six years of service.

**Professional Officer Course Early Release Program (POC-ERP).** This program allows active-duty airmen to apply for early separation to enter the junior or senior year of AFROTC. They must be able to complete all requirements within two academic years. This is not a scholarship program, but ROTC students qualify for a $150 monthly stipend and may qualify for a $1,000 incentive grant each semester.

**Medical Service Direct Appointment.** In this program, qualified airmen can apply for direct appointments for duty as officers in the medical specialties.

**Judge Advocate Direct Appointment.** This program makes provisions for qualified airmen to apply for direct appointments for duty as officers in the legal fields.

## ONE VERY IMPORTANT CONSIDERATION

One very important theme has a direct bearing on selection for a commissioning program—demonstration of outstanding potential to become an officer and the concurrence and recommendation by a commander. In a nutshell, this means that your performance, as reflected in your performance reports and your day-to-day efforts, must be outstanding and must clearly show that you have the proper aptitude, attitude, and motivation to succeed as an officer. When commanders make recommendations, they do so based on their personal observations, a review of your records, and the recommendations put forth by your supervisors. Their final decision will reflect the best interests of the Air Force; it's not always an automatic "yes, I concur."

I remember one young airman who talked with his commander about commissioning opportunities. The airman was very bright, enthusiastic, and very positive: "I've decided that I want to become an officer." He and the commander discussed several programs and options. After the airman left, the commander asked the first sergeant to contact the supervisors involved. Two days later, the supervisors (a senior master sergeant and a technical sergeant) came to see the commander. Their comments: "We think that Airman Smith is a bright and capable young man; however, we're concerned about his total commitment to the Air Force and his reasons for wanting to become an officer. He's qualified within his specialty, but he lacks initiative and sometimes imposes unfair workloads on his fellow airmen. This was reflected in his last performance report, which recommended improvements in several areas. In addition, he's told us that he wants a commission so he can be reassigned to another location."

The commander reviewed the airman's official personnel records and then discussed the situation with the airman. In summary, the commander said: "I know that you would like to become an officer, but after considering all factors, I have concluded it would be inappropriate for me to approve your request at this time. Approval may be appropriate at some future date if you can show improvement in the areas noted."

As you can see, the screening process considers many factors. Before candidates can be selected, they must first be recommended. So if you're seriously interested in a commissioning program, set your goals high and go for it, but don't neglect your duty performance in your present job. Your potential for future positions will always be assessed, in part, on your past record of performance.

## SOURCES OF ADDITIONAL INFORMATION

For information concerning the Air Force Academy and/or Air Force ROTC programs, access the official Air Force web site at www.af.mil or www.academyadmissions.com.

The base education office is a good source for further information.

# PART IV

# Personal Affairs

# 23

# The Family in the Air Force Community

Providing for the needs and well-being of a servicemember's family is recognized at every level as an essential factor in accomplishing the overall mission of the U.S. Air Force. Many family-oriented programs have evolved over a period of time; others have been implemented to keep pace with new developments and changes in force structure.

One point is commonly agreed upon at all levels: Long-term commitment to the USAF is strongly affected by the family's feelings of satisfaction with the Air Force way of life. The level of satisfaction usually has a strong and observable bearing on the military member's daily duty performance and ultimately on the decision to reenlist.

The composition and the needs of Air Force families have evolved and taken on many new dimensions over the past twenty years. Most of these changes can be traced to the shift from the draft to the all-volunteer force. In the past, the draft provided the personnel (mainly men) to meet the needs of the Air Force. With the coming of the all-volunteer force, personnel planners provided a wide range of new inducements to attract people to the USAF. As the range of new volunteers arrived, so did the range of needs, which were not previously provided for.

For example, the emergence of more single-parent families had a very definite effect on duty scheduling; prolonged periods of separation caused by temporary duty requirements were a particular problem. This also resulted in an increased need for child-care centers.

Also, as the number of dual-career families increased, more child-care centers were needed. Military reassignments meant the nonmilitary spouse had to stop working, resulting in partial loss of pay and benefits, an interruption in career progression within a profession, and loss of seniority. Even assignments when a husband and wife were both military members had to be considered more carefully.

In the "new" Air Force, more women were placed in nontraditional jobs, such as aircraft maintenance and security police. The full and effective use of trained women was a slow process, sometimes accompanied by resistance to change. Women also brought a new dimension: the "dependent husband" in the USAF community.

This range of new needs made it necessary to expand existing family-related programs and to develop additional ones.

## FAMILY SUPPORT CENTERS: THEIR ROLE AND THEIR SERVICES

*We have always been proud of the idea that the Air Force takes care of its own. Family Support Centers are an important part of this.*
—Gen. Charles A. Gabriel, former Chief of Staff, U.S. Air Force

Family Support Centers (FSCs), or Airman and Family Readiness Flights, have been expanded considerably at base level over the past few years. They are a result of the Air Force's recognition that family issues have a direct effect on the morale and productivity of Air Force members and on decisions for making the Air Force a career. They serve as a focal point for responding to family issues that affect the Air Force mission.

Their services include the following:
1. Information/referral center, where you can get information or specialized assistance.
2. Relocation assistance, for help when you're moving to another base.
3. Support during family separations.
4. Financial management programs.
5. Spouse employment programs, which offer information about job opportunities and programs on how to develop job-hunting skills.
6. Special-needs programs, such as single parents' groups.
7. Family skills, which offer programs on communication and enhancing a family's quality of life.
8. Private and professional assistance for personal crisis issues, marital, child-related, and so forth.

Family Support Centers provide something for everyone in the Air Force family, whether they are singles, couples, or families with children. The best way to see what they have to offer is to stop in and get acquainted. They may be able to help you. You may be able to help them if you have skills or experience that would be useful for programs they would like to offer. More on FSCs is found in chapter 26.

## SETTLING INTO A NEW COMMUNITY
The Air Force community offers many social, educational, and volunteer opportunities for men and women, both married and single. The Air Force community seeks to overcome isolationism, and allows all airmen to actively seek out and pursue their interests.

**Volunteer Work.** Many important programs in the Air Force community are made possible through the efforts of volunteer workers. The concept isn't unique to the USAF. It's really a reflection of American community life where, for generations, people from all walks of life have reached out to help others. It's also a way to meet other people who share similar experiences and to get experience for future employment. Within the USAF, thousands of people offer their time to support community services, such as the thrift shops, family services programs, Family Support Center programs, youth activities (such as sports and Scouts), and as Red Cross assistants in medical facilities. Some positions are full-time; others are part-time, sometimes for a few hours a week. Some volunteers also hold down a full-time job but still serve as Scout leaders or sports coaches. Many of these programs are not fully funded, so without volunteers they would have to be discontinued. If you are interested in volunteer work, it's best to contact the agency directly; it'll usually welcome you with open arms. Information is also available in the Family Support Center and periodically in the base newspaper.

**Employment Opportunities for Spouses.** Employment opportunities for spouses vary, depending on location and occupation. Working off base in a local community is common in the United States. If you'd like to work on base, your first stop should be the Civilian Personnel Office. Job openings are posted here and applications are taken. They also provide standard information handouts that describe available employment opportunities. Other on-base options include the Army and Air Force Exchange Service (AAFES), the commissary, banks, and credit unions. Overseas areas include all these plus teaching and administrative positions in the Department of Defense Dependent Schools (DODDS) system. Opportunities to work off base in overseas areas do exist, but they vary from country to country, based on the laws and customs of the host nation.

**Dispelling Some Myths.** When it comes to volunteer work and employment by spouses, two very popular myths always seem to circulate.

*The myth:* "What I do in the military community will have an effect on my spouse's career, especially when it comes to promotions."

*The reality:* Military success is determined by the servicemember's duty performance and adherence to Air Force standards. Support and encouragement from a spouse usually have a positive effect on that performance. Involvement in programs in the Air Force community is always recognized and appreciated, but this involvement is not directly linked to a member's potential for promotion. There are circumstances where a spouse's actions can indirectly have an adverse effect—instances of continued indebtedness, criminal acts, use of illegal drugs, and so forth—because of his or her potentially disrupting influence on the member's performance. When performance declines, career progression can be affected.

*The myth:* "I can't get a job because Air Force policy states that I have to support my husband's career."

*The reality:* According to the Air Force policy statement in effect since 1988, "It is Air Force policy that the choice of a spouse to pursue employment, to be a homemaker, to attend school, or to serve as a volunteer in the Air Force or local

**"I talked my wife into getting this job. It's part of my retirement program."**

community activities is a private matter and solely the decision of the individual concerned. No commander, supervisor, or other Air Force official will directly or indirectly impede or otherwise interfere with this decision. Neither the decision of the spouse in this matter, nor the marital status of the military member will be a factor used to affect the evaluation, promotion, or assignment of the military member, except under conditions specifically permitted by Air Force regulation (e.g., joint spouse assignments or personal hardship circumstances).

"Air Force spouses and members have a long tradition of service to their communities. Their individual and collective efforts have enhanced the quality of life in military and civilian communities around the world. This generous and willing participation in volunteer organizations, in clubs and in other support activities has contributed greatly to the morale and well being of the Air Force family. The Air Force welcomes and values this generosity of spirit. At the same time, the Air Force recognizes that voluntary service must be exactly that—voluntary, and must be so regarded by all Air Force members."

## CHILDREN'S NEEDS
The life of a military child is a mix of new places, new people, and new routines. It's also a life of many opportunities. Because they are exposed to a variety of

changing situations, children often mature much more quickly and become more self-reliant. As world travelers, they also have a much greater awareness of people and their cultures: similarities, differences, customs, history, and languages.

As children become older, each move usually becomes a little bit harder to make. New environments can pose a temporary threat. Children are very adaptable, however, and in most cases they tend to make the readjustment before parents do—sometimes before all the boxes are unpacked.

When you arrive at a new location, it's a good idea to provide your children with a miniorientation. At a minimum, they should know the following:

- Where mom or dad works (office, shop, or duty location) and how to get in touch with you (a duty telephone number).
- The telephone numbers of a relative or close friend in case they can't contact you.
- How to get in touch with the hospital, fire department, and security police.
- Some information about places you consider to be "no-go" areas: streets they shouldn't cross; off-limits areas, such as active flight lines; and so forth.

A smooth transition to a new environment comes easier with exposure to community programs. Most of the ones that affect kids revolve around their neighborhood friends, the schools, and special youth activities, such as sports, Scouts, and other programs. The base newspaper and the Family Support Center are excellent sources of information on what's happening locally. Your sponsor should be able to answer most general questions.

Any reference to community problems that affect children, such as vandalism or drugs, should be checked out through a reliable source. Each installation usually has a "rumor control" telephone number. Some stories may have substance; others may have been greatly exaggerated.

**DoD Schools.** When it comes time for school enrollment, it's usually necessary to furnish documents such as your children's birth certificates, shot records, and latest report cards or transcripts. It's a good idea to hand-carry these items with you whenever you're reassigned. A complete discussion on DoD schools is found in chapter 26.

**Child-Development Centers.** Most bases have child-development centers that offer full-day, part-day, and hourly care for children six months to eleven years of age. Some bases also provide infant programs for children of ages six weeks to six months. Most centers use theme programming to provide quality care and to encourage growth physically, emotionally, intellectually, and socially. As a service distinct and apart from child care, many bases offer structured preschool classes for two, three, or five days a week.

**Youth Activity Centers.** Youth Activity Centers offer a variety of specially supervised programs for children ages five through eighteen. Activities include a variety of sports programs and special activities, such as special interest clubs, dances, instructional classes (ballet, gymnastics, self-defense, and so on), and trips to local places of interest. Many youth centers feature game rooms, special interest rooms for teens, and snack bars.

**Children with Special Needs.** Some children may need additional attention, care, or teaching because they are affected by physical, learning, or emotional disabilities or speech and language impairments. The Air Force provides for these needs with the Children Have a Potential (CHAP) program. Under this program, an airman may receive an assignment or deferment from an assignment to establish a special-education or medical program for a handicapped child. Each request is reviewed on a case-by-case basis and reevaluated upon request each time a member is selected for reassignment.

**Single-Parent Families.** Single-parent families are commonly found (and accepted) throughout the Air Force. They exist when one parent is responsible for managing the affairs of a family without a partner or spouse. Military members in this category have "extended duty days" at home to fulfill the role of the absent partner. Sources of help and assistance include members of their extended families, coworkers, and neighbors; schools, child-care centers, and religious organizations; Family Support Centers, which often provide referral services; and single-parent support groups, for mutual support and assistance.

## PLANNING FOR FAMILY SEPARATIONS DURING DEPLOYMENTS AND TEMPORARY DUTY ASSIGNMENTS

The USAF conducts missions around the world. To support these requirements, sometimes it is necessary for military personnel to go away for short periods on unaccompanied tours of duty. A little preplanning can eliminate a lot of potential problems. Be sure to discuss the following with your family or designated representative:

1. Departure and return dates.
2. The mailing address at the temporary duty location. If you are overseas, make sure your spouse knows the number and combination for your mailbox.
3. Important local addresses, points of contact, and telephone numbers for routine matters and in case of an emergency. At a minimum they should include your commander and first sergeant, hospital, fire department, security forces, legal office, chaplain, the Family Support Center, and the Red Cross.
4. Dependent ID cards. Check them for expiration dates, and if necessary, get new ones from the customer service unit of the Military Personnel Section. ID cards are issued to children when they reach ten years of age; exceptions can be made on a case-by-case base when required.
5. The use of power of attorney. If you already have one, make sure it is current and still meets your needs. Some provide full powers to act in your absence; some provide limited powers. If you are a single parent, make sure it allows for medical care of children. The same applies for wills; ensure they are current. If in doubt, check with the base legal office. They can prepare both these documents for you at no expense.

6. Financial arrangements. For the military member: Have sufficient funds for expenses, but don't carry a lot of cash. Consider traveler's checks if you're going to leave your checkbook at home with your spouse. Pay known bills in advance, especially car insurance so it doesn't expire while you're away. For your family members: Make sure they have sufficient funds.

7. The family car. Check tires, oil, car insurance, and base-pass expiration dates. Let your spouse know whom to contact in case of problems.

8. Procedures for minor house repairs. If the house is rented, note the landlord's telephone number. If you live in base housing, make a note of the service call number in case a repairman needs to be called out to check heating, plumbing, appliances, and so forth.

9. The children's needs. It's a good idea to talk to them candidly. Tell them why you're going, how long you'll be gone, and when you'll be back. This will help put them at ease and let them understand that it's just a temporary absence. Single parents may have special considerations to take into account under the family care program, particularly if a child's temporary guardian does not have military entitlements and privileges—arranging access to the base, commissary, exchange, medical facilities, and so forth. The best sources of information for questions are your supervisor, the unit orderly room, and your first sergeant.

DOD policy requires servicemembers with responsibilities for family members to have a family care plan. Failure to produce a family care plan within 60 days of the discussion with the commander, supervisor, or commander's designated representative may result in disciplinary action and/or administrative separation. In addition to the required family care plan, military members are strongly encouraged to have a will.

Servicemembers who are single parents with custody of children and military couples with dependents must have a family care plan. Members who are solely responsible for the care of a spouse, elderly family member, or other adult family member with disabilities who is dependent upon the member for financial, medical, or logistical support (housing, food, clothing, and transportation) must also have a family care plan. This includes a family member with limited command of the English language or the inability to drive or gain access to basic life-sustaining facilities. Members whose family circumstances or personal status change are required to notify their commander as soon as possible, but no later than 30 days after any change in family circumstance or personal status that makes it necessary for them to establish a family care plan.

These plans must include provisions for short-term absences (such as TDY for schooling or training) and long-term absences (such as operational deployments) and designate a caregiver for the affected family member(s). Financial arrangements may include powers of attorney, allotments, and other documents necessary for logistical movement of the family or caregiver should it become necessary. A statement signed by the caretaker and the servicemember and stating that the caretaker has been thoroughly briefed on financial arrangements, logistical arrangements, military facilities, services, and benefits and entitlements of the family members must also be included. Additional items may be required to fit individual situations.

## AIR FORCE SOCIAL FUNCTIONS

Social functions in the U.S. Air Force include formal and informal gatherings in base facilities, private living quarters, and at locations in the surrounding community. Most are attended by those who really want to be involved, who enjoy each other's company, and want to mix and have fun. Nowadays, when people mention gatherings for "mandatory fun" they usually speak in terms of sympathy for senior officials who have full calendars of engagements, sometimes four and five nights a week.

Social courtesies in military circles are very similar to commonly accepted courtesies in civilian circles. Invitations are usually sent out for formal functions. A written response should be provided when requested; it helps the host make the necessary plans and arrangements. For informal occasions, people are usually invited in personal conversation, but never in front of someone who is not being invited.

Always ask your host before bringing other guests. Take children if it is a children's function (such as a Christmas or Halloween party), but not otherwise, unless they are specifically invited. Be punctual. Be yourself and go with the flow of the occasion.

At the social function, it's appropriate to rise when being introduced or when shaking hands, especially when the other individual is a woman, an older person, or a distinguished person. Formal terms of address for military personnel are noted in chapter 2, "Customs and Courtesies." Try to avoid too much shop talk. It's usually a common denominator in military circles and hard to steer clear of altogether. But it can be a real source of irritation, especially to a spouse, if it goes on throughout the evening.

Enjoy the occasion, but do not overindulge. Everyone has different tolerance levels. Having an occasional soft drink with ice is a good way to pace yourself. There's nothing wrong with politely turning down offers for another drink ("No thanks, I'm not drinking"). This can also pay dividends when it comes time to go home. Driving while drunk is not legal in the United States or overseas. Besides that, it can be very dangerous (even life-threatening) for you, your family, your friends, and other people on the roads. Don't overstay your welcome. And when it's time to leave, always remember to thank the host.

## WRITING HOME

Some people are quite good at writing home regularly. Others may do so only once or twice a year. How often you decide to write is an individual decision, of course, but family members will be anxious and concerned if they don't hear from you for long periods, especially if you are a long way from home. Many airmen away from home connect through internet services like Skype or Google Voice. The latest technologies allow real-time video conferencing and staying in touch has never been easier. Always be mindful of disclosing sensitive military information.

## SOURCES OF ADDITIONAL INFORMATION

Air Force Instruction 36-3009, *Airman and Family Readiness Centers.*

Air Force Instruction 36-2110, *Assignments,* for information concerning Children Have a Potential (CHAP) programs.

The website www.LettersfromDad.com provides tools for deploying men and women to keep in touch with loved ones while away from home.

You may also consult your supervisor, your first sergeant, or the Family Support Center.

# 24

# Medical Care

Servicemembers cannot function at peak performance if they are not fit and in good health. Individuals who are distracted by sickness or health problems of family members are also incapable of full concentration on their military duties. Consequently, the Air Force provides excellent medical and dental care to servicemembers and their families. Many consider medical and dental care as important benefits of service in the Air Force.

The idea of military medical care for the families of active-duty members of the uniformed services dates back to the late 1700s. In 1884, Congress directed that the "medical officers of the Army and contract surgeons shall whenever possible attend the families of the officers and soldiers free of charge." In 1997, it created Tricare, which replaced the Civilian Health and Medical Program for the United States (CHAMPUS) Armed Forces.

## TRICARE

Tricare is DOD's health-care program for active-duty airmen, their dependents, and retirees of the uniformed services. Medical and dental care for servicemembers is absolutely free of charge. If the required specialists are unavailable at your duty station, you will be medically evacuated to a regional military hospital or referred to local civilian physicians or hospitals. As the Air Force is concerned with preventive medicine, periodic medical and dental examinations are required of servicemembers. Frequency varies depending on job specialty. Flying personnel, for example, are given annual flight physicals. Fitness and weight programs, as well as antitobacco campaigns and emphasis on the moderate use of alcohol, are also efforts to maintain the health and fitness of servicemembers and their families.

Health care for dependents is provided by military clinics and hospitals on an as-available basis. Tricare's eleven DOD Health Service Regions coordinate regional health care between military treatment facilities and civilian health-care providers.

**Tricare Dependent Coverage.** The Tricare program offers eligible participants three options. In selecting one, it's important for you to understand what each program offers (and equally important, what each program does not offer). You can get copies of brochures, fact sheets, or handbooks that provide additional information and insight into each of the three options. They can usually be obtained from the health benefits adviser (HBA) at your nearest military medical facility, from the beneficiary counseling and assistance coordinator (BCAC) at your Tricare region's lead agent office, or from the regional Tricare contractor's local Tricare service center. You can also find information on the Tricare web site, at *www.tricare.osd.mil.* The three options are as follows.

*Tricare Standard.* Tricare Standard is the former CHAMPUS program. Under the Tricare Standard option, you can still use your nearby military hospital or clinic, if the facility has the space available, to provide services to you. Tricare Standard pays a share of the cost of covered health services that you obtain from a nonnetwork civilian health-care provider. There's no enrollment in Tricare Standard, but, as with the other Tricare options, you must be listed as eligible in the Defense Enrollment Eligibility Reporting System (DEERS) database in order to use Tricare Standard. The annual deductibles, cost shares, and benefits are the same as they were for CHAMPUS. Under this option, you have the most freedom to choose your provider of care, but your costs will be higher than with the other two Tricare options. You may also have to file your own claim forms and perhaps pay a little more for the care (up to 20 percent more than the allowable charge), if the provider you choose doesn't participate in Tricare Standard. If the provider does participate, he or she agrees to accept the Tricare Standard allowable charge as the full fee for the care you receive and will file the claims for you. To use Tricare Standard, just choose a physician or other Tricare-certified provider of care. Ask the provider if he or she participates in Tricare Standard.

(*Note:* A participating provider is one who agrees to accept the allowable charge as the full fee for the care that he or she provides to you. The participating provider is not signed up as part of the Tricare network. He or she participates voluntarily and may do so on a case-by-case basis. If you use a nonparticipating provider, that provider may bill you for his or her normal charges, up to 20 percent more than the Tricare Standard allowable charge.)

*Tricare Extra.* Tricare Extra, an expanded network of providers that offers reduced cost sharing, doesn't require enrollment and can be used on a case-by-case basis. Under Tricare Extra you do not have to pay an annual fee. It's exactly like

Tricare Standard, but you can seek care from a provider who's part of the Tricare network, get a discount on services, and pay reduced cost shares that, in most cases, are 5 percent below those of Tricare Standard. You won't have to file any claims when using network providers. However, you will have to meet the normal annual outpatient deductible as you would under Tricare Standard (i.e., $50 for one person or $100 for a family, for active-duty pay grades E-4 and below; $150 for one person or $300 for a family, for all other eligible persons). For assistance in locating a provider who's part of the Tricare Extra network, call a health-care finder, using your Tricare contractor's toll-free telephone number, or use the contractor's directory of providers, which is available at Tricare service centers, and in some cases, on the Tricare web site. These lists change frequently, so be sure to ask the provider if he or she is still in the network when you schedule an appointment. Under Tricare Extra, you can still use a military medical facility when space is available. You can move between the Tricare Extra and Tricare Standard options on a visit-by-visit basis.

*Tricare Prime.* Tricare Prime is a voluntary enrollment option. It is the only option that requires enrollment. Tricare Prime is very much like a civilian health maintenance organization (HMO). If you decide to get your care through Tricare Prime, you must enroll yourself and/or your family members in Prime. If you're an active-duty servicemember, you must enroll during in-processing, according to your command's policies and procedures. In Tricare Prime, you'll receive most of your care from military providers, or from civilian providers who belong to the Tricare Prime network. Parents or guardians must enroll newborns and newly adopted children in Tricare Prime as soon as possible after birth or adoption—and must also register them in DEERS—to ensure that they have uninterrupted coverage under Tricare Prime. Active-duty members and families don't have to pay an annual enrollment fee, nor do they have to pay co-pays or cost shares if they use a military medical facility or access care through Tricare Prime network providers. When you're enrolled in Tricare Prime, you'll choose (or will be assigned) a primary care manager (PCM), from whom you'll get most of your routine health care. Your PCM will manage all aspects of your care, including referrals to specialists, with the help of the local health-care finder (HCF). It's important to remember that your PCM and HCF must arrange for a referral when required, before you get specialized care.

*Tricare for Life.* The most sweeping improvements to the Department of Defense's health-care system in nearly thirty years began October 1, 2001, as legislated by the 2001 National Defense Authorization Act. If you are a uniformed service beneficiary who has attained the age of 65, are Medicare-eligible, and have purchased Medicare Part B, you will gain access to expanded medical coverage known as Tricare For Life. TFC is like a Medicare supplemental insurance policy, in that it pays for many of the medical and pharmaceutical expenses not covered by Medicare. There is no fee for Tricare For Life; it is a permanent health-care benefit.

For additional information about Tricare, contact your regional contractor's nearest Tricare service center, or call the health benefits adviser at the nearest military medical facility.

## DEERS

The Defense Enrollment Eligibility Reporting System is a worldwide database of military sponsors, families, and others who are entitled to certain health care and other benefits. The Department of Defense uses DEERS to check those who are eligible for Tricare health-care benefits. It's important for you to be familiar with its use and the need for you to keep the information that applies to you current in its database.

**Who Is Registered with DEERS?** Active-duty and retired military members are automatically enrolled, but they must take action to enroll their family members and make sure that they are correctly entered into the system. All information in the DEERS files—such as home addresses and information about spouses and children—is listed and updated only if the military sponsor specifically gives the information to DEERS.

**Keep Your DEERS Enrollment Up to Date.** Problems can arise when DEERS files are not updated by military sponsors. For example, Tricare contractors use home addresses in the DEERS files when they send information about health benefits to families. It is estimated that up to half of the addresses of active-duty military families in the DEERS files are incorrect, because DEERS files were not updated by sponsors when their families moved. When this happens, important information may be sent to a wrong address, and your family members may not receive it.

Problems can also arise when a military sponsor gets married, divorced, has a child, or adopts a child, and does not tell DEERS about the change. When this happens, claims for health care under Tricare may be denied because the DEERS files have no record of a new spouse or a child. It's also possible that a medical claim may be paid by mistake because there was no record in DEERS of a divorce or death that took place. When this happens, the government is required by law to get the money back from the agency or person to whom it was incorrectly paid, regardless of who was responsible for the mistake.

Military sponsors and family members should immediately report any changes in status (discharges, births, divorce, etc.) or location/home addresses to the nearest personnel office of any uniformed service. This will help you to avoid experiencing claims problems or having important information go to the wrong address.

Family members who are not enrolled or who are not sure about their enroll-ment should contact the nearest military personnel office of any uniformed service for assistance. To verify enrollment, call the DEERS office at one of the following toll-free telephone numbers:

DEERS 1-800-538-9552

Tricare Active Duty Programs 1-888-363-2273

Tricare for Life 1-866-773-0404

You can also find information at www.tricare.mil.

# 25

# Dollars and Sense

Money matters affect everyone—single, married, those embarking on a career, and those preparing to separate or retire. Here we'll take a look at some basic aspects of dollars and sense/cents in the military.

**THE JOINT UNIFORM MILITARY PAY SYSTEM (JUMPS)**

The Joint Uniform Military Pay System is a computerized pay system that automatically computes your pay entitlements, deductions, and leave based on information from local Accounting and Finance Offices (AFOs), Military Personnel Flight (MPF), and the Air Force Personnel Center (AFPC).

**When and How You Are Paid.** Air Force members can choose to be paid either once or twice a month. Once-a-month pay is computed from the first to the last calendar day of each month. Twice-a-month pay is computed for two periods: the first through the fifteenth calendar day, and the sixteenth through the last day of the month.

Paydays are the fifteenth calendar day of each month and the first day of the following month. If a payday falls on a Saturday, a Sunday, or a holiday, the payday is moved up to the workday before the weekend or the holiday.

During 1989, direct deposit of paychecks became a condition of employment in the Air Force. Under the Direct Deposit program (previously referred to as the SURE-PAY program), you are required to establish a direct-deposit account when you report to your first permanent duty station. Payments are then made to your personal savings or checking account, which can be in any U.S. financial institution (such as a bank, a credit union, or a savings and loan association). This system helps you avoid waiting in lines on paydays. It's also useful when you are sent on temporary duty; it reduces the prospect of delayed payments when you are at one location and your check is at another.

Local payments, whereby your local Accounting and Finance Office pays you directly by cash or check, are authorized under two circumstances:

- When new personnel are assigned to Basic Military Training School, Officer Training School, or other initial training courses.
- When it is clearly in the best interest of the servicemember and the government; for example, a waiver of the Direct Deposit program might be granted when an individual repeatedly demonstrates that he or she is incapable of handling a checking account.

**What You Are Paid.** The amount of money each member receives is computed as follows:

|  | | |
|---|---|---|
|  | **Entitlements** | Basic pay, allowances, and special and incentive pay |
| plus | **Miscellaneous payments** | Advances of pay or travel allowances, casual and partial payments, and sale of accrued leave |
| minus | **Deductions** | Taxes, life insurance, allotments |
| equals | **Net Pay** | The amount on your paycheck, also referred to as take-home pay |

**Payments.** Let's look at some of the ingredients more closely. There are several sources of what are called entitlements.

- *Basic pay* is based on your grade and years in service.
- *Allowances* are nontaxable payments for your welfare and the welfare of your dependents. They include the following:
  1. Basic Allowance for Subsistence (BAS): for enlisted members when government dining facilities are not available or when they are authorized to purchase meals outside government facilities. Most married personnel, personnel with dependents, and, in some instances, single personnel draw BAS.
  2. Basic Allowance for Housing (BAH): two rates, one for members with dependents and one for members without dependents. This allowance is not provided if you are assigned to government housing or quarters. In the United States, BAH is based on duty locations. In overseas areas, rates can be based on the fluctuation of foreign currency exchange rates and whether or not utilities are included as part of the rent. See your finance office for a list of rates.
  3. Family Separation Allowances (FSA): for added housing expenses incurred when airmen are separated from their dependents as a result of official duty requirements. The allowances compensate for the costs of maintaining quarters in two places.

4. Clothing Allowances: for repair and maintenance of military uniforms. In certain cases, personnel are entitled to civilian clothing allowances if civilian clothing is required to perform official duties.

5. Station Allowances outside the United States: for extra costs incurred when an airman is reassigned on a permanent change of station to places outside the continental United States. They include allowances for cost-of-living adjustments and temporary lodging.

- *Special pay* is provided to airmen who use specialized skills or who are assigned to specified locations (for example, Foreign Duty Pay and Overseas Extension Pay).

- *Bonus or contract pay* is provided to stimulate enlistments and reenlistments. Examples include enlistment bonuses for critically manned specialties, reenlistment bonuses, and proficiency pay to attract and retain highly qualified personnel in a designated Special Duty Assignment.

- *Incentive pay* is provided those who are required to perform certain hazardous duties. Examples include parachute duty, hazardous duty (flight), demolition duty, hostile fire duty, experimental stress duty, toxic fuel handling, and lab work with live, dangerous viruses or bacteria.

- *Miscellaneous payments* are made for three purposes. Amounts vary based on individual circumstances.

    1. Advances of pay or travel allowances are usually granted, on request, in conjunction with a permanent-change-of-station move. Up to three months of advance pay may be requested. Repayment is deducted from your future pay, usually spread over the following six-month period. For pay grades E-1 through E-4, the approval of your commander is required. If the desired payback period is greater than twelve months, then all members require the approval of their immediate commander. Advance travel allowances for permanent-change-of-station and temporary duty assignments are also permitted.

    2. Casual payments (to members away from their home stations) and partial payments (to personnel at their home stations) are made primarily under emergency situations. These payments are the exception rather than the rule. The amounts advanced are deducted from future paychecks.

    3. Accrued leave pay compensates for leave earned but not taken. One day's basic pay is provided for each day of unused leave. Up to sixty days may be "sold back" during a military career. Amounts received are subject to federal and state taxes.

**Deductions.** There are two general categories of deductions: voluntary and involuntary. Involuntary deductions are automatically taken out. They include the following:

1. Federal Insurance Contributions Act (FICA) and Medicare deductions, commonly referred to as Social Security tax.

2. Federal Income Tax Withholding (FITW).

3. State Income Tax Withholding (SITW).

4. U.S. Soldier's and Airmen's Home (USSAH) deductions, 50 cents per month for each enlisted member.

Other involuntary deductions include erroneous payments, loss or damage to government property, fines and forfeitures from disciplinary actions, court-ordered child support or alimony, charges for shipping excess household goods, and writing bad checks to the commissary, exchange, or nonappropriated fund activities (such as the NCO Club).

Voluntary deductions are taken out with your consent. They include allotments made to others on your authorization. The Defense Finance and Accounting Service (DFAS) sends checks to the persons or organizations you have designated as recipients, such as charities, home loans, insurance programs, support of dependents, and personal savings and investment programs. You may authorize up to fifteen allotments.

Premium payments for Servicemember's Group Life Insurance (SGLI) are also considered a voluntary deduction. SGLI is a low-cost, government-subsidized life insurance program. Each airman is entered into the program automatically but can discontinue coverage or request only partial coverage; either action must be requested in writing.

**Keeping Track of Your Pay.** Each military member is provided with a monthly copy of a DFAS Military Leave and Earnings Statement, a personal account of your pay status. In specialized blocks, it shows details of your entitlements, allotments, deductions, payments, taxes, indebtedness, and net pay. It also has a remarks section to inform you of any changes specifically made during the month.

DFAS Form 702, Defense Finance and Accounting Service Leave and Earnings Statement (LES), is a comprehensive statement of a member's entitlements, deductions, allotments, leave information, tax-withholding information, and Thrift Savings Plan (TSP) information. Verify and keep your LES each month. If your pay varies significantly and you do not understand why, or if you have any questions, consult your finance office. The LES is available electronically. Members use the myPay system to view the LES as well as to initiate changes to selected items affecting their pay. If you lose your myPay PIN, call 1-888-DFAS411 or visit your local finance office.

If you are paid twice a month and use the direct deposit system (check sent directly to bank), the DFAS also sends an abbreviated pay notice during the middle of the month, telling how much was deposited to your account at that time.

## THRIFT SAVINGS PLAN

The Thrift Savings Plan (TSP) is a retirement and investment plan that has been available to civilian government workers since 1987. Congress extended the plan in 2000 to include servicemembers who wish to save a portion of their pay that would be in addition to their regular retirement. Contributions to the plan come from pre-tax dollars, so there are no federal or state income taxes on contributions or earnings until they're withdrawn.

# MONTHLY BASIC PAY RATES FOR COMMISSIONED OFFICERS
## Effective January 1, 2011 (Senate Version)

| Rank | <2 | 2 | 3 | 4 | 6 | 8 | 10 | 12 | 14 | 16 | 18 | 20 | 22 | 24 | 26 | 28 |
|------|----|----|----|----|----|----|----|----|----|----|----|----|----|----|----|----|
| **COMMISSIONED OFFICERS** | | | | | | | | | | | | | | | | |
| O-10 | 0.00 | 0.00 | 0.00 | 0.00 | 0.00 | 0.00 | 0.00 | 0.00 | 0.00 | 0.00 | 0.00 | 15400.80 | 15475.80 | 15797.70 | 16358.40 | 16358.40 |
| O-9 | 0.00 | 0.00 | 0.00 | 0.00 | 0.00 | 0.00 | 0.00 | 0.00 | 0.00 | 0.00 | 0.00 | 13469.70 | 13663.80 | 13944.00 | 14433.00 | 14433.00 |
| O-8 | 9530.70 | 9842.70 | 10050.00 | 10107.90 | 10366.50 | 10798.20 | 10899.00 | 11308.80 | 11426.40 | 11779.80 | 12291.00 | 12762.30 | 13077.30 | 13077.30 | 13077.30 | 13077.30 |
| O-7 | 7919.10 | 8287.20 | 8457.30 | 8592.60 | 8837.70 | 9079.80 | 9359.70 | 9638.70 | 9918.60 | 10798.20 | 11540.70 | 11540.70 | 11540.70 | 11540.70 | 11599.50 | 11599.50 |
| O-6 | 5869.50 | 6448.50 | 6871.50 | 6871.50 | 6897.60 | 7193.40 | 7232.40 | 7232.40 | 7643.40 | 8370.30 | 8796.90 | 9222.90 | 9465.60 | 9711.30 | 10187.70 | 10187.70 |
| O-5 | 4893.00 | 5512.20 | 5893.80 | 5965.80 | 6203.70 | 6346.20 | 6659.40 | 6889.20 | 7186.20 | 7640.70 | 7856.70 | 8070.30 | 8313.30 | 8313.30 | 8313.30 | 8313.30 |
| O-4 | 4221.90 | 4887.30 | 5213.40 | 5286.00 | 5588.70 | 5913.30 | 6317.40 | 6632.10 | 6851.10 | 6976.50 | 7049.10 | 7049.10 | 7049.10 | 7049.10 | 7049.10 | 7049.10 |
| O-3 | 3711.90 | 4208.10 | 4542.00 | 4951.80 | 5188.80 | 5449.20 | 5617.80 | 5894.70 | 6039.00 | 6039.00 | 6039.00 | 6039.00 | 6039.00 | 6039.00 | 6039.00 | 6039.00 |
| O-2 | 3207.30 | 3652.80 | 4207.20 | 4349.10 | 4438.50 | 4438.50 | 4438.50 | 4438.50 | 4438.50 | 4438.50 | 4438.50 | 4438.50 | 4438.50 | 4438.50 | 4438.50 | 4438.50 |
| O-1 | 2784.00 | 2897.40 | 3502.50 | 3502.50 | 3502.50 | 3502.50 | 3502.50 | 3502.50 | 3502.50 | 3502.50 | 3502.50 | 3502.50 | 3502.50 | 3502.50 | 3502.50 | 3502.50 |

YEARS OF SERVICE

# MONTHLY BASIC PAY RATES FOR ENLISTED MEMBERS
## Effective January 1, 2011 (Senate Version)

| Rank | <2 | 2 | 3 | 4 | 6 | 8 | 10 | 12 | 14 | 16 | 18 | 20 | 22 | 24 | 26 | 28 |
|------|-----|------|------|------|------|------|------|------|------|------|------|------|------|------|------|------|
| **ENLISTED MEMBERS** | | | | | | | | | | | | | | | | |
| E-9 | 0.00 | 0.00 | 0.00 | 0.00 | 0.00 | 0.00 | 4634.70 | 4739.70 | 4872.00 | 5027.70 | 5184.60 | 5436.60 | 5649.30 | 5873.40 | 6215.70 | 6215.70 |
| E-8 | 0.00 | 0.00 | 0.00 | 0.00 | 0.00 | 3794.10 | 3961.80 | 4065.60 | 4190.40 | 4325.10 | 4568.40 | 4691.70 | 4901.70 | 5017.80 | 5304.60 | 5304.60 |
| E-7 | 2637.30 | 2878.50 | 2988.90 | 3135.00 | 3249.00 | 3444.60 | 3554.70 | 3750.90 | 3913.50 | 4024.50 | 4143.00 | 4189.20 | 4342.80 | 4425.60 | 4740.00 | 4740.00 |
| E-6 | 2281.20 | 2510.10 | 2620.80 | 2728.50 | 2840.70 | 3093.60 | 3192.30 | 3382.80 | 3441.00 | 3483.60 | 3533.40 | 3533.40 | 3533.40 | 3533.40 | 3533.40 | 3533.40 |
| E-5 | 2090.10 | 2230.20 | 2337.90 | 2448.30 | 2620.20 | 2800.50 | 2947.50 | 2965.50 | 2965.50 | 2965.50 | 2965.50 | 2965.50 | 2965.50 | 2965.50 | 2965.50 | 2965.50 |
| E-4 | 1916.10 | 2014.20 | 2123.40 | 2230.80 | 2325.90 | 2325.90 | 2325.90 | 2325.90 | 2325.90 | 2325.90 | 2325.90 | 2325.90 | 2325.90 | 2325.90 | 2325.90 | 2325.90 |
| E-3 | 1729.80 | 1838.70 | 1950.00 | 1950.00 | 1950.00 | 1950.00 | 1950.00 | 1950.00 | 1950.00 | 1950.00 | 1950.00 | 1950.00 | 1950.00 | 1950.00 | 1950.00 | 1950.00 |
| E-2 | 1644.90 | 1644.90 | 1644.90 | 1644.90 | 1644.90 | 1644.90 | 1644.90 | 1644.90 | 1644.90 | 1644.90 | 1644.90 | 1644.90 | 1644.90 | 1644.90 | 1644.90 | 1644.90 |
| E-1 | 1467.60 | | | | | | | | | | | | | | | |

**DEFENSE FINANCE AND ACCOUNTING SERVICE MILITARY LEAVE AND EARNINGS STATEMENT**

| ID | NAME (LAST, FIRST, MI)<br>JONES, JOHN J. | SOC. SEC. NO.<br>123-45-6789 | GRADE<br>E9 | PAY DATE<br>780316 | YRS SVC<br>24 | ETS<br>050524 | BRANCH<br>AF | ADSN/DSSN<br>4096 | PERIOD COVERED<br>1-30 SEP 11 |
|---|---|---|---|---|---|---|---|---|---|

| | ENTITLEMENTS | | DEDUCTIONS | | ALLOTMENTS | | SUMMARY | |
|---|---|---|---|---|---|---|---|---|
| | TYPE | AMOUNT | TYPE | AMOUNT | TYPE | AMOUNT | +AMT FWD | .00 |
| A | BASE PAY | 4251.30 | FEDERAL TAXES | 487.86 | COMB FED CAMPAIGN | 10.00 | +TOT ENT | 5,794.10 |
| B | BAS | 241.80 | FICA-SOC SECURITY | 263.58 | DISCRETIONARY ALT | 194.00 | | |
| C | BAH | 970.00 | FICA-MEDICARE | 61.64 | AFAF | 3.00 | -TOT DED | 3,098.89 |
| D | CLOTHING | 331.20 | SGLI FOR 250,000 | 20.00 | TRICARE DENTAL | 19.74 | | |
| E | | | AFRH | .50 | | | -TOT ALMT | 226.74 |
| F | | | TSP | 127.54 | | | -NET AMT | 2,468.47 |
| G | | | MID-MONTH-PAY | 2137.77 | | | | |
| H | | | | | | | -CR FWD | .00 |
| I | | | | | | | | |
| J | | | | | | | •EOM PAY | |
| K | | | | | | | | |
| L | | | | | | | | 2,468.47 |
| M | | | | | | | | |
| N | | | | | | | | |
| O | | | | | | | | |
| | TOTAL | 5794.10 | | 3098.89 | | 226.74 | DIEMS<br>780316 | RET PLAN<br>FINAL PAY |

| LEAVE | BF BAL | ERND | USED | CR BAL | ETS BAL | LV LOST | LV PAID | USE/LOSE | FED TAXES | WAGE PERIOD | WAGE YTD | M/S EX | ADD'L TAX | TAX YTD |
|---|---|---|---|---|---|---|---|---|---|---|---|---|---|---|
| | 8.5 | 30.0 | 27 | 11.5 | 91.0 | .0 | 50.0 | 0 | | 4123.76 | 36742.82 | M 00 | .00 | 4335.09 |

| FICA TAXES | WAGE PERIOD | SOC WAGE YTD | SOC TAX YTD | MED WAGE YTD | MED TAX YTD | STATE TAXES | ST | WAGE PERIOD | WAGE YTD | M/S EX | TAX YTD |
|---|---|---|---|---|---|---|---|---|---|---|---|
| | 4251.30 | 37879.20 | 2348.50 | 37879.20 | 549.23 | | TX | .00 | .00 | S 00 | .00 |

| PAY DATA | BAQ TYPE | BAQ DEPN | VHA ZIP | RENT AMT | SHARE | STAT | JFTR | DEPNS | 2D JFTR | BAS TYPE | CHARITY YTD | TPC | PACIDN |
|---|---|---|---|---|---|---|---|---|---|---|---|---|---|
| | W/DEP | CHILD | 78150 | .00 | 1 | R | | 0 | | STANDARD | 117.00 | | |

| Thrift Savings Plan (TSP) | BASE PAY RATE | BASE PAY CURRENT | SPEC PAY RATE | SPEC PAY CURRENT | INC PAY RATE | INC PAY CURRENT | BONUS PAY RATE | BONUS PAY CURRENT |
|---|---|---|---|---|---|---|---|---|
| | 3% | | 0% | | 0% | | 0% | |
| | | TSP YTD DEDUCTIONS<br>1136.38 | | DEFERRED<br>1136.38 | | EXEMPT<br>.00 | | |

| REMARKS | YTD ENTITLE | 49114.80 | YTD DEDUCT | 8553.70 |
|---|---|---|---|---|

CLOTHING MAINTENANCE      011001-020930(266)
BAH BASED ON W/DEP, ZIP 78150
BANK  RANDOLPH BROOKS FCU
ACCT # XXXXXXX

www.dfas.mil

DFAS Form 702, Jan 02

**Leave and Earnings Statement (Example)**

Participation in the TSP is optional. Unlike the civilian plan, servicemembers may contribute all or a percentage of any special pay, incentive pay, or bonus pay they receive. You can contribute from one percent to 100 percent of your special pays into the thrift plan. The total amount generally cannot exceed $16,500 for the year. Contributions from pay earned in a combat zone do not count against the $16,500 ceiling. Combat zone contributions are subject to a different limitation, which is twenty-five percent of pay or $49,000, whichever is less.

Like civilian employees in the program, servicemembers must choose how they want their money invested. Right now, there are five funds to choose from. The funds run the gamut of safe to riskier investments. Study each carefully before making your choice.

For more information, contact your finance office or view the thrift plan's uniformed services web site www.tsp.gov.

## AIR FORCE POLICIES CONCERNING LEAVE

Your leave status is also reflected on your Leave and Earnings Statement. The policy concerning its use is noted in Air Force Instruction 36-3003, *Military Leave Program*.

As a member of the armed forces, you accrue two and a half days of leave for each month of active duty. Leave is paid time off for thirty days each year. It can be taken all at once or at short intervals. Each request must be approved by your supervisor and, in some cases, by your commander; it is normally granted, except in cases where military necessity requires your presence. It's always important to watch your leave balance (number of days you have accrued and not used); as on the last day of September each year, any days in excess of sixty will be lost.

### Types of Leave

*Ordinary Leave.* Leave the Air Force grants you upon your request at any time during a fiscal year to the extent of the leave that you may earn during that fiscal year, plus your leave credit from previous years.

*Sick or Convalescent Leave.* Leave the Air Force grants you for absence because of illness or convalescence upon recommendation of medical authority. It is not chargeable as leave.

*Advance Leave.* The Air Force may grant you advance leave in anticipation of the future accrual of leave. Such leave would apply in cases of emergency leave and leave used when making a permanent-change-of-station (PCS) move.

*Emergency Leave.* Leave the Air Force may grant you upon assurance that an emergency exists and that granting of such leave will contribute to the alleviation of the emergency. The total leave advanced, including emergency leave, may not exceed forty-five days. The Air Force charges it against present or future accrued leave.

*Excess Leave.* Leave of up to thirty days that the Air Force grants you that is in excess of the amount you have accrued, and is, except for such advance or ordinary leave as specifically authorized, without pay and allowances, and that you may take only under exceptional circumstances upon authority of commanders. Excess leave is charged against leave accrued in the future.

*Prenatal and Postpartum Leave.* Normally, a woman who becomes pregnant while on active duty goes into "sick in quarters" status when directed by the attending physician. Time spent in the hospital for delivery is duty time. Following completion of inpatient care, the servicemember receives convalescent leave until her medical condition permits her to return to duty.

*Delays Enroute in Executing Travel.* The Air Force counts and charges as leave authorized delays stated in travel orders.

### General Leave Policies

*Day of Departure; Day of Return on Duty Days.* The Air Force will charge you both the day of departure and the day of return as leave unless you were present for duty all or nearly all of the normal working day on either the day of commencement or termination of the leave period.

*Day of Departure; Day of Return on Nonduty Days.* When you sign out on a nonduty day, the Air Force will charge that day as leave. When you sign in on a nonduty day, the Air Force will not charge that day as leave.

*Leave to Visit Outside the United States.* Air Force members may visit foreign countries as leave, either from the United States or from their overseas station. Such leaves are chargeable as ordinary leave.

To visit communist or communist-oriented countries, special procedures must be followed. Some specialties may be more affected than others, especially in cases where personnel have access to sensitive information. For information, contact your unit security manager, the customer service branch of the Military Personnel Flight (MPF), or your first sergeant.

**Application for Leave.** In 2002, airmen throughout the Air Force began using a simplified and automated on-line leave system called *LeaveWeb. LeaveWeb* allows airmen to submit leave requests, coordinate leave with supervisors and orderly rooms, receive approvals, and notify the finance office electronically, thus saving time and improving customer service. Although *LeaveWeb* is the standard, the paper form (AF Form 988, Leave Request/Authorization) is still used where electronic requests are not available.

## PERSONAL FINANCIAL MANAGEMENT PLANNING

In today's society, our quality of life in the present and sense of security in the future depend largely on our ability to manage our finances. And while money is a subject close to everyone's heart, few of us give serious forethought to financial planning. Some people live from paycheck to paycheck. Others believe they'll achieve financial comfort and security "someday," when they reach higher income levels. Neither of these approaches is realistic.

The first step in planning your financial future is to find out where you are today, by taking a close look at your net worth. Your net worth lets you know where you stand compared to your expectations. It is computed by adding up your assets (what you own or have saved) and subtracting your liabilities (what you owe). The accompanying worksheet includes items commonly considered; you may want to add or delete categories to suit your circumstances.

After you've computed your net worth you'll have a better idea of your financial strengths and weaknesses. This leads you to your second step: identifying your financial goals, where you'd like to be tomorrow. This phase is easy. Take a pencil and make a long list. Then put them in a priority sequence based on needs and wants (needs come first, wants come second). Try to further define each goal; make it specific and establish a target date for achieving it.

For example, if you'd like to have $10,000 cash at the end of a four-year enlistment, divide the sum by the number of pay periods available. If you just came in, you would have to save approximately $100 every two-week pay period to achieve this.

| **LEAVE REQUEST / AUTHORIZATION** | | | **SECTION I** | |
|---|---|---|---|---|
| (See Privacy Act Statement and General Instructions below) | TO: ACFP | 1. DATE OF REQUEST<br>1 Nov 2011 | 2. TYPE OF TRANSACTION<br>(1–5) (AFO Use Only) | |

| 3. SSN (6–14)<br>123-45-6789 | 4. NAME (Last, First, Middle Initial) (15–19)<br>Doe, John D. | | 5. GRADE<br>E–5 | 6. CURRENT LV BALANCE<br>30 | 6a. DOS<br>1 Dec 13 |
|---|---|---|---|---|---|

| 7. RECOMMEND CONVALESCENT LEAVE<br><br>FROM _____ TO _____<br><br><br>PROVIDER'S SIGNATURE & STAMP | 8. TYPE OF LEAVE<br>(Check one)<br><br>☐ Ordinary (A)<br>☐ Convalescent (F)<br><br>REMARKS: | ☐ Terminal (P)<br>☐ Emergency (D)<br>[X] Ordinary (A)<br>☐ Special (H) | ☐ Reenlistment (E)<br>☐ Graduation (J)<br>☐ Other (Specify)<br>☐ Permissive TDY (T) | PTDY Reason<br>(AFR 35–26,<br>Atch 1)<br>_____ |
|---|---|---|---|---|

Note: Block 8 shows Ordinary (A) checked [X], and Appellate Review (R).

| 9. NO. DAYS REQUESTED<br>(33–35)<br>5 | 10. LEAVE AUTH NO.<br>(37–43)<br>LX–1234 | 11. FIRST DAY/TIME OF LV STATUS<br>5 Nov 11/0001 | 12. FIRST DAY OF CHARGEABLE LV (47–52)<br>5 Nov 11 | 13. LAST DAY OF CHARGEABLE LV (53–58)<br>9 Nov 11 |
|---|---|---|---|---|

| 14. LEAVE AREA (36)<br>[X] CONUS  ☐ OS  ☐ OS to CONUS | 15. EMERGENCY PHONE NO.<br>( 512 ) 555-7878 | 16. LEAVE ADDRESS (Street, City, State, Zip Code, and Phone No.)<br>711 Main St. |
|---|---|---|
| 17. DUTY PHONE NO.<br>7-5034 | 18. UNIT<br>7110MS | 19. DUTY SECTION<br>OMP | Anytown, MN    12345<br>512-555-7878 |
| 20. DUTY LOCATION<br>Randolph AFB TX | | | |

**LEAVE REQUEST CERTIFICATION:** *I acknowledge that the leave requested by me will be charged against my leave account unless otherwise cancelled or corrected through Part III of this form. In addition, if I cannot earn enough leave before separation to cover this request, I consent to withholding from current pay, final pay, or any other pay due to satisfy this indebtedness. I understand that there is no actual debt until my final separation from the Air Force; however, I consent to this withholding of pay in anticipation of the indebtedness for the unearned portion of my leave balance. I further consent to such withholding at a rate sufficient to satisfy this indebtedness no later than my requested or projected separation date, and understand that this could result in the withholding of 100% of any current pay, final pay, or any other money due me. I have read the instructions on PART II.*

| 21. MEMBER'S SIGNATURE<br>*John D. Doe* | 22.<br>LEAVE IS  [X] APPROVED  ☐ DISAPPROVED  DATE  1 Nov 11 |
|---|---|
| 23. SUPERVISOR'S NAME AND GRADE (Print or Type)<br>JANE D. DOE, Major | 24. DUTY PHONE NO.<br>7-5034 | 25. SUPERVISOR'S SIGNATURE<br>*Jane D. Doe* |

| **SECTION II** (To be completed by supervisor / unit commander to authorize advance or excess leave) | | | | |
|---|---|---|---|---|
| 26. LEAVE AVAILABLE TO ETS<br>(From LES) | 27. ADVANCE LEAVE REQUESTED<br>(Block 9 minus 6) | 28. EXCESS LEAVE REQUESTED<br>(44–46) (Block 9 minus 26) | 29. TOTAL LEAVE APPROVED | |
| 30. UNIT HEADQUARTERS | 31. COMMANDER'S SIGNATURE / GRADE | 32. AUTHORIZATION DATE | 33. AUTHORITY FOR ADVANCE LEAVE OVER 30 DAYS | |

**PRIVACY ACT STATEMENT**

**AUTHORITY:** 10 U.S.C., Chapter 40; 37 U.S.C., Chapter 9; EO 9397, November 1943.

**PRINCIPAL PURPOSES:** To authorize military leave, document the start and stop of such leave; record address and telephone number where you may be contacted in case of emergency during leave; and certify leave days chargeable to you.

**ROUTINE USES:** Information may be disclosed to the Department of Justice, to federal, state, local or foreign law enforcement authorities for investigating or prosecuting a violation or potential violation of law; the American Red Cross for information concerning the needs of the member or dependents and relatives in emergency situations.

**DISCLOSURE:** Disclosure of SSN is voluntary. However, this form will not be processed without your SSN, since the Air Force identifies members by SSN for pay or leave purposes.

**GENERAL INSTRUCTIONS**

**(For emergency, reenlistment, convalescent, terminal, appellate review leave, and PTDY, see variations in AFM 177–373, Volume II, Ch 7.)**

1. THIS FORM MUST BE TYPED OR COMPLETED IN INK.
2. BEFORE SEPARATING PARTS I, II, AND III, COMPLETE THE FOLLOWING BLOCKS:
   a. Blocks 1 thru 5, 9, 12 thru 21, and 23 thru 25 are self-explanatory.
   b. Block 6, Current Leave Balance. Verify that the member has enough leave balance to cover the period of leave requested. This may be done by checking the member's LES or the orderly room's leave balance listing. Complete 6a when member requests leave with a planned return date within 30 days of DOS.
   c. Block 7. This block will be completed, signed, and stamped by the appropriate medical authority if convalescent leave is recommended.
   d. Block 8. For PTDY, state the paragraph number of the applicable reason for PTDY as stated in AFR 35–26 and in Remarks area give abbreviated description of purpose of PTDY. (For example: base baseball team.)
   e. Block 10. Leave Authorization Number. Supervisor or designee obtains a leave authorization number from the unit orderly room immediately before signing a leave approval and forwarding Part I to AFO. Do not get leave number earlier than 14 days before effective date.
   f. Block 11. First Day/Time of Leave Status. This is the earliest time a member can depart or sign up for space available transportation. If planned departure is on a non-duty day, enter the non-duty date and 0001 hours. If planned departure is on a duty day without performing the majority (more than 50%) of scheduled duty, enter the date and time when more than 50% of the scheduled duty will be completed. NOTE: Leave status is not necessarily chargeable leave. Date cannot be more than 1 day before the date in block 12. See also Part III, Instructions for Charging Leave.
   g. Block 22. For completion, use approval level required by AFR 35–26.
   h. Blocks 26–33. Complete only to authorize advance or excess leave. Blocks are self-explanatory except for blocks 27, 28, and 33.
   (1) Advance Leave (Block 27). If the requested leave exceeds the current balance but does not exceed the balance to ETS, the leave is advance leave. Complete Blocks 26–27 and forward the form (all parts) to the unit commander for approval. If a member requesting leave has a cumulative advance balance of 30 days, comply with AFR 35–9.
   (2) Excess Leave (Block 28). If the requested leave exceeds the balance to ETS, the leave is excess leave. Complete Blocks 26 and 28 and forward the form (all parts) to the unit commander for approval.
   (3) Authority for Advance Leave Over 30 Days (Block 33). Record message date/time group if approval was received by message.
3. AFTER INITIALLY COMPLETING THIS FORM:
   a. Separate Part I immediately after getting a leave authorization number and signing the form. Forward to the AFO using normal distribution unless the leave is terminal/separation or involves excess or advance leave. Forward these requests (all parts) to the unit for approval.
   b. Separate Part II and give to member.
   c. Hold Part III for completion after the member's return from leave. If member requests leave cancellation before any leave is taken, complete Section III of Part III and forward to your unit commander.
4. INSTRUCTIONS FOR COMPLETING AND PROCESSING PART III ARE PRINTED ON PART III.
5. GUIDELINES FOR CHARGING LEAVE AND INSTRUCTIONS FOR LEAVE ADJUSTMENTS ARE PRINTED ON PART III.

| AF Form 988, SEP 91 | PREVIOUS EDITION WILL BE USED | PART I — AFO COPY |
|---|---|---|

**Leave Request/Authorization**

## PERSONAL NET WORTH CALCULATION

| **Assets** | | **Liabilities** | |
|---|---|---|---|
| Funds available | | Major loans | |
| Cash on hand | $ _____ | Mortgage balance | $ _____ |
| Savings accounts | _____ | Car loan balance | _____ |
| Checking accounts | _____ | Cash loan balance | _____ |
| U.S. savings bonds | _____ | | |
| | | | |
| Money lent to others | _____ | Money owed to others | _____ |
| (to be paid back) | | | |
| | | | |
| Investments | | Unpaid bills | |
| Real estate | _____ | Credit cards | _____ |
| Stocks, bonds, etc. | _____ | Charge accounts | _____ |
| Life insurance | _____ | Insurance payments | _____ |
| (cash value) | | Taxes | _____ |
| | | Education payments | _____ |
| | | | |
| Property | | Other items owed | |
| Value of home | _____ | | _____ |
| Automobile | _____ | | _____ |
| Furniture | _____ | | _____ |
| Other items | _____ | | _____ |
| | | | |
| Total assets | $ _____ | Total liabilities | $ _____ |

|   |   |   |
|---|---|---|
| | **Total assets** | $ _____ |
| *minus* | **Total liabilities** | $ _____ |
| | | |
| *equals* | **Net worth** | $ _____ |

**Money Management and Budgeting.** After you've established your goals, it's time to take a look at your income and analyze your day-to-day spending habits. The best way to start is to keep a written record of your daily expenses for a couple of weeks or a month. This will tell you exactly where your money is going. People are frequently surprised at how rapidly the small expenses accumulate. Consider the following:

- A $15 compact disk (CD) per week would equate to $780 a year.
- A $4 lunch every day would equate to $1,460 a year.
- Spending $3 a day at the bar would equate to $1,095 a year.

These are trivial examples, but they add up to $3,335 a year. Necessary expenses? Perhaps. But there are more inexpensive options. The important point is that you need to develop an awareness of where your money is going and why. As you reduce the amounts spent for unnecessary items, you'll have more of your income left for the goals that you have established.

The next step is establishing a monthly budget. Write down your total income. Then figure out and write down your fixed expenses (food, lodging, transportation, and bills). Try to economize where possible. Then look at your flexible expenses (clothing, entertainment, impulse buying habits, and so forth). This is the area to economize in. One good way to start a savings program is to "pay yourself first," identifying a specified dollar amount as a fixed expense. Reevaluate your budget after a month or two. Look at the figures and review your goals to see if you are achieving them. Make adjustments where necessary.

While you're reviewing the document you used to develop your budget, it's a good idea to think about establishing a record-keeping system. It doesn't have to be anything fancy; maybe just a cardboard box with some file folders and envelopes. Contents can include items such as Leave and Earnings Statements, savings and checking statements, bills (those paid and those to be paid), receipts for major purchases, and copies of tax forms filed during previous years. By doing this, you can assure that all your important documents will be together and easy to find when you need them.

**Moonlighting.** Moonlighting means working a second job, often at night. Current policy allows Air Force members to have second jobs as long as they don't interfere with duties or create a conflict of interest with other members of the armed forces, the Department of Defense, or the U.S. government.

**Financial Institutions.** Financial institutions whose services you may require include banks, credit unions, and savings and loan associations. The type you choose to do business with will usually depend on its location, services, and service charges.

Almost everyone uses savings and checking accounts. The status of these accounts is usually sent to each customer with a written statement each month. The statement lists all the transactions—deposits, withdrawals, and interest or dividends credited—made during the period. It's important to check this statement for accuracy. Then check it against your checkbook balance; that will help you avoid writing checks when funds aren't available.

Balancing a checking account is a simple three-step process: (1) Write down the current dollar balance from your bank statement, (2) add any deposits you've made that are not reflected on the statement, and (3) subtract the total of outstanding checks. Your account is reconciled when the balance amount on your statement and the balance amount in your checkbook are the same. If the figures don't agree, double-check your computations and make sure you've included all deposits and withdrawals. If they still don't agree, discuss it with a customer service representative at the financial institution. Banks, too, can make mistakes from time to time.

Credit and loan services allow you to buy items that you may not have sufficient funds for. Associated costs include interest payments, loan fees, insurance fees, and late charges. Use of these services is commonplace, especially for large purchases such as a car or home. The best way to approach credit is make sure that you use it, not that it uses you. Shop around and compare costs. Get the items that you need, but don't overextend yourself financially.

The 2007 defense authorization bill included a provision capping annual interest rates on consumer credit loans—including so-called "payday loans"—to service members and their dependents at 36 percent. A payday loan is a small, short-term, high-interest-rate loan, typically of a few hundred dollars. They go by a variety of other names: cash advance loans, check advance loans, post-dated check loans, or deferred-deposit check loans. High interest rates and exorbitant fees make these loans a very bad idea.

**Cosigning for a Loan.** There may come a time when you will be asked by a friend or relative to be a cosigner on a loan agreement. Cosigners are usually required when a lending institution such as a bank or credit union considers the borrower (the person requesting the loan) a bad risk. When you cosign for another person's loan, your credit is added to the borrower's to reduce the risk. If the loan is then approved, you have a legal responsibility to repay the loan if the borrower defaults. Technically, you could be liable for missed payments, late fees, and demands for payment of any balance due. As you can see, cosigning for a loan can mean taking on a heavy responsibility and it's usually not a smart move.

If in spite of these warnings you feel you must help out, consider becoming a guarantor instead of a cosigner. This will make you only secondarily liable. If you are a guarantor, the lending institution can't ask you to repay the loan without first trying to have the borrower pay. In either case, read the small print of any agreement very carefully before you sign; seek an opinion from the Base Legal Office if necessary.

**Buying a House.** Buying a house is a major step in a person's life. In some cases it can yield many benefits and be a dream come true. In others, it can become a burden and turn into a financial nightmare. The decision to buy requires careful consideration of the circumstances.

A home purchase can be to your advantage when there are major income tax benefits, the house's value will appreciate significantly during the time you own it, or you are planning to keep the house for a long time, perhaps to live in when you retire.

A purchase may *not* be to your advantage if the payments are beyond your means, the mortgage has an adjustable interest rate and is subject to periodic increases, or you may be reassigned in the near future and the prospects do not look good for reselling the house at an increased price or finding a reliable tenant.

**The Personal Financial Management Program.** The Personal Financial Management Program (PFMP) was developed by the Air Force to help all Air Force people successfully manage their finances. It provides help in three primary ways:

1. Educational instruction courses on good money management in basic training and at permanent duty stations.
2. Counseling to meet individual needs or problems.
3. Information through different media, such as base newspapers and handouts. Special pamphlets also explain a range of financial subjects, such as buying with credit, buying a car, insurance, and estate planning. They use a commonsense approach and provide practical advice. These pamphlets are free and can usually be obtained from family support centers, personal affairs offices, and some accounting and finance offices.

## SOURCES OF ADDITIONAL INFORMATION

Consult the Air Force directives and pamphlets referred to in this chapter or your supervisor, first sergeant, or unit commander.

For questions on managing personal finances, consult the Family Support Center. The Base Legal Office or Staff Judge Advocate can answer questions on the legal aspects of financial responsibility. A good discussion of this is found in *Servicemember's Legal Guide,* published by Stackpole Books, 5067 Ritter Road, Mechanicsburg, PA 17055.

For a thorough discussion of managing your personal finances, consult *Armed Forces Guide to Personal Financial Planning,* published by Stackpole Books.

# 26

# Where to Go for Information, Assistance, or "Help!"

The U.S. Air Force has a broad system of customer service–oriented agencies that respond to the needs of its personnel and their families. Some are staffed by active-duty servicemembers and civilian employees, others by volunteers: family members, retirees, and people from the local community.

The agencies provide a wide range of services—from meeting physical needs to career aspirations; from helping people resettle at a new base to helping someone in financial difficulty; from ensuring equal opportunity and treatment to ensuring national security. Despite the variety in the end product, there's a common thread that runs through every organization: service to the individual and the Air Force community.

### AIR FORCE AID SOCIETY (AFAS)

Administered by the Personal Affairs Office, which is assigned to the Military Personnel Flight (MPF), the Air Force Aid Society (AFAS) was established to provide assistance for unforeseen financial emergencies. Each case is reviewed individually, and where aid is appropriate, it can be given as either a noninterest loan or an outright grant. For example, full or limited financial assistance may be provided to meet costs of rent, utilities, food, transportation, off-duty education, and funeral expenses.

### AREA DEFENSE COUNSELS (ADCs)

Located at every major base, Area Defense Counsels (ADCs) are Air Force lawyers whose primary responsibility is to act as defense counsel for military personnel undergoing courts-martial. They also are available to advise personnel who have been administered Article 15 punishment or recommended for administrative discharge, and when a suspect in a criminal investigation asks to see a lawyer.

## THE CIVILIAN PERSONNEL OFFICE

As manager of the personnel system for the civilian workforce, the Civilian Personnel Office implements programs, classifies applicants according to their qualifications, places personnel in positions, and provides overall program management—training, appraisal, equal opportunity, labor relations, performance awards, pay, travel, leave, promotions, and so on.

## THE MILITARY PERSONNEL SECTION (MPS)

The Military Personnel Section is the office of primary responsibility for all base-level personnel actions involving military members and their dependents. The customer service branch is the focal point for all general inquiries. In most cases they will be able to act on and complete your requests. If not, they will refer you to a personnel representative from one of the following four sections:

1. The Customer Assistance Section, which includes the customer service branch, the records center, and personal affairs.
2. The Personnel Utilization Section, which includes assignments, manning control, and personnel readiness.
3. The Career Progression Section, which includes promotion and testing, classification and training, and on-the-job training.
4. The Quality Force Section, which includes separations and reenlistments, performance reports, maintenance of all unfavorable information files (UIFs), and all records of special disciplinary actions.

## THE EDUCATION OFFICE

The Education Office provides information about a wide range of educational opportunities, primarily at the college level. For more information, see chapter 16, "Training and Education."

## EDUCATION PROGRAMS/SCHOOLING
## FOR DEPENDENT CHILDREN

In the United States, some schools may be located on bases; however, most children attend schools in surrounding civilian communities. In overseas areas, the Department of Defense Dependent Schools (DODDS) network provides elementary and secondary education for children in kindergarten through twelfth grade. Their schools are staffed with American teachers, and the curriculum and standards are comparable with those in the United States. If DODDS facilities are not available, children may attend private or locally operated schools; when this is approved, costs are paid for by the government. Students who wish to continue their education can attend a university of their choice or participate in college-level courses offered on their sponsor's base on a space-available basis. In these cases, all costs are absorbed by the sponsor or dependent. Information about student grants and loans, from federal and Air Force sources, is usually available at base education centers.

More and more families are home-educating their children. Homeschoolers in the military are in a unique situation when they find themselves stationed overseas.

Unlike in the states, homeschoolers overseas rarely have access to English libraries, sports, various extracurricular activities, and other supplemental classes and courses found in the United States. The law allows homeschoolers to receive equal access to Department of Defense schools (DODEA) without having to follow the normal registration of their student as a DODEA student. On November 6, 2002, the Department of Defense issued the policy memorandum regarding homeschooling. The policy states that "DODEA recognizes that homeschooling is a sponsor's right and can be a legitimate alternative form of education for the sponsor's dependents. . . ." The costs are entirely born by the family and there are no government entitlements if you should choose this option. Home-educating is not for everybody, but those who are dedicated to it often find the flexibility and choices make for a more stable home life when moving from station to station. More information can be found at Home School Legal Defense Association's web site, www.hslda.org.

## FAMILY SERVICES

Family Services is a people-oriented program administered by volunteers from Air Force families, both active-duty and retired. Primarily they provide assistance to personnel arriving and departing from a base. Of special note is their "loan-out" program: You can check out, free of charge, household items you need to keep you going until your items arrive or after your things have been shipped when you're being reassigned. Items range from small kitchen accessories to baby furniture to linens. Some offices maintain brochures with information about other bases. They also arrange emergency services when possible, such as baby-sitting and transportation.

## AIRMAN AND FAMILY READINESS FLIGHTS

Family Support Service Centers (FSCs) have been renamed to reflect a change in focus and scope to accommodate the Total Force concept. The new Airman and Family Readiness Flights (A&FR flights) now provide consultation services to commanders and assist in developing policies, services, and processes which enhance individual, family, and community readiness. They continue to function to help provide support and assistance to military members (single or married) and their immediate families. They serve as one-stop centers for reliable information, courses, and services. Sometimes they help by encouraging people to see other referral agencies that can provide more specialized assistance or counseling. The following are some examples of normal services:

1. Personal Financial Management Program courses in the following areas:
   - Basic budgeting, addressing the need for and techniques of developing a personal or family budget. Topics include goal development, spending plans, savings plans, estate planning, and retirement planning.
   - Checkbook maintenance, giving instruction on how to open and maintain a checking account.

- Personal financial planning, including the need for long-term planning and the probable results of successful planning versus the results of failing to plan for the future.
- Smart car buying, giving instruction on purchasing or leasing a new or used vehicle, including prepurchase research, advertising gimmicks, price negotiations, and trade-in decisions and negotiations.
- Social Security registration, in which representatives from the Social Security Administration provide guidance and assistance in completing applications for new or replacement Social Security numbers. This reduces the stress of lines at the agency's offices and offers convenient service to base personnel.

2. The Transition Assistance Program (TAP) equips separating or retiring members and their families with the skills and knowledge required to make a smooth, successful transition to another career or retirement.

3. Employee Resource Programs offer workshops and other assistance:
   - An interview workshop provides job seekers with information and practical experience in conducting an effective job interview.
   - A job search workshop takes participants through the entire job-search process, from initial preparation to interviewing.
   - A mini employment workshop has representatives from the local community explain the essentials of an effective job search.
   - A positive image workshop has representatives from the local community outline tips for successful dressing for interviews and appropriate ways of presenting yourself to the business world.
   - A résumé workshop provides job seekers with current information and firsthand experience in developing résumés and cover letters.
   - An SF-171 workshop provides information on how to complete the form, federal service hiring procedures, employment opportunities, and veterans benefits.
   - A state employment workshop covers details of obtaining employment at the state level.
   - A temp workshop offers information from various temporary employment agency representatives, who discuss how they fill job openings, some of which can become permanent positions.
   - Additionally, there is a Resource Area that contains tools and resources to ease job hunting. It may include job vacancy listings; pamphlets and books on employment subjects; videos on careers, résumé writing, and interviewing techniques; educational opportunities; employment trends and projections; and word-processing programs to prepare cover letters, résumés, and job applications.

4. Training in Marriage Enrichment (TIME) teaches couples how to make marriage more effective, rewarding, and satisfying.

5. Parenting programs offer assistance in the following areas:
   - Systematic Training for Effective Parenting (STEP) offers three pro-grams: STEP (Early Childhood) gives parents a better understanding of children under six years old and presents factors that influence their behavior and development. STEP (6–12 years) helps parents relate to children in this age group through discussion and practice. STEP (Teens) offers a down-to-earth way to meet the challenges of raising teenagers. Topics include peer pressure, education and career plans, sexuality, using the family car, and drinking and drug use.
   - Siblings without Rivalry teaches parents how to help children resolve conflicts and get along better with brothers and sisters. The courses iden-tify what causes hostility between children and what kinds of attitudes and language you should use to decrease hostile actions.
   - Strengthening Stepfamilies offers information, skills, and practical advice for successful living when two families are united as one.
   - Single Parents' Support Groups offer an opportunity for single parents to share their experiences raising children without the aid of a partner while coping with the stresses of military life.
6. The Airman's Attic program offers donated clothes, furniture, and house-hold goods for staff sergeants and below at no charge. (This program is usually through the Family Support Center, but at some locations it is aligned under other base activities.)
7. Relocation service, helping new families settle in and helping those prepar-ing for a move.
8. Services for special-need families (single parents, special-education require-ments, and cultural orientation programs for non-English-speaking family members).
9. Referral and aid for families in crisis.
10. Spouse employment training, consultation, and job information (career planning, writing a résumé, preparing for a job interview).
11. Support during separation, when the military member is going away on temporary duty or on a remote tour.
12. Information about overseas areas, such as language courses, customs requirements, cultural differences and sensitivities, and what items to ship and what not to ship. Brochures, guides, and some videos are available on bases worldwide.

## HOUSING OFFICES

Housing offices handle the assignment and maintenance of on-base housing, prior-ity for which is based on your grade, date of arrival, number of dependents, and units available. They maintain lists of available off-base housing or rental agents. They also help mediate in cases of landlord-tenant disputes. At some locations, they provide information on the purchase of a home (what's available, veterans benefits, and financing).

Many bases now have privatized the housing areas. This was meant to save the military the costs and responsibility of managing their own housing.

## LEGAL ASSISTANCE

Legal assistance is provided by the Staff Judge Advocate's Office, also referred to as the Base Legal Office. Active-duty members and their dependents are eligible to receive assistance, as are retirees and sometimes civil service employees, when time permits. Assistance is restricted to matters of a personal nature (not for businesses) or a civil nature (not criminal matters; they are referred to the Area Defense Counsel). Each Judge Advocate (lawyer) is a graduate of an accredited law school and has been admitted to the bar (authorized to practice law) in at least one state or territory. Because of their duty status in the USAF (usually as a commissioned officer), they are not allowed to represent military clients in any state or federal court. However, they can, with your permission, provide advice and assistance (such as writing letters or contacting other people on your behalf). Primary services provided by the Base Legal Office are help with financial claims, consumer matters, wills and powers of attorney, taxes, insurance, separation and divorce, and military justice issues. Walk-in service is provided for common needs; appointments are given for more complex issues.

## MEDICAL AND DENTAL CARE

Medical and dental care is provided to all active-duty members. Dependents are provided full medical care in military and civilian hospitals under the Uniformed Services Health Benefit Program (USHBP). Under this program, care is available anywhere in the world in a uniformed service medical facility (Air Force, Army, Navy, and certain public health facilities) subject to the availability of space and facilities and type of specialized care required. Dependents are also eligible for care under Tricare (see chapter 24 for more information).

Air Force medical facilities vary in size. There are small facilities, such as medical aid stations and dispensaries. There are larger facilities, such as clinics, hospitals, and regional medical centers. One special aspect of the medical system is the air evacuation program. It operates worldwide through the use of specially modified aircraft. Its purpose is to bring patients to medical centers that provide specialized treatment when care is not available locally.

Full dental care is provided to active-duty members. Dependents receive limited care. In the United States, supplementary insurance is offered to cover most needs. In overseas areas, dependents are usually provided with an annual examination during their sponsor's birth month. If follow-up work is needed, appointments are made on a space-available basis.

## THE AIR FORCE OFFICE OF SPECIAL INVESTIGATIONS (OSI)

OSI usually has a detachment office at each major installation. It is responsible for the following:

1. Investigations of espionage, sabotage, and subversion.
2. Counterintelligence.
3. Major criminal matters.
4. Liaison and assistance to other United States and foreign government agencies, when requested.
5. Protection of senior distinguished visitors and dignitaries, both foreign and domestic, when requested by proper authority.
6. Internal security investigations.

## PERSONAL AFFAIRS OFFICES

Personal Affairs Offices are located in the Military Personnel Flight (MFP). They provide a variety of information and assistance in matters concerning government and personal passports, visas, the Air Force Aid Society, casualty assistance, veterans benefits, and travel in foreign countries.

## POSTAL SERVICES

Postal services are provided by the U.S. Postal Service at most bases in the United States. At overseas installations, services are provided at Air Force Post Offices (APOs), operated by USAF airmen. The scope of service includes delivery of mail to individually assigned post office boxes, parcel post, stamp sales, postal insurance, and money orders. Delivery of first-class mail to overseas areas usually takes four to seven days. Larger packages and newspaper or magazine subscriptions can take a while longer, depending on how they are sent. Airmail comes quickly. Boat mail comes slowly.

## PUBLIC AFFAIRS OFFICES (PAOs)

Public Affairs Offices provide information in three different forums:

1. The internal information program to inform members of the Air Force and their dependents about current developments.
2. The public information program to give the public unclassified information about the Air Force: stories, statements, interviews, speeches.
3. The community relations program to obtain support for the unit's mission in the local community.

## RED CROSS

Representatives of the Red Cross are available at all major overseas bases twenty-four hours a day. In the United States, representatives are available either on base or in the local civilian community. They can provide military members and their dependents with financial aid for emergency situations (such as for food, clothing, or shelter); verification of doctors' reports on family members who are ill; travel and maintenance loans or grants for military personnel on emergency leave; and counseling assistance on related problems.

## RELIGIOUS PROGRAMS
Religious programs are provided through a network of base chapels and chaplains representing many denominations. Chaplains are accredited clergymen and women who serve on active duty as commissioned officers. Their programs include worship services and masses, religious education for adults and children, weddings, baptisms, confirmations, spiritual retreats, choirs, Bible study groups, youth and young adult fellowships, women's groups, and special conferences. They interact with and provide humanitarian support and guidance to other agencies, such as the hospital, the Red Cross, and Family Support Centers. They also provide confidential counseling and referral services.

## SECURITY FORCES
The security forces have two primary segments: security and law enforcement. The security branch is committed to safeguarding operational resources (such as aircraft). The law enforcement branch acts as a community police force, conducting investigations, responding to inquiries, implementing crime prevention programs, manning gate guard positions, monitoring traffic control, and so forth. Most bases provide a special telephone number for assistance.

## MILITARY EQUAL OPPORTUNITY OFFICES
Military Equal Opportunity Offices serve as a focal point for programs and counseling related to drug and alcohol abuse control, human relations education, and equal opportunity and treatment.

## THRIFT SHOPS
Staffed by volunteers, usually from the Noncommissioned Officers' Wives Club and the Officers' Wives Club, thrift shops provide a community service by selling—at very reasonable prices—articles no longer needed by military members and their dependents: clothing, furniture, small appliances, toys, and other miscellaneous items. A small commission charge (usually 15 percent of the purchase price) for each sale is put back into charities in the local Air Force community.

## SOURCES OF ADDITIONAL INFORMATION
Consult the organization listed. If you're unsure where it's located, look in the base telephone directory, which usually lists telephone numbers and building numbers.

Consult the Airman and Family Readiness Flight, your supervisor, or your unit's first sergeant or commander. Each is familiar with the referral agencies and can probably help you select the one that best meets your needs.

# 27

# Off-Duty Pursuits

When people think about the armed forces they usually think in general terms about the on-duty aspects and the tangible conditions, such as pay, job security, medical care, education, and retirement benefits. Yet one of the major benefits, not always recognized as such, is a package of off-duty pursuits and benefits that can't be matched by many major corporations in the world. This package includes a worldwide system of shopping facilities; a full range of morale, welfare, and recreation programs; optional membership in private associations and clubs; and the opportunity to travel extensively in the United States and overseas. The extent of these programs varies from base to base and is usually governed by the size of the installation. To gain access to these facilities and programs, all you need is a current military identification (ID) card.

## SHOPPING FACILITIES

Shopping facilities are provided worldwide under the control of the Army and Air Force Exchange Service (AAFES) and the Air Force Commissary Service (AFCOMS). Their mission is to supply and control retail outlets whose size, inventory, and services are consistent with the size of the population served. Merchandise provided varies from necessity to convenience items. Everything is competitively priced and, in most cases, is less expensive than similar products off base. Some of their primary outlets, services, and facilities include the following:

*Base Exchanges* (also referred to as the BX or the Main Exchange). Normally the largest shopping facility on each base. Merchandise available includes most of the items you would find in any large department store off base: clothing, appliances, jewelry, health and beauty aids, stationery, toys, greeting cards, candy, and so forth. Customer service sections offer mail-order services, gift wrapping, and other services.

*Commissaries.* Large grocery stores with selections comparable to their stateside equivalents. In overseas areas, most packaged, frozen, and canned goods come from U.S. sources; some of the meat, poultry, dairy, and produce items are acquired from local areas. All goods must pass rigid inspections and health controls.

*Exchange Concessions.* Smaller individual outlets that offer specialized services: laundromats, service stations, barber and beauty shops, dry cleaning, photo processing, tailor, repair shops (electrical, watch, shoe), and television and video rentals. At some overseas locations, facilities are available for souvenir and gift shops and approved agents who sell new U.S. cars.

*Foodlands or Shopettes.* Small, quick-service convenience stores with smaller inventories: food, beverages, health and beauty aids, and stationery.

*Furniture Centers, Garden Centers, and Sports Centers.* Sometimes called the BXtra, these are specialized outlets that carry a specific range of merchandise. Furniture outlets, in particular, are usually found in overseas areas.

*Military Clothing Sales Stores.* Sell military uniforms, insignia, badges, devices, and related items.

*Package Liquor Stores.* Primarily found in overseas locations, where they are referred to as Class VI Stores. A selection of American and foreign liquors and wines are sold at low prices. Purchases and quantities are controlled under a ration card system. Since most of the items are sold on a tax-free basis, rules and procedures vary from country to country.

*Stars and Stripes Bookstores.* Found primarily in overseas locations. They offer a wide selection of reading material, including newspapers, magazines, and hard- and softcover books. In addition, they are usually the place to buy college textbooks for off-duty education programs.

## AIR FORCE SERVICES

The Air Force Services programs have evolved over the years and are considered to be an integral part of the Air Force way of life. They represent an assortment of self-supporting activities that provide services to enhance the morale of military members and their families. They do this at minimum expense to the Air Force community and "reinvest" their earnings to improve and operate their respective programs. Examples of programs include the following:

*Aero Clubs.* Offer safe, low-cost flying in light aircraft. Local instructors are usually available to provide courses for personnel who wish to obtain a private pilot's license for this type of aircraft.

*Audio/Photo Clubs.* Very popular in overseas areas. They offer a comprehensive range of stereo equipment, televisions and video equipment, cameras, and in some cases, computer equipment.

*Base Theaters.* Show a wide range of popular motion pictures at reduced rates. The facilities are also used for visiting shows and large briefings, such as commander's calls.

*Bowling Lanes.* Vary in size based on location. Some small, remote Air Force stations have two-lane alleys. Larger installations have facilities comparable with some of the best in the civilian community. Often included are automatic pinspotters, foul lights, and overhead score projectors. Snack bars and pro shops offering bowling accessories are usually available in the large facilities. Both organized leagues and open bowling are scheduled.

*Child Development Centers (CDC).* Offer services for full- or part-day care, including nursery, preschool, and play-school programs. With the increase in the number of single-parent families, these centers have received additional emphasis during recent years. Many new facilities have been built, and high standards have been set to assure the best quality of care. Types of programs and ages accepted may vary based on size of the staff and facility.

*Golf Courses.* Available on some installations. They range from standard nine-hole and eighteen-hole courses down to miniature courses. Pro shops and snack bars are commonly found.

*Gymnasiums, Fitness, and Sports Centers.* Provide coed facilities for varsity, intramural, and individual endeavors. Scope of services is normally determined by the size of the installation. May include basketball courts, exercise and weight rooms, steam and sauna rooms, handball and squash courts, tennis courts, swimming pools, outdoor tracks, and football, softball, and soccer fields. Schedules are adjusted seasonally. Opportunities also exist for varsity competitions (base teams) to participate with other local and interservice teams.

*Hobby Shops.* Organized either individually or collectively in a complex. Popular examples include craft and ceramics shops, photo shops (for rental of cameras and use of a lab to process and develop film), wood hobby shops, and auto hobby shops (operated by experienced personnel, with an extensive range of tools for checkout on the premises and facilities, ranging from work bays with hydraulic lifts to wash racks and paint booths).

*Libraries.* Contain a wide variety of books, magazines, newspapers, recordings, and other media that can be used for pleasure or self-improvement. Many have recently acquired video and computer equipment, with software, to complement education programs.

*Open Mess Facilities (NCO and Airmen's Clubs).* Facilities provided for members usually include a main lounge, a dining room, a casual bar, and a game room. Services may include floor shows, dances, take-out food, and support for special events, such as awards banquets and squadron parties. Also included are check-cashing facilities and foreign currency exchange at overseas installations. At some locations, separate facilities, such as "The Top Three Club," may exist for senior noncommissioned officers.

*Recreation Centers or Community Activities Centers.* Offer a wide range of activities and entertainment. Depending on the size of the installation, they usually have three main areas: a large room with a stage (suitable for conferences or large functions), a game room (pool tables, Ping-Pong tables, musical instruments, records, CDs, tapes, and cards), and a television lounge. The "Rec Center" is usually the primary location for special programs, such as shows, plays, tournaments, coin and stamp clubs, chess clubs, square dancing, and so forth. Local tours to surrounding areas are frequently organized and offered. Overseas centers normally provide reimbursable telephone services for personnel who want to make calls to the United States. Free refreshments or concession snack bar facilities are commonly available.

*Recreation Supply.* Issues, stores, and maintains all athletic equipment and supplies for teams or individuals. Also provides equipment you can check out for a small fee, usually for seventy-two hours, including softball and baseball equipment, camping equipment (tents, sleeping bags, stoves, and coolers), tennis rackets, horseshoe sets, fishing equipment, and golf clubs. Sometimes gardening equipment, such as lawn mowers and weed eaters, is available.

*Rod and Gun Clubs.* Offer facilities for skeet and trap shooting, and make arrangements for fishing and hunting excursions in surrounding areas. These clubs usually offer a sports equipment shop and snack bar or restaurant.

*Youth Centers.* Provide facilities for leisure activities for base youths between ages six and eighteen. Activities offered usually include sports and social programs, dances, arts and crafts, and Scouting programs.

## CLUBS AND PRIVATE ASSOCIATIONS

Each installation has a number of self-supporting private community-service groups that cater to sports, religious, fraternal, and special interest groups. Examples include the following:

Air Force Association Chapters
Air Force Sergeants Association Chapters
Alcoholics Anonymous
American Legion Chapters
Barbershop Groups (singing)
Booster Clubs (for sports activities)
Bowling Associations
Chess Clubs
Choirs and Singing Groups
Coin and Stamp Clubs
Computer User Clubs
Darts Teams
Drama Clubs
Investment Clubs
Little League
Marriage Encounter Groups

Martial Arts Clubs
Masonic Lodges
Model Airplane Clubs
Motorcycle Clubs
NCO Association Chapters
Parent Teacher Associations
Scouting Programs: Cubs through
    Explorers, Brownies through
    Girl Scouts
Square Dancing Clubs
Swim Clubs
Toastmasters
Officers' Wives' Clubs
    Spouses Clubs,
    Protestant Women of the Chapel,
    Council of Catholic Wives

The list of private associations lengthens or shortens from time to time, depending on the needs of the local population. Where similar interests exist, people are encouraged to join together and start an organization.

## OVERSEAS ACTIVITIES

American communities overseas traditionally offer a wider range of leisure activities than stateside bases. Two very special pluses about being overseas are opportunities to travel and to make friends with people of other cultures.

To enjoy an overseas tour, try to achieve a balance among duty commitments, touring and traveling, and getting involved in local base or community life. Try to avoid becoming a "barracks rat," staying in your dormitory room or house and never going anywhere. People who do this miss a lot of great opportunities. Their tours of duty drag out and they often find themselves counting the day until their return to the United States.

One of the best ways to get acquainted with an overseas country is to go to the Recreation Center and sign up for one of the newcomers' tours. They're inexpensive and are geared for both singles and families. Some are day trips; others take advantage of long weekends. Trips are usually organized around the following:

1. Local attractions.
2. A specific theme, such as shopping for antiques, visiting ancient churches or castles, going to live entertainment shows, eating out at traditional restaurants, stopping at local pubs or taverns, or visiting a local McDonald's or Pizza Hut.
3. Sporting events, either watching or participating, ranging from skiing in the Alps or deep-sea fishing to international events such as the Olympics or World Cup soccer matches.

You can watch for upcoming events by reading the base newspaper or contacting the base's Community Relations Advisor. These positions are sometimes created by the host government to help personnel and their families settle in. They can advise on shopping, transportation, traveling, education, and many other aspects of local life. They can also introduce you to local clubs and organizations and provide information on facilities where you can pursue your hobbies and recreational interests while you are stationed there.

For the more adventurous, you can consult local travel agents or even plan your own itineraries. Many countries have national tourist offices, which routinely provide free literature, such as maps and brochures, and will do their best to answer your travel questions. The following are some of the most frequently used offices:

British Tourist Authority, 551 Fifth Avenue, Suite 701, New York, NY
    10176-0799
French Government Tourist Office, 444 Madison Avenue, #16, New York,
    NY 10022

German National Tourist Office, 122 East 42nd Street #2000, New York, NY
10168

Ireland Tourist Board, 757 Third Avenue, New York, NY 10017

Italian Government Tourist Office, 630 Fifth Avenue, Room 1565, New York,
NY 10111

Netherlands Board of Tourism, 355 Lexington Avenue, New York, NY 10017

Spanish National Tourism Office, 665 Fifth Avenue, New York, NY 10022

Swiss National Tourist Office, 608 Fifth Avenue, New York, NY 10020

Another way to access these tourist offices is through the Internet. One of the best sites is Tourism Offices Worldwide Directory (TOWD). It can be accessed at *www.towd.com*. This directory is your guide to official tourist information sources. It lists only official government tourism offices, conventions and visitors bureaus, chambers of commerce, and similar agencies that provide free, accurate, and unbiased travel information to the public. This database contains almost 1,400 entries.

You can also access a broad range of travel information on the web by using a search engine, such as *Yahoo*™. Just type in the web site address *(www.yahoo.com)* and you will then be able to access the recreation and travel sections. These will take you to hundreds of links for countries, cities, transportation, lodging, and so forth.

Another common way to enjoy travel overseas is to plan your itinerary so that you can take advantage of facilities at other U.S. military installations. This is commonly referred to as base-hopping. It's especially useful if you're traveling by car and have a periodic need to convert dollars to the local currency, want to service the car, or take advantage of exchange or medical entitlements. Billeting can sometimes be arranged on a space-available basis. Some overseas activities and installations that offer special recreational facilities or that are located close to major cities are noted below. Use the telephone numbers listed to contact the base operator or a billeting office.

### England

RAF Lakenheath, 48th Tactical Fighter Wing, APO AE 09464, commercial phone Eriswell, 3131, DSN 226-1110 or 3131. Located north of Newmarket, about seventy miles north of London.

### Germany

Germany has a U.S. Armed Forces Recreation Area with extensive recreational programs and facilities. It is located in the beautiful surroundings of the Bavarian Alps, south of Munich by the Austrian border. Activities for all seasons are planned for singles, couples, and families with children. A full range of support activities is also available (exchanges, commissaries, medical, child-care centers, and so forth). For additional information, write to Garmisch-Partenkirchen, Armed Forces Recreation Center, APO AE 09053-5000, or visit www.edelweisslodge andresort.com/home.html.

## Hawaii

Bellows Air Force Station, HI 96853, commercial phone (808) 259-7271. Recreation area with 104 furnished beach cottages, located on the eastern coast of the island of Oahu.

Hale Koa Hotel, Fort DeRussy, HI 96815, commercial phone (808) 955-0555, toll-free (800) 367-6027. Located on Waikiki Beach, by Honolulu.

Hickam AFB, 15th ABW, Honolulu, HI 96853, commercial phone (808) 449-2603, DSN 430-0111. Located next to the Honolulu International Airport.

Kilauea Armed Forces Recreation Center, Hawaii Volcanoes National Park, HI 96718, commercial phone (808) 543-2658, DSN R1 1101-00. Located on the island of Hawaii, the "Big Island."

Waianae Army Recreation Center, Waianae, HI 96792, commercial phone (808) 696-2494 or 2883. Located on the northeast coast of the island of Oahu.

## Italy

Camp Darby, 8th Support Group, APO AE 09613-5000, commercial phone (0586) 93001, DSN 633-8371. Located in northwestern Italy, by the city of Pisa.

Naples, Naval Support Activity, FPO AE 09619-5000, commercial phone (081) 724-4379, DSN 621-1100. Located in Naples, south of Rome; recreation center located in Carney Park, three miles from base.

Vincenza, Hq USA/SETAF, APO AE 09630-5000, commercial phone (0444) 500333, DSN 634-1000. Located between the cities of Venice and Milan.

## Japan

Sanno Joint Services Transient Billeting Facility, APO AP 96337-0110, commercial phone 581-6741. Located in the Akasaka district of downtown Tokyo.

Yokota Air Base, 374 MSS, APO AP 96328-5123, commercial phone 0425-52-2511, DSN 248-1101. Located approximately thirty miles from Tokyo.

## Korea

Naija Hotel and R&R Center, U.S. Army Garrison, Korea, APO AP 96205-0427, commercial phone Seoul, 73-5580. Located in downtown Seoul, close to the capitol building.

U.S. Army Garrison, Yongson, Hq U.S. 8th Army, U.S. Forces, Korea, and United Nations Command, APO AP 96205-0177, commercial phone 293-0-4448, DSN 315 262-1101. Located in the Yongson district of Seoul.

## Scotland

U.S. Naval Security Group Activity, FPO AE 09419-1200, commercial phone Edzell, 431, DSN 229-1110. Located near the town of Edzell in the Scottish highlands (limited facilities).

**Spain**

Rota, U.S. Naval Station, FPO AE 09645-5500, commercial phone 862780, DSN
727-1110. Located south of Seville on Spain's southern coast.

## FURLOUGH FARES AND SPACE-AVAILABLE TRAVEL

For those of you who would rather not travel by car, there are two other special
options to pursue. Active-duty personnel and their dependents are eligible to ask
for furlough fares. These are special discounted travel rates offered by major air-
lines, bus companies, railways, rental car agencies, and hotel chains. The amount
of discount can vary from company to company, anywhere from 10 to 60 percent
of the standard rate. A valid ID card and your leave authorization slip are usually
required to obtain the special rates.

The second option is space-available travel, often referred to as "Space-A" or
"catching a hop." This system lets military members and their families travel on
government aircraft when there are extra seats available. Base Operations and Air
Mobility Command (AMC) Passenger Terminals are your primary points of contact for this kind of travel. They can provide information about frequency of
flights, destinations, and travel requirements.

There are some basic guidelines for Space-A travel. Space is always subject to
mission requirements. There's a priority system for passengers, based on urgency
of need and duty status. Those on emergency leave are normally processed first,
then passengers in a duty status, passengers in a leave status, and retirees. Members may sign up in advance to get priority within their category. To do so, they
must present an ID card and either special orders or a copy of their leave authorization form. In some instances, passports, visas, and shot records may also be
required. Military members can travel on a space-available basis in the United
States even with their dependents. When traveling, active duty personnel must usually travel in uniform; however, the policy may change depending on current threat
levels and destinations. Consult your local MPS for current information. There are
also special R&R opportunities from time to time such as for Operation Iraqi Freedom personnel and their families. If you might qualify, ask about them when
checking on reservations.

These rules may seem somewhat restrictive at first glance, but they are necessary to provide some general controls and ensure the smooth and equitable operation of the system. Thousands of people travel this way every week. And in the
long run, almost everyone's in agreement about one thing: People who can fly
from California to Japan or from New Jersey to England at no cost don't really
mind a little bit of red tape.

## SOURCES OF ADDITIONAL INFORMATION

Contact the shopping facilities and Air Force Services programs referred to in
this chapter.

Contact the Air Mobility Command (AMC) passenger service terminal or base operations for information on space-available travel on government aircraft.

For overseas travel, contact the Base Recreation Center or the Personal Affairs Branch of the Military Personnel Section (MPS).

A good source of information on temporary military lodging and Space-A air opportunities is Military Living Publications. For information on their publications, write to Military Living Publications, P.O. Box 2347, Falls Church, VA 22042, or call (703) 237-0203. Military Living will send a free welcome kit to anyone on orders to the Washington, D.C., area.

For a thorough discussion of installations in the continental United States and overseas, consult *Guide to Military Installations,* published by Stackpole Books, 5067 Ritter Road, Mechanicsburg, PA 17055.

You can also access the web sites for each of the military installations or recreation centers listed. These web site addresses can be found in Air Force Link, www.af.mil.

# 28

# Veterans Benefits

There comes a time in every career, be it long or short, to consider other career options. Some changes are pursued by choice. Others may be necessitated by conditions that are beyond any one individual's ability to control.

Events such as the dissolution of the Soviet Union, the emergence of small regional conflicts, advances in technology, and reductions in federal funding levels resulted in the need to restructure the U.S. Armed Forces and make significant reductions in the number of personnel who serve. In order to draw down the numbers of active-duty personnel, the services developed a wide range of voluntary and involuntary separation programs that offer special benefits and incentives in order to ease the transition from military to civilian life. In addition to the programs offered by the armed forces, there are various benefits available to veterans and their dependents that are administered by local, state, and federal government agencies and private organizations.

This chapter provides an overview into some of the primary benefit programs and sources of support available to eligible veterans.

## THE TRANSITION ASSISTANCE PROGRAM

The Labor Department has established the Transition Assistance Program (TAP) to assist servicemembers who are scheduled for separation from active duty. The program establishes a partnership with the Department of Defense, Department of Veterans Affairs, and Labor Department to provide employment and training information to servicemembers within 180 days of separation. Three-day workshops to assist in civilian employment are conducted at military installations. Additional counseling is available to disabled veterans. For additional information, contact VETS, Department of Labor, 200 Constitution Avenue, NW, Room S1313, Washington, DC 20210, or call (202) 219-5573.

## REEMPLOYMENT RIGHTS

Under the Veterans' Reemployment Rights (VRR) law, as noted in chapter 43 of Title 38, U.S. Code, a person who left a civilian job to enter active duty in the armed forces, either voluntarily or involuntarily, may be entitled to return to his or her civilian job after discharge or release from active duty. Four requirements must be met in order for a veteran to pursue employment rights:

1. The person must have been employed in other than a temporary civilian job.
2. The person must have left the civilian job for the purpose of entering military service.
3. The person must not remain on active duty longer than four years, unless the period beyond four years is at the request and for the convenience of the federal government and the military discharge form carries this statement. (In some cases, the limitation may be extended to six years.)
4. The person must be discharged or released from active duty under honorable conditions.

Under this law, returning veterans are to be placed in the job as if they had remained continuously employed instead of going on active duty. This means that the person may be entitled to benefits that are generally based on seniority (such as pay increases, pensions, missed promotions, and missed transfers). The law also protects a veteran from discharge without just cause for one year from the date of reemployment.

A veteran must apply to the preservice employer within ninety days following separation from active duty. If the veteran is hospitalized or recuperating when discharged, the ninety-day application period begins upon release from the hospital or completion of recuperation, which may last up to one year. Applications for reemployment should be given verbally or in writing to a person who is authorized to represent the company for hiring purposes. A record should be kept of when and to whom the application was given.

Questions on the VRR law, or requests for assistance in attaining reemployment if there are problems with private employers or state or local governments, should be directed to the Department of Labor's director for Veterans Employment and Training (DVET) for the state in which the employer is located. For additional information, consult telephone directories under U.S. Department of Labor, or call (866) 4-USA-DOL for the appropriate DVET telephone number.

## JOB-FINDING ASSISTANCE

Assistance in finding jobs is provided to veterans through state employment offices throughout the country. These offices have special veterans offices that provide veterans with free job counseling, testing, training referral, and placement services, as well as information about unemployment compensation, job marts, and on-the-job and apprenticeship training opportunities.

## EMPLOYMENT IN THE FEDERAL GOVERNMENT

The federal government has over 2 million civilian positions representing approximately nine hundred different occupations. Annual salary levels range from $12,000 for entry-level positions to $80,000 for more senior positions. These positions are located in the major federal agencies: the Legislative Branch, Judiciary, Executive Office of the President, Department of Agriculture, Department of Commerce, Department of Defense, Department of Education, Department of Energy, Department of Health and Human Services, Social Security, Department of Housing and Urban Development, Department of the Interior, Department of Justice, Department of Labor, Department of State, Department of Transportation, Department of the Treasury, Department of Veterans Affairs, Environmental Protection Agency, General Services Administration, National Aeronautics and Space Administration, Office of Personnel Management, Small Business Administration, Central Intelligence Agency, and Federal Bureau of Investigation.

There are two primary programs that provide veterans with special access to federal employment opportunities:

1. The Vietnam-Era Veterans Readjustment Assistance Act of 1974 enacted into law the *Veterans Readjustment Appointment (VRA) authority,* which provides for the U.S. policy of promoting maximum job opportunities within the federal government for qualified disabled veterans. The VRA authority allows agencies to make noncompetitive appointments, at their discretion, to federal jobs for Vietnam-era and post–Vietnam-era veterans. These appointments lead to conversion to career or career-conditional employment upon satisfactory completion of two years' service. Veterans seeking VRA appointments should apply directly to the federal agency where they are seeking employment.

2. The *Disabled Veterans Affirmative Action Program (DVAAP)* is administered by the Office of Personnel Management. All federal agencies and departments are required to establish action plans to facilitate the recruitment, employment, and advancement of disabled veterans. Eligible veterans may receive veterans preference in federal employment, which provides for additional points added to passing scores in examinations, first consideration for certain jobs, and preference for retention in reduction-in-force actions.

If you are interested in these benefits or other federal employment opportunities, contact the personnel offices of the federal agencies in which you wish to be employed. Information may also be obtained by contacting the Federal Employment Information Centers of the U.S. Office of Personnel Management. The centers are listed in the telephone books under U.S. Government. Veterans may also obtain a nationwide listing of the Federal Employment Information Centers by writing to the U.S. Office of Personnel Management, Federal Employment Information Center, 1900 E Street NW, Washington, DC 20415.

## AFFIRMATIVE ACTION PROGRAM

Employers with federal contracts or subcontracts of $10,000 or more are required to take affirmative action to employ and advance Vietnam-era and special disabled veterans. Legislative requirements are administered by the U.S. Department of Labor's Office of Federal Contract Compliance Programs (OFCCP).

## SMALL BUSINESS ADMINISTRATION

Ever thought about starting your own business? The Small Business Administration (SBA) has a number of programs designed to help foster and encourage small business enterprises, including businesses owned or operated by veterans. The SBA provides business training, conferences, one-on-one counseling, advocacy, surety bonding, government procurement, and financial management assistance. In each SBA field office there is a veterans affairs officer who is designated as the contact person to assist veterans in dealings with the SBA. Information on SBA programs is available without charge from any of the approximately one hundred field offices. For the address of the nearest SBA office, check the U.S. Government section of your local telephone directory, or use the agency's national toll-free number, (800) 827-5722.

## UNEMPLOYMENT COMPENSATION

Unemployment compensation is available for ex-servicemembers to provide a weekly income for a limited period of time to help them meet basic needs while searching for employment. The amount and duration of payments are governed by state laws, which vary considerably. Benefits are paid from federal funds. Ex-servicemembers should apply at their nearest state employment office immediately after leaving military service. Copies of military discharge forms (DD Form 214) are required to help determine eligibility for programs.

## DEPARTMENT OF VETERANS AFFAIRS (VA) BENEFITS

The Department of Veterans Affairs (VA) is a federal agency whose primary role is providing benefits to those who have served their country in the active military, naval, or air service and to their dependents. The VA has improved access and increased its awareness campaign to veterans.

Eligibility for most VA benefits is based on the type of discharge from active military service and, in some cases, minimum periods of time served as specified by law. Honorable and general discharges qualify veterans for most VA benefits. Dishonorable and some bad-conduct discharges issued by general courts-martial bar VA benefits. Those who enlisted in the military after September 7, 1980, and officers commissioned or who entered active military service after October 16, 1981, must have completed two years of active duty or the full period of their initial service obligation to be eligible for most VA benefits. Veterans with service-connected disabilities or those discharged for disability or hardship near the end of their service obligation are not held to this provision.

You can file a claim for VA benefits in person, through a veterans service organization, or through the mail. In order to file a claim with the VA, you must submit a copy of your service discharge form (DD Form 214), which documents service dates and type of discharge, or provide your full name, military service number, branch of service, and dates of service. Once a claim is filed, the VA will set up a file number (Social Security numbers are presently used for this purpose) to track all of your future claims actions. This file number is often referred to as a C number.

**Types of VA Benefits.** The VA offers an extensive range of benefits, some of which must be applied for within a specified period of time. The following are the most frequently sought after:

- *Disability compensation.* Disability compensation is monetary benefits paid to veterans who are disabled by injury or disease incurred or aggravated during active military service in the line of duty. This compensation is paid in monthly payments based on the degree of a veteran's disability. Expressed as a percent, they run from 0 to 100 percent in 10 percent increments. Current rates range from $112 for a 10 percent disability to $2,393 for a 100 percent disability rating. The dollar amounts of these benefits, which are not subject to federal or state income tax, are usually changed each year by Congress. Higher amounts may be awarded to veterans who have suffered certain specific, severe disabilities. These are granted on a case-by-case basis. Federal law prohibits the award of VA disability compensation that can be received when a veteran receives military retirement pay, except to the extent that an equal amount of military retirement pay is waived. Special entitlements can be granted to certain disabled veterans. These include the following:
  1. Special allowances, such as specialty adapted housing grants, housing insurance, adaptive equipment for automobiles or other conveyances, and clothing allowances for veterans who use prosthetic or orthopedic appliances.
  2. Allowances for dependents are granted for service-connected disabled veterans who are rated at 30 percent or more.
  3. Former prisoners of war who were incarcerated for at least thirty days are entitled to a presumption of service connection for disabilities resulting from certain diseases or ailments if manifested to a degree of 10 percent at any time after active service.
- *Non-service-connected (NSC) disability pensions.* Monetary benefits can be paid, in some instances, to veterans who have ninety days or more of wartime service; were separated from such service for a service-connected disability and became permanently and totally disabled from reasons not traceable to military service; or are over sixty-five years old. NSC pensions are not paid when a veteran's income and estate and that of his or her spouse and dependent children is so large that it is reasonable that some of

it could be used for living expenses or when their income exceeds the applicable limit under federal law.

- *Medical care.* Medical care is provided to veterans on either a mandatory or a discretionary basis. Mandatory care is provided to those who have adjudicated service-connected medical or dental conditions. Discretionary care is provided to other categories of veterans with non-service-connected disabilities if space and facilities are available after providing care to service-connected veterans. Non-service-connected veterans can be charged for discretionary care based on their level of income, which is determined by a review of VA Form 10-10f, "Financial Worksheet," filled out at the time care is requested. The VA has the authority to compare income information provided by veterans with information obtained from the Department of Health and Human Services and the Internal Revenue Service. The types of services available at VA medical facilities include, but are not limited to, inpatient and outpatient medical, surgical, and psychiatric care; dental care; nursing home; domiciliary; pharmacy; prosthetics; blind aids and services; drug/alcohol treatment; beneficiary travel; and special physical examinations for Agent Orange, ionizing radiation, and/or problems incurred in the Persian Gulf.
- *Medical Care for Dependents and Survivors.* The Civilian Health and Medical Program of the Department of Veterans Affairs (CHAMPVA) helps pay for medical services and supplies obtained from civilian sources by eligible dependents and survivors of certain veterans. The following are eligible for CHAMPVA benefits, provided they are not eligible for care under Tricare (the Civilian Health and Medical Programs of the Uniformed Services) or Medicare:
  1. The spouse or child of a veteran who has a permanent and total service-connected disability.
  2. The surviving spouse or child of a veteran who died as a result of a service-connected condition or who at the time of death was permanently and totally disabled from a service-connected condition.
  3. The surviving spouse or child of a person who died while on active military service in the line of duty.
  4. A surviving spouse who remarries may qualify for care after the subsequent marriage is terminated.
     Care under the CHAMPVA program is not normally provided in VA medical facilities. For additional information, apply to the Health Administration Center, 300 South Jackson, Suite 444, Denver, CO 80206, or call (800) 733-8387.
- *Education and training programs* that include counseling and funding are available for veterans, servicemembers, and eligible dependents. See chapter 16, "Training and Education," for an overview of GI Bill programs and benefits. The Vocational Rehabilitation Program provides training and reha-

bilitation services to veterans who have a compensable service-connected disability and a need for such services in order to overcome an employment handicap. Under this program, up to forty-eight months or more may be authorized in colleges, universities, vocational schools, on-farm, on-job, or apprenticeship programs, and special rehabilitation facilities. The VA will pay for tuition, books, fees, supplies, and equipment and will also provide employment assistance following completion of the program.

- *Guaranteed loans* for the purchase and refinancing of homes, condominiums, and manufactured homes may be obtained by eligible veterans and unmarried surviving spouses. The VA guarantees part of the total loan so a veteran may obtain a mortgage with a competitive interest rate—without a down payment, if the lender agrees.
- *Post-traumatic stress disorder (PTSD)* is an anxiety disorder that can occur after you have been through a traumatic event. A traumatic event is anything horrible and scary that you see or that happens to you. During this type of event, you think that your life or others' lives are in danger. You may feel afraid or feel that you have no control over what is happening. Because of our military's involvement around the world, new concerns for our veteran's health have required increased treatment and awareness. As a result, the VA has devoted more resources to address the effects of PTSD. See www.ptsd.va.gov, the National Center for treatment of Post-traumatic Stress Disorder website, for more information.

**Points of Contact within the Department of Veterans Affairs.** The type of benefit you are interested in obtaining will determine whom you should contact to obtain additional information. In general, the VA has four primary sources:

1. *Vet centers* are located throughout the country. They provide veterans with counseling to assist in readjusting to civilian life. Assistance includes group, individual, and family counseling; community outreach; and education. Vet center staff can also help veterans find services from the VA and non-VA sources if needed.
2. *VA Regional Offices (VAROs)* process claims for VA benefits and administer those benefits, which include disability compensation, pension, home loan guaranty, life insurance, education, vocational training for disabled veterans, burial benefits, and survivor's compensation, pension, and education.
3. *VA Medical Centers (VAMCs)* are the immediate sources for obtaining information regarding medical care. Through a national network, they provide all types of medical care. Many of the VA Medical Centers also operate smaller outpatient clinics at separate geographical locations. These smaller clinics can make referrals for a wider range of care in the larger VA Medical Centers.
4. *VA national cemeteries* can provide information about eligibility of veterans and dependents for burial benefits.

Veterans and dependents from throughout the country may obtain information on VA benefits from regional offices by calling a toll-free number, (800) 827-1000. Callers are then automatically connected to the closest VA regional office, where a veterans benefits advisor (VBA) will direct the caller to an appropriate program manager. Other toll-free VA telephone services available in all states include the following:

CHAMPVA: (800) 733-8387
Debt Management Center: (800) 827-0648
VA Education Benefits: 1-888-GIBILL-1 (1-888-442-4551)
Life insurance: (800) 669-8477
Prisoner of War (POW) Hotline: (800) 821-8139. (Calls are received in a twenty-four-hour service center in Washington, D.C., which in turn coordinates with local VA Medical Centers and regional offices in arranging benefits assistance and resolving differences.)
Radiation Helpline: (800) 827-0365
Telecommunication Device for the Deaf (TDD): (800) 829-4833

You can also use your local telephone directory, which lists the addresses and commercial telephone numbers of all VA facilities in your area, under Department of Veterans Affairs in the Federal or U.S. Government section.

Many states also offer benefits to veterans. These are independent of federal benefits and may differ from state to state. Eligibility for state benefits usually requires that the state be a veteran's place of residence or home of record at the time of enlistment. For further information, consult your local telephone directory under the state government listing section.

Department of Veterans Affairs Regional Offices (VAROs) and VA Medical Centers (VAMCs) that can provide you with assistance are listed on the VA website, www.va.gov.

## OBTAINING VA ASSISTANCE WHILE OVERSEAS

Virtually all VA monetary benefits (compensation, pension, educational assistance, and burial allowances) are payable regardless of place of residence or nationality. Beneficiaries residing in foreign countries should contact the nearest American embassy or consulate for information and claims assistance. In Canada, the local office of Veterans Affairs Canada should be contacted.

There are some program limitations in foreign jurisdictions that you should be aware of. These include the following:

- Reimbursed fee-basis medical care, including prosthetic services, is available to veterans outside of the United States for treatment of adjudicated, service-connected disabilities and conditions related to those disabilities. Prior to treatment, an authorization must be obtained from the nearest American embassy or consulate. In emergency situations, treatment should be reported within seventy-two hours.

## VETERANS BENEFITS TIMETABLE

| Time | Benefits | Where to apply |
|------|----------|----------------|
| 90 days | REEMPLOYMENT | Former employer |
| Limited time | UNEMPLOYMENT COMPENSATION: The amount of benefit and payment period vary among states. Apply soon after separation. | State employment service |
| 120 days or up to one year if totally disabled | INSURANCE: SGLI (Servicemember's Group Life Insurance), a five-year nonrenewable term policy, may be converted to VGLI (Veterans Group Life Insurance). | Servicemember's Group Life Insurance, 213 Washington St., Newark, N.J. 07102-9990 |
| Two years (from date of notice of VA disability rating) | GI INSURANCE: Life insurance (up to $10,000) is available for veterans with service-connected disabilities. Veterans who are totally disabled may apply for a waiver of premiums on these policies. | Any VA office |
| One year (from date of notice of eligibility for premium waiver) | SUPPLEMENTAL INSURANCE: An additional $20,000 policy is available for those veterans who are under age sixty-five, eligible for waiver of premiums, and have Service Disabled Veterans Insurance. However, no waiver can be granted on the additional insurance. | Any VA office |
| Ten years from release | EDUCATION: Educational assistance depends upon period of service. | Any VA office |
| Twelve years (generally from date of discharge) | VOCATIONAL REHABILITATION: For disabled vets, VA will pay tuition, fees, and the cost of books, tools, and other program expenses, as well as provide a monthly living allowance. Upon completion of the vocational rehabilitation program, VA will assist in finding employment. | Any VA office |
| No time limit | GI HOME LOANS: VA will guarantee a loan for the purchase of a home, farm with a residence, manufactured home, or condominium. | Any VA office |

- Nursing-home care is not available in foreign jurisdictions.
- Home loan guarantees are available only in the United States and selected territories and possessions.
- Educational benefits are limited to approved degree-granting programs in institutions of higher learning.

## VETERANS SERVICE ORGANIZATIONS

Veterans service organizations (VSOs) provide a wide range of services to help veterans obtain the benefits they are entitled to. The states maintain state veterans service agencies that provide assistance, and there are also over thirty national organizations. The following are some of the larger organizations that have national service offices throughout the country:

- American Legion (AL). Membership: 3,000,000. National headquarters: P.O. Box 1055, Indianapolis, IN 46206, telephone (317) 635-8411. Washington headquarters: 1608 K Street NW, Washington, DC 20006, telephone (202) 861-2711.
- Disabled American Veterans (DAV). Membership: 1,300,727. National headquarters: 3725 Alexandria Pike, Cold Springs, KY 41076, telephone (606) 441-7300. Washington headquarters: 807 Maine Avenue SW, Washington, DC 20024, telephone (202) 554-3506.
- Non-Commissioned Officers Association (NCOA). Membership: 160,000. National headquarters: 10635 IH 35 North, San Antonio, TX 78233, telephone (512) 653-6161. Washington headquarters: 225 N. Washington Street, Alexandria, VA 22314, telephone (703) 549-0311.
- Paralyzed Veterans of America (PVA). Membership: 19,000. This organization serves the special needs of veterans of military service who have catastrophic paralysis caused by spinal cord injury or disease. National headquarters: 801 18th Street NW, Washington, DC 20006, telephone (202) 872-1300.
- Veterans of Foreign Wars of the United States (VFW). Membership: 2,400,000. National headquarters: 406 West 34th Street, Kansas City, MO 64111, telephone (816) 756-3390. Washington headquarters: 200 Maryland Avenue NE, Washington, DC 20002, telephone (202) 543-2239.
- Vietnam Veterans of America, Inc. (VVA). Membership: 40,100. National headquarters: 2001 S Street NW, Suite 700, Washington, DC 20009, telephone (202) 265-8019.

## SOURCES OF ADDITIONAL INFORMATION

Consult with the Military Personnel Section (MPS) or the Family Support Center at your present active-duty location concerning transition programs.

Visit www.ptsd.va.gov for information on post-traumatic stress disorder (PTSD).

Contact the local, state, or national government or private veterans organizations as referenced in this chapter. The United States Department of Veterans Affairs (VA) web site is www.va.gov. It offers extensive information on programs and benefits that are available for veterans. The web site also has blank forms (such as applications for benefits) that can be downloaded for your use.

For a thorough discussion of veterans benefits, consult *Veteran's Guide to Benefits,* Stackpole Books, 5067 Ritter Road, Mechanicsburg, PA 17055.

# 29

# Answers to
# 25 Commonly Asked Questions

*1. What is the policy on taking leave?*

As a member of the armed forces, you get credit for two and a half days' leave for each month of active duty under honorable conditions. This equates to thirty days a year, which can be taken at one time or broken up into smaller amounts throughout the year. Requests must be approved by your supervisor and, in some cases, your commander. Airmen worldwide can now take advantage of a simplified and automated online leave system called *LeaveWeb*. *LeaveWeb* streamlines the leave process by allowing airmen to submit leave requests and approvals electronically, saving time and improving customer service. Requests are normally granted for the period of time requested except when military necessity requires your presence. Most supervisors have a projected leave schedule based on information from their personnel. The best way to secure the days you would like is to provide your supervisor with plenty of advance notice. The best way to be disappointed is to wait until the last moment, when the workload is heavy and several other people from your duty section are on leave or in a temporary duty status at other locations.

*2. What should I do if I'm experiencing pay problems?*

Errors do not occur very often. Those that do happen are usually temporary delays caused by a change in a person's status, the date the change was brought to the attention of Accounting and Finance personnel, and the time required for processing the change in the automated computer pay system. Once corrected, payments are usually made within the following thirty days. If you're experiencing pay problems, you should contact the military pay branch at your local Accounting and Finance Office. Take your most recent Leave and Earnings Statement (LES); it can help identify potential problems and expedite their correction.

3. *What's the best way for my parents or family to contact me in case of an emergency?*

Tell them to contact their local Red Cross. There are almost thirty-three hundred offices in chapters on or near military installations all over the world. Your local Red Cross office is listed in the local or base telephone directory, or call the American Red Cross Armed Forces Emergency Service Center toll-free at 1-877-272-7337. They will verify the situation and rapidly transmit a message to you through the local Red Cross representative at your base.

4. *It's hard for me to get up in the morning. What should I do to make sure I get to work on time?*

If possible, ask a friend to stop by on the way to work. If not, take a look at the clocks you're using. Heavy sleepers tend to go back to sleep after they let the alarms on mechanical wind-up clocks unwind. Electric alarm clocks and clock radios with alarms are the best bet. Place them a good distance from the bed, so you have to get up to turn them off. If you seem to be waking up late on a regular basis, it might be because you're staying up too late the night before. If so, try hitting the sack a little bit earlier.

5. *What should I do if I have problems getting along with my coworkers or my supervisor?*

If the problem is a minor or one-time occurrence, it's probably nothing to be seriously concerned about. If problems recur and seem to center around major disagreements or conflicts, then you need to think about your actions and ask yourself to what degree you may be causing the problem; think of the possible solutions and talk openly and honestly with your supervisor or those concerned, or discuss the situation with someone else in your chain of command. Your unit's first sergeant is in a good position to provide insight and help resolve these kinds of issues.

6. *Why do Air Force personnel have to work long hours?*

In the Air Force environment, exercises, unforeseen workloads, and unprogrammed personnel losses can result in situations where unit commanders and supervisors are compelled to extend standard workdays or workweeks to meet mission requirements. When this happens for an extended period of time, higher headquarters is usually contacted to reevaluate requirements or provide manning assistance.

7. *How should I get ready for the movers when I'm being reassigned to another base? What should I do if my furniture or personal possessions are damaged en route?*

At base level, the Transportation Management Office (TMO) will schedule your move and provide you with specific information about procedures. You can start to make formal arrangements once you've received printed copies of your reassignment orders. Weight allowances are established based on grade and in some cases the location you are being reassigned to. Your possessions will usually be sent two ways—one for household goods (furniture and other possessions) and another for unaccompanied baggage (also referred to as hold baggage), which includes smaller possessions and items that you will need shortly after arrival to initially set up a household.

Before the movers come, have your belongings organized based on the way you want them shipped. For example, put the items you want to be shipped in unaccompanied baggage in one room, put the clothing and documents you intend to hand-carry in suitcases or a briefcase in another area, and so forth. Safeguard items of high value (jewelry, cash). Make sure everything is properly identified and recorded on the mover's inventory sheet, with its condition correctly annotated (scratched, worn, broken). Get a copy of the inventory before the movers leave. If you are asked to sign additional forms, read them carefully, and ask the movers to provide you with a personal copy if possible.

When your shipment is delivered, know where you want each item placed. Check off each item on the inventory to assure everything is accounted for. Assure that the movers make note of any damaged or missing articles.

Loss and damage claims should be filed as soon as possible after delivery of the shipment. Specific instructions will be provided by the Transportation Management Office. In general, you may be expected to provide estimates and receipts for repairs and replacements; keep anything that's been damaged until the claim has been resolved or awarded.

*Note:* Some bases refer to their Traffic Management Offices (TMO) as Personal Property Shipping Offices (PPSO) or Joint Personal Property Shipping Offices (JPPSO) in cases where multiple locations or joint forces are supported.

8. *How are military couples assigned?*

Military couples are assigned in accordance with the policy outlined in Air Force Instruction 36-2110, *Assignments.* The general policy is to assign military couples when possible to locations in the continental United States (CONUS) and overseas, where they can maintain a joint residence. When it is not possible, each member is considered to be serving in his or her own right and must fulfill the obligations inherent to all Air Force members. One important step is to complete Air Force Form 1048, "Military Spouse Information," which advises personnel planners of a military couple's status and the fact that they want to be considered for a joint assignment. A primary factor governing joint assignments is the need at a location for both members' Air Force specialties.

9. *How can I get reassigned or released from an assignment if I have a problem that needs to be taken care of?*

Requests for a humanitarian reassignment are outlined in Air Force Instruction 36-2110, *Assignments.* They are considered on a case-by-case basis. Some cases may be incompatible with continued military service, and a hardship discharge, rather than reassignment or deferment, may be more appropriate.

A humanitarian or permissive humanitarian application may be approved in situations such as the recent death of spouse or child, when spouse or child has a disease and prolonged hospital or outpatient treatment has begun or is scheduled (for example, certain orthopedic and tuberculosis cases), terminal illness of a family member where death is imminent (within two years), and when reassignment or deferment is considered essential to an effective child advocacy program.

Normally, applications are disapproved in cases of threatened separation, divorce action, or action to pursue child custody; when climatic conditions or geographic areas adversely affect health of family member if the problem is of a recurring nature (for example, asthma or allergies); a housing shortage or home ownership problem; a financial or management problem related to off-duty employment, spouse's employment, private business activities, or settling of estates; and parents or parents-in-law suffering chronic disease or disability (problems of this nature are commonly encountered).

Applications are available electronically on the virtual MPF (vMPF) which can be accessed on the AFPC website (http://afpc.af.mil). Personnel seeking reassignment under such conditions should seek initial counsel from the customer service branch at the MPS or from their supervisor or their unit's first sergeant or commander.

10. *What is overseas culture shock?*

Overseas culture shock isn't always easy to recognize, because it affects different people in different ways. In general, it's an uncomfortable disorienting experience caused by living in a foreign country. Some people don't experience it at all. Others can have symptoms ranging from homesickness, irritability, and resentment to bitterness, hostility, and depression. Cultural adaptation usually has four phases:

*Phase 1: Initial euphoria.* Most people begin their new overseas assignment with great expectations and a positive outlook.

*Phase 2: Irritation and hostility.* During this phase, big and little differences that exist in the foreign country's culture become sources of frustration. Some people can feel uncomfortable, isolated, and even helpless.

*Phase 3: Gradual adjustment.* This comes as people become more familiar and at ease with local customs.

*Phase 4: Adaptation.* People accept and enjoy doing things in the host country. This can include travel, eating out, enjoying local customs, and even communicating in the foreign language. People in this phase, both military members and their families, feel right at home and actually miss certain aspects of the foreign culture when they're reassigned.

Most people move rapidly to the third and fourth phases. In overseas areas, many Airman and Family Readiness Centers and Recreation Centers offer programs to make cultural adaptation an easy and enjoyable experience.

11. *What's Air Force policy if my spouse wants to work?*

The Air Force fully supports the work aspirations of spouses, whether that work is in the home or in a commercial enterprise. Airman and Family Readiness Centers offer a wide range of programs to support these aspirations, including information about local job and career opportunities, job-hunting skills, and résumé preparation.

12. *I've been thinking about reenlisting, but I can't make up my mind. What should I do?*

It's a decision that, in some ways, only you can make. First, you should talk with your unit career advisor. He or she can tell you if you are eligible to reenlist; some people are not, based on their past performance and the Air Force's quality force program. They can also tell you what career fields and job opportunities are available. Then it's a matter of weighing the pros and cons of staying in, and talking it over with close friends and family members.

The Air Force offers a lot in terms of challenge, career progression, education and training, travel, and benefits for members and their families. It also requires involvement, commitment, and some degree of personal sacrifice. Most first-term airmen decide to reenlist during their last six months. Sometimes it helps to visit home (or wherever you plan to live after you get out). Places can change, as can opportunities. Your personal outlook has also evolved over the past few years. Your original plans may not seem so attractive now. Weigh all the factors concerned and you'll be in a much better position to make a final decision.

13. *What are some of the benefits of military retirement?*

Some of the most commonly cited benefits are as follows: retirement pay, which ranges from 40 to 75 percent of your base pay for your grade at the time of retirement; medical care; unlimited exchange, commissary, and theater privileges in the United States and overseas, where not limited by Status of Forces Agreements; federal benefits administered by the Department of Veterans Affairs; the Survivor Benefit Plan; membership privileges in open messes; Worldwide space-available travel on Department of Defense aircraft; and Air Force Aid Society assistance.

14. *Can I volunteer to help with youth activities, such as sports and Scouting programs, if I'm single?*

Yes. There are no limitations based on grade or marital status. Many single airmen have skills and experience in such programs and find that their involvement with children is personally rewarding and greatly appreciated by those in the Air Force community.

15. *What's Air Force policy for time off from duty to participate in Air Force–related sports programs?*

The Air Force supports participation in regularly sponsored sports programs. The mission comes first, but supervisors are encouraged to adjust duty schedules for men and women when possible. Highly skilled athletes may also be selected to participate in specialized training programs to prepare for interservice, national, and international competitions, such as the Olympics and the Pan-American Games. At base level, the focal point for details on Air Force sports programs is the base gymnasium or fitness center.

16. *How can I exercise my right to vote when I'm in the service?*

If you reside in your home state where you are registered to vote, you would vote in the normal way. If you reside elsewhere, you would vote by using an absentee ballot. Each commander appoints a voting officer who helps personnel, their spouses, and dependents register with the state they are eligible to vote in. Registration is done by submitting a Standard Form (SF) 76, Federal Post Card Application (FPCA). The FPCA is accepted by all states and territories as an application for registration and request for absentee ballot. It is postage free when placed in the U.S. mail. You may also send a written request for a ballot to your county, city, town, or parish clerk. The on-line FPCA (OFPCA) is available at the Federal Voting Assistance Program's (FVAP) web site, *www.fvap.gov*, but must be completed, printed out, signed, dated, and placed in an envelope affixed with proper postage, and mailed to your local election official. All states and territories, with the exception of American Samoa, Guam, and Ohio accept the OFPCA.

The Air Force Personnel Center (AFPC) provides information for personnel about voting and the opportunities to exercise the right to vote, including opportunities for absentee voting on its web site, *www.afpc.af.mil/library/airforcevoting*.

17. *What should I do if I'm approached by someone who wants access to classified or sensitive information?*

Verify his or her right to have access. It must be based on an official need to know and possession of a security clearance for the level of classified information involved. It is not automatically granted because of the requestor's position or rank. If the request is made from outside official channels (by another American citizen or from a citizen of a foreign country), you should immediately inform your supervisor, commander, or the nearest Air Force Office of Special Investigation (AFOSI).

18. *Should I write my representative in Congress if I have a complaint?*

Every citizen has a right to write to elected representatives and should be encouraged to do so. But it's also important to focus on the reason for writing. Many times a complaint, if surfaced, can be resolved much more quickly at the unit level. The Air Force has established programs locally to help solve real or perceived problems that affect the morale and welfare of assigned personnel and their dependents. If you do not find sufficient help within your unit or any of the support agencies on base, the Inspector General's (IG) office can assist in resolving your problem or handling your complaint. Although anybody can contact the IG office at any time with concerns or complaints, again, it is usually best to try and resolve it at the lowest level or with the most appropriate agency. This may not always be possible, which is why the IG is available for assistance. Issues brought to the IG are usually handled by a senior officer, civilian, or senior noncommissioned officer on each base who is appointed as the Inspector General. When contacted, he or she looks into all the facts of a given situation and calls other affected agencies or personnel if required. Where issues can be resolved, they usually are. When congressional complaints are filed, the base will provide a written response to the congressional representative based on a review of the facts and the options available.

19. *What is a chain of command?*

The chain of command is an organized structure of authority. This structure is well suited to resolve problems at the lowest possible level. Each link in the chain of command is a level of responsibility and authority, extending from the President, as Commander in Chief, down to each supervisory level in the Air Force. Each level in the chain is responsible for a lower level and accountable to a higher level. The chain of command is used for performing official duties in support of the mission and also to help resolve problems and issues of concern to individual members. At the unit level, your upward chain starts with your immediate supervisor and goes through the unit's first sergeant to the commander. Most of the questions and concerns are resolved at this level.

20. *Can I contest a performance report that I think is inaccurate and might be unfair, unjust, and prejudicial to my career?*

Yes. Appeals and requests for changes to reports can be made after the reports have been entered into the personnel system and have been made a matter of record. Procedures are outlined in Air Force Instruction 36-2603, *Air Force Board for Correction of Military Records,* and Air Force Instruction 36-2401, *Correcting Officer and Enlisted Evaluation Reports.* Each request is considered on its own merits. The customer service branch in the Military Personnel Section (MPS) is the focal point for initial information and assistance.

21. *What's Air Force policy on the use of alcohol?*

The use of alcohol is acceptable, when it is not restricted by public law or military directives. The Air Force does not investigate private drinking habits unless they affect public behavior, duty performance, or physical or mental health. Driving under the influence (DUI) is not tolerated. Violators are subject to apprehension and punishment under the Uniform Code of Military Justice (UCMJ). Programs are available through the Military Equal Opportunity Office to help personnel resolve alcohol-related problems.

22. *What does it mean if I've been counseled?*

It depends on the purpose. Counseling is conducted to provide feedback on performance and career opportunities, to assure that Air Force standards are understood and maintained, and to advise personnel about other sources of help if they need specialized assistance. Some examples include the orientation of new personnel, training evaluations, and disciplinary problems. Counseling can be done orally or in writing.

Written counselings usually record specific facts or a problem, the cause of the problem (if known), the outcome (actions being taken or planned), and the signatures of the counselor and the individual being counseled. The overall intent is to provide help. Supervisors are specifically encouraged to conduct written counseling in cases where adverse trends (such as disciplinary problems or failure to meet Air Force standards) continue over a period of time. When appropriate, they may be forwarded to a unit's first sergeant or commander.

### 23. *What is a letter of reprimand?*

A letter of reprimand is a formal act of censure that rebukes an offender for misconduct. It is primarily given by commanders in cases not serious enough to warrant Uniform Code of Military Justice (UCMJ) action or for conduct that is not technically criminal but is, in the commander's opinion, not conducive to the effective performance of the mission. It's also a way to deal with people on first offenses (inexperienced personnel or those with good past behavior). In this method, a member is formally advised in writing of the mistakes of judgment and warned of the future consequences if there is a recurrence. If a pattern of irresponsibility continues, a commander may consider other actions, such as an Article 15.

The actual letter contains narrative statements, the commander's signature, and a place for the member's signature, referred to as the acknowledgment indorsement. The acknowledgment indorsement does not mean agreement by the member, but only receipt and understanding of the contents of the letter.

### 24. *What is an Article 15?*

Article 15 of the Uniform Code of Military Justice (UCMJ) is a procedure used by military commanders to impose punishment for minor offenses on military members under their command. It's often referred to as nonjudicial punishment because the punishment is not imposed by a court of justice. In the Air Force, any member from the grade of airman basic to general officer can be punished under the provisions of this article.

The purpose of Article 15 is to give commanders a means for maintaining morale, discipline, and efficiency within their units, as well as the flexibility to punish members for offenses not serious enough to warrant court-martial proceedings. Under this system, the primary objective is the rehabilitation of the offender, but in cases where the offender is beyond rehabilitation the punishment may be intended to be punitive or to serve as a deterrent to others.

The types of punishment that can be given are proscribed based on the grade of the commander. Examples range from forfeiture of pay, reduction in grade, and imposition of additional duties, to restriction and placement in correctional custody. Commanders also have the authority to suspend, mitigate, and set aside punishments.

When a commander contemplates giving an Article 15, he or she considers the nature of the offense, the age and prior service record of the accused, and the recommendations of key personnel (supervisors, first sergeants, and representatives from the legal office). Airmen who receive an Article 15 will not automatically be discharged from the service or denied reenlistment. Those decisions are based on performance over a period of time.

25. *What happens to Air Force members who are caught using illegal drugs?*

When drug use is substantiated, the outcome is determined on a case-by-case basis. Nonjudicial punishment (an Article 15) can be administered. A court-martial may be requested. Fines can be levied. Stripes can be taken. Administrative discharges under other-than-honorable conditions may be requested. Confinement may be considered for possession. Prison terms for dealing drugs normally range from fifteen months to three or more years. Local rehabilitation programs are available and must be successfully completed before reenlistment is considered. In most cases, retention in the service is not favorably considered.

Why is the outcome so rough? The Air Force has a heavy responsibility to the nation and the American people. The use of drugs by any member compromises that responsibility. To condone their use could result in dangerous consequences.

Supervisors and commanders won't have much sympathy for those who are caught. Excuses that won't fly: "I made a mistake, but I have an outstanding record." "I don't know how it got there." "I didn't use it while I was on duty." "I was only using it off base." "It's only his word against mine."

Substantiated drug abuse may also have spinoff effects after the Air Force: on future employment, existing marital relationships, and child custody proceedings.

# Appendices

# Appendix A

# Professional Reading Guide

## THE CHIEF OF STAFF'S PROFESSIONAL READING PROGRAM

> *The inscription on the Eagle and Fledglings statue at our U.S. Air Force Academy reminds us that "Man's flight through life is sustained by the power of his knowledge." I believe knowledge isn't a final destination—something we "get" and hold on to forever—but is instead a never-ending pursuit.*
> —Gen. T. Michael Moseley, Air Force Chief of Staff

In 1996 Gen. Ronald Fogleman created the CSAF Professional Reading Program to develop a common frame of reference among Air Force members—officers, enlisted, and civilians. The goal was to help each of us become better, more effective advocates of air and space power.

The CSAF's Professional Reading Program can help launch a career-long reading program or can be used to supplement your previous knowledge. The books cover an expanse of topics. The majority of books detail air and space power from its genesis to recent times. Other books provide great examples of leadership to illustrate qualities airmen should emulate. The more books you read, the better you will understand the background behind the Air Force's core competencies, and the better equipped you will be to form and express your own opinions.

Mr. Herman Wolk, senior Air Force historian, asserts that "the CSAF's Reading Program emphasizes the crucial role played by the United States Air Force in American military history during the past century. . . . Reading these books fosters an important understanding that the advances in aviation technology have had on the evolution of air and space power," Wolk said. "They dramatically reveal how air and space power have transformed the battlefield through long-range precision engagement, international relations and national security policy."

You can access the complete reading list at www.af.mil/information/csafreading, and each of these books will be available through the Air University schools and Air Force libraries.

## CSAF READING LIST—FY11

### Our Military Heritage
- *The All Americans* by Lars Anderson
- *Fighter Pilot: The Memoirs of Legendary Ace Robin Olds* by Robin Olds, Christina Olds, and Ed Rasimus
- *Red Eagles: America's Secret MiGs* by Steve Davies
- *Cataclysm: General Hap Arnold and the Defeat of Japan* by Herman S. Wolk

### Strategic context
- *Monsoon: The Indian Ocean and the Future of American Power* by Robert Kaplan
- *Cyber War: The Next Threat to National Security and What to Do About It* by Richard Clarke and Robert Knake
- *The Return of History and the End of Dreams* by Robert Kagan
- *Technology Horizons: A Vision for the Air Force Science and Technology* by Dr. Werner Dahm
- *A Savage War of Peace: Algeria 1954–1962* by Alistair Horne
- *Descent into Chaos: The United States and the Disaster in Pakistan, Afghanistan, and Central Asia* by Ahmed Rashid

### Leadership
- *Three Cups of Tea: One Man's Mission to Promote Peace . . . One School at a Time* by Greg Mortenson and David Oliver Relin
- *Partners in Command: George Marshall and Dwight Eisenhower in War and Peace* by Mark Perry
- *The Lost Peace: Leadership in a Time of Horror and Hope, 1945–1953* by Robert Dallek
- *Secrets of Special Ops Leadership: Dare the Impossible; Achieve the Extraordinary* by William Allen Cohen

### Other Important Reading
The following works provide additional insight into the international military arena, the history of the USAF, and career development. Most of these titles can be obtained from your base library (either directly or through an interlibrary loan), your base exchange, a Stars and Stripes bookstore, or the publisher. The letters in parentheses indicate reading ease: E = easy; A = average; D = difficult.

*Air Power Journal.* Professional journal of the United States Air Force. Published bimonthly by Government Printing Office, Washington, DC. A journal designed to stimulate professional thought concerning aerospace doctrine, strategy, tactics, and related matters.

Atkinson, Rick. *Crusade: The Untold Story of The Persian Gulf War.* New York: Houghton Mifflin Company, 1993. Balanced and well-written journalistic account of Operation Desert Storm. (E)

Baker, David. *The Shape of Wars to Come.* New York: Stein and Day, 1982. The author is a technical information consultant to NASA and has been deeply involved in future mission planning. He describes the work presently going on in antisatellite techniques, discusses the possibilities of lasers and charged-particle-beam weapons, and speculates on the ultimate threats from space. (A)

Boettcher, Thomas D. *Vietnam: The Valor and the Sorrow.* Boston: Little, Brown and Company, 1985. The author has written a highly readable account of the American involvement in Vietnam. Beginning with the North Vietnamese struggle against French imperialism, Boettcher leads the reader through an analysis of the key events and major participants involved in America's struggle in Southeast Asia. Superb illustrations complement a comprehensive and even-handed account of the Vietnam conflict. (E)

Builder, Carl H. *The Icarus Syndrome.* New Brunswick, NJ: Transaction Publishers, 1993. A provocative and critical look at the role of airpower in theory in the development of the U.S. Air Force. (A)

Burrows, William E. *Deep Black: Space Espionage and National Security.* New York: Random House, 1987. Controversial and unverifiable look at space-based intelligence operations. (A)

Copp, DeWitt S. *A Few Great Captains.* New York: Doubleday, 1980. Written under the auspices of the Air Force Historical Foundation, this is a history of pre-WWII U.S. airpower that catches the drama and excitement of that early era. (A)

Copp, DeWitt S. *Forged in Fire.* New York: Doubleday, 1982. This sequel to *A Few Great Captains* covers WWII. It looks at the men who developed American airpower, surveys strategic bombing in Europe, and relates the quest for an independent Air Force. (A)

Douhet, Guilio. *The Command of the Air.* Translated by Dino Ferrari. Washington, DC: Office of Air Force History, 1983 (1942). The first and most passionate exposition of a comprehensive air warfare theory. (A)

Hackett, John Winthrop. *The Profession of Arms.* London: Times Publishing Co., 1963. Traces the development, meaning, and implications of our military traditions while offering perceptive observations on training, discipline, and professionalism. (A)

Hallion, Richard P. *Storm over Iraq: Air Power and the Gulf War.* Washington, DC: Smithsonian Institution Press, 1992. This book argues that the Gulf War air campaign marked a revolution in military conflict: the ascendancy of airpower in warfare. (A)

Puryear, Edgar F. *Stars in Flight.* Novato, CA: Presidio Press, 1981. The biographer of *Nineteen Stars* addresses Air Force leadership, and his subjects are the first five Air Force Chiefs: Arnold, Spaatz, Vanderberg, Twining, and White. Similarities and differences among these individuals are examined as well as the differences between air command and ground command. The questions considered are, How did they get to the top?; How did they lead while on the way to the top?; and How did they run the show when they reached the top? (E)

Smith, Perry M. *Assignment Pentagon: The Insider's Guide to the Potomac Puzzle Palace.* Elmsford, NY: Pergamon Press, Inc., second edition, 1993. This book is a "must read" for personnel at all levels who are or will be working in the Pentagon. It's also of value for anyone who will be assigned to an intermediate headquarters. Content stresses effective staff work and communication. Of special note is the chapter titled "Rules of Thumb: Helpful Hints on How to Get Ready to Work, Survive, and Thrive." (E)

Smith, Perry. M. *Taking Charge: Making the Right Choices.* Garden City, NY: Avery Publishing Group, 1988. This book by Major General Smith provides exceptional insight into leadership roles in large and complex organizations. The content is well organized and presented in an easy-to-read format. Of special note are the segments on decision making and communication. (E)

Sun Tzu Wu. *The Art of War.* New York: Oxford University Press, 1971. This short military treatise written in the sixth century B.C. lays down a set of basic military principles dealing with strategy, tactics, communications, supply, etc. The basic nature of Sun Tzu's tenets gives them a lasting relevance. (E)

United States Air Force. *AFM 1-1, Volumes I and II: Basic Aerospace Doctrine of the United State Air Force.* Washington, DC: Government Printing Office, March 1992. Volume I contains the current definitive statement of U.S. Air Force basic doctrine. Volume II contains a set of background essays explaining and supporting current Air Force basic doctrine. (A)

## CAREER DEVELOPMENT GUIDES AND MILITARY/USAF-RELATED PUBLICATIONS FROM STACKPOLE BOOKS:

Benton, Col. Jeffrey C. (USAF, Ret.). *The Air Force Officer's Guide,* 34th Edition. Provides Air Force officers and those on their way to joining the officer corps the facts they need to get ahead.

Cline, Lydia Sloan. *Today's Military Wife: Meeting the Challenges of Service Life,* 5th Edition. A down-to-earth sourcebook with practical advice on how to get the most out of military life.

Cragg, SGM Dan (USA, Ret.). *Guide to Military Installations,* 6th Edition. Comprehensive guide to the location, facilities, housing, climate, and customs of major military installations in the United States and overseas.

McIntosh, William A. *Guide to Effective Military Writing,* 3rd Edition. A handbook for getting things written quickly, correctly, and easily.

*Roots of Strategy: The Five Greatest Military Classics of All Time.* Edited by BG T. R. Phillips.

*Roots of Strategy Book 2.* Three classics in one volume by du Picq, Clausewitz, and Jomini.

*Roots of Strategy Book 3.* Three more-recent classics: *Defense,* the *Power of Personality,* and *Surprise.*

*Roots of Strategy Book 4.* Four classics on airpower and seapower by Mahan, Corbett, Douhet, and Mitchell. Edited by David Jablonsky.

Tomes, LTC Jonathan P. (USA). *The Servicemember's Legal Guide,* 4th Edition. Everything you and your family need to know about the law.

Belknap, Col. Margaret H. (USA), and Maj. F. Michael Marty (USA). *Armed Forces Guide to Personal Financial Planning,* 6th Edition. Strategies for managing your budget, savings, insurance, taxes, and investments.

# Appendix B

# Key References

The publications identified in this appendix are the primary references that were used to develop this book. They are provided for your use to gain additional insight or conduct additional research in a specific area.

**ABBREVIATIONS**
AFDIR = Air Force Directory
AFH = Air Force Handbook
AFI = Air Force Instruction
AFMAN = Air Force Manual
AFMD = Air Force Mission Directive
AFPAM = Air Force Pamphlet
AFPD = Air Force Policy Directive
DODD = Department of Defense Directive
DODI = Department of Defense Instruction
DODM = Department of Defense Manual
DODR = Department of Defense Regulation
FEMA Pub = Federal Emergency Management Agency Publication
JCS Pub = Joint Chiefs of Staff Publication
JFTR = Joint Federal Travel Regulation

**DIRECTIVES**
AFDIR 37-144, *Air Force Privacy Act Systems of Records Notices*
AFH 33-337, *The Tongue and Quill*
AFI 10-301, *Responsibilities of Air Reserve Component Forces*
AFI 10-1101, *Operations Security*
AFI 31-501, *Personnel Security Program Management*
AFI 32-6001, *Family Housing Management*
AFI 33-114, *Software Management*
AFI 33-119, *Electronic Mail (E-Mail) Management and Use*

AFI 33-129, *Transmission of Information via the Internet*
AFI 33-332, *Air Force Privacy Act Program*
AFI 33-360, Volume 1, *Publications Management Program*
AFI 35-101, *Public Affairs Policies and Procedures*
AFI 36-1201, *Discrimination Complaints*
AFI 36-2110, *Assignments*
AFI 36-2113, *The First Sergeant*
AFI 36-2201, Vols. 1–6, *Developing, Managing, and Conducting Training*
AFI 36-2209, *Survival and Code of Conduct Training*
AFI 36-2301, *Professional Military Education*
AFI 36-2306, *The Education Services Program*
AFI 36-2401, *Correcting Officer and Enlisted Evaluation Reports*
AFI 36-2403, *The Enlisted Evaluation System*
AFI 36-2502, *Airman Promotion Program*
AFI 36-2603, *Air Force Board for Correction of Military Records*
AFI 36-2604, *Service Dates and Dates of Rank*
AFI 36-2605, *Air Force Military Personnel Testing System*
AFI 36-2606, *Reenlistment in the United States Air Force*
AFI 36-2608, *Military Personnel Records Systems*
AFI 36-2618, *The Enlisted Force Structure*
AFI 36-2626, *Airman Retraining Program*
AFI 36-2706, *Military Equal Opportunity and Treatment Program*
AFI 36-2803, *The Air Force Awards and Decorations Program*
AFI 36-2805, *Special Trophies and Awards*
AFI 36-2903, *Dress and Personal Appearance of Air Force Personnel*
AFI 36-2906, *Personal Financial Responsibilities*
AFI 36-2907, *Unfavorable Information File (UIF) Program*
AFI 36-2908, *Family Care Plans*
AFI 36-2909, *Professional and Unprofessional Relationships*
AFI 36-2923, *Aeronautical Duty and Occupational Badges*
AFI 36-3003, *Military Leave Program*
AFI 36-3009, *Family Support Center Program*
AFI 36-3014, *Clothing Allowance for Air Force Personnel*
AFI 37-131, *Freedom of Information Act Program*
AFI 38-101, *Air Force Organization*
AFI 40-102, *Tobacco Use in the Air Force*
AFI 40-501, *The Air Force Fitness Program*
AFI 40-502, *The Weight and Body Fat Management Program*
AFI 41-115, *Authorized Health Care and Health Care Benefits in the Military Health Services (MHS)*
AFI 44-121, *Alcohol and Drug Abuse Prevention and Treatment (ADAPT) Program*

AFI 51-202, *Nonjudicial Punishment*
AFI 51-504, *Legal Assistance, Notary, and Preventive Law Programs*
AFI 51-902, *Political Activities by Members of the U.S. Air Force*
AFI 51-903, *Dissident and Protest Activities*
AFI 51-904, *Complaints of Wrongs Under Article 138, Uniform Code of Military Justice*
AFI 90-201, *Inspector General Activities*
AFI 90-301, *Inspector General Complaints*
AFI 91-202, *The U.S. Air Force Mishap Prevention Program*
AFI 91-204, *Safety Investigations and Reports*
AFMAN 33-326, *Preparing Official Communication*
AFMAN 36-2108, *Enlisted Classification*
AFMAN 37-123, *Management of Records*
AFMAN 37-139, *Records Disposition Schedule*
AFMD 2, *Air Combat Command*
AFMD 3, *Air Education and Training Command*
AFMD 4, *Air Force Materiel Command*
AFMD 5, *Air Force Space Command*
AFMD 6, *Air Force Special Operations Command*
AFMD 8, *Pacific Air Forces*
AFMD 9, *United States Air Forces in Europe*
AFMD 11, *Air Force Reserve*
AFPAM 36-2241, *Professional Development Guide*
AFPAM 36-2607, *Applicants' Guide to the Air Force Board for Correction of Military Records (AFBCMR)*
AFPAM 36-2627, *Airman and NCO Performance Feedback System (EES)*
AFPD 10-3, *Air Reserve Component Forces*
AFPD 10-11, *Operations Security*
AFPD 31-5, *Personnel Security Program Policy*
AFPD 32-60, *Housing*
AFPD 36-21, *Utilization and Classification of Air Force Military Personnel*
AFPD 36-22, *Military Training*
AFPD 36-23, *Military Education*
AFPD 36-24, *Military Evaluations*
AFPD 36-27, *Social Actions*
AFPD 36-28, *Awards and Decorations Program*
AFPD 36-29, *Military Standards*
AFPD 40-5, *Fitness and Weight Management*
AFPD 71-1, *Criminal Investigations and Counterintelligence*
AFPD 90-2, *Inspector General—The Inspection System*
AFPD 90-3, *Inspector General—Complaints Program*
AFPD 91-2, *Safety Programs*

AFPD 91-3, *Occupational Safety and Health*

AFSSI 5102, *The Computer Security (COMPUSEC) Program (projected to be AFI 33-202)*

DODI 1010.15, *Smoke-Free Workplace*

DODD 1315.7, *Military Personnel Assignments*

DODD 1327.5, *Leave and Liberty*

DODI 1342.19, *Family Care Plans*

DODI 1342.22, *Family Centers*

DODD 1350.2, *Military Equal Opportunity Programs*

DODD 5410.18, *Community Relations*

DODD 7000.14-R, Volume 7A, *Financial Management Regulation, Military Pay, Policies and Procedures*

DOD GEN 6P, *Voting Assistance Guide*

DOD 5500.7-R, *Joint Ethics Regulation*

JCS Pub 1-02, *Department of Defense Dictionary of Military and Associated Terms Public Law 99-433, 1 October 1986, as amended (Title X)*

JFTR, *Joint Federal Travel Regulation*

*Manual for Courts-Martial*

*Uniform Code of Military Justice (UCMF)*

*U.S. Code,* Title 10, *Armed Forces*

# Appendix C

# Major USAF Installations

**Altus AFB,** Okla. 73523-5000; 120 mi. SW of Oklahoma City. Phone: 580-482-8100; DSN 866-1110. Majcom: AETC. Host: 97th Air Mobility Wing. Mission: trains aircrew members for C-17 and KC-135 aircraft. History: activated January 1943; inactivated May 1945; reactivated January 1953. Area: 6,593 acres. Runways: 13,440 ft., 9,000-ft. parallel runway, and 3,515-ft. assault strip. Altitude: 1,381 ft. Personnel: permanent party military, 1,333; DOD civilians, 1,285 Housing: single family, 797; visiting, VOQ/VAQ, 315; TLF, 30. Clinic.

**Andersen AFB,** Guam, APO AP 96543-5000; 2 mi. N of Yigo. Phone: (cmcl, from CONUS) 671-366-1110; DSN 315-366-1110. Majcom: PACAF. Host: 36th Wing. Mission: Pacific center for power projection, regional cooperation, and multinational training; serves as a logistic support and staging base for aircraft operating in the Pacific and Indian Oceans. Major tenants: Det. 5, 22nd Space Operations Sq. (AFSPC); 613th Contingency Response Gp. (AMC); 734th Air Mobility Sq. (AMC); Helicopter Combat Support Sq. 5 (US Navy). History: activated 1945. Named for Gen. James Roy Andersen, who was chief of staff, Hq. AAF, Pacific Ocean Areas, and lost at sea in February 1945. Area: 20,270 acres. Runways: 11,182 ft. and 10,555 ft. Altitude: 612 ft. Personnel: permanent party military, 1,762; DOD civilians, 1,561. Housing: single family, officer, 236, enlisted, 1,153; unaccompanied, UOQ, 74, UAQ/UEQ, 1,018; visiting, VOQ, 23, VAQ/VEQ, 519, TLF, 232. Clinic.

**JB (Joint Base) Andrews AFB,** Md. 20762-5000; 10 mi. SE of Washington, D.C. Phone: 301-981-1110; DSN 858-1110. Majcom: AMC. Host: 89th Airlift Wing. Mission: gateway to nation's capital and home of Air Force One. Provides worldwide airlift for the President, vice president, top US officials, and foreign heads of state. Also responsible for Presidential support and base operations; supports all branches of the armed services, several major commands, and federal agencies. Major tenants: Air Force Flight Standards Agency; Hq. AFOSI; AFOSI Academy; Air National Guard Readiness Center; 113th Wing (ANG), F-16; 459th ARW (AFRC), KC-135; Naval Air Facility; Marine Aircraft Gp. 49, Det. A; Air

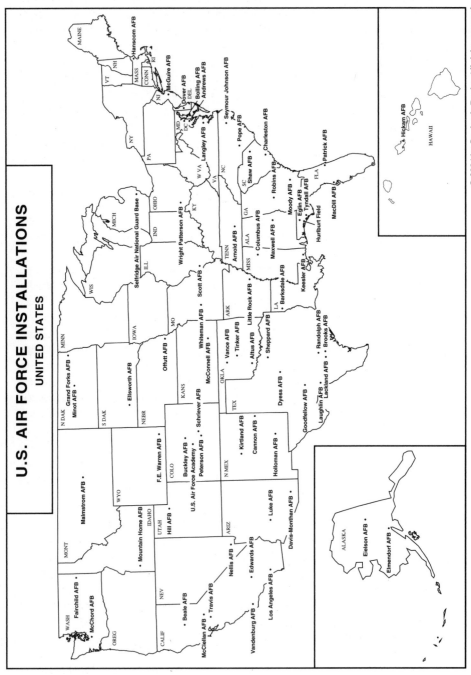

U.S. AIR FORCE INSTALLATIONS
UNITED STATES

Force Review Boards Agency. History: activated May 1943. Named for Lt. Gen. Frank M. Andrews, military air pioneer and WWII commander of the European Theater, killed in aircraft accident May 3, 1943 in Iceland. Area: 6,853 acres. Runways: 9,755 ft. and 9,300 ft. Altitude: 281 ft. Personnel: permanent party military, 5,502; DOD civilians, 3,247. Housing: single family, officer, 383 (including 96 govt. leased), enlisted, 1,667 (including 318 govt.-leased); unaccompanied, UAQ/UEQ, 923; visiting, VOQ, 136, VAQ/VEQ, 66, TLF, 68. Hospital.

**Arnold AFB,** Tenn. 37389; approx. 7 mi. SE of Manchester. Phone: 931-454-4204; DSN 340-4204. Majcom: AFMC. Host: Arnold Engineering Development Center. Mission: supports acquisition and sustainment of aerospace systems by conducting flight simulation research, development, and evaluation testing for DOD, other government agencies, and commercial aerospace firms with the world's largest complex of wind tunnels, jet and rocket engine test cells, space simulation chambers, and hyperballistic ranges. History: base dedicated June 25, 1951. Named for Gen. of the Army H.H. "Hap" Arnold, wartime Chief of the Army Air Forces. Area: 39,081 acres. Runway: 6,000 ft. Altitude: 1,100 ft. Personnel: permanent party military, 58; DOD civilians, 240. Housing: single family, officer, 12, enlisted, 28; visiting, 40. Medical aid station and small VA clinic.

**Aviano AB,** Italy, APO AE 09604; adjacent to Aviano, 50 mi. N of Venice. Phone: (cmcl, from CONUS) 011-39-0434-66-7111; DSN 632-1110. Majcom: USAFE. Host: 31st Fighter Wing. Mission: maintains two LANTIRN-equipped F-16 fighter squadrons, the 510th and the 555th, and 603rd Air Control Sq. Major tenants: Hq. 401st Air Expeditionary Wing (USAFE). Geographically Separated Units (GSUs): Det. 2, 401st AEW Pristina (Kosovo) Serbia; Det. 1, 401st AEW, Sarajevo, Bosnia; 774th Expeditionary Air Base Gp., Istres AB, France; 31st RED HORSE Flt. and 31st Munitions Sq., Camp Darby, Italy; 31st Munitions Support Sq., Ghedi AB, Italy; 99th Ex. Recon. Sq., RAF Akrotiri, Cyprus; 496th Air Base Sq., Morón AB, Spain. History: one of the oldest Italian air bases, dating to 1911. USAF began operations 1954. Area: 1,467 acres. Runway: 8,596 ft. Altitude: 413 ft. Personnel: permanent party military, 3,700; DOD civilians, 164. Housing: 681 govt.-leased (189 officer, 592 enlisted); unaccompanied, UAQ/UEQ, 812; visiting, 74, DV, 6. Clinic (contracted with local hospital).

**Barksdale AFB,** La. 71110-5000; in Bossier City. Phone: 318-456-1110; DSN 781-1110. Majcom: ACC. Host: 2nd Bomb Wing. Mission: B-52H operations and training. Major tenants: 8th Air Force (ACC); 917th Wing (AFRC), A-10, B-52H; 8th Air Force Museum. History: activated Feb. 2, 1933. Named for Lt. Eugene H. Barksdale, WWI airman killed in an August 1926 crash. Area: 22,000 acres (18,000 acres reserved for recreation). Runway: 11,756 ft. Altitude: 166 ft. Personnel: permanent party military, 5,300; DOD civilians, 1,800. Housing: single family, officer, 135, enlisted, 594; unaccompanied, 876; visiting, VOQ, 118, VAQ, 102, TLF, 24. Superclinic.

**Beale AFB,** Calif. 95903-5000; 13 mi. E of Marysville. Phone: 530-634-3000; DSN 368-1110. Majcom: ACC. Host: 9th Reconnaissance Wing. Mission:

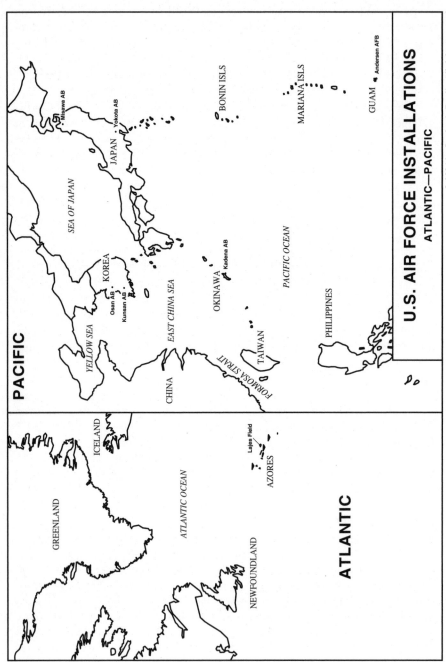

U-2, KC-135, and Global Hawk missions. Major tenants: 940th ARW (AFRC), KC-135; 7th Space Warning Sq. (AFSPC), PAVE PAWS; 548th Intelligence Gp. (ACC). History: originally US Army's Camp Beale; transferred to Air Force in 1948; became Air Force base in April 1951. Named for Brig. Gen. E.F. Beale, Indian agent in California prior to Civil War. Area: 22,944 acres. Runway: 12,000 ft. Altitude: 113 ft. Personnel: permanent party military, 3,742; DOD civilians, 718. Housing: single family, officer, 159, enlisted, 1,294; unaccompanied, 545; visiting, VOQ, 53, VAQ/VEQ, 125, TLF, 46. Clinic.

**JB Bolling AFB,** D.C. 20032-5000; 3 mi. S of US Capitol. Phone: 703-545-6700; DSN 227-0101. Host: 11th Wing, which includes the USAF Band and USAF Honor Guard. Mission: Provides support responsibilities for Hq. USAF and 40,000 USAF members worldwide. Major tenants: Air Force Chief of Chaplains; Air Force District of Washington; Air Force Surgeon General; Air Force Medical Operations Agency; Defense Intelligence Agency; Air Force Legal Services Agency; 497th Intelligence Gp. (ACC). History: activated October 1917. Named for Col. Raynal C. Bolling, first high-ranking Army Air Service officer killed in WWI. Area: 607 acres. Runway: Helipad only. Altitude: 20 ft. Personnel: permanent party military, 1,408; DOD civilians, 822. Housing: single family, officer, 285, enlisted, 950; unaccompanied, UAQ/UEQ, 262; visiting, VOQ, 62, VAQ/VEQ, 87, TLF, 100. Clinic.

**Buckley AFB,** Colo. 80011-9524; 8 mi. E of Denver. Phone: 720-847-9011 DSN 847-9011. Majcom: AFSPC. Host: 460th Space Wing. Mission: provides to combatant commanders superior global surveilllance, worldwide missile warning, homeland defense, and expeditionary forces. Focal point for transition to Space Based Infrared System. Major tenants: 2nd SWS, 140th Wing (ANG); Aerospace Data Facility; Navy/Marine Reserve Center; Air Reserve Personnel Center; Army Aviation Support Facility; Defense Finance and Accounting Center-Denver. History: activated April 1, 1942 as a gunnery training facility. Named for 1st Lt. John H. Buckley, a WW I flier, killed Sept. 17, 1918. ANG assumed control from US Navy in 1959. Became active duty Air Force base Oct. 2, 2000. Area: 3,832 acres. Runway: 11,000 ft. Altitude: 5,663 ft. Personnel: permanent party military, 3,114; DOD civilians, 3,365. Housing: unaccompanied, UAQ/UEQ, 380 Clinic.

**Cannon AFB,** N.M. 88103-5000; 7 mi. W of Clovis. Phone: 505-784-1110; DSN 681-1110. Majcom: ACC. Host: 27th FW. Mission: F-16 operations. History: activated August 1942. Named for Gen. John K. Cannon, WWII commander of all Allied air forces in the Mediterranean Theater and former commander, Tactical Air Command. Area: 3,789 acres, excluding range. Runways: 10,000 ft. and 8,200 ft. Altitude: 4,295 ft. Personnel: permanent party military, 3,126; DOD civilians, 610. Housing: single family, officer, 143, enlisted, 1,501; unaccompanied, 835; visiting, 57, TLF, 36. Ambulatory care clinic.

**JB Charleston AFB,** S.C. 29404-5000; 10 mi. from downtown Charleston. Phone: 843-963-2100; DSN 673-2100. Majcom: AMC. Host: 437th AW. Mission: C-17 operations. Major tenant: 315th AW (AFRC assoc.), C-17. History: activated October 1942; inactivated March 1946; reactivated August 1953. Area: 6,033 acres

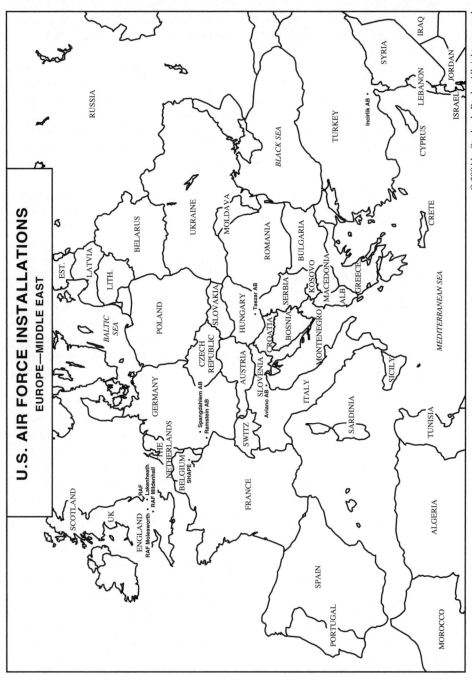

## U.S. AIR FORCE INSTALLATIONS
### EUROPE—MIDDLE EAST

(including auxiliary airfield). Runway: 9,000 ft.; joint-use airfield. Altitude: 46 ft. Personnel: permanent party military, 3,553; DOD civilians, 962. Housing: single family, officer, 148, enlisted, 1,178; unaccompanied, UAQ/UEQ, 587; visiting, VOQ, 156, VAQ/VEQ, 40, TLF, 40. Clinic.

**Columbus AFB,** Miss. 39710-1000; 7.5 mi. NW of Columbus. Phone: 662-434-7322; DSN 742-110. Majcom: AETC. Host: 14th Flying Training Wing. Mission: Specialized Undergraduate Pilot Training (T-1, T-37, T-38). History: activated 1942 for pilot training. Area: 5,325 acres. Runways: 12,000 ft., 8,000 ft., and 6,300 ft. Altitude: 219 ft. Personnel: permanent party military, 1,409; DOD civilians, 585. Housing: single family, 538; unaccompanied, UOQ, 234, UAQ/UEQ, 166; visiting, 73, DV, 4, TLF, 20. Clinic.

**Davis-Monthan AFB,** Ariz. 85707-5000; within Tucson. Phone: 520-228-1110; DSN 228-1110. Majcom: ACC. Host: 355th Wing. Mission: A-10 combat crew training; OA-10 and FAC HC-130 training and operations; EC-130H; HH-60 Pavehawk; and CSAR operations. Major tenants: 12th Air Force (ACC); Aerospace Maintenance and Regeneration Center (AFMC), DOD's single location for regeneration, maintenance, parts reclamation, preservation, storage, and disposal of excess DOD and government aerospace vehicles; 943rd Rescue Gp. (AFRC), HH-60; 55th ECG (ACC); 563rd RQG (AFSOC); US Customs and Border Protection. History: activated 1927. Named for two local aviators: 2nd Lt. Samuel H. Davis, killed Dec. 28, 1921, and 2nd Lt. Oscar Monthan, killed March 27, 1924. Area: 10,633 acres. Runway: 13,643 ft. Altitude: 2,404 ft. Personnel: permanent party military, 6,671; DOD civilians, 3,197. Housing: single family, officer, 125, enlisted, 1,129; unaccompanied, 756; visiting, VOQ, 20, VAQ/VEQ, 61, DV, 165, TLF, 50. Clinic.

**Dover AFB,** Del. 19902-7209; 6 mi. SE of Dover. Phone: 302-677-3000; DSN 445-3000. Majcom: AMC. Host: 436th AW. Mission: C-5 operations; operates largest DOD aerial port facility; houses military's East Coast mortuary. Major tenant: 512th AW (AFRC assoc.). History: activated December 1941; inactivated 1946; reactivated February 1951. Area: 3,908 acres. Runways: 12,900 ft. and 9,600 ft. Altitude: 28 ft. Personnel: permanent party military, 3,350; DOD civilians, 1,040. Housing: single family, officer, 139, enlisted, 866; unaccompanied, UAQ/UEQ, 533; visiting, VOQ, 238, VAQ/VEQ, 34, TLF, 19. Clinic.

**Dyess AFB,** Tex. 79607-1980; WSW border of Abilene. Phone: 325-696-1110; DSN 461-1110. Majcom: ACC. Host: 7th BW. Mission: B-1 operations. Major tenant: 317th Airlift Gp. (AMC), C-130. History: activated April 1942; deactivated December 1945; reactivated as Abilene AFB September 1955. In December 1956, renamed for Lt. Col. William E. Dyess, WWII fighter pilot who escaped from a Japanese prison camp, killed in P-38 crash in December 1943. Area: 6,342 acres (including off-base sites). Runway: 13,500 ft. Altitude: 1,789 ft. Personnel: permanent party military, 4,884; DOD civilians, 412. Housing: single family, officer, 153, enlisted, 824; unaccompanied, 808; visiting, 160, TLF, 39. Clinic.

**Edwards AFB,** Calif. 93524; adjacent to Rosamond. Phone: 661-277-1110; DSN 527-3510. Majcom: AFMC. Host: 95th Air Base Wing. Mission: The Air Force Flight Test Center is AFMC's center of excellence for conducting and supporting research, development, test, and evaluation of aerospace systems from concept to combat. It operates the US Air Force Test Pilot School and is home to NASA's Dryden Research Center and considerable test activity conducted by America's commercial aerospace industry. Major tenants: AFRL's Propulsion Directorate (AFMC); Dryden Flight Research Center (NASA); USMC Air Reserve helicopter squadrons and detachments HMM 764 and HMH 769. History: activities began in September 1933 when the Muroc Bombing and Gunnery Range was established. In 1942, it was designated Muroc Army Air Base. Renamed in 1949 for Capt. Glen W. Edwards, killed June 5, 1948 in crash of a YB-49 "Flying Wing." Area: 301,000 acres. Runways: 21, from 4,000 to 39,000 ft. Altitude: 2,302 ft. Personnel: permanent party military, 1,701; DOD civilians, 3,471. Housing: single family, officer, 194; enlisted, 603. Medical and dental clinics.

**Eglin AFB,** Fla. 32542; 2 mi. SW of the twin cities of Niceville and Valparaiso; 7 mi. NE of Fort Walton Beach. Phone: 850-882-1110; DSN 872-1110. Majcom: AFMC. Host: 96th ABW. Mission: supporting the Eglin Air Armament Center and associate units with traditional military services as well as civil engineering, personnel, logistics, communications, computer, medical, security, and all other host services. Major tenants: AFRL's Munitions Directorate (AFMC); 33rd FW (ACC), F-15; 53rd Wing (ACC); 919th Special Operations Wing (AFRC) at Duke Field, MC-130; Air Force Armament Museum; Army 6th Ranger Training Battalion; Naval School Explosive Ordnance Disposal. History: activated 1935. Named for Lt. Col. Frederick I. Eglin, WWI flier killed in aircraft accident Jan. 1, 1937. Area: 463,452 acres. Eglin is the nation's largest Air Force base in terms of acreage, covering an area roughly two-thirds the size of Rhode Island. Runways: 12,000 ft. and 10,000 ft. Altitude: 85 ft. Personnel: permanent party military, 7,854; DOD civilians, 3,884 (excluding Hurlburt Field). Housing: single family, officer, 218, enlisted, 2,116; unaccompanied, UAQ/UEQ, 1,212; visiting, VOQ, 169, VAQ/VEQ, 156, TLF, 87. Hospital.

**Eielson AFB,** Alaska 99702-5000; 26 mi. SE of Fairbanks. Phone: 907-377-1110; DSN 317-377-1110. Majcom: PACAF. Host: 354th FW. Mission: F-16C/D and A/OA-10 operations. Major tenants: Arctic Survival School (AETC); 168th Air Refueling Wing (ANG), KC-135; 353rd Combat Training Sq. History: activated October 1944. Named for Carl Ben Eielson, Arctic aviation pioneer who died in an Arctic rescue mission in November 1929. Area: 19,790 acres (including 16 remote sites, 63,195 acres). Runway: 14,500 ft. Altitude: 534 ft. Personnel: permanent party military, 2,930; DOD civilians, 633. Housing: single family, officer, 181, enlisted, 1,243; unaccompanied, UOQ, 8, UAQ, 522, UEQ, 16; visiting, VOQ, 206, VAQ/VEQ, 328, TLF, 40. Outpatient clinic.

**Ellsworth AFB,** S.D. 57706-5000; 12 mi. ENE of Rapid City. Phone: 605-385-5056; DSN 675-5056. Majcom: ACC. Host: 28th BW. Mission: B-1 operations. Major tenants: Det. 21, Belle Fourche Electronic Scoring Site; Det. 8, 372nd Training Sq. (AETC); Det. 226, AFOSI. History: activated January 1942 as Rapid City AAB; renamed June 13, 1953 for Brig. Gen. Richard E. Ellsworth, killed March 18, 1953 in RB-36 crash. Area: 5,411 acres. Runway: 13,500 ft. Altitude: 3,276 ft. Personnel: permanent party military, 3,144; DOD civilians, 451. Housing: single family, officer, 311, enlisted, 1,535, unaccompanied, 728; visiting, 80, TLF, 29. Clinic.

**JB Elmendorf AFB,** Alaska 99506-5000; bordering Anchorage. Phone: 907-552-1110; DSN 317-552-1110. Majcom: PACAF. Host: 3rd Wing. Mission: C-12, C-130, E-3 Airborne Warning and Control System, F-15C/D, and F-15E operations. Hub for air traffic to and from Far East. Major tenants: Alaskan Command; 11th Air Force (PACAF); Alaskan NORAD Region. History: activated July 1940. Named for Capt. Hugh Elmendorf, killed Jan. 13, 1933. Area: 13,100 acres. Runways: 10,000 ft. and 7,500 ft. Altitude: 213 ft. Personnel: permanent party military, 6,642; DOD civilians, 898. Housing: single family, officer, 172, enlisted, 1,640; unaccompanied, UAQ/UEQ, 1,044; visiting, VOQ, 196, VAQ/VEQ, 203, TLF, 86. Hospital.

**Fairchild AFB,** Wash. 99011-9588; 10 mi. WSW of Spokane. Phone: 509-247-1110; DSN 657-1110. Majcom: AMC. Host: 92nd Air Refueling Wing. Mission: KC-135R operations. Major tenants: 2nd SS (ACC) Munition Maintenance; 336th Training Gp. (USAF Survival School, AETC); 141st ARW (ANG), KC-135E. History: activated January 1942. Named for Gen. Muir S. Fairchild, USAF vice chief of staff at his death in 1950. Area: 5,823 acres; 530,205 acres used for survival school. Runway: 13,901 ft. Altitude: 2,426 ft. Personnel: permanent party military, 2,759; DOD civilians, 787. Housing: single family, officer, 144, enlisted, 1,092; unaccompanied, UAQ/UEQ, 642; visiting, VOQ, 85, VAQ/VEQ, 222, TLF, 18. Clinic.

**F.E. Warren AFB,** Wyo. 82005-5000; adjacent to Cheyenne. Phone: 307-773-1110; DSN 481-1110. Majcom: AFSPC. Host: 90th SW. Mission: Minuteman III ICBMs; UH-1N. Major tenants: 20th Air Force (AFSPC); Air Force ICBM Museum. History: activated as Ft. D.A. Russell July 4, 1867; under Army jurisdiction until 1949, when reassigned to USAF; renamed in 1930 for Francis Emory Warren, Wyoming Senator and first state governor. Area: 5,866 acres. Missile site area covering more than 12,600 sq. mi. in Wyoming, Colorado, and Nebraska. Runway: none. Altitude: 6,142 ft. Personnel: permanent party military, 3,078; DOD civilians, 1,017. Housing: single family, officer, 114, enlisted, 717; unaccompanied, officer, 12, enlisted, 767; visiting, 30, TLF, 39. Clinic.

**Goodfellow AFB,** Tex. 76908-4410; SE of San Angelo. Phone: 325-654-3231; DSN 477-3231. Majcom: AETC. Host: 17th Training Wing. Mission: trains intelligence, fire protection, and special instruments personnel for US military and DOD and international agencies. Major tenants: 344th Military Intelligence Battalion (Army); Center for Information Dominance det. (Navy); USMC det.; NCO Academy. History: activated January 1941. Named for Lt. John J. Goodfellow Jr., WWI observation airplane pilot killed in combat Sept. 14, 1918. Area: 1,136 acres. Runway: none. Altitude: 1,900 ft. Personnel: permanent party military, 1,387; DOD civilians, 689. Housing: single family, officer, 2, enlisted, 296; unaccompanied, UOQ, 51, UAQ/UEQ, 206; visiting, VOQ, 206, VAQ/VEQ, 351, TLF, 31. Clinic.

**Grand Forks AFB,** N.D. 58205-5000; 16 mi. W of Grand Forks. Phone: 701-747-3000; DSN 362-3000. Majcom: AMC. Host: 319th ARW. Mission: KC-135R operations. History: activated 1956. Named after town of Grand Forks, whose citizens bought the property for the Air Force. Area: 5,418 acres. Runway: 12,351 ft. Altitude: 911 ft. Personnel: permanent party military, 1,986; DOD civilians, 366. Housing: single family, officer, 168, enlisted, 1,036; unaccompanied, UAQ/UEQ, 587; visiting, VOQ, 31, VAQ/VEQ, 17, TLF, 27. Hospital.

**Hanscom AFB, Mass.** 01731-5000; 17 mi. NW of Boston. Phone: 781-377-4441; DSN 478-5980. Majcom: AFMC. Host: 66th ABW. Mission: Electronic Systems Center manages development and acquisition of command and control systems. Major tenants: AFRL's Space Vehicles Directorate-Hanscom; AFRL's Sensors Directorate-Hanscom. History: activated 1941. Named for Laurence G. Hanscom, a pre-WWII advocate of private aviation, killed in a lightplane accident in 1941. Area: 846 acres. Runway: no flying mission; transient USAF aircraft use runways of Laurence G. Hanscom Field, state-operated airfield adjoining the base. Altitude: 133 ft. Personnel: permanent party military, 1,229; DOD civilians, 2,051. Housing: single family, officer, 314, enlisted, 383; unaccompanied, UAQ/UEQ, 122; visiting, 148, TLF, 47. Clinic.

**JB Pearl Harbor-Hickam AFB,** Hawaii 96853-5000; 9 mi. W of Honolulu. Phone: 808-449-7110 (Oahu military operator); DSN 315-449-7110. Majcom: PACAF. Host: 15th AW. Mission: provides base and logistical support for 140 associate and tenant units in Hawaii and other Pacific-region locations; airlift for commander, PACOM, and commander, PACAF; and maintenance and refueling support for aircraft transiting between the US mainland and the western Pacific. Major tenants: PACAF; 13th AF/Kenney Warfighting Hq. (Provisional); 154th Wing (ANG), C-17, C-130, F-15, KC-135R; Joint POW/MIA Accounting Command. History: activated September 1938. Named for Lt. Col. Horace M. Hickam, aviation pioneer killed in crash Nov. 5, 1934. Formed a joint base with Naval Station Pearl Harbor in 2010. Area: 2,761 acres. Runways: Four joint-use runways shared with Honolulu Arpt.: 12,357 ft., 12,000 ft., 9,000 ft., and 6,952 ft. Altitude: 13 ft. Personnel: permanent party military, 5,016; DOD civilians, 1,405. Housing: single family, officer, 553, enlisted, 1,628; unaccompanied, UAQ/UEQ, 588; visiting, VOQ, 149, VAQ/VEQ, 83, TLF, 40. Clinic.

**Hill AFB,** Utah 84056-5990; 25 mi. N. of Salt Lake City. Phone: 801-777-1110; DSN 777-1110. Majcom: AFMC. Host: 75th ABW. Mission: Ogden Air Logistics Center provides worldwide engineering and logistics management for F-16s; maintains the A-10, C-130, and F-16; handles logistics management and maintenance for Minuteman ICBMs; provides sustainment and logistics support for space and C3I programs; overhauls and repairs landing gear for all USAF (and

70 percent of DOD) aircraft; leading provider of rocket motors, small missiles, air munitions and guided bombs, photonics imaging and reconnaissance equipment, simulators and training devices, avionics, hydraulics and pneudraulics instruments, and software. Major tenants: 388th FW (ACC); 419th FW (AFRC), F-16; Hill Aerospace Museum; Defense Enterprise Computing Center (DISA); Defense Distribution Depot Hill Utah; Defense Logistics Agency; 372nd Recruiting Gp. (USAF). History: activated 1940. Named for Maj. Ployer P. Hill, killed Oct. 30, 1935 while test flying the first B-17. Area: 6,797 acres; manages 962,076 acres (Utah Test and Training Range). Runway: 13,500 ft. Altitude: 4,789 ft. Personnel: permanent party military, 6,200; DOD civilians, 17,000. Housing: single family, officer, 178, enlisted, 960; unaccompanied, UAQ/UEQ, 786; visiting, VOQ, 13, VAQ/VEQ, 147, TLF, 61. Clinic.

**Holloman AFB,** N.M. 88310; 8 mi. SW of Alamogordo. Phone: 505-572-1110; DSN 572-1110. Majcom: ACC. Host: 49th FW. Mission: F-117A operations; Basic Expeditionary Airfield Resources (BEAR Base Assets) and two air transportable clinics. Major tenants: 46th Test Gp. (AFMC); 4th Space Control Sq. (AFSPC); German Air Force Flying Training Center. History: activated 1941. Named for Col. George Holloman, guided-missile pioneer. Area: 58,000 acres. Runways: 12,000 ft., 10,500 ft., and 8,000 ft. Altitude: 4,350 ft. Personnel: permanent party military, 3,751; DOD civilians, 1,049. Housing: single family, officer, 190, enlisted, 1,223; unaccompanied, 945; visiting, 192, TLF, 49. Clinic.

**Hurlburt Field,** Fla. 32544-5000; 5 mi. W of Fort Walton Beach. Phone: 850-884-7464; DSN 579-7464. Majcom: AFSOC. Host: 16th Special Operations Wing. Mission: specialized airpower, equipped with AC-130H/U, MC-130E/H, MC-130P (located at Eglin), MH-53J/M, U-28A. Major tenants: AFSOC; 823rd RED HORSE Sq.; USAF Combat Weather Center; USAF Special Operations School; Joint Special Operations University; 505th Command and Control Wing; 605th Test and Evaluation Sq.; 25th Information Operations Sq.; 18th Flight Test Sq.; 720th Special Tactics Gp.; Det. 3, 342nd Training Sq. History: activated 1943. Named for Lt. Donald W. Hurlburt, WWII pilot killed Oct. 1, 1943. Area: 6,600 acres. Runway: 6,900 ft. Altitude: 38 ft. Personnel: permanent party military, 7,340; DOD civilians, 800. Housing: single family, officer, 52, enlisted, 628; unaccompanied, UAQ/UEQ, 1,231; visiting, VOQ, 163, VAQ/VEQ, 51, TLF, 24. Clinic.

**Incirlik AB,** Turkey, APO AE 09824; 6 mi. E of Adana. Phone: (cmcl, from CONUS) 011-90-322-316-6060; DSN (from CONUS) 676-6060. Majcom: USAFE. Host: 39th ABW. Mission: provides full spectrum, forward operating base support to expeditionary forces. History: activated May 1954. Present unit began operations March 1966. Incirlik, in Turkish, means fig orchard. Area: 3,400 acres. Runway: 10,000 ft. Altitude: 240 ft. Personnel: permanent party military, 1,358; DOD civilians, 696. Housing: single family, 750; unaccompanied, UOQ, 105, UEQ, 756; visiting, VOQ, 91, VAQ/VEQ, 192, DV, 18, TLF, 80. Clinic.

**Kadena AB,** Japan, APO AP 96368-5000; 15 mi. N of Naha. Phone: (cmcl, from CONUS) 011-81-6117-34-1110; DSN 315- 634-1110. Majcom: PACAF.

Host: 18th Wing. Mission: E-3, F-15C/D, KC-135R, and HH-60 operations. Major tenants: 353rd Special Operations Gp. (AFSOC); 390th Intelligence Sq.; 82nd Reconnaissance Sq. (ACC); 733rd Air Mobility Support Sq. (AMC); Commander, Fleet Activities Okinawa (Navy). History: occupied by US forces in April 1945. Named for city of Kadena, Okinawa. Area: 11,210 acres. Runway: 12,100 ft. Altitude: 146 ft. Personnel: permanent party military, 8,000; DOD civilians, 1,800. Housing: single family, officer, 1,677, enlisted, 5,800; unaccompanied, UOQ, 47, UAQ/UEQ, 2,080; visiting, VOQ, 226, VAQ/VEQ, 222, TLF, 122. Clinic.

**Keesler AFB,** Miss. 39534-5000; located in Biloxi. Phone: 228-377-1110; DSN 597-1110. Majcom: AETC. Host: 81st TRW. Mission: conducts Air Force, joint service, and international training for basic electronics, communications electronic systems, communications computer systems, air traffic control, airfield management, command post, air weapons control, weather, precision measurement, education and training, financial management and comptroller, information management, manpower and personnel, and medical, dental, and nursing specialties. Major tenants: 2nd Air Force (AETC); 45th Airlift Sq. (AETC), C-21; 403rd Wing (AFRC), C-130, WC-130. History: activated June 12, 1941. Named for 2nd Lt. Samuel R. Keesler Jr., a native of Mississippi and WWI aerial observer killed in action Oct. 9, 1918. Area: 3,554 acres, excluding off-base housing. Runway: 6,600 ft. Altitude: 33 ft. Personnel: permanent party military, 3,956; DOD civilians, 3,483. Housing: single family, officer, 280, enlisted, 1,551; unaccompanied, UAQ/UEQ, 809; visiting, 1,306, TLF, 79. Keesler Medical Center.

**Kirtland AFB,** N.M. 87117-5606; SE quadrant of Albuquerque. Phone: 505-853-0011; DSN 263-0011. Majcom: AFMC. Host: 377th ABW. Mission: provide world-class nuclear surety, expeditionary forces, and support to base operations. Major tenants: 498th Armament Systems Wing (AFMC); 58th SOW (AETC), HC-130, MC-130, HH-60, MH-53, UH-1, receiving CV-22 in 2006; Airborne Laser Program Office; Air Force Nuclear Weapons and Counterproliferation Agency; Air Force Pararescue and Combat Officer School; Air Force Office of Aerospace Studies; Air Force Operational Test and Evaluation Center; Air Force Research Laboratories (AFMC); 150th FW (ANG), F-16; Defense Threat Reduction Agency; Nuclear Weapons Center (AFMC); Nuclear Weapons Directorate (AFMC); Sandia National Laboratories; National Nuclear Security Administration (DOE); Space and Missile Systems Center Det. 12 (AFSPC); Defense Nuclear Weapons School; Air Force Inspection Agency; Air Force Safety Center. History: activated January 1941. Named for Col. Roy C. Kirtland, aviation pioneer who died May 2, 1941. Area: 52,678 acres. Runways: two, each 13,000 ft.; 10,000 ft.; and 6,000 ft. Altitude: 5,352 ft. Personnel: permanent party military, 3,057; DOD civilians, 3,459. Housing: single family, officer, 136, enlisted, 892; unaccompanied, UAQ/UEQ, 828; visiting, VOQ, 181, VAQ/VEQ, 216, DV, 38, TLF, 39. Air Force-VA joint medical center.

**Kunsan AB,** South Korea, APO AP 96264-5000; 8 mi. SW of Kunsan City. Phone: (cmcl, from CONUS) 011-82-63-470-1110; DSN 782-1110. Majcom:

PACAF. Host: 8th FW. Mission: F-16C/D operations; home of the "Wolf Pack" and the first active overseas F-16 wing (September 1981). Major tenants: US Army's Charlie and Delta Batteries, 2nd Battalion, 1st Air Defense Artillery; US Army Contracting Command Korea. History: built by the Japanese in 1938. Area: 2,157 acres. Runway: 9,000 ft. Altitude: 29 ft. Personnel: permanent party military, 2,550; DOD civilians, 31. Housing: unaccompanied, UOQ, 245, UAQ/UEQ, 2,475; visiting, VOQ, 26, VAQ/VEQ, 60. Clinic.

**Lackland AFB,** Tex. 78236-5000; 8 mi. SW of downtown San Antonio. Phone: 210-671-1110; DSN 473-1110. Majcom: AETC. Host: 37th TRW. Mission: One of the largest USAF training wings. Provides basic military training for civilian recruits entering Air Force, ANG, and AFRC; conducts courses in ground combat (base support) functions, English language training for international and US military students, and specialized maintenance and security training in Spanish to military forces and government agencies from 26 Latin American nations. Major tenants: Air Intelligence Agency; 433rd AW (AFRC); 149th FTW (ANG); 67th Information Operations Wing (ACC); National Security Agency/Central Security Service Texas; 59th Medical Wing; Air Force Security Forces Center; Force Protection Battlelab; Cryptologic Systems Gp. History: activated 1941. Named for Brig. Gen. Frank D. Lackland, early commandant of Kelly Field .ying school, who died in 1943. Area: 9,572 acres. Runway: 11,550 ft. Altitude: 691 ft. Personnel: permanent party military, 20,303; DOD civilians, 7,797. Housing: single family, officer, 151, enlisted, 1,060; unaccompanied, enlisted, 1,477; visiting, 2,838, TLF, 96. Wilford Hall Medical Center.

**Lajes Field,** Azores, Portugal, APO AE 09720-5000; Terceira Island, 900 mi. W of Portugal. Phone: (cmcl, from CONUS) 011-351-295-57-1110; DSN from US 535-1110, from Europe 312-535-1110. Majcom: USAFE. Host: 65th ABW. Mission: provides support to US and allied aircraft and personnel transiting the Atlantic, through US military and host-nation coordination. Major tenants: 65th ABW; 729th AMS (AMC). History: US operations began at Lajes Field 1943. Area: 1,192 acres. Runway: 10,865 ft. Altitude: 180 ft. Personnel: permanent party military, 655; DOD civilians, 151. Housing: single family, officer, 80, enlisted, 336; unaccompanied, UOQ, 20, UAQ/UEQ, 269; visiting, 252, TLF, 30. Clinic.

**JB Langley AFB,** Va. 23665-5000; 3 mi. N of Hampton. Phone: 757-764-1110; DSN 574-1110. Majcom: ACC. Host: 1st FW. Mission: F-15 and F-22A air dominance operations. Major tenants: Air Combat Command; Air Force Rescue Coordination Center; Aerospace C2ISR Center; USAF Heritage of America Band; 480th Intelligence Wg. (ACC); Air and Space Expeditionary Force Center (ACC). History: activated Dec. 30, 1916. Langley is the first military base in the US purchased and built specifically for military aviation. Named for aviation pioneer and scientist Samuel Pierpont Langley, who died in 1906. Area: 2,900 acres. Runway: 10,000 ft. Altitude: 11 ft. Personnel: permanent party military, 8,057; DOD civilians, 2,264. Housing: single family, officer, 328, enlisted, 1,053; unaccompanied, 1,053; visiting, VOQ, 78, VAQ/VEQ, 153, TLF, 60. Hospital.

**Laughlin AFB,** Tex. 78843-5000; 6 mi. E of Del Rio. Phone: 830-298-3511; DSN 732-1110. Majcom: AETC. Host: 47th FTW. Mission: SUPT (T-1, T-6, T-38). History: activated July 1942. Named for 1st Lt. Jack Thomas Laughlin, Del Rio native, B-17 pilot, killed Jan. 29, 1942. Area: 5,343 acres. Runways: 8,858 ft., 8,316 ft., and 6,236 ft. Altitude: 1,081 ft. Personnel: permanent party military, 929; DOD civilians, 982. Housing: single family, officer, 298, enlisted, 218; unaccompanied, UOQ, 320, UAQ/UEQ, 184; visiting, 96, TLF, 20. Clinic.

**Little Rock AFB,** Ark. 72099-4940; 17 mi. NE of Little Rock (Jacksonville). Phone: 501-987-1110; DSN 731-1110. Majcom: AETC. Host: 314th AW. Mission: largest C-130 training base in the world; trains crew members from all services and 28 allied nations. Major tenants: 463rd Airlift Gp. (AMC), C-130; 189th AW (ANG), C-130; US Air Force Mobility Weapons School (AMC); Hq. Ark. ANG. History: activated Oct. 9, 1955. Area: 6,130 acres. Runway: 12,000 ft. Altitude: 310 ft. Personnel: permanent party military, 5,340; DOD civilians, 570. Housing: single family, officer, 185, enlisted, 1,286; unaccompanied, 840; visiting, VOQ, 102, VAQ/VEQ, 52. Clinic.

**Los Angeles AFB,** Calif. 90245-4657; in El Segundo, 3 mi. SE of Los Angeles Arpt.; base housing and support facilities 18 mi. S of the main base, in San Pedro. Phone: 310-363-1110; DSN 833-1110. Majcom: AFSPC. Host: Space and Missile Systems Center. Mission: responsible for research, development, acquisition, on-orbit testing, and sustainment of military space and missile systems. History: activated as Air Research and Development Command's Western Development Division July 1, 1954. Area: 112 acres at Los Angeles AFB and 127 acres at Ft. MacArthur Military Family Housing Annex. Runway: none. Altitude: 95 ft. Personnel: permanent party military, 1,076; DOD civilians, 1,257. Housing: 645 units, TLF, 25. Clinic.

**Luke AFB,** Ariz. 85309-5000; 20 mi. WNW of downtown Phoenix. Phone: 623-856-1110; DSN 896-1110. Majcom: AETC. Host: 56th FW. Mission: F-16 operations; conducts USAF and allied F-16 pilot and crew chief training. Major tenant: 944th FW (AFRC), F-16. History: activated 1941. Named for 2nd Lt. Frank Luke Jr., observation balloon-busting ace of WWI and first American aviator to receive the Medal of Honor, killed in action Sept. 29, 1918. Luke is the largest fighter training base in the world. Area: 4,200 acres, plus 1.9 million-acre Barry M. Goldwater Range. Runways: 10,000 ft. and 9,910 ft. Altitude: 1,090 ft. Personnel: permanent party military, 5,008; DOD civilians, 935. Housing: single family, 724; unaccompanied, UAQ/UEQ, 730; visiting, 186, TLF, 84. Clinic.

**MacDill AFB,** Fla. 33621-5000; on the Interbay Peninsula in southern Tampa. Phone: 813-828-1110; DSN 968-1110. Majcom: AMC. Host: 6th AMW. Mission: KC-135 operations; provides worldwide air refueling and combatant commander support. Major tenants: SOCOM; CENTCOM; Joint Communications Support Element; NOAA Aircraft Operations Center. History: activated April 15, 1941. Named for Col. Leslie MacDill, killed in aircraft accident Nov. 8, 1938. Area: 5,767 acres. Runways: 11,420 ft. and 7,167 ft. Altitude: 6 ft. Personnel: permanent party military, 3,650; DOD civilians, 1,417. Housing: single family, officer, 45, enlisted, 629; unaccompanied, UAQ/UEQ, 610; visiting, VOQ, 112, VAQ/VEQ, 130, TLF, 5. Hospital.

**Malmstrom AFB,** Mont. 59402-5000; 1.5 mi. E of Great Falls. Phone: 406-731-1110; DSN 632-1110. Majcom: AFSPC. Host: 341st SW. Mission: Minuteman III ICBM operations, UH-1N. Major tenant: 819th RED HORSE Sq. (ACC). History: activated Dec. 15, 1942. Named for Col. Einar A. Malmstrom, WWII fighter commander killed in air accident Aug. 21, 1954. Site of SAC's first Minuteman wing. Area: 3,716 acres, plus about 23,500 sq. mi. for missile sites. Runway: closed. Altitude: 3,460 ft. Personnel: permanent party military, 3,382; DOD civilians, 607. Housing: single family, officer, 210, enlisted, 974; unaccompanied, UAQ/UEQ, 834; visiting, 53, TLF, 30. Clinic.

**Maxwell AFB,** Ala. 36112-5000; 1 mi. WNW of Montgomery. Phone: 334-953-1110; DSN 493-1110. Majcom: AETC. Host: 42nd ABW. Mission: Air University conducts professional military, graduate, and professional continuing education for precommissioned and commissioned officers, enlisted personnel, and civilians. Major tenants: Air University; Air War College; Air Command and Staff College; Air University Library; College of Aerospace Doctrine, Research, and Education; School of Advanced Air and Space Studies; Air Force Officer Accession and Training Schools; Ira C. Eaker College for Professional Development; College for Enlisted Professional Military Education; Community College of the Air Force; Air Force Institute for Advanced Distributed Learning; Squadron Officer College; Civil Air Patrol; 908th AW (AFRC), C-130; Air Force Historical Research Agency; Air Force Doctrine Center; Headquarters Operations and Sustainment Systems Gp.; USAF Counterproliferation Center. History: activated 1918. Named for 2nd Lt. William C. Maxwell, killed in air accident Aug. 12, 1920. Area: 4,221 acres (includes Gunter Annex). Runway: 8,000 ft. Altitude: 172 ft. Personnel: permanent party military, 3,466; DOD civilians, 5,395. Housing: single family, officer, 372, enlisted, 588; unaccompanied, UAQ/UEQ, 280; visiting, 2,304, TLF, 30. Clinic.

**JB Lewis-McChord AFB,** Wash. 98438-1109; 8 mi. S of Tacoma. Phone: 253-982-1110; DSN 382-1110. Majcom: AMC. Host: 62nd AW. Mission: C-17 operations. Base is adjacent to Ft. Lewis, its primary customer for strategic airlift worldwide. Major tenant: 446th AW (AFRC assoc.). History: activated May 5, 1938. Named for Col. William C. McChord, killed Aug. 18, 1937. Formed a joint base with Ft. Lewis in 2010. Area: 4,639 acres. Runway: 10,100 ft. Altitude: 4,639 ft. Personnel: permanent party military, 3,750; DOD civilians, 1,128. Housing: single family, officer, 113, enlisted, 867; unaccompanied, UOQ, 2, UAQ/UEQ, 752; visiting, VOQ, 68, VAQ/VEQ, 232, TLF, 20. Dispensary. Madigan Army Medical Center is located 4 mi. SE.

**McConnell AFB,** Kan. 67221-5000; SE corner of Wichita. Phone: 316-759-6100; DSN 734-1110. Majcom: AMC. Host: 22nd ARW. Mission: KC-135 operations. Major tenants: 184th ARW (ANG); 931st Air Refueling Gp. (AFRC assoc.).

History: activated June 5, 1951. Named for the three McConnell brothers, WWII B-24 pilots from Wichita—Lt. Col. Edwin M. McConnell (died Sept. 1, 1997), Capt. Fred J. McConnell (died in a private airplane crash Oct. 25, 1945), and 2nd Lt. Thomas L. McConnell (killed July 10, 1943). Area: 3,533 acres. Runways: two, 12,000 ft. each. Altitude: 1,371 ft. Personnel: permanent party military, 2,722; DOD civilians, 403. Housing: single family, officer, 83, enlisted, 506; unaccompanied, UAQ/UEQ, 615; visiting, VOQ, 42, VAQ/VEQ, 44, TLF, 45. Clinic.

**JB McGuire AFB,** N.J. 08641-5000; 18 mi. SE of Trenton. Phone: 609-754-1100; DSN 650-1100. Majcom: AMC. Host: 305th AMW. Mission: C-17 and KC-10 operations. Major tenants: 21st Expeditionary Mobility Task Force (AMC); Air Mobility Warfare Center, Ft. Dix, N.J.; N.J. Civil Air Patrol; 108th ARW (ANG), KC-135; 514th AMW (AFRC assoc.). History: adjoins Army's Ft. Dix. Formerly Ft. Dix AAB; activated as Air Force base 1949. Named for Maj. Thomas B. McGuire Jr., P-38 pilot, second leading US ace of WWII, Medal of Honor recipient, killed in action Jan. 7, 1945. Formed a joint base with Ft. Dix and NAES Lakehurst in 2009. Area: 3,598 acres. Runways: 10,001 ft. and 7,129 ft. Altitude: 133 ft. Personnel: permanent party military, 5,189, DOD civilians, 3,812. Housing: single family, officer, 223, enlisted, 1,658; unaccompanied, UAQ/UEQ, 1,162; visiting, VOQ, 33, VAQ/VEQ, 385, TLF, 55. Clinic.

**Minot AFB,** N.D. 58705-5000; 13 mi. N of Minot. Phone: 701-723-1110; DSN 453-1110. Majcom: ACC. Host: 5th BW. Mission: B-52 operations. Major tenant: 91st SW (AFSPC), Minuteman III, UH-1N. History: activated January 1957. Named after the city of Minot, whose citizens donated $50,000 toward purchase of the land for USAF. Area: 4,732 acres, plus additional 330 acres for missile sites spread over 8,500 sq. miles. Runway: 13,200 ft. Altitude: 1,668 ft. Personnel: permanent party military, 5,370; DOD civilians, 569. Housing: single family, officer, 324, enlisted, 1,521; unaccompanied, 813; visiting, 51, TLF, 15. Clinic.

**Misawa AB,** Japan, APO AP 96319-5000; within Misawa city limits. Phone: (cmcl, from CONUS) 011-81-176-53-5181 ext. 226-3075; DSN 315-226-5181. Majcom: PACAF. Host: 35th FW. Mission: F-16C/D operations. Major tenants: 301st Intelligence Sq. (ACC); Naval Air Facility; Naval Security Gp. Activity; 750th Military Intelligence Det. (Army); Co. E, US Marine Support Battalion; Northern Air Defense Force (JASDF). History: occupied by US forces September 1945. Area: 3,865 acres. Runway: 10,000 ft. Altitude: 119 ft. Personnel: permanent party military, 3,769; DOD civilians, 398. Housing: single family, officer, 298, enlisted, 1,810; unaccompanied, UOQ, 40, UAQ/UEQ, 951; visiting, VOQ, 82, VAQ/VEQ, 44, TLF, 40. Hospital.

**Moody AFB,** Ga. 31699-5000; 10 mi. NNE of Valdosta. Phone: 229-257-1110; DSN 460-1110. Majcom: AFSOC. Host: 347th Rescue Wing. Mission: HC-130 and HH-60 operations. Major tenants: 479th Flying Training Gp. (AETC); 820th Security Forces Gp. (ACC). History: activated June 1941. Named for Maj. George P. Moody, killed May 5, 1941. Area: 6,050 acres. Runways: 9,300 ft. and

8,000 ft. Altitude: 235 ft. Personnel: permanent party military, 5,349; DOD civilians, 439. Housing: single family, officer, 32, enlisted, 271; unaccompanied, 714; visiting, VOQ, 37, VAQ/VEQ, 19, TLF, 32. Clinic.

**Mountain Home AFB,** Idaho 83648-5000; 50 mi. SE of Boise. Phone: 208-828-6800; DSN 728-6800. Majcom: ACC. Host: 366th FW. Mission: F-15C/D, F-15E, and F-16CJ/D operations. Major tenants: Air Warfare Battlelab; 266th Range Sq. History: activated August 1943. Area: 9,112 acres. Runway: 13,500 ft. Altitude: 3,000 ft. Personnel: permanent party military, 3,985; DOD civilians, 535. Housing: single family, officer, 175, enlisted, 1,170; unaccompanied, 883; visiting, VOQ, 43, VAQ/VEQ, 54, TLF, 15. Hospital.

**Nellis AFB,** Nev. 89191-5000; 8 mi. NE of Las Vegas. Phone: 702-652-1110; DSN 682-1110. Majcom: ACC. Host: 99th ABW. Mission: USAF Warfare Center manages advanced pilot training and tactics development and integrates test and evaluation programs. Its 98th Range Wing oversees a 15,000 sq.-mile Nellis Range Complex and two emergency airfields. 57th Wing, A-10A, F-15C/D/E, F-16C/D, HH-60G, and Predator MQ-1/9 UAV. 57th Wing missions include Red Flag exercises (414th Combat Training Sq.); graduate-level pilot training (USAF Weapons School); support for Army exercises (549th Combat Training Sq.); training for international personnel in joint firepower procedures and techniques (Hq. USAF Air Ground Operations School); and USAF Air Demonstration Sq. (Thunderbirds). 53rd Wing, at 17 locations nationwide, serves as focal point for combat air forces in electronic warfare, armament and avionics, chemical defense, reconnaissance, and aircrew training devices, and operational testing and evaluation of proposed new equipment and systems. 505th Command and Control Wing builds the predominant air and space command and control ability for combined joint warfighters through training, testing, exercising, and experimentation. Major tenants: Aerospace Integration Center; Triservice Reserve Center; 58th and 67th Intelligence Gp. (ACC); 58th and 66th RQS (AFSOC); 820th RED HORSE Sq. (ACC); and 896th Munitions Sq. (AFMC). History: activated July 1941 as Las Vegas AAF with Army Air Corps Flexible Gunnery School; closed 1947; reopened 1948. Named for 1st Lt. William H. Nellis, WWII P-47 fighter pilot, killed Dec. 27, 1944. Area: Main base is 14,000 acres. NRC occupies 3 million acres of restricted air-land use and an additional 7,000 sq.-mile military operating area shared with civilian aircraft. Runways: 10,119 ft. and 10,051 ft. Altitude: 1,868 ft. Personnel: permanent party military, 8,636; DOD civilians, 3,748. Housing: single family, officer, 88, enlisted, 1,190; unaccompanied, 1,190; visiting, VOQ, 340, VAQ/VEQ, 354, TLF, 60. Air Force-VA joint hospital.

**Offutt AFB,** Neb. 68113-5000; 8 mi. S of Omaha. Phone: 402-294-1110; DSN 271-1110. Majcom: ACC. Host: 55th Wing. Mission: provides worldwide reconnaissance, intelligence, information warfare, treaty verification, and command and control to warfighting commanders and national leadership. Major tenants: STRATCOM; Joint Intelligence Center (STRATCOM); Air Force Weather Agency; National Airborne Operations Center (JCS); USAF Heartland of America

Band. History: activated 1896 as Army's Ft. Crook. Landing field named for 1st Lt. Jarvis J. Offutt, WWI pilot who died Aug. 13, 1918. Area: 4,039 acres. Runway: 11,700 ft. Altitude: 1,048 ft. Personnel: permanent party military, 5,741; DOD civilians, 1,984. Housing: single family, officer, 344, enlisted, 2,256; unaccompanied, 793; visiting, 171, TLF, 60. Clinic.

**Osan AB,** South Korea, APO AP 96278-5000; 38 mi. S of Seoul. Phone: (cmcl, from CONUS) 011-82-31-661-1110; DSN 315-784-1110. Majcom: PACAF. Host: 51st FW. Mission: A/OA-10, C-12, and F-16C/D operations. Major tenants: 7th Air Force (PACAF); 5th RS (ACC); 31st SOS (AFSOC); 33rd Rescue Sq. (PACAF); 303rd Intelligence Sq. (AIA); 731st Air Mobility Sq. (AMC); Charlie and Delta Batteries, 1st Battalion, 43rd Air Defense Artillery (Army). History: originally designated K-55; runway opened December 1952. Renamed Osan AB in 1956 for nearby town that was the scene of first fighting between US and North Korean forces in July 1950. Area: 1,674 acres. Runway: 9,000 ft. Altitude: 38 ft. Personnel: permanent party military, 5,700; DOD civilians, 280. Housing: single family, 211; unaccompanied, UOQ, 457, UAQ/UEQ, 3,615; visiting, VOQ, 57, VAQ/VEQ, 20, DV, 350, TLF, 15. Hospital.

**Patrick AFB,** Fla. 32925-3237; 2 mi. S of Cocoa Beach. Phone: 321-494-1110; DSN 854-1110. Majcom: AFSPC. Host: 45th SW. Mission: supports DOD, NASA, Navy (Trident), and other government agency and commercial missile and space programs. Host responsibilities include Cape Canaveral AFS and tracking stations on Antigua and Ascension islands. Major tenants: Defense Equal Opportunity Management Institute; Air Force Technical Applications Center; 920th Rescue Wing (AFRC), HC-130, HH-60; 2nd Brigade, 87th Division (Army); Naval Ordnance Test Unit (Navy); Joint Task Force for Joint STARS at Melbourne, Fla. History: activated 1940. Named for Maj. Gen. Mason M. Patrick, Chief of AEF's Air Service in WWI and Chief of the Air Service/Air Corps, 1921-27. Area: 2,341 acres. Runway: 9,000 ft. Altitude: 9 ft. Personnel: permanent party military, 3,109; DOD civilians, 1,766. Housing: single family, enlisted, 550; unaccompanied, UAQ/UEQ, 204; visiting, VOQ, 52, VAQ/VEQ, 163, TLF, 51. Clinic.

**Peterson AFB,** Colo. 80914-5000; at eastern edge of Colorado Springs. Phone: 719-556-7321; DSN 834-7321. Majcom: AFSPC. Host: 21st SW. Mission: provides missile warning and space control; detects, tracks, and catalogs objects in space. Major tenants: NORAD; AFSPC; NORTHCOM; US Army Space and Missile Defense Command; 302nd AW (AFRC), C-130. History: activated 1942. Named for 1st Lt. Edward J. Peterson, killed Aug. 8, 1942. Area: 1,277 acres. Runway: shared with city. Altitude: 6,200 ft. Personnel: permanent party military, 6,152; DOD civilians, 2,302. Housing: single family, officer, 103, enlisted, 384; unaccompanied, UAQ/UEQ, 704; visiting, VOQ, 100, VAQ/VEQ, 54, TLF, 68. Clinic.

**Pope AFB,** N.C. 28308-2391; 12 mi. NNW of Fayetteville. Phone: 910-394-1110; DSN 424-1110. Majcom: AMC. Host: 43rd AW. Mission: C-130 operations. Adjoins Army's Ft. Bragg and provides intratheater combat airlift and close air support for airborne forces and other personnel, equipment, and supplies. Major tenants: 23rd Fighter Gp. (ACC), A/OA-10; 18th Air Support Operations Gp. (ACC); 21st and 24th STSs (AFSOC); USAF Combat Control School. History: activated 1919. Named after 1st Lt. Harley H. Pope, WWI pilot, killed Jan. 7, 1919. Area: 2,198 acres. Runway: 7,500 ft. Altitude: 218 ft. Personnel: permanent party military, 3,166; DOD civilians, 559. Housing: single family, officer, 84, enlisted, 543; unaccompanied, UAQ/UEQ, 668; visiting, VOQ, 8, VAQ/VEQ, 159, TLF, 22. Clinic.

**RAF Lakenheath,** UK, APO AE 09461-5000; 70 mi. NE of London; 25 mi. NE of Cambridge. Phone: (cmcl, from CONUS) 011-44-1638-52-3000; DSN 226-1110. Majcom: USAFE. Host: 48th FW (USAFE). Mission: F-15C/D and F-15E operations. GSU: 85th Group, NAS Ke.avik, Iceland. History: activated 1941. US forces arrived August 1948; the 48th FW arrived January 1960. Named after nearby village. Area: 2,290 acres. Runway: 9,000 ft. Altitude: 32 ft. Personnel: permanent party military, 4,500; DOD civilians, 250; Housing: single family, officer, 196, enlisted, 1,869; unaccompanied, UAQ/UEQ, 984; visiting, VOQ, 88, VAQ/VEQ, 48, TLF, 33. Regional medical center.

**RAF Mildenhall,** UK, APO AE 09459-5000; 20 mi. NE of Cambridge. Phone: (cmcl, from CONUS) 011-44-1638-54-3000; DSN 238-3000. Majcom: USAFE. Host: 100th ARW. Mission: KC-135R operations. Major tenants: 16th Air Force (USAFE); 352nd SOG (AFSOC), MC-130, MH-53; 95th RS (ACC); 488th Intelligence Sq. (ACC); Naval Air Facility. History: activated 1934; US presence began July 1950. Named after nearby town. Area: 1,144 acres. Runway: 9,227 ft. Altitude: 33 ft. Personnel: permanent party military, 3,053; DOD civilians, 331. Housing: single family, officer, 64, enlisted, 137; unaccompanied, UAQ/UEQ, 783; visiting, 328, TLF, 36.

**Ramstein AB,** Germany, APO AE 09094-0385; adjacent to the city of Ramstein, 10 mi. W of Kaiserslautern. Phone: (cmcl, from CONUS) 011-49-6371-47-1110; DSN 314-480-1110. Majcom: USAFE. Host: 86th AW. Mission: C-20, C-21, C-40, and C-130E operations; provides expeditionary airlift for first-in base opening capabilities; 86th AW commander also serves as commander of the Kaiserslautern Military Community; also at Ramstein is the 435th Air Base Wing and the 38th Combat Support Wing. The 435th ABW provides expeditionary combat support and quality of life services for the Kaiserslautern community; the 38th CSW provides mission support to geographically separated units delivering American and European alliance combat support. Major tenant: USAFE. History: activated and US presence began 1953. Area: 3,212 acres. Runways: 10,498 ft. and 8,015 ft. Altitude: 782 ft. Personnel: permanent party military, 13,876; DOD civilians, 7,544. Housing: single family, officer, 473, enlisted, 4,588; unaccompanied, UOQ, 32, UAQ/UEQ, 1,795; visiting, 547, TLF, 70. Clinic.

**Randolph AFB,** Tex. 78150-5000; 17 mi. NE of San Antonio. Phone: 210-652-1110; DSN 487-1110. Majcom: AETC. Host: 12th FTW. Mission: conducts T-1, T-6, T-37, and T-38 instructor pilot training and combat systems officer training in the T-43. Major tenants: AETC; 19th Air Force; Air Force Personnel Center; Air Force Manpower Agency; Air Force Services Agency; Air Force Recruiting Service. History: dedicated June 1930. Named for Capt. William M. Randolph, killed Feb. 17, 1928. Area: 5,044 acres. Runways: two, 8,350 ft. each. Altitude: 761 ft. Personnel: permanent party military, 4,626; DOD civilians, 4,318. Housing: single family, officer, 218, enlisted, 427; unaccompanied, UOQ, 200, UEQ, 276; visiting, VOQ, 376, VAQ/VEQ, 164, TLF, 30. Clinic.

**Robins AFB,** Ga. 31098; 15 mi. SSE of Macon at Warner Robins. Phone: 478-926-1110; DSN 468-1001. Majcom: AFMC. Host: 78th ABW. Mission: Warner Robins Air Logistics Center provides worldwide logistics management for the C-5, C-17, C-130, E-8, F-15, U-2, and various special operations forces aircraft and helicopters. Support for general-purpose computers, avionics, missiles, aircraft propellers, vehicles, airborne electronic warfare and communications equipment, airborne bomb- and gun-directing systems, fire-fighting equipment, Joint Tactical Information Distribution System, and emergency software programming of Air Force, other DOD, and allied electronic warfare systems. Major tenants: Air Force Reserve Command; 116th Air Control Wing (ACC), E-8; 19th ARG (AMC), KC-135; 5th Combat Communications Gp. (ACC). History: activated March 1942. Named for Brig. Gen. Augustine Warner Robins, an early chief of the Materiel Division of the Army Air Corps, who died June 16, 1940. Area: 8,700 acres. Runway: 12,000 ft. Altitude: 294 ft. Personnel: permanent party military, 6,210; DOD civilians, 13,815. Housing: single family, officer, 108, enlisted, 1,043; visiting, VOQ, 134, VAQ/VEQ, 157, TLF, 50. Clinic.

**Schriever AFB,** Colo. 80912-5000; 10 mi. E of Colorado Springs. Phone: 719-567-1110; DSN 560-1110. Majcom: AFSPC. Host: 50th SW. Mission: command and control of DOD satellites. Major tenants: Joint National Integration Center; Space Battlelab; 310th Space Gp. (AFRC). History: designated as Falcon AFB June 1988. Renamed in June 1998 for Gen. Bernard A. Schriever. Area: 3,840 acres. Runway: none. Altitude: 6,267 ft. Personnel: permanent party military, 2,000; DOD civilians, 627. Housing: none. Medical and dental clinics.

**Scott AFB,** Ill. 62225-5000; 6 mi. ENE of Belleville. Phone: 618-256-1110; DSN 576-1110. Majcom: AMC. Host: 375th AW. Mission: C-9 and C-21 operations. Major tenants: TRANSCOM; AMC; 18th Air Force; Air Force Communications Agency; Defense Information Technology Contracting Office; 126th ARW (ANG), KC-135; 932nd AW (AFRC), C-9. History: activated June 14, 1917. Named for Cpl. Frank S. Scott, the first enlisted man to die in an aircraft accident, killed Sept. 28, 1912. Area: 3,230 acres. Runways: 10,000 ft. and 8,000 ft. (joint-use airfield). Altitude: 453 ft. Personnel: permanent party military, 5,364; DOD civilians, 5,032. Housing: single family, officer, 298, enlisted, 1,122; unaccompanied, UAQ/UEQ, 569; visiting, VOQ, 222, VAQ/VEQ, 173, TLF, 60. Hospital.

**Seymour Johnson AFB,** N.C. 27531; within city limits of Goldsboro. Phone: 919-722-1110; DSN 722-1110. Majcom: ACC. Host: 4th FW. Mission: F-15E operations and training. Major tenant: 916th ARW (AFRC), KC-135R. History:

activated June 12, 1942. Named for Navy Lt. Seymour A. Johnson, Goldsboro native, killed March 5, 1941. Area: 3,558 acres. Runway: 11,758 ft. Altitude: 110 ft. Personnel: permanent party military, 6,409; DOD civilians, 1,091. Housing: single family, officer, 150, enlisted, 1,210; unaccompanied, 652; visiting, VOQ, 63, VAQ/VEQ, 40, DV, 10, TLF, 49. Clinic.

**Shaw AFB,** S.C. 29152-5000; 8 mi. WNW of Sumter. Phone: 803-895-1110; DSN 965-1110. Majcom: ACC. Host: 20th FW. Mission: F-16CJ operations. Major tenants: 9th Air Force (ACC); CENTCOM Air Forces. History: activated Aug. 30, 1941. Named for 1st Lt. Ervin D. Shaw, one of the first Americans to see air action in WWI, killed in France July 9, 1918. Area: 121,930 acres. Runways: 10,000 ft. and 8,000 ft. Altitude: 242 ft. Personnel: permanent party military, 5,200; DOD civilians, 938. Housing: single family, officer, 164, enlisted, 1,042; unaccompanied, 1,112; visiting, 97, TLF, 39. Hospital (no emergency room).

**Sheppard AFB,** Tex. 76311-5000; 5 mi. N of Wichita Falls. Phone: 940-676-1110; DSN 736-2511. Majcom: AETC. Host: 82nd TRW. Mission: second largest of AETC's four technical training centers. Conducts resident training in aircraft maintenance, aircraft avionics, aerospace propulsion, fuels, ammo and munitions, armament, aerospace ground equipment, life support, civil engineering, communications, and various medical and dental specialties; provides instruction in a wide range of specialties at more than 40 USAF installations worldwide. Major tenant: 80th FTW (AETC), conducts T-37 and T-38 UPT, instructor pilot training in the Euro-NATO Joint Jet Pilot Training program, and Introduction to Fighter Fundamentals course with AT-38 aircraft. History: activated June 14, 1941. Named for US Sen. Morris E. Sheppard, who died April 9, 1941. Area: 6,158 acres. Runways: 13,100 ft., 10,000 ft., 7,000 ft., and 6,000 ft. Altitude: 1,019 ft. Personnel: permanent party military, 3,248; DOD civilians, 1,208. Housing: single family, officer, 200, enlisted, 1,010; unaccompanied, UOQ, 196, UAQ/UEQ, 396; visiting, 1,584, TLF, 95. Clinic.

**Spangdahlem AB,** Germany, APO AE 09126-5000; 20 mi. NE of Trier; 9 mi. E of Bitburg. Phone: (cmcl, from CONUS) 011-49-6565-61-1110; DSN 452-1110. Majcom: USAFE. Host: 52nd FW. Mission: A/OA-10A and HARM-equipped F-16CJ operations; air control squadron operations with logistics responsibilities at dozens of GSUs. History: built by the French in 1951 and turned over to US in 1952. Named after nearby town. Area: 1,616 acres. Runway: 10,000 ft. Altitude: 1,196 ft. Personnel: permanent party military, 5,252; DOD civilians, 171. Housing: single family, officer, 126, enlisted, 1,299; unaccompanied, UAQ/UEQ, 856, UOQ, 8; visiting, 114, TLF, 52. Hospital.

**Tinker AFB,** Okla. 73145-3010; 8 mi. SE of Oklahoma City. Phone: 405-732-7321; DSN 884-1110. Majcom: AFMC. Host: 72nd ABW. Mission: Oklahoma City Air Logistics Center manages and repairs the engines that power cruise missiles and a variety of Air Force and Navy aircraft. The center also accomplishes aircraft modifications and repairs and maintains bombers, refuelers, and reconnaissance aircraft, including the B-1, B-2, B-52, C/KC-135, E-3 AWACS, and E-6

Mercury. Major tenants: 552nd Air Control Wing (ACC), E-3; Navy Strategic Communications Wing One, E-6; 507th ARW (AFRC), KC-135; 513th Air Control Gp. (AFRC assoc.), E-3; Defense Information Systems Agency; Defense Logistics Agency; Defense Distribution Center Oklahoma; 3rd Combat Communications Gp. (ACC); 38th Engineering Installation Gp. (AFMC). History: activated March 1942. Named for Maj. Gen. Clarence L. Tinker, who went down at sea June 7, 1942 while leading group of LB-30 bombers against Japan. Area: 5,033 acres. Runways: 11,100 ft. and 10,000 ft. Altitude: 1,291 ft. Personnel: permanent party military, 9,174; DOD civilians, 15,911. Housing: single family, officer, 107, enlisted, 587; unaccompanied, UAQ/UEQ, 1,220; visiting, VOQ, 109, VAQ/VEQ, 50, TLF, 40. Clinic.

**Travis AFB,** Calif. 94535-5000; 50 mi. NE of San Francisco at Fairfield. Phone: 707-424-1110; DSN 837-1110. Majcom: AMC. Host: 60th AMW. Mission: C-5 and KC-10 operations. Major tenants: 615th Contingency Response Wing; 15th Expeditionary Mobility Task Force (AMC); 349th AMW (AFRC assoc.); USAF Band of the Golden West; Air Museum. History: activated May 17, 1943. Named for Brig. Gen. Robert F. Travis, killed Aug. 5, 1950. Area: 6,383 acres. Runways: two, approx. 11,000 ft. each. Altitude: 62 ft. Personnel: permanent party military, 5,800; DOD civilians, 3,811. Housing: single family, officer, 177, enlisted, 1,143; unaccompanied, UAQ/UEQ, 1,627; visiting, VOQ, 139, VAQ/VEQ, 212, TLF, 84. David Grant Medical Center.

**Tyndall AFB,** Fla. 32403-5000; 12 mi. E of Panama City. Phone: 850-283-1113; DSN 523-1113. Majcom: AETC. Host: 325th FW. Mission: F-15 and F-22 operations; trains USAF F-15 and F-22 pilots. Major tenants: 1st Air Force (ANG); Southeast Air Defense Sector (ANG); 53rd Weapons Evaluation Gp. (ACC); Air Force Civil Engineer Support Agency. History: activated Dec. 7, 1941. Named for 1st Lt. Frank B. Tyndall, WWI fighter pilot killed July 15, 1930. Area: 29,102 acres. Runways: 10,000 ft., 9,000 ft., and 7,000 ft. Altitude: 18 ft. Personnel: permanent party military, 5,280; DOD civilians, 687. Housing: single family, officer, 111, enlisted, 737; unaccompanied, UAQ/UEQ, 448; visiting, 648, TLF, 52. Clinic.

**US Air Force Academy,** Colo. 80840-5025; N of Colorado Springs. Phone: 719-333-1110; DSN 333-1110. Host: USAFA. Mission: inspires and develops outstanding young men and women to become Air Force officers with knowledge, character, and discipline. History: established April 1, 1954. Moved to permanent location August 1958. Area: 18,500 acres. Runways: 4,500 ft., 3,500 ft., and 2,300 ft. Altitude: 7,200 ft. Personnel: permanent party military, 1,890; DOD civilians, 1,995. Housing: single family, officer, 231, enlisted, 978; unaccompanied, 130; visiting, 90, TLF, 30. Hospital.

**Vance AFB,** Okla. 73705-5000; 3 mi. SSW of Enid. Phone: 580-213-5000; DSN 448-7110. Majcom: AETC. Host: 71st FTW. Mission: provides Joint SUPT in T-1, T-6, T-37, and T-38 aircraft. History: activated November 1941. Named for Lt. Col. Leon R. Vance Jr., Enid native, 1939 West Point graduate, and Medal of

Honor recipient, killed July 26, 1944. Area: 3,066 acres. Runways: 9,200 ft., 9,200 ft., and 5,001 ft. Altitude: 1,307 ft. Personnel: permanent party military, 700; DOD civilians, 225. Housing: single family, officer, 115, enlisted, 115; unaccompanied, UOQ, 202, UAQ/UEQ, 108; visiting, 64, TLF, 10. Clinic.

**Vandenberg AFB,** Calif. 93437-5000; 8 mi. NNW of Lompoc. Phone: 805-606-1110; DSN 276-1110. Majcom: AFSPC. Host: 30th SW. Mission: conducts polar-orbiting space launches and supports R&D tests and launch range operations for DOD, USAF, and NASA space, ballistic missile, and aeronautical systems and commercial space launches; provides test support for DOD space and ICBM systems; furnishes facilities and essential services to more than 36 aerospace contractors. Major tenants: 14th Air Force (AFSPC); 381st Training Gp. (AETC); 576th Flight Test Sq. (Space Warfare Center). History: originally Army's Camp Cooke. Activated October 1941; taken over by USAF June 7, 1957. Renamed for Gen. Hoyt S. Vandenberg, USAF's second Chief of Staff. Area: 98,400 acres. Runway: 15,000 ft. Altitude: 367 ft. Personnel: permanent party military, 2,680; DOD civilians, 1,100. Housing: single family, officer, 403, enlisted,1,566; unaccompanied, dorm rooms, 670, UOQ, 43, UAQ/UEQ, 59; visiting, VOQ, 111, VAQ/VEQ, 124, DV, 18, TLF, 26. Clinic.

**Whiteman AFB,** Mo. 65305-5000; 2 mi. S of Knob Noster. Phone: 660-687-1110; DSN 975-1110. Majcom: ACC. Host: 509th BW. Mission: B-2 operations. Major tenants: 442nd FW (AFRC), A/OA-10; 1st Battalion, 135th Aviation Regiment (ARNG); Mobile Inshore Undersea Warfare Unit 114 (Navy Reserve). History: activated 1942. Named for 2nd Lt. George A. Whiteman, .rst pilot to die in aerial combat during the attack on Pearl Harbor. Area: 4,993 acres. Runway: 12,400 ft. Altitude: 871 ft. Personnel: permanent party military, 5,246; DOD civilians, 2,492. Housing: single family, officer, 116, enlisted, 968; unaccompanied, 674; visiting, VOQ, 52, VAQ/VEQ, 35, TLF, 31. Clinic.

**Wright-Patterson AFB,** Ohio 45433; 10 mi. ENE of Dayton. Phone: 937-257-1110; DSN 787-1110. Majcom: AFMC. Host: 88th ABW. Mission: Aeronautical Systems Center develops, acquires, modernizes, and sustains aerospace systems. Major tenants: Air Force Materiel Command; Development and Fielding Systems Gp.; Air Force Research Laboratory (AFMC); Air Force Security Assistance Center (AFMC); 445th AW (AFRC), C-141 (converting to C-5); Air Force Institute of Technology (AETC); National Museum of the US Air Force. History: originally separate, Wright Field and Patterson Field were merged and redesignated Wright-Patterson AFB Jan. 13, 1948. Named for aviation pioneers Orville and Wilbur Wright and for 1st Lt. Frank S. Patterson, killed June 19, 1918. The Wright brothers did much of their early flying on Huffman Prairie, now in Area C of the present base. The prairie is part of the Dayton Aviation Heritage National Historical Park. Site of US Air Force Marathon, held annually on Saturday nearest Sept. 18. Area: 8,357 acres. Runway: 12,600 ft. Altitude: 824 ft. Personnel: permanent party military, 6,698; DOD civilians, 10,199. Housing: single family, officer, 914, enlisted, 1,098; unaccompanied, UAQ/UEQ, 300; visiting, 414, TLF, 41. Wright-Patterson Medical Center.

**Yokota AB,** Japan, APO AP 96328-5000; approx. 8 mi. W of downtown Tokyo. Phone: (cmcl, from CONUS) 011-81-311-755-1110; DSN 315-225-1110. Majcom: PACAF. Host: 374th AW. Mission: C-21, C-130, and UH-1N operations. Primary aerial port in Japan. Major tenants: US Forces, Japan; 5th Air Force (PACAF); 730th AMS (AMC); Det. 1, Air Force Band of the Paci.c-Asia; American Forces Network Tokyo; DFAS-Japan. History: opened as Tama AAF by the Japanese in 1939. Area: 1,750 acres. Runway: 11,000 ft. Altitude: 457 ft. Personnel: permanent party military, 3,414; DOD civilians, 199. Housing: single family, officer, 683, enlisted, 1,956; unaccompanied, UOQ, 184, UAQ/UEQ, 896; visiting, VOQ, 202, VAQ/VEQ, 23, TLF, 189. Hospital.

# Appendix D

# USAF Fitness Charts

## DETERMINING FITNESS SCORE
Fitness level is determined by adding aerobic fitness, body composition, push-up, and crunch component points.

| FITNESS LEVEL | TOTAL SCORE |
|---------------|-------------|
| Excellent     | ≥ 90        |
| Good          | 75–89.9     |
| Marginal      | 70–74.9     |
| Poor          | < 70        |

Members must complete *all* components unless medically exempted. If a member is medically exempted from any component, the total score is calculated as follows:

$$\frac{\text{Total component points achieved}}{\text{Total possible points}} \times 100$$

| COMPONENT | POSSIBLE POINTS |
|-----------|-----------------|
| Aerobic   | 50              |
| Body Comp | 30              |
| Push-ups  | 10              |
| Crunches  | 10              |

## DETERMINING BODY COMPOSITION
To measure abdominal circumference, locate the upper hip bone and the top of the right iliac crest. Place a measuring tape in a horizontal plane around the abdomen at the level of the iliac crest. Before reading the tape measure, ensure that the tape is snug, but does not compress the skin, and is parallel to the floor. The measurement is made at the end of a normal expiration.

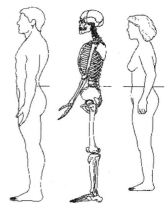

## MEN UNDER 30

### CARDIO ENDURANCE

| 1.5-Mile Run Time (min.) | Health Risk Category | Component Points |
|---|---|---|
| ≤9:12 | Low-Risk | 60.0 |
| 9:13 - 9:34 | Low-Risk | 59.7 |
| 9:35 - 9:45 | Low-Risk | 59.3 |
| 9:46 - 9:58 | Low-Risk | 58.9 |
| 9:59 - 10:10 | Low-Risk | 58.5 |
| 10:11 - 10:23 | Low-Risk | 57.9 |
| 10:24 - 10:37 | Low-Risk | 57.3 |
| 10:38 - 10:51 | Low-Risk | 56.6 |
| 10:52 - 11:06 | Low-Risk | 55.7 |
| 11:07 - 11:22 | Low-Risk | 54.8 |
| 11:23 - 11:38 | Low-Risk | 53.7 |
| 11:39 - 11:56 | Low-Risk | 52.4 |
| 11:57 - 12:14 | Low-Risk | 50.9 |
| 12:15 - 12:33 | Low-Risk | 49.2 |
| 12:34 - 12:53 | Moderate Risk | 47.2 |
| 12:54 - 13:14 | Moderate Risk | 44.9 |
| 13:15 - 13:36 | Moderate Risk | 42.3 |
| 13:37 - 14:00 | High Risk | 39.3 |
| 14:01 - 14:25 | High Risk | 35.8 |
| 14:26 - 14:52 | High Risk | 31.7 |
| 14:53 - 15:20 | High Risk | 27.1 |
| 15:21 - 15:50 | High Risk | 21.7 |
| 15:51 - 16:22 | High Risk | 15.5 |
| 16:23 - 16:57 | High Risk | 8.3 |
| ≥16:58 | High Risk | 0.0 |

### BODY COMPOSITION

| Abdominal Circumference (inches) | Health Risk Category | Component Points |
|---|---|---|
| ≤32.5 | Low-Risk | 20.0 |
| 33.0 | Low-Risk | 20.0 |
| 33.5 | Low-Risk | 20.0 |
| 34.0 | Low-Risk | 20.0 |
| 34.5 | Low-Risk | 20.0 |
| 35.0 | Low-Risk | 20.0 |
| 35.5 | Moderate Risk | 17.6 |
| 36.0 | Moderate Risk | 17.0 |
| 36.5 | Moderate Risk | 16.4 |
| 37.0 | Moderate Risk | 15.8 |
| 37.5 | Moderate Risk | 15.1 |
| 38.0 | Moderate Risk | 14.4 |
| 38.5 | Moderate Risk | 13.5 |
| 39.0 | Moderate Risk | 12.6 |
| 39.5 | High Risk | 11.7 |
| 40.0 | High Risk | 10.6 |
| 40.5 | High Risk | 9.4 |
| 41.0 | High Risk | 8.2 |
| 41.5 | High Risk | 6.8 |
| 42.0 | High Risk | 5.3 |
| 42.5 | High Risk | 3.7 |
| 43.0 | High Risk | 1.9 |
| ≥43.5 | High Risk | 0.0 |

### MUSCLE FITNESS

| 1 minute Push-up (# reps) | Component Points | 1 minute Crunch (# reps) | Component Points | 1 minute Push-up (# reps) | Component Points | 1 minute Crunch (# reps) | Component Points |
|---|---|---|---|---|---|---|---|
| ≥67 | 10.0 | ≥58 | 10.0 | 39 | 6.5 | 32 | 1.5 |
| 62 | 9.5 | 55 | 9.5 | 38 | 6.3 | 31 | 1.3 |
| 61 | 9.4 | 54 | 9.4 | 37 | 6.0 | 30 | 1.0 |
| 60 | 9.3 | 53 | 9.2 | 36 | 5.8 | ≤29 | 0.0 |
| 59 | 9.2 | 52 | 9.0 | 35 | 5.5 | | |
| 58 | 9.1 | 51 | 8.8 | 34 | 5.3 | | |
| 57 | 9.0 | 50 | 8.7 | 33 | 5.0 | | |
| 56 | 8.9 | 49 | 8.5 | 32 | 4.8 | | |
| 55 | 8.8 | 48 | 8.3 | 31 | 4.5 | | |
| 54 | 8.8 | 47 | 8.0 | 30 | 4.3 | | |
| 53 | 8.7 | 46 | 7.5 | 29 | 4.0 | | |
| 52 | 8.6 | 45 | 7.0 | 28 | 3.8 | | |
| 51 | 8.5 | 44 | 6.5 | 27 | 3.5 | | |
| 50 | 8.4 | 43 | 6.3 | 26 | 3.0 | | |
| 49 | 8.3 | 42 | 6.0 | 25 | 2.8 | | |
| 48 | 8.1 | 41 | 5.5 | 24 | 2.5 | | |
| 47 | 8.0 | 40 | 5.0 | 23 | 2.3 | | |
| 46 | 7.8 | 39 | 4.5 | 22 | 2.0 | | |
| 45 | 7.7 | 38 | 4.0 | 21 | 1.8 | | |
| 44 | 7.5 | 37 | 3.5 | 20 | 1.7 | | |
| 43 | 7.3 | 36 | 3.3 | 19 | 1.5 | | |
| 42 | 7.2 | 35 | 3.0 | 18 | 1.0 | | |
| 41 | 7.0 | 34 | 2.5 | ≤17 | 0.0 | | |
| 40 | 6.8 | 33 | 2.0 | | | | |

## MEN 30–39

### CARDIO ENDURANCE

| 1.5-Mile Run Time (min.) | Health Risk Category | Component Points |
|---|---|---|
| ≤9:34 | Low-Risk | 60.0 |
| 9:35 - 9:58 | Low-Risk | 59.3 |
| 9:59 - 10:10 | Low-Risk | 58.6 |
| 10:11 - 10:23 | Low-Risk | 57.9 |
| 10:24 - 10:37 | Low-Risk | 57.3 |
| 10:38 - 10:51 | Low-Risk | 56.6 |
| 10:52 - 11:06 | Low-Risk | 55.7 |
| 11:07 - 11:22 | Low-Risk | 54.8 |
| 11:23 - 11:38 | Low-Risk | 53.7 |
| 11:39 - 11:56 | Low-Risk | 52.4 |
| 11:57 - 12:14 | Low-Risk | 50.9 |
| 12:15 - 12:33 | Low-Risk | 49.2 |
| 12:34 - 12:53 | Low-Risk | 47.2 |
| 12:54 - 13:14 | Moderate Risk | 44.9 |
| 13:15 - 13:36 | Moderate Risk | 42.3 |
| 13:37 - 14:00 | Moderate Risk | 39.3 |
| 14:01 - 14:25 | High Risk | 35.8 |
| 14:26 - 14:52 | High Risk | 31.7 |
| 14:53 - 15:20 | High Risk | 27.1 |
| 15:21 - 15:50 | High Risk | 21.7 |
| 15:51 - 16:22 | High Risk | 15.5 |
| 16:23 - 16:57 | High Risk | 8.3 |
| ≥16:58 | High Risk | 0.0 |

### BODY COMPOSITION

| Abdominal Circumference (inches) | Health Risk Category | Component Points |
|---|---|---|
| ≤32.5 | Low-Risk | 20.0 |
| 33.0 | Low-Risk | 20.0 |
| 33.5 | Low-Risk | 20.0 |
| 34.0 | Low-Risk | 20.0 |
| 34.5 | Low-Risk | 20.0 |
| 35.0 | Low-Risk | 20.0 |
| 35.5 | Moderate Risk | 17.6 |
| 36.0 | Moderate Risk | 17.0 |
| 36.5 | Moderate Risk | 16.4 |
| 37.0 | Moderate Risk | 15.8 |
| 37.5 | Moderate Risk | 15.1 |
| 38.0 | Moderate Risk | 14.4 |
| 38.5 | Moderate Risk | 13.5 |
| 39.0 | Moderate Risk | 12.6 |
| 39.5 | High Risk | 11.7 |
| 40.0 | High Risk | 10.6 |
| 40.5 | High Risk | 9.4 |
| 41.0 | High Risk | 8.2 |
| 41.5 | High Risk | 6.8 |
| 42.0 | High Risk | 5.3 |
| 42.5 | High Risk | 3.7 |
| 43.0 | High Risk | 1.9 |
| ≥43.5 | High Risk | 0.0 |

### MUSCLE FITNESS

| 1 minute Push-up (# reps) | Component Points | 1 minute Crunch (# reps) | Component Points | 1 minute Push-up (# reps) | Component Points | 1 minute Crunch (# reps) | Component Points |
|---|---|---|---|---|---|---|---|
| ≥57 | 10.0 | ≥54 | 10.0 | 31 | 6.5 | 30 | 2.0 |
| 52 | 9.5 | 51 | 9.5 | 30 | 6.0 | 29 | 1.8 |
| 51 | 9.4 | 50 | 9.4 | 29 | 5.5 | 28 | 1.5 |
| 50 | 9.3 | 49 | 9.2 | 28 | 5.3 | 27 | 1.3 |
| 49 | 9.2 | 48 | 9.0 | 27 | 5.0 | 26 | 1.0 |
| 48 | 9.2 | 47 | 8.8 | 26 | 4.8 | ≤25 | 0.0 |
| 47 | 9.1 | 46 | 8.7 | 25 | 4.5 | | |
| 46 | 9.0 | 45 | 8.5 | 24 | 4.0 | | |
| 45 | 8.9 | 44 | 8.3 | 23 | 3.8 | | |
| 44 | 8.8 | 43 | 8.0 | 22 | 3.7 | | |
| 43 | 8.7 | 42 | 7.5 | 21 | 3.5 | | |
| 42 | 8.6 | 41 | 7.0 | 20 | 3.0 | | |
| 41 | 8.5 | 40 | 6.5 | 19 | 2.5 | | |
| 40 | 8.3 | 39 | 6.0 | 18 | 2.3 | | |
| 39 | 8.0 | 38 | 5.8 | 17 | 2.0 | | |
| 38 | 7.8 | 37 | 5.5 | 16 | 1.8 | | |
| 37 | 7.7 | 36 | 5.0 | 15 | 1.5 | | |
| 36 | 7.5 | 35 | 4.0 | 14 | 1.3 | | |
| 35 | 7.3 | 34 | 3.8 | 13 | 1.0 | | |
| 34 | 7.0 | 33 | 3.5 | ≤12 | 0.0 | | |
| 33 | 6.8 | 32 | 3.0 | | | | |
| 32 | 6.7 | 31 | 2.5 | | | | |

## MEN 40–49

### CARDIO ENDURANCE

| 1.5-Mile Run Time (min.) | Health Risk Category | Component Points |
|---|---|---|
| ≤9:45 | Low-Risk | 60.0 |
| 9:46 - 10:10 | Low-Risk | 59.8 |
| 10:11 - 10:23 | Low-Risk | 59.5 |
| 10:24 - 10:37 | Low-Risk | 59.1 |
| 10:38 - 10:51 | Low-Risk | 58.7 |
| 10:52 - 11:06 | Low-Risk | 58.3 |
| 11:07 - 11:22 | Low-Risk | 57.7 |
| 11:23 - 11:38 | Low-Risk | 57.1 |
| 11:39 - 11:56 | Low-Risk | 56.3 |
| 11:57 - 12:14 | Low-Risk | 55.4 |
| 12:15 - 12:33 | Low-Risk | 54.3 |
| 12:34 - 12:53 | Low-Risk | 53.1 |
| 12:54 - 13:14 | Low-Risk | 51.5 |
| 13:15 - 13:36 | Low-Risk | 49.8 |
| 13:37 - 14:00 | Moderate Risk | 47.7 |
| 14:01 - 14:25 | Moderate Risk | 45.2 |
| 14:26 - 14:52 | Moderate Risk | 42.3 |
| 14:53 - 15:20 | High Risk | 38.8 |
| 15:21 - 15:50 | High Risk | 34.7 |
| 15:51 - 16:22 | High Risk | 29.9 |
| 16:23 - 16:57 | High Risk | 24.2 |
| 16:58 - 17:34 | High Risk | 17.4 |
| 17:35 - 18:14 | High Risk | 9.4 |
| ≥18:15 | High Risk | 0.0 |

### BODY COMPOSITION

| Abdominal Circumference (inches) | Health Risk Category | Component Points |
|---|---|---|
| ≤32.5 | Low-Risk | 20.0 |
| 33.0 | Low-Risk | 20.0 |
| 33.5 | Low-Risk | 20.0 |
| 34.0 | Low-Risk | 20.0 |
| 34.5 | Low-Risk | 20.0 |
| 35.0 | Low-Risk | 20.0 |
| 35.5 | Moderate Risk | 17.6 |
| 36.0 | Moderate Risk | 17.0 |
| 36.5 | Moderate Risk | 16.4 |
| 37.0 | Moderate Risk | 15.8 |
| 37.5 | Moderate Risk | 15.1 |
| 38.0 | Moderate Risk | 14.4 |
| 38.5 | Moderate Risk | 13.5 |
| 39.0 | Moderate Risk | 12.6 |
| 39.5 | High Risk | 11.7 |
| 40.0 | High Risk | 10.6 |
| 40.5 | High Risk | 9.4 |
| 41.0 | High Risk | 8.2 |
| 41.5 | High Risk | 6.8 |
| 42.0 | High Risk | 5.3 |
| 42.5 | High Risk | 3.7 |
| 43.0 | High Risk | 1.9 |
| ≥43.5 | High Risk | 0.0 |

### MUSCLE FITNESS

| 1 minute Push-up (# reps) | Component Points | 1 minute Crunch (# reps) | Component Points | 1 minute Push-up (# reps) | Component Points | 1 minute Crunch (# reps) | Component Points |
|---|---|---|---|---|---|---|---|
| ≥44 | 10.0 | ≥50 | 10.0 | 19 | 4.5 | 26 | 2.5 |
| 40 | 9.5 | 47 | 9.5 | 18 | 4.0 | 25 | 2.3 |
| 39 | 9.4 | 46 | 9.4 | 17 | 3.8 | 24 | 2.0 |
| 38 | 9.2 | 45 | 9.2 | 16 | 3.5 | 23 | 1.5 |
| 37 | 9.1 | 44 | 9.1 | 15 | 3.0 | 22 | 1.0 |
| 36 | 9.0 | 43 | 9.0 | 14 | 2.8 | ≤21 | 0.0 |
| 35 | 8.8 | 42 | 8.8 | 13 | 2.5 | | |
| 34 | 8.5 | 41 | 8.7 | 12 | 2.3 | | |
| 33 | 8.4 | 40 | 8.5 | 11 | 2.0 | | |
| 32 | 8.3 | 39 | 8.0 | 10 | 1.5 | | |
| 31 | 8.1 | 38 | 7.8 | 9 | 1.0 | | |
| 30 | 8.0 | 37 | 7.5 | ≤8 | 0.0 | | |
| 29 | 7.5 | 36 | 7.0 | | | | |
| 28 | 7.3 | 35 | 6.5 | | | | |
| 27 | 7.2 | 34 | 6.0 | | | | |
| 26 | 7.0 | 33 | 5.8 | | | | |
| 25 | 6.5 | 32 | 5.5 | | | | |
| 24 | 6.0 | 31 | 5.0 | | | | |
| 23 | 5.8 | 30 | 4.5 | | | | |
| 22 | 5.5 | 29 | 4.0 | | | | |
| 21 | 5.0 | 28 | 3.5 | | | | |
| 20 | 4.8 | 27 | 3.0 | | | | |

## MEN 50–59

### CARDIO ENDURANCE

| 1.5-Mile Run Time (min.) | Health Risk Category | Component Points |
|---|---|---|
| ≤10:37 | Low-Risk | 60.0 |
| 10:38 - 11:06 | Low-Risk | 59.7 |
| 11:07 - 11:22 | Low-Risk | 59.4 |
| 11:23 - 11:38 | Low-Risk | 59.0 |
| 11:39 - 11:56 | Low-Risk | 58.5 |
| 11:57 - 12:14 | Low-Risk | 58.0 |
| 12:15 - 12:33 | Low-Risk | 57.3 |
| 12:34 - 12:53 | Low-Risk | 56.5 |
| 12:54 - 13:14 | Low-Risk | 55.6 |
| 13:15 - 13:36 | Low-Risk | 54.5 |
| 13:37 - 14:00 | Low-Risk | 53.3 |
| 14:01 - 14:25 | Low-Risk | 51.8 |
| 14:26 - 14:52 | Low-Risk | 50.0 |
| 14:53 - 15:20 | Moderate Risk | 47.9 |
| 15:21 - 15:50 | Moderate Risk | 45.4 |
| 15:51 - 16:22 | Moderate Risk | 42.4 |
| 16:23 - 16:57 | High Risk | 39.0 |
| 16:58 - 17:34 | High Risk | 34.9 |
| 17:35 - 18:14 | High Risk | 30.0 |
| 18:15 - 18:56 | High Risk | 24.3 |
| 18:57 - 19:43 | High Risk | 17.5 |
| 19:44 - 20:33 | High Risk | 9.5 |
| ≥20:34 | High Risk | 0.0 |

### BODY COMPOSITION

| Abdominal Circumference (inches) | Health Risk Category | Component Points |
|---|---|---|
| ≤32.5 | Low-Risk | 20.0 |
| 33.0 | Low-Risk | 20.0 |
| 33.5 | Low-Risk | 20.0 |
| 34.0 | Low-Risk | 20.0 |
| 34.5 | Low-Risk | 20.0 |
| 35.0 | Low-Risk | 20.0 |
| 35.5 | Moderate Risk | 17.6 |
| 36.0 | Moderate Risk | 17.0 |
| 36.5 | Moderate Risk | 16.4 |
| 37.0 | Moderate Risk | 15.8 |
| 37.5 | Moderate Risk | 15.1 |
| 38.0 | Moderate Risk | 14.4 |
| 38.5 | Moderate Risk | 13.5 |
| 39.0 | Moderate Risk | 12.6 |
| 39.5 | High Risk | 11.7 |
| 40.0 | High Risk | 10.6 |
| 40.5 | High Risk | 9.4 |
| 41.0 | High Risk | 8.2 |
| 41.5 | High Risk | 6.8 |
| 42.0 | High Risk | 5.3 |
| 42.5 | High Risk | 3.7 |
| 43.0 | High Risk | 1.9 |
| ≥43.5 | High Risk | 0.0 |

### MUSCLE FITNESS

| 1 minute Push-up (# reps) | Component Points | 1 minute Crunch (# reps) | Component Points | 1 minute Push-up (# reps) | Component Points | 1 minute Crunch (# reps) | Component Points |
|---|---|---|---|---|---|---|---|
| ≥44 | 10.0 | ≥46 | 10.0 | 18 | 5.8 | 22 | 3.5 |
| 39 | 9.5 | 43 | 9.5 | 17 | 5.5 | 21 | 3.0 |
| 38 | 9.4 | 42 | 9.4 | 16 | 5.3 | 20 | 2.5 |
| 37 | 9.4 | 41 | 9.2 | 15 | 5.0 | 19 | 2.0 |
| 36 | 9.3 | 40 | 9.1 | 14 | 4.5 | 18 | 1.8 |
| 35 | 9.3 | 39 | 9.0 | 13 | 4.0 | 17 | 1.5 |
| 34 | 9.2 | 38 | 8.8 | 12 | 3.8 | 16 | 1.3 |
| 33 | 9.2 | 37 | 8.7 | 11 | 3.5 | 15 | 1.0 |
| 32 | 9.1 | 36 | 8.5 | 10 | 3.0 | ≤14 | 0.0 |
| 31 | 9.1 | 35 | 8.0 | 9 | 2.0 | | |
| 30 | 9.0 | 34 | 7.8 | 8 | 1.8 | | |
| 29 | 8.8 | 33 | 7.5 | 7 | 1.5 | | |
| 28 | 8.5 | 32 | 7.3 | 6 | 1.0 | | |
| 27 | 8.3 | 31 | 7.0 | ≤5 | 0.0 | | |
| 26 | 8.2 | 30 | 6.5 | | | | |
| 25 | 8.0 | 29 | 6.3 | | | | |
| 24 | 7.5 | 28 | 6.0 | | | | |
| 23 | 7.3 | 27 | 5.5 | | | | |
| 22 | 7.2 | 26 | 5.0 | | | | |
| 21 | 7.0 | 25 | 4.5 | | | | |
| 20 | 6.5 | 24 | 4.0 | | | | |
| 19 | 6.0 | 23 | 3.8 | | | | |

## MEN 60+

### CARDIO ENDURANCE

| 1.5-Mile Run Time (min.) | Health Risk Category | Component Points |
|---|---|---|
| ≤11:22 | Low-Risk | 60.0 |
| 11:23 - 11:56 | Low-Risk | 59.7 |
| 11:57 - 12:14 | Low-Risk | 59.4 |
| 12:15 - 12:33 | Low-Risk | 59.0 |
| 12:34 - 12:53 | Low-Risk | 58.5 |
| 12:54 - 13:14 | Low-Risk | 58.0 |
| 13:15 - 13:36 | Low-Risk | 57.3 |
| 13:37 - 14:00 | Low-Risk | 56.5 |
| 14:01 - 14:25 | Low-Risk | 55.6 |
| 14:26 - 14:52 | Low-Risk | 54.5 |
| 14:53 - 15:20 | Low-Risk | 53.3 |
| 15:21 - 15:50 | Low-Risk | 51.8 |
| 15:51 - 16:22 | Low-Risk | 50.0 |
| 16:23 - 16:57 | Moderate Risk | 47.9 |
| 16:58 - 17:34 | Moderate Risk | 45.4 |
| 17:35 - 18:14 | Moderate Risk | 42.4 |
| 18:15 - 18:56 | High Risk | 39.0 |
| 18:57 - 19:43 | High Risk | 34.9 |
| 19:44 - 20:33 | High Risk | 30.0 |
| 20:34 - 21:28 | High Risk | 24.3 |
| 21:29 - 22:28 | High Risk | 17.5 |
| 22:29 - 23:34 | High Risk | 9.5 |
| ≥23:35 | High Risk | 0.0 |

### BODY COMPOSITION

| Abdominal Circumference (inches) | Health Risk Category | Component Points |
|---|---|---|
| ≤32.5 | Low-Risk | 20.0 |
| 33.0 | Low-Risk | 20.0 |
| 33.5 | Low-Risk | 20.0 |
| 34.0 | Low-Risk | 20.0 |
| 34.5 | Low-Risk | 20.0 |
| 35.0 | Low-Risk | 20.0 |
| 35.5 | Moderate Risk | 17.6 |
| 36.0 | Moderate Risk | 17.0 |
| 36.5 | Moderate Risk | 16.4 |
| 37.0 | Moderate Risk | 15.8 |
| 37.5 | Moderate Risk | 15.1 |
| 38.0 | Moderate Risk | 14.4 |
| 38.5 | Moderate Risk | 13.5 |
| 39.0 | Moderate Risk | 12.6 |
| 39.5 | High Risk | 11.7 |
| 40.0 | High Risk | 10.6 |
| 40.5 | High Risk | 9.4 |
| 41.0 | High Risk | 8.2 |
| 41.5 | High Risk | 6.8 |
| 42.0 | High Risk | 5.3 |
| 42.5 | High Risk | 3.7 |
| 43.0 | High Risk | 1.9 |
| ≥43.5 | High Risk | 0.0 |

### MUSCLE FITNESS

| 1 minute Push-up (# reps) | Component Points | 1 minute Crunch (# reps) | Component Points | 1 minute Push-up (# reps) | Component Points | 1 minute Crunch (# reps) | Component Points |
|---|---|---|---|---|---|---|---|
| ≥30 | 10.0 | ≥42 | 10.0 | 7 | 2.5 | 18 | 3.5 |
| 28 | 9.5 | 39 | 9.5 | 6 | 2.0 | 17 | 3.0 |
| 27 | 9.3 | 38 | 9.4 | 5 | 1.5 | 16 | 2.5 |
| 26 | 9.0 | 37 | 9.2 | 4 | 1.0 | 15 | 2.0 |
| 25 | 8.8 | 36 | 9.1 | ≤3 | 0.0 | 14 | 1.8 |
| 24 | 8.5 | 35 | 9.0 | | | 13 | 1.5 |
| 23 | 8.0 | 34 | 8.9 | | | 12 | 1.3 |
| 22 | 7.5 | 33 | 8.8 | | | 11 | 1.2 |
| 21 | 7.0 | 32 | 8.6 | | | 10 | 1.0 |
| 20 | 6.5 | 31 | 8.5 | | | ≤9 | 0.0 |
| 19 | 6.3 | 30 | 8.0 | | | | |
| 18 | 6.0 | 29 | 7.8 | | | | |
| 17 | 5.8 | 28 | 7.5 | | | | |
| 16 | 5.5 | 27 | 7.3 | | | | |
| 15 | 5.3 | 26 | 7.0 | | | | |
| 14 | 5.0 | 25 | 6.8 | | | | |
| 13 | 4.8 | 24 | 6.5 | | | | |
| 12 | 4.5 | 23 | 6.3 | | | | |
| 11 | 4.3 | 22 | 6.0 | | | | |
| 10 | 4.0 | 21 | 5.5 | | | | |
| 9 | 3.5 | 20 | 5.0 | | | | |
| 8 | 3.0 | 19 | 4.0 | | | | |

## FEMALE UNDER 30

### CARDIO ENDURANCE

| 1.5-Mile Run Time (min.) | Health Risk Category | Component Points |
|---|---|---|
| ≤10:23 | Low-Risk | 60.0 |
| 10:24 - 10:51 | Low-Risk | 59.9 |
| 10:52 - 11:06 | Low-Risk | 59.5 |
| 11:07 - 11:22 | Low-Risk | 59.2 |
| 11:23 - 11:38 | Low-Risk | 58.9 |
| 11:39 - 11:56 | Low-Risk | 58.6 |
| 11:57 - 12:14 | Low-Risk | 58.1 |
| 12:15 - 12:33 | Low-Risk | 57.6 |
| 12:34 - 12:53 | Low-Risk | 57.0 |
| 12:54 - 13:14 | Low-Risk | 56.2 |
| 13:15 - 13:36 | Low-Risk | 55.3 |
| 13:37 - 14:00 | Low-Risk | 54.2 |
| 14:01 - 14:25 | Low-Risk | 52.8 |
| 14:26 - 14:52 | Low-Risk | 51.2 |
| 14:53 - 15:20 | Moderate Risk | 49.3 |
| 15:21 - 15:50 | Moderate Risk | 46.9 |
| 15:51 - 16:22 | Moderate Risk | 44.1 |
| 16:23 - 16:57 | High Risk | 40.8 |
| 16:58 - 17:34 | High Risk | 36.7 |
| 17:35 - 18:14 | High Risk | 31.8 |
| 18:15 - 18:56 | High Risk | 25.9 |
| 18:57 - 19:43 | High Risk | 18.8 |
| 19:44 - 20:33 | High Risk | 10.3 |
| ≥20:34 | High Risk | 0.0 |

### BODY COMPOSITION

| Abdominal Circumference (inches) | Health Risk Category | Component Points |
|---|---|---|
| ≤29.0 | Low Risk | 20.0 |
| 29.5 | Low Risk | 20.0 |
| 30.0 | Low Risk | 20.0 |
| 30.5 | Low Risk | 20.0 |
| 31.0 | Low Risk | 20.0 |
| 31.5 | Low Risk | 20.0 |
| 32.0 | Moderate Risk | 17.6 |
| 32.5 | Moderate Risk | 17.1 |
| 33.0 | Moderate Risk | 16.5 |
| 33.5 | Moderate Risk | 15.9 |
| 34.0 | Moderate Risk | 15.2 |
| 34.5 | Moderate Risk | 14.5 |
| 35.0 | Moderate Risk | 13.7 |
| 35.5 | Moderate Risk | 12.8 |
| 36.0 | High Risk | 11.8 |
| 36.5 | High Risk | 10.7 |
| 37.0 | High Risk | 9.6 |
| 37.5 | High Risk | 8.3 |
| 38.0 | High Risk | 6.9 |
| 38.5 | High Risk | 5.4 |
| 39.0 | High Risk | 3.8 |
| 39.5 | High Risk | 2.0 |
| ≥40.0 | High Risk | 0.0 |

### MUSCLE FITNESS

| 1 minute Push-up (# reps) | Component Points | 1 minute Crunch (# reps) | Component Points | 1 minute Push-up (# reps) | Component Points | 1 minute Crunch (# reps) | Component Points |
|---|---|---|---|---|---|---|---|
| ≥47 | 10.0 | ≥54 | 10.0 | 21 | 6.0 | 30 | 3.0 |
| 42 | 9.5 | 51 | 9.5 | 20 | 5.8 | 29 | 2.8 |
| 41 | 9.4 | 50 | 9.4 | 19 | 5.5 | 28 | 2.5 |
| 40 | 9.3 | 49 | 9.0 | 18 | 5.0 | 27 | 2.0 |
| 39 | 9.2 | 48 | 8.9 | 17 | 4.5 | 26 | 1.8 |
| 38 | 9.1 | 47 | 8.8 | 16 | 4.3 | 25 | 1.7 |
| 37 | 9.0 | 46 | 8.6 | 15 | 4.0 | 24 | 1.5 |
| 36 | 8.9 | 45 | 8.5 | 14 | 3.5 | 23 | 1.0 |
| 35 | 8.8 | 44 | 8.0 | 13 | 3.0 | ≤22 | 0.0 |
| 34 | 8.6 | 43 | 7.8 | 12 | 2.8 | | |
| 33 | 8.5 | 42 | 7.5 | 11 | 2.5 | | |
| 32 | 8.4 | 41 | 7.0 | 10 | 2.0 | | |
| 31 | 8.3 | 40 | 6.8 | 9 | 1.5 | | |
| 30 | 8.2 | 39 | 6.5 | 8 | 1.0 | | |
| 29 | 8.1 | 38 | 6.0 | ≤7 | 0.0 | | |
| 28 | 8.0 | 37 | 5.5 | | | | |
| 27 | 7.5 | 36 | 5.3 | | | | |
| 26 | 7.3 | 35 | 5.0 | | | | |
| 25 | 7.2 | 34 | 4.5 | | | | |
| 24 | 7.0 | 33 | 4.3 | | | | |
| 23 | 6.5 | 32 | 4.0 | | | | |
| 22 | 6.3 | 31 | 3.5 | | | | |

## FEMALE 30–39

### CARDIO ENDURANCE

| 1.5-Mile Run Time (min.) | Health Risk Category | Component Points |
|---|---|---|
| ≤10:51 | Low-Risk | 60.0 |
| 10:52 - 11:22 | Low-Risk | 59.5 |
| 11:23 - 11:38 | Low-Risk | 59.0 |
| 11:39 - 11:56 | Low-Risk | 58.6 |
| 11:57 - 12:14 | Low-Risk | 58.1 |
| 12:15 - 12:33 | Low-Risk | 57.6 |
| 12:34 - 12:53 | Low-Risk | 57.0 |
| 12:54 - 13:14 | Low-Risk | 56.2 |
| 13:15 - 13:36 | Low-Risk | 55.3 |
| 13:37 - 14:00 | Low-Risk | 54.2 |
| 14:01 - 14:25 | Low-Risk | 52.8 |
| 14:26 - 14:52 | Low-Risk | 51.2 |
| 14:53 - 15:20 | Low-Risk | 49.3 |
| 15:21 - 15:50 | Moderate Risk | 46.9 |
| 15:51 - 16:22 | Moderate Risk | 44.1 |
| 16:23 - 16:57 | Moderate Risk | 40.8 |
| 16:58 - 17:34 | High Risk | 36.7 |
| 17:35 - 18:14 | High Risk | 31.8 |
| 18:15 - 18:56 | High Risk | 25.9 |
| 18:57 - 19:43 | High Risk | 18.8 |
| 19:44 - 20:33 | High Risk | 10.3 |
| ≥20:34 | High Risk | 0.0 |

### BODY COMPOSITION

| Abdominal Circumference (inches) | Health Risk Category | Component Points |
|---|---|---|
| ≤29.0 | Low Risk | 20.0 |
| 29.5 | Low Risk | 20.0 |
| 30.0 | Low Risk | 20.0 |
| 30.5 | Low Risk | 20.0 |
| 31.0 | Low Risk | 20.0 |
| 31.5 | Low Risk | 20.0 |
| 32.0 | Moderate Risk | 17.6 |
| 32.5 | Moderate Risk | 17.1 |
| 33.0 | Moderate Risk | 16.5 |
| 33.5 | Moderate Risk | 15.9 |
| 34.0 | Moderate Risk | 15.2 |
| 34.5 | Moderate Risk | 14.5 |
| 35.0 | Moderate Risk | 13.7 |
| 35.5 | Moderate Risk | 12.8 |
| 36.0 | High Risk | 11.8 |
| 36.5 | High Risk | 10.7 |
| 37.0 | High Risk | 9.6 |
| 37.5 | High Risk | 8.3 |
| 38.0 | High Risk | 6.9 |
| 38.5 | High Risk | 5.4 |
| 39.0 | High Risk | 3.8 |
| 39.5 | High Risk | 2.0 |
| ≥40.0 | High Risk | 0.0 |

### MUSCLE FITNESS

| 1 minute Push-up (# reps) | Component Points | 1 minute Crunch (# reps) | Component Points | 1 minute Push-up (# reps) | Component Points | 1 minute Crunch (# reps) | Component Points |
|---|---|---|---|---|---|---|---|
| ≥46 | 10.0 | ≥45 | 10.0 | 19 | 7.5 | 21 | 2.5 |
| 40 | 9.5 | 42 | 9.5 | 18 | 7.0 | 20 | 2.0 |
| 39 | 9.4 | 41 | 9.4 | 17 | 6.8 | 19 | 1.8 |
| 38 | 9.3 | 40 | 9.0 | 16 | 6.5 | 18 | 1.5 |
| 37 | 9.3 | 39 | 8.8 | 15 | 6.0 | 17 | 1.3 |
| 36 | 9.2 | 38 | 8.5 | 14 | 5.0 | 16 | 1.2 |
| 35 | 9.1 | 37 | 8.3 | 13 | 4.5 | 15 | 1.0 |
| 34 | 9.1 | 36 | 8.2 | 12 | 4.3 | ≤14 | 0.0 |
| 33 | 9.0 | 35 | 8.0 | 11 | 4.0 | | |
| 32 | 8.9 | 34 | 7.8 | 10 | 3.5 | | |
| 31 | 8.9 | 33 | 7.5 | 9 | 3.0 | | |
| 30 | 8.8 | 32 | 7.0 | 8 | 2.0 | | |
| 29 | 8.7 | 31 | 6.8 | 7 | 1.5 | | |
| 28 | 8.6 | 30 | 6.5 | 6 | 1.0 | | |
| 27 | 8.6 | 29 | 6.0 | ≤5 | 0.0 | | |
| 26 | 8.5 | 28 | 5.5 | | | | |
| 25 | 8.3 | 27 | 5.0 | | | | |
| 24 | 8.2 | 26 | 4.5 | | | | |
| 23 | 8.0 | 25 | 4.0 | | | | |
| 22 | 7.9 | 24 | 3.5 | | | | |
| 21 | 7.8 | 23 | 3.3 | | | | |
| 20 | 7.6 | 22 | 3.0 | | | | |

## FEMALE 40–49

### CARDIO ENDURANCE

| 1.5-Mile Run Time (min.) | Health Risk Category | Component Points |
|---|---|---|
| ≤11:22 | Low-Risk | 60.0 |
| 11:23 - 11:56 | Low-Risk | 59.9 |
| 11:57 - 12:14 | Low-Risk | 59.8 |
| 12:15 - 12:33 | Low-Risk | 59.6 |
| 12:34 - 12:53 | Low-Risk | 59.4 |
| 12:54 - 13:14 | Low-Risk | 59.1 |
| 13:15 - 13:36 | Low-Risk | 58.7 |
| 13:37 - 14:00 | Low-Risk | 58.2 |
| 14:01 - 14:25 | Low-Risk | 57.7 |
| 14:26 - 14:52 | Low-Risk | 56.9 |
| 14:53 - 15:20 | Low-Risk | 56.0 |
| 15:21 - 15:50 | Low-Risk | 54.8 |
| 15:51 - 16:22 | Low-Risk | 53.3 |
| 16:23 - 16:57 | Moderate Risk | 51.4 |
| 16:58 - 17:34 | Moderate Risk | 49.0 |
| 17:35 - 18:14 | Moderate Risk | 45.9 |
| 18:15 - 18:56 | High Risk | 42.0 |
| 18:57 - 19:43 | High Risk | 37.1 |
| 19:44 - 20:33 | High Risk | 30.8 |
| 20:34 - 21:28 | High Risk | 22.9 |
| 21:29 - 22:28 | High Risk | 12.8 |
| ≥22:29 | High Risk | 0.0 |

### BODY COMPOSITION

| Abdominal Circumference (inches) | Health Risk Category | Component Points |
|---|---|---|
| ≤29.0 | Low Risk | 20.0 |
| 29.5 | Low Risk | 20.0 |
| 30.0 | Low Risk | 20.0 |
| 30.5 | Low Risk | 20.0 |
| 31.0 | Low Risk | 20.0 |
| 31.5 | Low Risk | 20.0 |
| 32.0 | Moderate Risk | 17.6 |
| 32.5 | Moderate Risk | 17.1 |
| 33.0 | Moderate Risk | 16.5 |
| 33.5 | Moderate Risk | 15.9 |
| 34.0 | Moderate Risk | 15.2 |
| 34.5 | Moderate Risk | 14.5 |
| 35.0 | Moderate Risk | 13.7 |
| 35.5 | Moderate Risk | 12.8 |
| 36.0 | High Risk | 11.8 |
| 36.5 | High Risk | 10.7 |
| 37.0 | High Risk | 9.6 |
| 37.5 | High Risk | 8.3 |
| 38.0 | High Risk | 6.9 |
| 38.5 | High Risk | 5.4 |
| 39.0 | High Risk | 3.8 |
| 39.5 | High Risk | 2.0 |
| ≥40.0 | High Risk | 0.0 |

### MUSCLE FITNESS

| 1 minute Push-up (# reps) | Component Points | 1 minute Crunch (# reps) | Component Points | 1 minute Push-up (# reps) | Component Points | 1 minute Crunch (# reps) | Component Points |
|---|---|---|---|---|---|---|---|
| ≥38 | 10.0 | ≥41 | 10.0 | 12 | 5.5 | 17 | 3.0 |
| 33 | 9.5 | 38 | 9.5 | 11 | 5.0 | 16 | 2.5 |
| 32 | 9.4 | 37 | 9.4 | 10 | 4.5 | 15 | 2.3 |
| 31 | 9.2 | 36 | 9.2 | 9 | 4.0 | 14 | 2.0 |
| 30 | 9.1 | 35 | 9.1 | 8 | 3.5 | 13 | 1.5 |
| 29 | 9.0 | 34 | 9.0 | 7 | 3.0 | 12 | 1.3 |
| 28 | 8.9 | 33 | 8.8 | 6 | 2.0 | 11 | 1.2 |
| 27 | 8.8 | 32 | 8.5 | 5 | 1.5 | 10 | 1.0 |
| 26 | 8.7 | 31 | 8.3 | 4 | 1.0 | ≤9 | 0.0 |
| 25 | 8.6 | 30 | 8.2 | ≤3 | 0.0 | | |
| 24 | 8.6 | 29 | 8.0 | | | | |
| 23 | 8.5 | 28 | 7.5 | | | | |
| 22 | 8.4 | 27 | 7.0 | | | | |
| 21 | 8.3 | 26 | 6.8 | | | | |
| 20 | 8.2 | 25 | 6.4 | | | | |
| 19 | 8.1 | 24 | 6.0 | | | | |
| 18 | 8.0 | 23 | 5.5 | | | | |
| 17 | 7.8 | 22 | 5.0 | | | | |
| 16 | 7.5 | 21 | 4.5 | | | | |
| 15 | 7.0 | 20 | 4.0 | | | | |
| 14 | 6.5 | 19 | 3.5 | | | | |
| 13 | 6.0 | 18 | 3.3 | | | | |

## FEMALE 50–59

### CARDIO ENDURANCE

| 1.5-Mile Run Time (min.) | Health Risk Category | Component Points |
|---|---|---|
| ≤12:53 | Low-Risk | 60.0 |
| 12:54 - 13:36 | Low-Risk | 59.8 |
| 13:37 - 14:00 | Low-Risk | 59.6 |
| 14:01 - 14:25 | Low-Risk | 59.3 |
| 14:26 - 14:52 | Low-Risk | 58.9 |
| 14:53 - 15:20 | Low-Risk | 58.4 |
| 15:21 - 15:50 | Low-Risk | 57.7 |
| 15:51 - 16:22 | Low-Risk | 56.8 |
| 16:23 - 16:57 | Low-Risk | 55.6 |
| 16:58 - 17:34 | Low-Risk | 54.0 |
| 17:35 - 18:14 | Low-Risk | 51.9 |
| 18:15 - 18:56 | Moderate Risk | 49.2 |
| 18:57 - 19:43 | Moderate Risk | 45.5 |
| 19:44 - 20:33 | High Risk | 40.7 |
| 20:34 - 21:28 | High Risk | 34.3 |
| 21:29 - 22:28 | High Risk | 25.9 |
| 22:29 - 23:34 | High Risk | 14.7 |
| ≥23:35 | High Risk | 0.0 |

### BODY COMPOSITION

| Abdominal Circumference (inches) | Health Risk Category | Component Points |
|---|---|---|
| ≤29.0 | Low Risk | 20.0 |
| 29.5 | Low Risk | 20.0 |
| 30.0 | Low Risk | 20.0 |
| 30.5 | Low Risk | 20.0 |
| 31.0 | Low Risk | 20.0 |
| 31.5 | Low Risk | 20.0 |
| 32.0 | Moderate Risk | 17.6 |
| 32.5 | Moderate Risk | 17.1 |
| 33.0 | Moderate Risk | 16.5 |
| 33.5 | Moderate Risk | 15.9 |
| 34.0 | Moderate Risk | 15.2 |
| 34.5 | Moderate Risk | 14.5 |
| 35.0 | Moderate Risk | 13.7 |
| 35.5 | Moderate Risk | 12.8 |
| 36.0 | High Risk | 11.8 |
| 36.5 | High Risk | 10.7 |
| 37.0 | High Risk | 9.6 |
| 37.5 | High Risk | 8.3 |
| 38.0 | High Risk | 6.9 |
| 38.5 | High Risk | 5.4 |
| 39.0 | High Risk | 3.8 |
| 39.5 | High Risk | 2.0 |
| ≥40.0 | High Risk | 0.0 |

### MUSCLE FITNESS

| 1 minute Push-up (# reps) | Component Points | 1 minute Crunch (# reps) | Component Points | 1 minute Push-up (# reps) | Component Points | 1 minute Crunch (# reps) | Component Points |
|---|---|---|---|---|---|---|---|
| ≥35 | 10.0 | ≥32 | 10.0 | 9 | 5.0 | 9 | 1.8 |
| 30 | 9.5 | 30 | 9.5 | 8 | 4.5 | 8 | 1.7 |
| 29 | 9.4 | 29 | 9.0 | 7 | 4.0 | 7 | 1.5 |
| 28 | 9.3 | 28 | 8.9 | 6 | 3.5 | 6 | 1.0 |
| 27 | 9.2 | 27 | 8.8 | 5 | 3.0 | ≤5 | 0.0 |
| 26 | 9.1 | 26 | 8.6 | 4 | 2.0 | | |
| 25 | 9.0 | 25 | 8.5 | 3 | 1.0 | | |
| 24 | 8.8 | 24 | 8.0 | ≤2 | 0.0 | | |
| 23 | 8.7 | 23 | 7.6 | | | | |
| 22 | 8.6 | 22 | 7.0 | | | | |
| 21 | 8.6 | 21 | 6.5 | | | | |
| 20 | 8.5 | 20 | 6.0 | | | | |
| 19 | 8.4 | 19 | 5.5 | | | | |
| 18 | 8.3 | 18 | 5.3 | | | | |
| 17 | 8.2 | 17 | 5.0 | | | | |
| 16 | 8.1 | 16 | 4.5 | | | | |
| 15 | 8.0 | 15 | 4.3 | | | | |
| 14 | 7.5 | 14 | 4.0 | | | | |
| 13 | 7.0 | 13 | 3.6 | | | | |
| 12 | 6.5 | 12 | 3.0 | | | | |
| 11 | 6.0 | 11 | 2.5 | | | | |
| 10 | 5.5 | 10 | 2.0 | | | | |

## FEMALE 60+

### CARDIO ENDURANCE

| 1.5-Mile Run Time (min.) | Health Risk Category | Component Points |
|---|---|---|
| ≤14:00 | Low-Risk | 60.0 |
| 14:01 - 14:52 | Low-Risk | 59.8 |
| 14:53 - 15:20 | Low-Risk | 59.5 |
| 15:21 - 15:50 | Low-Risk | 59.1 |
| 15:51 - 16:22 | Low-Risk | 58.6 |
| 16:23 - 16:57 | Low-Risk | 57.9 |
| 16:58 - 17:34 | Low-Risk | 57.0 |
| 17:35 - 18:14 | Low-Risk | 55.8 |
| 18:15 - 18:56 | Low-Risk | 54.2 |
| 18:57 - 19:43 | Low-Risk | 52.1 |
| 19:44 - 20:33 | Moderate Risk | 49.3 |
| 20:34 - 21:28 | Moderate Risk | 45.6 |
| 21:29 - 22:28 | Moderate Risk | 40.8 |
| 22:29 - 23:34 | High Risk | 34.4 |
| 23:35 - 24:46 | High Risk | 26.0 |
| 24:47 - 26:06 | High Risk | 14.8 |
| ≥26:07 | High Risk | 0.0 |

### BODY COMPOSITION

| Abdominal Circumference (inches) | Health Risk Category | Component Points |
|---|---|---|
| ≤29.0 | Low Risk | 20.0 |
| 29.5 | Low Risk | 20.0 |
| 30.0 | Low Risk | 20.0 |
| 30.5 | Low Risk | 20.0 |
| 31.0 | Low Risk | 20.0 |
| 31.5 | Low Risk | 20.0 |
| 32.0 | Moderate Risk | 17.6 |
| 32.5 | Moderate Risk | 17.1 |
| 33.0 | Moderate Risk | 16.5 |
| 33.5 | Moderate Risk | 15.9 |
| 34.0 | Moderate Risk | 15.2 |
| 34.5 | Moderate Risk | 14.5 |
| 35.0 | Moderate Risk | 13.7 |
| 35.5 | Moderate Risk | 12.8 |
| 36.0 | High Risk | 11.8 |
| 36.5 | High Risk | 10.7 |
| 37.0 | High Risk | 9.6 |
| 37.5 | High Risk | 8.3 |
| 38.0 | High Risk | 6.9 |
| 38.5 | High Risk | 5.4 |
| 39.0 | High Risk | 3.8 |
| 39.5 | High Risk | 2.0 |
| ≥40.0 | High Risk | 0.0 |

### MUSCLE FITNESS

| 1 minute Push-up (# reps) | Component Points | 1 minute Crunch (# reps) | Component Points | 1 minute Push-up (# reps) | Component Points | 1 minute Crunch (# reps) | Component Points |
|---|---|---|---|---|---|---|---|
| ≥21 | 10.0 | ≥31 | 10.0 | | | 7 | 4.3 |
| 19 | 9.5 | 28 | 9.5 | | | 6 | 4.0 |
| 18 | 9.4 | 27 | 9.4 | | | 5 | 3.5 |
| 17 | 9.0 | 26 | 9.0 | | | 4 | 2.5 |
| 16 | 8.8 | 25 | 8.9 | | | 3 | 2.0 |
| 15 | 8.5 | 24 | 8.8 | | | ≤≤1 | 0.0 |
| 14 | 8.0 | 23 | 8.7 | | | | |
| 13 | 7.5 | 22 | 8.6 | | | | |
| 12 | 7.0 | 21 | 8.5 | | | | |
| 11 | 6.5 | 20 | 8.4 | | | | |
| 10 | 6.0 | 19 | 8.3 | | | | |
| 9 | 5.7 | 18 | 8.2 | | | | |
| 8 | 5.3 | 17 | 8.0 | | | | |
| 7 | 5.0 | 16 | 7.8 | | | | |
| 6 | 4.5 | 15 | 7.5 | | | | |
| 5 | 4.0 | 14 | 7.3 | | | | |
| 4 | 3.0 | 13 | 7.0 | | | | |
| 3 | 2.0 | 12 | 6.5 | | | | |
| 2 | 1.0 | 11 | 6.0 | | | | |
| ≤1 | 0.0 | 10 | 5.5 | | | | |
| | | 9 | 5.3 | | | | |
| | | 8 | 4.5 | | | | |

# Appendix E

# USAF Acronyms and Abbreviations

| | |
|---|---|
| **A1C** | airman first class |
| **AA&E** | arms, ammunition, and explosives |
| **AAF** | Army Air Force |
| **AAFES** | Army and Air Force Exchange Service |
| **AB** | airman basic; air base |
| **ACC** | Air Combat Command |
| **ACE** | Allied Command Europe |
| **ACTS** | Air Corps Tactical School |
| **AD** | active duty |
| **ADAPT** | alcohol and drug abuse prevention and treatment |
| **ADAPTPM** | ADAPT program manager |
| **ADC** | Area Defense Counsel; Air Defense Command |
| **ADSC** | Active Duty Service Commitment |
| **AECP** | Airman Education and Commissioning Program |
| **AEF** | air and space expeditionary force; American Expeditionary Force |
| **AETC** | Air Education and Training Command |
| **AEW** | aerospace expeditionary wing |
| **AFAS** | Air Force Aid Society |
| **AFBCMR** | Air Force Board for Correction of Military Records |
| **AFCFM** | Air Force career field manager |
| **AFEM** | Armed Forces Expeditionary Medal |
| **AFGCM** | Air Force Good Conduct Medal |
| **AFHRA** | Air Force Historical Research Agency |
| **AFHRI** | Air Force Enlisted Heritage Research Institute |
| **AFIA** | Air Force Inspection Agency |
| **AFIT** | Air Force Institute of Technology |
| **AFLSA** | Air Force Longevity Service Award |
| **AFMC** | Air Force Materiel Command |
| **AFMIA** | Air Force Manpower and Innovation Agency |

| | |
|---|---|
| **AFOEA** | Air Force Organizational Excellence Award |
| **AFOMS** | Air Force Occupational Measurement Squadron |
| **AFOR** | Air Force Overseas Ribbon |
| **AFOSI** | Air Force Office of Special Investigations |
| **AFOUA** | Air Force Outstanding Unit Award |
| **AFPC** | Air Force Personnel Center |
| **AFR** | Air Force Reserve |
| **AFRC** | Air Force Reserve Command |
| **AFRH** | Armed Forces Retirement Home |
| **AFROTC** | Air Force Reserve Officer Training Corps |
| **AFS** | Air Force specialty |
| **AFSC** | Air Force specialty code |
| **AFSM** | Armed Forces Service Medal |
| **AFSNCOA** | Air Force Senior NCO Academy |
| **AFSOC** | Air Force Special Operations Command |
| **AFSPC** | Air Force Space Command |
| **AFTR** | Air Force Training Ribbon |
| **AGR** | active guard or reserve |
| **ALS** | airman leadership school |
| **AMC** | Air Mobility Command |
| **AMJAMS** | Automated Military Justice Analysis and Management System |
| **Amn** | airman |
| **ANG** | Air National Guard |
| **AOR** | area of responsibility |
| **ARC** | American Red Cross; Air Reserve Component |
| **ASCP** | Airman Scholarship and Commissioning Program |
| **AT** | antiterrorism |
| **ATC** | Air Traffic Controller |
| **ATM** | automated teller machine |
| **AWACS** | Airborne Warning and Control System |
| **AWOL** | absent without official leave |
| **BAH** | basic allowance for housing |
| **BAS** | basic allowance for subsistence |
| **BDU** | battle dress uniform |
| **BHS** | behavioral health survey |
| **BMT** | basic military training |
| **BOP** | base of preference |
| **BTZ** | below the zone |
| **C3** | command, control, and communications |
| **C³I** | command, control, and communications, and intelligence |
| **C⁴** | command, control, and communications, and computer systems |

| | |
|---|---|
| **CAA** | career assistance advisor |
| **CAFSC** | control Air Force specialty code |
| **CAREERS** | Career Airman Reenlistment Reservation System |
| **CASF** | composite air strike force |
| **CB** | chemical-biological |
| **CC** | cost center |
| **CCAF** | Community College of the Air Force |
| **CCCA** | common core compliance area |
| **CCM** | command chief master sergeant; cost center manager |
| **CCRC** | common core readiness criteria |
| **CCT** | combat controller |
| **CDC** | career development course |
| **CEM** | chief enlisted manager |
| **CENTAF** | U.S. Air Force Central Command |
| **CEPME** | College for Enlisted Professional Military Education |
| **CFC** | Combined Federal Campaign |
| **CFETP** | career field education and training plan |
| **CHAMPUS** | Civilian Health and Medical Program of the Uniformed Services |
| **CI** | compliance inspection; counterintelligence |
| **CIA** | Central Intelligence Agency |
| **CINC** | commander in chief |
| **CJCS** | Chairman, Joint Chiefs of Staff |
| **CJR** | career job reservation |
| **CLEP** | College-Level Examination Program |
| **CMC** | Commandant of the Marine Corps |
| **CMSAF** | Chief Master Sergeant of the Air Force |
| **CMSgt** | chief master sergeant |
| **COLA** | cost-of-living adjustment |
| **COMPUSEC** | computer security |
| **COMSEC** | communications security |
| **CONUS** | continental United States |
| **CPR** | cardiopulmonary resuscitation |
| **CRA** | clothing replacement allowance |
| **CRO** | change of rating official |
| **CSA** | Chief of Staff, U.S. Army |
| **CSAF** | Chief of Staff, U.S. Air Force |
| **CSS** | commander support staff |
| **CTO** | commercial travel office |
| **DANTES** | Defense Activity for Nontraditional Education Support |
| **DCS** | deputy chief of staff |
| **DFAS** | Defense Finance and Accounting Service |
| **DIEMS** | date initially entered military service |

| | |
|---|---|
| **DLA** | Defense Logistics Agency |
| **DOB** | date of birth |
| **DOD** | Department of Defense |
| **DOR** | date of rank |
| **DOS** | date of separation |
| **DOT** | Department of Transportation |
| **DR** | demand reduction |
| **DRU** | direct reporting unit |
| **DSST** | DANTES subject standardized test |
| **DTRA** | Defense Threat Reduction Agency |
| **DUI** | driving under the influence |
| **DVR** | data verification record |
| **DWI** | driving while intoxicated |
| **E&T** | education and training |
| **EAD** | extended active duty; entrance on active duty |
| **EES** | Enlisted Evaluation System |
| **EFMP** | Exceptional Family Member Program |
| **EFT** | electronic funds transfer |
| **ELT** | extended long OS tour |
| **E-mail** | electronic mail |
| **ELA** | educational leave of absence |
| **EML** | environmental and morale leave |
| **EMSEC** | emissions security |
| **EOT** | equal opportunity and treatment |
| **EPA** | Environmental Protection Agency |
| **EPR** | enlisted performance report |
| **EQUAL** | Enlisted Quarterly Assignments Listing |
| **ETIC** | estimated time in commission |
| **ETS** | expiration of term of service |
| **EXORD** | execution order |
| **FAC** | functional account code |
| **FAP** | Family Advocacy Program |
| **FBI** | Federal Bureau of Investigation |
| **FICA** | Federal Insurance Contributions Act |
| **FIP** | fitness improvement program |
| **FITW** | federal income tax withholding |
| **FMB** | Financial Management Board |
| **FOA** | field operating agency |
| **FOIA** | Freedom of Information Act |
| **FOUO** | for official use only |
| **FPCON** | force protection condition |
| **FSA** | family separation allowance |
| **FSA-R** | FSA reassignment |

| | |
|---|---|
| **FSA-T** | FSA temporary |
| **FSC** | family support center |
| **FSH** | family separation, basic allowance for housing |
| **FSO** | financial services office |
| **FSSA** | family subsistence supplemental allowance |
| **FSTR** | full spectrum threat response |
| **FTA** | first-term airmen |
| **FVAP** | Federal Voting Assistance Program |
| **FWA** | fraud, waste, and abuse |
| **FWG** | financial working group |
| **FY** | fiscal year |
| **GCE** | ground crew ensemble |
| **GCM** | general court-martial |
| **GHQ** | general headquarters |
| **HAWC** | health and wellness center |
| **HAZMAT** | hazardous material |
| **HDL** | high-density lipoprotein |
| **HQ AFPC** | Headquarters, Air Force Personnel Center |
| **HRE** | human relations education |
| **HSI** | health services inspection |
| **HUMINT** | human intelligence |
| **HYT** | high year of tenure |
| **IA** | information assurance |
| **ICBM** | intercontinental ballistic missile |
| **IDS** | Integrated Delivery System |
| **IG** | Inspector General |
| **IMA** | individual mobilization augmentee |
| **INFOCON** | information operations condition |
| **IO** | information operations |
| **IRA** | individual retirement account |
| **IRR** | individual ready reserve |
| **ISD** | instructional system development |
| **ISP** | Internet service provider |
| **ISR** | intelligence, surveillance, reconnaissance |
| **IW** | information warfare |
| **JCS** | Joint Chiefs of Staff |
| **JFACC** | joint forces air component commander |
| **JFTR** | Joint Federal Travel Regulation |
| **JMUA** | Joint Meritorious Unit Medal |
| **JQS** | job qualification standard |
| **JTF** | joint task force |
| **JV** | Joint Vision |
| **LES** | leave and earnings statement |

| | |
|---|---|
| **LOA** | letter of admonishment |
| **LOAC** | law of armed conflict |
| **LOC** | letter of counseling; line of communication |
| **LOD** | line of duty |
| **LOE** | letter of evaluation |
| **LOR** | letter of reprimand |
| **LOW** | law of war |
| **LOX** | liquid oxygen |
| **Lt Col** | lieutenant colonel |
| **MAAG** | Military Assistance Advisory Group |
| **MAC** | Military Airlift Command |
| **MAJCOM** | major command |
| **MALT** | monetary allowance in lieu of transportation |
| **MCM** | Manual for Courts-Martial |
| **MDS** | Manpower Data System |
| **MEO** | military equal opportunity; most effective organization |
| **MFIP** | monitored fitness improvement program |
| **MFR** | memorandum for record |
| **MGIB** | Montgomery GI Bill |
| **MilPDS** | Military Personnel Data System |
| **MKTS** | military knowledge and testing |
| **MO** | manpower and organization |
| **MOPP** | mission-oriented protective posture |
| **MPS** | military personnel section |
| **MR** | memorandum for record |
| **MRE** | military rule of evidence |
| **MSF** | Motorcycle Safety Foundation |
| **MSgt** | master sergeant |
| **MSO** | military service obligation |
| **MTF** | military treatment facility; medical treatment facility |
| **MTP** | master training plan |
| **MTW** | major theater war |
| **NAF** | numbered Air Force |
| **NATO** | North Atlantic Treaty Organization |
| **NBC** | nuclear, biological, and chemical |
| **NBCC** | nuclear, biological, chemical, and conventional |
| **NCO** | noncommissioned officer |
| **NCOA** | noncommissioned officer academy |
| **NCORP** | NCO Retraining Program |
| **NDAA** | National Defense Authorization Act |
| **NDSM** | National Defense Service Medal |
| **NJP** | nonjudicial punishment |
| **NORAD** | North American Aerospace Defense Command |

| | |
|---|---|
| **NOTAM** | Notice to Airmen |
| **NPSP** | New Parent Support Program |
| **NSI** | nuclear surety inspection |
| **OBAD** | operating budget authority document |
| **OJT** | on-the-job training |
| **OPLAN** | operations plan |
| **OPORD** | operations order |
| **OPR** | office of primary responsibility; officer performance report |
| **OPSEC** | operations security |
| **ORI** | operational readiness inspection |
| **ORM** | operational risk management |
| **OS** | overseas |
| **OSD** | Office of the Secretary of Defense |
| **OSHA** | occupational safety and health administration |
| **OSI** | Office of Special Investigations |
| **OTS** | Officer Training School |
| **PA** | Privacy Act |
| **PACAF** | Pacific Air Forces |
| **PACOM** | Pacific Command |
| **PAS** | personnel accounting symbol |
| **PC** | personal computer |
| **PCA** | permanent change of assignment |
| **PCM** | primary care manager |
| **PCS** | permanent change of station |
| **PDA** | personal digital assistant |
| **PDS** | permanent duty station; personnel data system |
| **PECD** | promotion eligibility cutoff date |
| **PERSTEMPO** | personnel tempo |
| **PES** | promotion eligibility status |
| **PFC** | private first class |
| **PFE** | promotion fitness examination |
| **PFMP** | Personal Financial Management Program |
| **PFW** | performance feedback worksheet |
| **PIF** | personnel information file |
| **PIN** | personal identification number |
| **PJ** | pararescue |
| **P.L.** | public law |
| **PL1** | Protection Level 1 |
| **PL2** | Protection Level 2 |
| **PL3** | Protection Level 3 |
| **PL4** | Protection Level 4 |
| **PME** | professional military education |
| **POV** | privately owned vehicle |

| | |
|---|---|
| **POW** | prisoner of war |
| **PPE** | personal protective equipment |
| **PRP** | Personnel Reliability Program |
| **PSN** | promotion sequence number |
| **PT** | physical training |
| **PTDY** | permissive TDY |
| **QRP** | Qualified Recycling Program; Quality Retraining Program |
| **QT** | qualification training |
| **RA** | resource advisor |
| **RAC** | risk assessment code |
| **RAM** | random antiterrorism measure |
| **RAP** | Recruiter Assistance Program |
| **RCM** | Rules for Court Martial; responsibility center manager |
| **RDP** | recommendation for decoration printout |
| **RHIP** | rank has its privileges |
| **RIC** | record of individual counseling |
| **RIP** | Report of Individual Personnel |
| **RMS** | resource management system |
| **RNLTD** | report not later than date |
| **ROE** | rules of engagement |
| **ROTC** | Reserve Officer Training Corps |
| **SA** | substance abuse |
| **SAC** | Strategic Air Command |
| **SACS** | Southern Association of Colleges and Schools |
| **SAF** | Secretary of the Air Force |
| **SAM** | surface-to-air missile |
| **SAV** | staff assistance visit |
| **SBP** | survivor benefit plan |
| **SCG** | security classification guide |
| **SCM** | summary court-martial |
| **SDI** | special duty identifier |
| **SEA** | senior enlisted advisor |
| **SECAF** | Secretary of the Air Force |
| **SECDEF** | Secretary of Defense |
| **SEI** | special experience identifier |
| **SelRes** | selected reserve |
| **SFIP** | self-directed fitness improvement program |
| **SG** | surgeon general |
| **SGLI** | servicemembers group life insurance |
| **SII** | special interest item |
| **SITW** | state income tax withholding |
| **SJA** | staff judge advocate |
| **SKT** | specialty knowledge test |

| | |
|---|---|
| **SLA** | special leave accrual |
| **SMSgt** | senior master sergeant |
| **SNCO** | senior noncommissioned officer |
| **SOAR** | Scholarships for Outstanding Airmen to ROTC |
| **SOF** | special operations force |
| **SPCM** | special court-martial |
| **SrA** | senior airman |
| **SRB** | selective reenlistment bonus |
| **SRID** | senior rater identification |
| **SROE** | standing rules of engagement |
| **SRP** | Selective Reenlistment Program |
| **SSgt** | staff sergeant |
| **STEP** | Stripes for Exceptional Performers |
| **STS** | specialty training standard |
| **TA** | tuition assistance |
| **TAC** | Tactical Air Command |
| **TAFMS** | total active federal military service |
| **TDP** | TRICARE Dental Program |
| **TDY** | temporary duty |
| **TEMSD** | Total Enlisted Military Service Date |
| **TFW** | tactical fighter wing |
| **TIG** | time in grade |
| **TIS** | time in service |
| **TJAG** | The Judge Advocate General |
| **TMF** | traffic management flight |
| **TMO** | traffic management office |
| **TO** | technical order |
| **TOS** | time on station |
| **TRW** | tactical reconnaissance wing |
| **TSCA** | Top Secret control account |
| **TSCO** | Top Secret control officer |
| **TSgt** | technical sergeant |
| **TSP** | Thrift Savings Plan |
| **TT** | treatment team |
| **TTM** | treatment team meeting |
| **U&TW** | utilization and training workshop |
| **UCMJ** | Uniform Code of Military Justice |
| **UETM** | unit education and training manager |
| **UFPM** | unit fitness program manager |
| **UGT** | upgrade training |
| **UIF** | unfavorable information file |
| **UMD** | unit manning document |
| **UN** | United Nations |

| | |
|---|---|
| **UOCAVA** | Uniformed and Overseas Citizens Absentee Voting Act |
| **UOTHC** | under other than honorable conditions |
| **UPMR** | unit personnel management roster |
| **URE** | unit review exercise |
| **USAAF** | U.S. Army Air Forces |
| **USAF** | United States Air Force |
| **USAFA** | United States Air Force Academy; U.S. Air Force Association |
| **USAFE** | U.S. Air Forces in Europe |
| **USAFR** | U.S. Air Force Reserves |
| **USAFSE** | USAF supervisory examination |
| **U.S.C.** | United States Code |
| **USEUCOM** | U.S. European Command |
| **USSR** | Union of Soviet Socialist Republic |
| **UTM** | unit training manager |
| **UXO** | unexploded ordnance |
| **VA** | Veterans Affairs |
| **VAO** | voting assistance officer |
| **VCJCS** | Vice Chairman, Joint Chief of Staff |
| **VEAP** | Veterans Education Assistance Program |
| **VIP** | very important person |
| **WAC** | Women's Army Corps |
| **WAPS** | Weighted Airman Promotion System |
| **WASP** | Women Airforce Service Pilots |
| **WBFMP** | Weight and Body Fat Management Program |
| **WEAR** | we are all recruiters |
| **WMD** | weapons of mass destruction |
| **WOC** | wing operations center |
| **WR** | war reserve |
| **WWI** | World War I |
| **WWII** | World War II |

# Index

# About the Author

Boone Nicolls served in the United States Air Force in the grades of Airman Basic to Master Sergeant. His more than twenty-four years' service were predominantly in Aerospace Defense Command, Air Defense Weapons Center, Air Mobility Command, and Air Education and Training Command. His maintenance and flight experience includes T-33 crew chief, F-101 TOW system operator, and C-141 combat crew instructor/examiner flight engineer. As a flight superintendent, he managed thirty airmen in seven different functional areas. He earned his Chief Enlisted Air Crew Wings in the course of accumulating 7,600 flying hours, of which 97 hours were in the F-101, 240 hours in the C-141A, and the balance in the C-141B. He flew seven combat missions during the Persian Gulf War and served for several years as an installation-level deputy and chief inspector general.

Master Sergeant Nicolls is a graduate of the USAF Noncommissioned Officer Academy, Squadron Officer School, and both the Army and Air Force Inspector General Schools. He holds several associate degrees, including two from the Community College of the Air Force, a B.A. degree in Vocational Education from Southern Illinois University, and a paralegal degree. He and his family reside in Victory, Oklahoma.